JAGUAR

JAGUAR

LORD MONTAGU OF BEAULIEU

Quiller Press
London

This edition first published in Great Britain 1982 by
Quiller Press Ltd
11a Albemarle Street
London W1

Copyright © 1961, 1962, 1967, 1981 and 1982 by the
Rt. Hon. Lord Montagu of Beaulieu

Fourth revised edition printed by The Anchor Press Ltd
and bound by Wm Brendon & Son Ltd
both of Tiptree, Essex, England

ISBN 0 907621 01 5

This book is dedicated to
Sir William Lyons
and all those who made this story

CONTENTS

ACKNOWLEDGMENTS

EVEN when one is dealing with relatively recent history such as the saga of the Jaguar car, the amount of research entailed is likely to be prodigious if any standard of accuracy is to be maintained. I must therefore acknowledge my debt of gratitude to all those who assisted me in obtaining that extra information which makes a book such as this worthwhile:

I wish to set on record my indebtedness to the following journals: *The Autocar*, *The Motor*, *The Light Car*, *The Motor Cycle*, *Motor Cycling*, *Motor Sport*, and *Autosport*, not only for furnishing invaluable background material, but also for permission to quote from their pages. I must also express my thanks to Sir William Lyons for giving me personal attention and full facilities to visit the Jaguar factory, and for authorizing his staff to co-operate to the maximum in every way on the preparation of this book. Their friendliness and help at all times was boundless, despite the flood of questions aimed at them. Special thanks must go to the late E. W. Rankin, to his successors R. E. Berry and Andrew Whyte, and to all the members of the Press Office staff, for coping so manfully and so patiently with our 'Elephant's child' curiosity. Though at the time they were pre-occupied with the launching of the new E-type, they devoted countless hours to ferreting out forgotten facts, and never complained, however recondite the query. I must also thank the late Colonel Rixon Bucknall, who not only gave generously of his vast fund of Jaguar lore accumulated in many years of enthusiastic ownership, but was also kind enough to read the whole manuscript, making numerous helpful suggestions, and correcting a number of mistakes. William Boddy, Editor of *Motor Sport*, also gave much of his valuable time to the reading of the manuscript, allowing me the benefit of his encyclopaedic knowledge of all matter relating to sports and racing cars; while Rodney Crouch, then Secretary of the Jaguar Drivers' Club, gave me every encouragement, and acted as a 'post-office' for many enthusiasts who also offered their services.

Others, too, have brought their specialized knowledge to bear on various sections of the book. Mr C. W. Hayward of Firth Cleveland Ltd., for many years closely associated with the Swallow Sidecar Co., kindly read the first chapter for me, as did that great authority on all motorcycling matters, the late Graham Walker, former Editor of *Motor Cycling* and subsequently Motorcycle Curator of the Montagu Motor Museum; while Ronald Watson and C. G. Bennett of Watsonian Sidecars Ltd. were most helpful in tying up the later history of Swallow sidecars. Mrs E. L. Robbins went to a great deal of time and trouble—including a lengthy interview—to give her reminiscences of the earliest days of Swallow and S.S.

For much of the background of Chapter 2, I am indebted to the late F. J. Eric Findon, for many years Editor of *The Light Car*, whose unique knowledge helped fill many gaps. B. Alan Hill of Standard-Triumph contributed much valuable information on his company's relations with the Swallow Coachbuilding Co. Ltd. and S.S. Cars Ltd. Kenneth Ball of Autobooks saved me many hours of difficult research by donating a vast file of Swallow and S.S. advertisements culled from the weekly motoring press of the 1930s, and William E. Summers, S.S. and Jaguar Technician to the Classic Car Club of America, furnished much illuminating material on the early history of the cars on the other side of the Atlantic. Mr B. H. Vanderveen was responsible for the detailed information on the experimental W.D. vehicles made in the Second World War.

While most of the more recent material comes from Jaguars and from the files of the contemporary press, Philip Turner of *The Motor* generously presented me with all his notes on part of the *marque*'s competition history, sorted and ready to use. Despite other very heavy commitments, Stirling Moss, the late Ron Flockhart, T.E.B. Sopwith and Ronald Adams answered numerous questions on their competition experiences with Jaguar cars; while Brian Lister went to a great deal of trouble to answer questions on the history of the Lister-Jaguar. To the late David Murray I owe the information relating to the distinguished exploits of *Ecurie Ecosse*; Max Trimble contributed a fascinatingly detailed account of his competition career on C- and D-type cars; and the late Norman Buckley was equally helpful in furnishing the background story of his marine exploits with twin-overhead camshaft Jaguar engines.

The following also were most helpful, and some of them went to much trouble to show me their cars:

S. Alper (Sprite Ltd.), G. F. Boughton (Brown and Mallalieu Ltd.), W. Brass, D. H. Clarke, A. L. H. Dawson (The Nuffield Organization), Miss D. P. A. Day, Major H. M. Farmer, U.S.A.F. (Retd.), the late Dennis C. Field, A.M.I.E.E. (Research Historian, The Veteran Car Club of Great Britain), A. F. Rivers Fletcher, Major D. G. Gershon, G. Geoffrey Haigh, C. J. Hellberg (Carbodies Ltd.), E. W. Ife (FIAT [England] Ltd.), J. R. T. Gibson Jarvie, Harold Karslake, C. Longden-Thurgood, T. J. Lovell (Tube Investments Ltd.), Cyril Mann, Charles Lam Markmann, F. W. Mead, G. L. Miller (H. Miller & Co. Ltd.), Norman J. Milne (Austin Motor Co. Ltd.), F. Wilson McComb (*Safety Fast*), C. M. Needham, the late S. H. Newsome, J.P., J. D. Paton, Derek Pine, P. de F. C. Pycroft, M. Reeves, H. N. Ryan, W. R. Scott, D. P. E. Taylor, Edward Walker, W. G. L. Ward (Joseph Lucas Ltd.), I. Webb, B.E.M. (Blacknell Sidecars Ltd.), G. H. Wiltsher (Alvis Ltd.) and Captain G. Liston Young (The FIAT Register).

I should also like to thank the numerous other people who wrote to me offering help. Space precludes the mention of their names, but their sympathy and interest was much appreciated.

I am also grateful to L. G. Firmin, who not only devoted hours of his valuable time to assistance on the appendixes, but also loaned rare items from his personal motoring library. Additional thanks are due to Colonel Rixon Bucknall for providing the excellent index. Finally, I must thank my publishers, who have as usual interpreted deadlines with a generosity that has made such a book possible.

MONTAGU

INTRODUCTION

'The car of the future has arrived. Swift as the wind—silent as a shadow come the new S.S. Jaguars: 1½-litre and 2½-litre models that impart a new meaning to 'high performance'—a deeper satisfaction to pride of ownership.'

S.S. Jaguar advertisement, October 1935

IT was September 1935, and the Motor Show—the penultimate one of the series to be held at Olympia—lay three weeks ahead.

Nineteen thirty-five had been an eventful year—the year of Mussolini's colonial exploits in Abyssinia, of Sanctions, and of a call to rearmament, ending in a political landslide that was destined to drive the Labour Party into the wilderness for ten years. Income tax was 5s. 6d. in the pound, petrol cost 1s. 5d. per gallon, and the British Empire (as yet no mere Commonwealth) was celebrating the Silver Jubilee of King George V with imperial pomp. Motorists were beginning to feel the impact of the energetic Mr Leslie Hore-Belisha at the Ministry of Transport, and roads were sprouting orange-topped beacons. The 30 m.p.h. speed limit was in its infancy, compulsory driving tests had just come into force, and work was restarting on road developments such as the North Oxford and Winchester by-passes, which had been lying neglected since the economic blizzard of 1931.

Recovery was in the air, and the 1936 season brought a notable crop of new cars. The Nuffield Group, Rootes and Standard had subjected their ranges to stylistic face-lifts, Rileys had a vee-eight, Jowett a flat-four, and Rolls-Royce the twelve-cylinder 'Phantom III'. Already there were rumours of a *four*-wheeled Morgan, and in a small engineering works on the Kingston by-pass the finishing touches were being put to the last true Vintage sports car design—the H.R.G. On the Continent, FIAT's 1500 and Peugeot's 402 were combining independent front suspension with aerodynamic shape, both cars having faired-in headlamps. Yet the belle of the 1935 London Show was a strictly conventional motor car, with semi-elliptic front springing, traditional styling, and a wheel not too far from each corner—the S.S. Jaguar.

Other cars had been made which would carry four people in comfort at 85 m.p.h.: elegance of line had already reached its pinnacle in the middle 1930s, though often at the expense of practicality as well as a price of the order of £1,500, the equivalent of £4,000 today: but nobody had hitherto ventured to offer untemperamental performance in a sports saloon of this size for only £385. Well might the British public ask: 'How on earth did Bill Lyons do it?'

Only thirteen years before, the name of Lyons had been unknown except perhaps to a few family motorcyclists who were allergic to the stodgy perambulator styling of contemporary coachbuilt sidecars. Even five years back, the name of Swallow stood only for sidecars and for a series of curvaceous sports bodies on popular chassis, presented in bright duo-tone colours, at a time when maroon, black and brown were deemed a generous choice by the mass producers. The S.S. car had been thrust upon the market in October 1931, at the depth of the Depression. It had, on paper, little more than eye-appeal; it seated only two people; yet it sold, and had steered its sponsors into a strong position in the tricky specialist car market in four short seasons, of which the first two, certainly, were unhealthy ones for the British motor industry at large. Those four years had seen at least three eminent makers of high-grade cars—Invicta, Star, and Sunbeam—go to the wall, while even such solidly-established concerns as Morris and Rover had felt the cold. Others, notably Lagonda, Riley and Triumph, weathered the storm only to run into trouble in the ensuing calm. Yet the S.S. company came through, unassisted by the safely-entrenched sidecar business.

Admittedly they had been assemblers rather than manufacturers, but then so had Morris before them, and it is an indication of strength that these two famous firms progressed from assembly to manufacture, and not the other way round. True, Morris absorbed his suppliers, whereas Jaguar incorporated fewer and fewer mechanical components of other people's design as time went on. It is intriguing if a little ironic, to observe that a company which started life by building bodies round other makers' mechanical components nowadays makes its own 'works', and goes 'outside' for its coachwork.

How does Bill Lyons (or Sir William, as he has been since 1956) do it? After the 1936 Jaguar, there was the 3½-litre '100' model, giving the magic 100 m.p.h. with complete tractability, all for £445: there was the amazing XK120, 30 m.p.h. faster, and endowed with a twin-overhead-camshaft engine of a type hitherto reserved for near-racing machinery: there was the Mk. VII, a 'king-size sedan' which gave the American public everything that their native product offered, luggage space included, plus a close-ratio gearbox and the old-world appointments associated with British bespoke coachwork: there were the Cs and Ds, five times victorious at Le Mans, yet perfectly usable, weather permitting, upon the public roads: there was the 3·4-litre, a full four-seater saloon with 120 m.p.h. performance, and disc brakes to match this speed: and 1961 saw the staggering E-type, a 150 m.p.h. coupé in the *Gran Turismo* tradition, at half the price of its nearest competitor. Purchase tax and a heavy export demand rendered all too many of these vehicles inaccessible to the British motorist, but it is sobering to reflect that in 1939 any motorist desirous of acquiring road performance in the XK class had to expend £1,400-odd on a 3·3-litre supercharged Bugatti. The basic price of the XK120—always assuming that one was procurable at all—was only £998, in the inflationary year of 1950, when the pound was worth half as much as it was pre-war.

In 1936 S.S. Cars Ltd. turned out just under 2,500 vehicles, of which perhaps 7% were exported. In 1959, production was running at about 20,000 a year, and something over half these were earning currency for Britain overseas, especially in the United States. In 1960, the great recession year for Britain's motor industry, Jaguar alone of the major British manufacturers maintained full production.

In the Jaguar's first year of life, it was the victim of rude nicknames such as 'The Bentley of Wardour Street'. One *didn't* run one—though some thirteen thousand people were doing so unrepentantly by 1939. Forty years later, the Jaguar was correct executive wear, and chauffeur-driven automatic XJ 4.2s and 5.3s had finally ousted the towering limousines from parking lots reserved for the captains of industry.

This is a success story: the tale of how a small body shop, turning out 'customized' versions of family saloons, rose to a position only just below the 'Big Five' in Britain's motor industry, and gave that industry a foothold in the Western hemisphere from which Volkswagen and 'compact' alike have been unable to dislodge it. There is a Jaguar *mystique*, just as much as there is a Rolls-Royce or a Bugatti *mystique*. But it is a question of production engineering, and makers who have tried to compete with the Coventry firm on their own ground have either dug their own graves or sought success elsewhere.

Today the company is better equipped than ever before to seek perfection in its products. For the first time for many years Jaguar is a limited company with its own board of directors and a full management team completely in control of manufacturing operations.

Demand for Jaguar products has survived changes of fashion, recession, the energy crisis, and the ever rising costs of living.

This is a small and objective tribute to the team who made such success possible.

MONTAGU

JAGUAR

Blackpool (Cocker Street) factory (*circa* 1927).

CHAPTER 1

Sidecarriages

1920–45

'Swallow models are always the choice of the discriminating purchaser who realizes that absolute reliability and smart appearance mean more to him than the saving of a little initial outlay, a sum which could soon be expended after purchase on an inferior article.'

Swallow sidecar catalogue, 1931

MAN may originate a sport: soon, however, he is smitten with the desire to share it with woman.

Thus the motorcycle, brought into being to satisfy the dual need for a powered bicycle and for a lighter, simpler and speedier machine than the early light car, the *voiturette*, led inevitably to a vehicle made for two. The designers of the early 1900s tried two different approaches. There was the trailer, a light wicker chair mounted upon two cycle wheels, and towed astern. This was anything but sociable, and had an embarrassing penchant for detaching itself and its occupant on corners. The alternative was the forecarriage, a two-wheeled attachment which was clamped onto the front forks of a conventional motorcycle frame. This had the merit of fairly efficient suspension, via C or coil springs under the wicker seat: it was also firmly bolted to the basic structure and was therefore less liable to part company in the course of normal motoring. Alas!, by nature of its position, it planted the beloved out in the open, exposed not only to accidents but to thick road dust.

Curiously enough, nobody seems to have considered the obvious solution of the sidecarriage until 1902—perhaps people were discouraged by that vertiginous contrivance the Sociable Safety Bicycle, which presented problems of balance beyond the average man in the street. The first sidecar was in fact produced and patented by Graham Bros. of Enfield late in 1902, though *Motor Cycling and Motor* observed at the time that Messrs Graham's idea bore an uncanny resemblance to a cartoon of theirs entitled *Love Laughs at Motor Difficulties* which has been published a week or two before the first pictures of the 'Liberty' sidecarriage were released. In any case, the invention was a simple one, combining the firm attachment of the forecarriage with the relative safety of the trailer—the lady was now

housed in a wicker basket attached to a triangular chassis, which was in its turn affixed to the nearside of the motorcycle.

Not that the sidecar was immediately accepted. In 1903, there were still plenty of other solutions. While Components Ltd., of Birmingham, were marketing the original 'Liberty' design, and Lyons of London (no connection with Sir William) were countering with the 'Trafalgar', specially designed to mate with their own brand of motorcycle, Mills-Fulford, later to be a great name in the sidecar world, were offering a 'Duadcar' at ten guineas, which was 'adaptable for use as a sidecarriage or trailer'. Peacocks of Clerkenwell sought the best of both worlds with an odd contrivance known as the Carpeviam motor sociable, a kind of embryonic A.C., priced at under £100, and a Mr Wakeman was promoting a pedal-equipped trailer. 'What,' he challenged, 'is a fellow to do when he takes a lady out for a ride and his engine breaks down, and how is he to get home?' Evidently the 'fellows' did not appreciate his sentiments as we hear no more of him in this context.

However, the sidecar was the best solution, and in the long run it was not only cheaper than the fore-carriage—it was lighter. By 1906, Brown Bros. were cataloguing both species of carriage as adjuncts to their 3½ h.p. motorcycle, the forecar version costing £50, and the sidecar type only £48. Meanwhile, the three-wheelers were slowly evolving along a path that was to lead to the cyclecars of 1910—acquiring water-cooling, wheel-steering, and weight. The 1906 Lagonda tricar, though it ran in competitions under A.C.U. rules, was more car than motorcycle, and thereafter the sidecar was left in sole possession of the passenger motorcycle market.

In the last five years of the Edwardian era, the sybarites took over. Motorcycles were becoming more powerful, and the girl friends less spartan in outlook. In 1910, Mead and Deakin of Birmingham, later to win fame with their overhead-camshaft Rhode car, produced the Canoelet, first of the coach-built sidecars. They were quick to cash in on the public's willingness to pay twelve guineas for comfort and enclosure, instead of being jolted around in a glorified dog-basket for the sake of five pounds saved. It is true that a *de luxe* sidecar of 1914 came equipped with a ponderous cape cart hood and side-screens of fearsome opacity, but the idea of sociability was set at nought by the noise level of the average Edwardian motorcycle. Streamlining, too, was having its influence. In 1912, Montgomery's were offering a 'shell-type' sports model with wicker body, but it looked wrong, even though the frame was carried outside the wheel, in the manner of Hudson's 1948 'step-down' car design.

The adaptation of the sidecar to military purposes finally relegated wicker to its proper role in the manufacture of arty-crafty furniture. Fragile and susceptible to distortion in wet weather, it faded quietly out of the picture. Brown Bros. listed twelve different sidecar body types in 1920, only one of which was made of wicker—despite a saving of £6 10s. on the cheapest coachbuilt model, the primitives had disappeared from their catalogue four years later. The coachbuilt sidecarriage had come to stay, and it was never seriously challenged again till the advent of glass fibre in the 1950s, despite a determined onslaught around 1928 by the devotees of Mr Weymann's system of fabric construction.

In the immediate post-war boom, which supported some dozen sidecar constructors, nobody noticed William Walmsley. The son of a wealthy Cheshire coal-merchant, he manifested no interest in coal, and amused himself by buying war-surplus Triumph motorcycles in crates. These he stripped down and reconditioned in the garage of his parents' home at Woodsmoor, Stockport. Walmsley was not attracted to the ponderous perambulator style affected by the conventionalists, and reasoned that he could sell his rebuilt models better if he equipped them with 'chairs' which combined comfort and sporting lines. To this end he built his first Swallow sidecar, and christened it 'Otasel'. It certainly looked it.

The side and bottom ribs were made of ash, and the octagonal panelling was of polished aluminium. This Zeppelin-like body was mounted on a chassis bought from Haydens of Birmingham. Further sporting touches were added by the use of a polished aluminium disc wheel, and luxury was ensured by the provision of a close-fitting coupé hood which reduced visibility to nil.

The beginning: the Swallow sports sidecar of 1921.

At this stage, the Swallow sidecar could hardly be called a commercial venture. The chassis apart, Walmsley made everything himself, upholstery and trimming being handled first by his sister, and later by his wife. Output was one a week, the price of the sidecar alone being thirty-two guineas.

Late in 1920, Walmsley senior sold his coal business, and the family moved to Blackpool. At first, the sidecar venture continued at the same leisurely tempo, but among the Walmsley's neighbours was a Mr W. Lyons, who ran a piano business in the town. His twenty-year-old son William was about as interested in selling pianos as young Walmsley had been on the subject of coal, but he was an enthusiastic motor cyclist, taking part in many competitions, including hill-climbs and sprints on the nearby Southport sands. He was attracted by the stylish lines of Walmsley's aluminium sidecar, and bought one.

William Lyons was quick to see a future in the Swallow sidecar. If they could turn out ten a week, he argued, instead of just·one, they could market them at an economic price. Walmsley agreed. There was, however, a fly in the ointment. Lyons was not yet of age, and he had to wait some weeks before the Swallow Sidecar Co. was floated. Capital was £1,000, covered by bank guarantees furnished by the fathers of the two young partners. Although both parents supported the scheme enthusiastically, they could hardly have foreseen that this was the first and last occasion on which the young William Lyons was to seek outside financial assistance; still less that in thirty-eight years from that day he would be the head of a concern turning out some six hundred cars and buses a week from two internationally-famous factories, not in out-of-the-way Blackpool, but in Coventry, the car-manufacturing capital of England.

Operations were transferred from the Walmsleys' garage to a new small factory in Bloomfield Road. A staff of about twelve workmen was taken on.

In November 1922, *The Motor Cycle* published an illustrated description of the octagonal Swallow Sports model. Electric or acetylene lighting was optional, and chassis for these first production sidecars were made by Montgomery's of Coventry, themselves active as makers of complete sidecars in those days. Unlike manufacturers such as Hughes, Swallows did not go in much for competition, though Lyons and Walmsley supported local trials. They might advertise, as they did as late as 1933, that their 'Semi-Sports' model was ideal for 'competition purposes and sporting events', but they did not build 'chairs' for the International Six Days' Trials, and their impact on racing was confined to the Sidecar T.T.s of 1924 and 1925. In the former year, they figured prominently in the results, Harry Reed finishing second on a Swallow-equipped 344 c.c. Dot–J.A.P., and Tinkler bringing a Matador–Blackburne with Swallow 'chair' into third place. Reed remained loyal to Swallow in 1925, though he changed his mount to a Matador.

In these early years, however, Swallow built up a reputation as style leaders. They did not pioneer either coachbuilt bodies or electric lighting, though they undoubtedly led the field with aluminium panelling. The Lyons–Walmsley combination made their

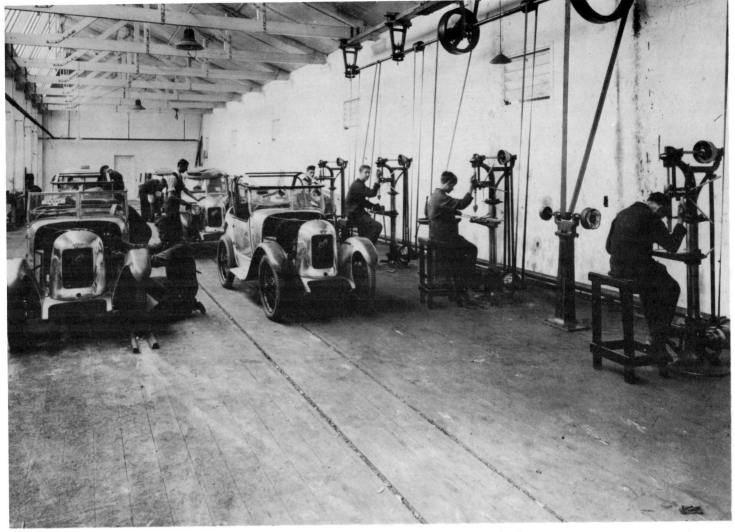

Body mounting department, Foleshill, 1929. The cars are Austins.

name as superb packagers. They established the sidecar, for the first time, as a thing of beauty rather than an ugly, utilitarian encumbrance born of the motorcyclist's need to reconcile family obligations with his innate contempt for cars and his reluctance to commit himself to the extra expenditure. Even in those early days Lyons had an instinctive knowledge of a design's commercial potentialities. He knew exactly what he wanted, and what the public would buy. In the smooth, sporting lines of these Zeppelin-shaped sidecars can be detected the genesis of the Jaguar as we know it.

Nineteen twenty-four saw pentagonal panels, introduced in the interests of cost-cutting—a lightweight touring model cost £22 10s., as against eighteen guineas for Millford's 'Popular'. The more luxurious Coupé de luxe set the purchaser back £30, for which he got a hammock-type seat, a Triplex screen, and space for luggage

in the pointed tail. At the 1923 Motorcycle Show, the little Blackpool firm not only hired a stand, they also had the satisfaction of seeing their sidecars displayed by four manufacturers—Brough Superior, Coventry Eagle, Dot, and Matador. George Brough incidentally, exhibited one of the costlier octagonal Coupés de Luxe, which style was to be the standard 'chair' listed on Broughs for four seasons, from 1924 to 1927.

In 1925, touring model prices started at £22 10s., though a lighter 'racer' was available at £16. Balloon tyres became an option on touring models. A year later, the expanding concern moved to new premises in Cocker Street, Blackpool, where they rented a building owned by the elder Walmsley. Even at this stage, though, only thirty-odd people were employed, among them a schoolgirl typist named Alice Fenton, who was to become Jaguar's Home Sales Director before her untimely death in 1960.

In the later 'twenties, there were to be two significant developments, though at the time they were overshadowed by the tremendous impact of the first Austin Seven Swallow two-seater, in the spring of 1927. The first of these was the purchase by Nottingham Police of a number of Brough Superior motorcycles with Swallow sidecars—a far cry to the white Jaguar saloons which later patrolled M.1, but in fact the first link between Lyons and the guardians of the Law. Meanwhile, the ever-enterprising William Lyons, in conjunction with Charles Hayward, who had supplanted Montgomerys as chassis suppliers, had set a firm foot in the export door.

Left-hand-drive is now almost universal outside the Commonwealth countries. It was, however, by no means so firmly established in 1925. America apart, right-hand steering was all too often the order of the day, even a firm as big as FIAT turning out r.h.d. cars for the home market. A few of Britain's specialist manufacturers, notably Invicta and Lanchester, were prepared to build l.h.d. cars, but generally the foreign customer, as *The Autocar* complained at the time, had either to put up with r.h.d., or pay for a special conversion after delivery. Lyons and Hayward, however, had other ideas. Already Swallow's energetic Swiss agent, Emil Frey of Zurich, was selling quite a few sidecars, and these sold even better after Hayward introduced his Universal chassis, which permitted attachment to either side of the motorcycle frame, and paved the way for the l.h.d. sidecar. M. Frey, incidentally, is still active, selling Jaguars in Switzerland.

Swallows were paying the penalty of leadership by 1927, their semi-sports at £16 16s. enjoying competition from Whitley's 'Dazzler' at £18 15s., Hughes' 'Super Sports' at £24 and Millford's 'Tourer Sports' at £19 19s. Twin-axle frames were made available for the heavier Swallow models, and in 1928 the firm offered a 'Launch' model, though almost alone among the sidecar makers, they eschewed fabric covering. Though they succumbed to this

The Standard element: By 1931 Swallow was fitting their saloon style to the four- and six-cylinder Standard chassis. This shot was taken in 1930, and therefore shows fours only.

vogue to the extent of one model in the 1930 range, William Lyons steered clear of the prevailing fashion, and he was proved right.

In 1928, the growth of the car body business, by then working on FIAT as well as Austin chassis, resulted in a move to Foleshill, Coventry, and thereafter the sidecar business began to take a back seat. That year Lyons and Walmsley adopted pneumatic upholstery and the rise of speedway racing resulted also in the addition of a special dirt track model to the range. In 1931, by which time the firm had revealed its change of direction by renaming itself the Swallow Coachbuilding Co. Ltd, the duotone cellulose finishes introduced on the cars had been applied to the basic sidecar line, though the devotees of plain aluminium could still keep their coach-work clean with Swallow Aluminium Polish (at 1s. 9d. a tin).

The Depression came and went. The 1931 Motor Show saw the first S.S. car, and the sidecars finally ceased to be the predominant interest. Not that they were abandoned, by any means. Sentiment may have been one cause for their retention, and it is possible that up to 1933-4 production was kept flowing by Lyons as an insurance against any possible setbacks in the promotion of the controversial S.S., but there is no doubt whatsoever that the Swallow directorate were loath to abandon a venture which 'more or less ran itself', and occupied little space in a factory which the booming car business was fast outgrowing. Even in 1930, production was running at around one hundred sidecars a week.

Right up to the outbreak of the second World War, Swallow sidecars remained in production. Perhaps their styling was less sensational, in the same way that the quieter lines of the 1936 Jaguar supplanted the long-bonneted flamboyance of the 1932 S.S.I. Certainly the more conservative firms followed their lead, and the days of the one-wheeled mailcart were over. Swallow incorporated Vauxhall-type flutes on a very successful design in the early 1930s, and in 1934 they offered a comprehensive range, made up of eleven variants of eight basic models, utilizing three frame types, light, standard, and 'Heavy Duty Colonial'. Prices ranged from a semi-sports at £12 12s. 0d. to a *de luxe* launch at £21. In this year also, a subsidiary company, S.S. Cars Ltd., was formed to take over the motor-car side of the business, and by a curious irony this offshoot was ultimately to crowd its progenitor out of Coventry.

In 1931, Mills-Fulford took over the manufacture of chassis for Swallow; their work was transferred in 1935 to Grindlays of Coventry, who continued as suppliers up to the outbreak of war. In 1936, Swallow again broke fresh ground with a pretty 'Ranelagh' swept-tail streamline saloon. This had an adjustable windscreen, four safety-glass windows, and a roof hinging towards the offside complete with a fabric roll-top. A full-depth door and a separate luggage compartment rounded off a luxurious *ensemble*, which cost £31 10s.

But the writing was on the wall. *The Motor Cycle* might observe chauvinistically in 1937 that Swallow sidecars were 'produced in the same factory as the famous S.S. car bodies', but they were a good twelve months out of date. William Lyons was fast becoming a manufacturer instead of a bodybuilder, and the S.S. Jaguar, though it used a 'bought-out' engine and gearbox, was conceived as an entity and not just as an ingenious packaging job on a mass-produced chassis. In spite of which *The Motor* was reporting, as late as February 1937, that some five hundred sidecar bodies were being turned out a week.

The War completed the transformation. As long as Lyons was a relatively small specialist producer, it was good economic policy to turn out perhaps four thousand sidecars a year, secure in the know-

The £1,000 look. The high cab and cycle fenders robbed the original 1932 model S.S.I of the elegance of its successors, but even so it appeared faster than its genuine 70 mph top speed, and nobody could believe the price – £310. Laudau irons were in fashion in 1932.

ledge that his products had a following. But his ultimate ambition was not only to design his own mechanical components, but to build them himself, and valuable space could not be spared for the limited manufacture of wood-framed jobs. During the War, the company changed its character without deserting any of its objectives, and the sidecars had to go. In March 1945, the first step was taken by altering the firm's name to Jaguar Cars Ltd., and the report on war production issued three months later referred to Swallow Coachbuilding merely as 'an associated company', though it did stress that Swallow had supplied large numbers of box sidecars to the Admiralty, the Army, the Royal Air Force, and the National Fire Service.

Sentiment could no longer be served, and by the end of 1945 the assets of Swallow Coachbuilding had been sold to the Helliwell Group.

The rest of the story is interesting if only for its complexity. Helliwells transferred operations to their own factory at Walsall Airport, and added Swallow to a diversity of industrial interests which included a project to build American light aircraft under licence. Three years later they disposed of the company to Tube Investments Ltd., who continued the sidecars as well as making two interesting incursions into vehicle manufacture. The first of these was the Swallow 'Gadabout', a scooter powered by a 125 c.c. Villiers two-stroke engine, which was also offered in commercial guise, complete with Swallow box sidecar. Unfortunately, this arrived a little in advance of the scooter boom which hit Britain in 1955, and these models were quietly dropped at the end of 1951. The Walsall factory reverted to sidecars for another three years before trying again, this time with a luxury sports car. Wisely, they did not attempt to compete with their distant cousins, the Jaguars, but their choice of the two-litre class was scarcely more felicitous, as the Triumph TR2 was already firmly established, and there was additional competition from the slightly bigger Austin-Healey '100'. Swallow's 'Doretti', named, it was said, after the daughter of their American distributor, used the mechanical components and suspension units of the Triumph in a special rigid frame of their own

S.S. Club Meet, 1936, assembled a selection of models past and present. Heading the procession are a 1934 S.S.I coupé, and one of the first 2½-litre S.S. Jaguar saloons.

Narrow grille and close-set headlamps characterized the original S.S.I of 1932.

design. Despite roadster bodywork more luxurious than that of either of its two competitors, the 'Doretti' was not alarmingly heavy, scaling 19¼ cwt. as against the 18½ cwt. of the Triumph and Austin-Healey. It was a trifle slower, recording 100·2 m.p.h. in the hands of *The Motor*, whereas the starker TR2 attained 107·3 m.p.h. Unfortunately, it was quite a lot more expensive than the Triumph, the basic price being £777 at a time when a TR2 could be bought for a mere £625. A change of policy brought 'Doretti' production to an end in March 1955, sales up to that time having been quite encouraging. The Walsall factory reverted to sidecars, and in October 1956, the Swallow Coachbuilding Co. (1935) Ltd. was purchased by Watsonian. Operations were transferred once more, this time to Watsonian's factory at Greet, Birmingham, where the Swallow line is still being produced.

The cars had come on the scene in 1927, and had only started to take the lion's share of the business in 1929. But the roots of the Jaguar business as we now know it go back to the earliest days at Bloomfield Road.

CHAPTER 2

The Packagers

1927–31

'Scientifically constructed to give great strength with minimum weight, the body in-corporates an ingenious disappearing hood and side curtains which are absolutely draught-proof . . . just like a fixed head. Carefully designed seating with a semi-horizontal spring steering wheel gives the driver a gorgeous feeling of supreme control at all speeds.'
Wolseley Swallow advertisement,
January 1931

'Personally I find 200 miles in the train more fatiguing than the same distance in the Swallow Hornet, and vastly more boring.'
A. G. Douglas Clease, The Autocar, May 1931

By 1926, the Swallow Sidecar Co. was established on a sound commercial basis, and also stood in the front rank of stylists of the sidecarriage. Henceforward, they were to interest themselves increasingly in cars.

Up to the middle 1920s, specialist coachwork had been largely the preserve of the bigger and more illustrious houses, who executed their art upon such luxury chassis as Rolls-Royce, Daimler, Hispano-Suiza and Packard. Not that these concerns were confined to London, for Arnold and Cockshoot in Manchester, Rippon at Huddersfield, Mann, Egerton at Norwich, Marshalsea at Taunton, and Bridges at Cirencester, to name but a few, catered for the provincial customer who preferred to support local craftsmanship. But in the main, the big names catered for the client who employed a chauffeur. Occasionally, they would execute a smart runabout for his wife, and such firms as Sanders of Hitchin made pleasing little doctors' coupés on medium-priced chassis like the Bean Twelve and 10/15 FIAT, but no attempt was made to produce such carrosserie in series —in fact, such practices would have been as insulting to the customer as making two identical hats for two different ladies. If one wanted sporting bodywork, one either went to a manufacturer who listed such a style in his catalogue, or bought one's own chassis and had a 'one-off' executed thereon by one's favourite coachbuilder. In any case, individuality was still relatively cheap, and even if one had to buy a 'bread-and-butter' car, there was still a formidable variety at one's beck and call . . . and they all looked different.

By the late 'twenties, stereotyped styling had crept in, and the era of the box-shaped saloon was in full swing. True, the rage for long bonnets, heralded by the 1929 Cord, was not far away, but for style, 1927 probably represented the nadir as far as British cars were concerned.

Lyons and Walmsley were packagers—that is to say, they took depressingly utilitarian motor-cars from the £200 price bracket, and dressed them up in such a form that they appealed to the aesthetically sensitive of both sexes. Wisely, being bodybuilders rather than engineers, they left the mechanical components untouched, relying upon the cars' lines to suggest speed that was not always there. The packager can flourish in any market where design is stereotyped, as in late-Vintage England, or the choice hopelessly limited, as in modern Italy. Much as I personally like the *Millecento* FIAT, I must admit that one example looks very much like another; this type enjoyed an absolute monopoly of its price class for twenty-two years, and the result has been the most fertile and original packaging industry in the world. The same uniformity of design has had different results in America, where the 'customizers' do weird and wonderful things by lowering roof-lines and painting bodies in exotic candy stripes.

Let us consider what material the two partners at Swallow had to contend with. The Austin Seven, though it has acquired a certain baroque charm in old age, was always a foursquare object innocent of frills. The design staff at Lingotto, having produced the very advanced Tipo 509 FIAT complete with four-wheel brakes and overhead-camshaft engine for the 1924 Paris Salon, left it severely alone for five years, in which time its angular appearance was hopelessly outmoded; and that worthy and indestructible little machine, the worm-drive Standard Nine, possessed a high-shouldered radiator of Edwardian aspect, towering fabric bodywork, and artillery wheels. The Wolseley Hornet in its original form did not pretend to be anything other than a Morris 'Minor' with two extra cylinders and the resultant extra footage of bonnet, while Swift of Coventry, though they sought to trick out their *de luxe* models with two-tone paint and coloured wire wheels, were a homely concern marketing a homely product. These family saloons might have hearts of gold, and some of them did: but they could never hope to sell on sex-appeal.

Not that Lyons and Walmsley were pioneers, either. For many years, small firms all over the world had been doing their best to disguise the Model T Ford's spindly appearance, and the Maiflower Motor Co. of Gloucester even acquired the status of a separate make in the early 1920s with their Ford conversion. From 1924 onwards, Cecil Kimber had been evolving M.G.s from that excellent but pedestrian contrivance, the Morris-Oxford, and by the time Swallows had transferred part of their allegiance to four wheels, Kimber had attained the right to a stand of his own in the car section at Olympia. Kimber, however, was to concentrate on performance, whereas Lyons aimed at making a car look exactly right, and encouraged the chassis manufacturer to provide any extra horses that might be needed. Other packagers were to arise: the Jensen brothers, working on their Avon Standards, and later on the Ford V8: Beauvais, who evolved the 'Kaye Don' Singers, the later Avons, and the Crossley 'Regis', and Ghia with his coupé on the 1956 Volkswagen chassis. But of this army of beautifiers, only Lyons, Kimber, and the Jensens rose from the art of gilding the lily to large-scale production of specialist cars conceived in their entirety by themselves.

Lyons waited until 1927 to explore this new market. He had bought himself a second-hand Austin Seven, and in this little car he recognized an ideal basis for special coachwork. In the spring of 1927 he was ready with the original Swallow Austin. A wooden frame was used, coachwork being panelled in aluminium, and staff was imported from the Midlands to assist in the construction of these bodies. The shortcomings of the basic Austin frame, which did not extend aft of the rear wheels, were met by strengthening the chassis side-members with angle iron—the only major modification made at Blackpool.

However, the finished article was recognizable only as an Austin by the badge on the radiator, the starting-handle orifice and the transverse front spring. The original Swallow Seven had a neat bulbous-tailed two-seater body, the stylish rear quarters housing the battery, the spare wheel, and (in theory, anyway) baggage. Whereas the standard Austin wore combined head and side lamps outrigged from the scuttle, the Blackpool variation had conventionally mounted headlamps, and side lamps set on top of the true cycle-type front wings, which turned with the wheels. This pleasing *ensemble* was crowned by an attractive rounded nose, reminiscent of the contemporary Morris and A.C., which matched the contours of the tail.

Nor was this all. The Austin Seven of the period had a bare dashboard, most of the space being occupied by an admonitory list of patents incorporated in the car, as a deterrent to would-be infringer

First time out: One of the S.S.I team in the 1933 Alpine Trial passes a Bugatti.

—but the Swallow version had a fully equipped panel, neatly laid out by the standards of the day. The complete car listed at £174, £10 more buying a hardtop that was not only detachable, but would hinge up to give easy access in wet weather. The Baby Austin had been transformed from a doughty and reliable 'pram on wheels' into a potential *concours* winner.

As yet there was no idea of large-scale production: Swallows thus admitting that Sir Herbert Austin's blessing had yet to be obtained. Later, Parkers of Manchester became the first distributors, followed by Henlys. Cars were still coach-painted, cellulose not appearing as standard till 1931, by which time operations had been transferred to Coventry. Later owners have confirmed that these early cars had their chassis painted only where it was visible.

The Austin was announced in May 1927, but three months later, Lyons had added another string to his bow, in the shape of a Morris-Cowley Swallow two-seater at £210, £10 extra being charged for wire wheels. As on the Austins, the steering wheel was lowered and raked, and the same system of body construction was used. Lines were enhanced by the lengthened scuttle, the vee windscreen, the polished mahogany dashboard with regrouped instruments, and the Ace wheel discs. The general effect was reminiscent of the contemporary M.G. but the Morrises, unlike the Austins, were finished in cellulose.

By this time, however, the M.G., though far costlier at £340, was well established, and Lyons abandoned this type after only a few had been made. These were distributed by Brown and Mallalieu, the Blackpool Morris agents, for whom Lyons had worked for a while before going into partnership with Walmsley. Though William Lyons was to have further dealings with the Morris interests, he never catalogued another body on a Morris chassis. The Austin-type Swallow saloon body fitted to an o.h.c. 'Minor' chassis in November 1930 was a 'one-off'.

The switch to car body production was marked by a change in the company's title, which became 'The Swallow Sidecar and Coachbuilding Co.' in 1927. By 1928, production was well under way, and Austin chassis were being procured direct from Birmingham—unfortunately, in batches of fifty, or rather more than the small works could handle at a time. Nonetheless, output of open and sidecar bodies rose rapidly to twelve a week, before the move from Blackpool to Coventry was made in 1928. Changes in design for the 1928 season included the abandonment of the hinged roof on the open two-seater, though the hardtop was still detachable; the adoption of full-size wings in place of the flimsy cycle-type; and the fitting of a vee-screen with openable panel on the driver's side (a concession to Lancashire fogs?). The standard two-seater cost £175, the coupé £185, and for £190 one could have the car with both hard and soft tops. The saloon cost £187 10s. By this time Henlys were handling the car in the South, and Parkers in the North, and the breed was so well established that in January 1930, Lyons made his first sale to a Royal client, H.H. The Sultan of Perak, who ordered an Austin saloon in purple and black. This famous saloon, the best-known

product of the pre-S.S. days, joined the range in November 1928, complete with domed roof, and tasteful duo-tone colour scheme with the unusual 'pen-nib' colour separation. At a time when blacks, browns, and dark blues were still deemed sufficient in the lower price brackets, the Swallows came out in a riot of colours, the 1932 Austin Swallow catalogue specifying the following combinations: black and apple green, black and Carnation red, Nile blue and ivory, apple green and ivory, Carnation red and ivory, cream and apple green, cream and Carnation red, or cream and Nile blue. *The Autocar* summarized the company's achievements as packagers in March 1929:

'The designers have contrived not only to make the car *look* bigger than it is, but to *feel* bigger. It handles well, is stable in cornering, and holds even a fairly rough road to a rather surprising extent for this type of car.'

Hardly sentiments which one would usually apply to the Austin Seven, excellent car though it was! Lyons and Walmsley had good reason for satisfaction.

Meanwhile, Lyons had taken a big step. He had decided to put the manufacture of car bodies first, and to carry out this plan successfully, it was imperative to move nearer to his sources of supply. Nineteen twenty-eight saw the firm established in part of a former munitions factory in Foleshill, Coventry, and these Holbrook Lane works covered the company's immediate capacity for expansion. Even so, Lyons' share of the site had extended to some thirteen acres by 1934. To him must go all the credit for making the move when he did, and this was the first step on the road that was to lead to the Jaguar, and to the run of post-war victories at Le Mans.

The next two seasons, which wrought destruction among the smaller car manufacturers and left few of the survivors unscathed, saw Lyons and Walmsley build up a steady business. Sidecars continued to sell, and the Depression almost *helped* Swallows. Specializing as they did in well-packaged and inexpensive light cars, they picked up customers from the higher income groups, who found that, the slump notwithstanding, they could still buy a car that did not look like everyone else's. Female clients poured in, for not only did the curvaceous contours and tasteful colour scheme take their fancy, but in addition they were being offered something that not only caught the eye, but was easy to drive. The average Vintage sports car, though eminently tractable in the hands of an experienced driver, was inclined to be heavy on the controls, and was possessed of a clutch and gearchange which needed knowing. The Austin Seven was, of course, foolproof, and the Swallow saloon was endowed with such pleasing little touches as a 'ladies' companion' built into the cubby-hole lid.

Swallows appeared at the Motor Show for the first time in 1929. The Austin was prominent, but it shared the stand with sports saloons on three different light car chassis—the FIAT Tipo 509A and Standard Big Nine at £250 apiece, and the Swift Ten at £275. Their bodies were modelled on the original Austin of 1928, but, given

The rare S.S.I drophead coupé was a mid-year introduction in 1935, and only a few were made. Some crossed the Atlantic, and this survivor was owned in California during the 1950s.

frames that extended well over the rear axles, the resulting designs suggested speed, and, cunningly, an underslung chassis, though in fact the cars were unmodified and untuned. The penalty was a perilously shallow windscreen of the type that reduces me to claustrophobia. However, the Swallows were to set a fashion for the next two or three years, and they were certainly no worse in this respect than some of their imitators. The FIAT appeared in the makers' English catalogue as a standard model, but disappeared after a few months, when the 509A was supplanted by the larger and stodgier Tipo 514. Between fifty and seventy were made, as far as I am able to ascertain—incidentally, they were the ordinary 509A model, and not the rare sports 509S.

Some 150 bodies were made on the Swift chassis in 1930 and 1931, production ceasing only when Swifts went out of business. The 'sports' chassis was used, but as this differed from the 'touring' version mainly in the provision of wire wheels as standard, it could hardly be called a sports car. Owners spoke of an honest 65 m.p.h., though. But the most important development was the alliance with Standard, then making a brisk recovery from low water in the dynamic hands of Captain J. P. Black, who had taken over in 1929. The chassis of the original Standard Swallow was unmodified apart from the provision of wire wheels, but, unlike the FIAT and Swift, it was given a face-lift by the use of a vee-radiator with chromium-plated shell, in which could be detected not only vestiges of the later

1932 S.S. style, but an almost exact prototype for the radiator used on Standard's own 1931 models. Chromium plate, incidentally, was adopted for the first time on Swallow's 1930 range.

For 1931 the Austins, the Swift and the Standard Nine were continued. The Austins acquired ship-type scuttle ventilators, the original split-bench front seat on the saloon gave way to the bucket type, and the uncompromisingly round nose was given the fashionable vee-effect by raising the radiator and adding a chromium-plated bar down the middle. There were, however, two new models from Foleshill.

The Wolseley 'Hornet' furnished the firm with the basis for a new style of open body. Introduced in the middle of the 1930 season, the 'Hornet' was an ugly beast reminiscent of an elongated Morris 'Minor', but it offered a smooth and flexible six-cylinder engine in a really compact vehicle at a really low price—£185. All too often, the 'Hornet' is cited as the archetype of popular motoring in the 'nasty thirties', but it could accelerate from a standing start on top gear, and thus endeared itself to the ladies. Properly maintained, the overhead-camshaft engine was reliable, and it had already attracted the attention of a whole army of specialist bodybuilders. Swallows furnished it with a pretty sports two-seater body. This had a tail with curves more restrained than the Austin's, and sold at £220. Apart from raked steering, and oversize tyres—the latter, as I know from personal experience, a desirable modification on

'Hornets'—it used the standard chassis, and was said to be good for over 70 m.p.h. No less a critic than A. G. Douglas Clease observed that its driver was 'comfortable in body and in mind', and it is significant that Clease later drove S.S. cars in many rallies. More important, it was the first six-cylinder car to pass through Swallow's works, and students of history cannot help but notice that ever since the company has shown a marked preference for the 'six' as against the 'four' and the 'eight'. The Wolseley Swallows sold quite well, despite the fact that they competed with the special-bodied 'Hornets' put out by Eustace Watkins, Wolseley's London distributors. To my eye, the Swallows were prettier, if less functional, than any of the whole array of sporting bodies on this chassis, and they lacked the bonnet straps, soup-plate instruments and other 'sporty' paraphernalia of the period.

In May 1931, a second 'six' purred its way into the Swallow catalogue, in the shape of a larger Standard Swallow on the 16 h.p. 'Ensign' chassis. Thanks to the admirable proportions of Swallow coachwork, it was hard to distinguish this from its smaller sister.

Even at £275 (£282 10s. with sliding roof) sales were not spectacular, but the big Swallow marked the beginnings of an association with the six-cylinder Standard engine, a unit which was to establish Lyons as a serious car manufacturer, and form the basis of every Jaguar engine made up to 1948.

Maurice Sampson and F. Gordon Crosby, who were doing a round trip of Britain's motor industry for *The Autocar* during the Depression, called in at Foleshill *en route* and published their findings in February 1931. They were suitably impressed by the ability of the small staff to make up thirty body frames a day, by the remarkably brisk rate of output in those dreary times, and by the cleanliness of the factory. They noted with approval that paint was kept properly mixed by an ingenious drum on which the tins were rotated at speed. Sliding roofs were now virtually universal on saloon bodies, but there were no assembly lines, bodies being transferred on trestles from the trimming shop for attachment to the waiting chassis. One suspects that the visit must have taken place late in 1930, for paint and varnish were still in use, and cellulose took its place in 1931.

Standards, as was their wont in those days of yearly models, were among the first British firms to announce their 1932 programme, and the Swallow Coachbuilding Co. Ltd.—the 'sidecar' was dropped from the title in 1930, and never reappeared even after the divorce with the car interests—was quick to inform the public that no changes were being made to their four- and six-cylinder Swallow variants. The Austins likewise escaped unchanged, apart from the provision of safety glass all round, but prices were slashed from £165 to £150 in the case of the two-seater, and from £187 10s. to £165 in the case of the saloon. The hardtop coupé still featured in the range, these later Austins being described as 'the sports chassis, with sports silencer and fishtail'. In these days of cumulative purchase tax, it is interesting to note how cheaply the gimmick-minded could load their cars with extras such as a coloured radiator muff (£1), a spring steering wheel with coloured rim (£1 15s.), a Hobson 'Telegage' (£2 19s. 6d.), an eight-day clock (£2 2s.), and a spotlamp (£1 12s. 6d. including fitting). One is surprised to find electric trafficators offered even as an extra, at £2 7s. 6d. fitted, but more alarming to the modern motorist is the realization that, unless one was prepared to part with an extra 35s. on the purchase price, one's headlamps would not dip. The Wolseley range was augmented by a smart four-seater sports, which had more than a look of the future S.S. I tourer.

The colour advertisement which Lyons inserted in the motoring press to launch these models depicted the Standard Swallow saloon, but a goodly portion of his space was devoted to this tantalizing copy:

> 'S.S. is the name of a new car that's going to thrill the hearts of the motoring public, and the trade alike. It's something utterly new ... different ... better. Long ... low ... very low ... and very FAST! At the Show, or before, two S.S. coupés of surpassing beauty will be presented. WAIT! ... THE S.S. IS COMING!'.

A jaded England, which had just slipped off the Gold Standard, waited.

Above: The police take an interest. Bolton Constabulary's first S.S.II, a 1935 tourer.

Below: Prototype sports car. The first S.S.90 of 1935, with the Hon. Brian Lewis at the wheel.

CHAPTER 3

Non-Standard Standards

1932–35

'In a stereotyped age, the S.S. stands alone—boldly individualistic—daring to be different. At a time when mere cheapness is frequently of greater account than worth, the S.S. note of quality is insistent. While affinity between appearance and performance tends to become less, the S.S. proffers both—in full measure.'

S.S. catalogue, October 1934

'Excruciatingly rakish little sedans, they appealed largely to the same types that went for yellow Auburns in this country.'

Ralph Stein, *Sports Cars of the World*, 1952

SWALLOWS kept their promise. The new S.S. duly appeared at the Olympia Show in October 1931, and sparked off a flood of controversy. From the earliest days, Lyons blazoned his ideals in the forewords to his catalogues and in press advertising, but even now the world is not quite sure what it thinks of the first complete cars from Foleshill. *The Motor* praised 'a radiator of outstanding design', but *The Scribe*, writing in *The Autocar*, preferred to sit on the fence, with the observation that:

'Anyone who was not ultra-smart in appearance, clean cut, and well groomed, would look as absurd in a S.S. Sixteen as would a costermonger in a choker, sitting in a Rolls-Royce *coupé de ville*.'

Ralph Stein's comments on yellow Auburns were typical of a more critical and Vintage-club-ridden era, and even so whimsical a writer as the late W. H. Charnock summed the S.S. up as 'a real cad's car' in *Motor Sport* in 1953. Some people even cast aspersions on the originality of the design, hinting that the car derived from the L–29 Cord of 1929, by which view they showed a remarkable ignorance of the past trend of Lyons' policy and concept of body design.

Be that as it may, the S.S. was a *fait accompli*, and carried the ridiculously low price-tag of £310, for which the customer could have a car conforming to what Americans of the 1960s would term the 'Classic formula'—i.e. a bonnet at least half as long as the whole vehicle.

Not that the S.S. represented a new idea—it was rather the logical development of what Lyons and Walmsley had been doing first at Cocker Street, and then at Foleshill, over the past four years. It did not mark the transformation of the Swallow Coachbuilding Co. from body-builders to manufacturers, for chassis were still purchased complete, and were only offered up to their bodies in the Swallow factory. But it did establish their product as a *marque* in its own right, even if it had to languish for three seasons among the special *carrosserie* in Olympia's National Hall before being promoted to a place among the manufacturers in the Grand Hall. (*The Autocar*, to its credit, adopted a more realistic attitude, listing the S.S. as a separate make as early as February 1932.) But whatever officialdom might think, the S.S. was designed as an entity, even if it did use a large proportion of stock components; and the work was not undertaken by Lyons and Walmsley for Standards. The Standard Motor Co.'s co-operation was vital to the success of the project, but they were suppliers, and not sponsors.

Previous Swallow-bodied cars had been family saloons packaged in such a way that they not only looked bigger, faster, and costlier, but actually performed better. It became obvious that there was a future in a specialist car at a low price, and that two litres was a good size—big enough to give a satisfying performance without elaborate tuning, yet small enough to dodge the burden of the horsepower tax. This followed the lead of Cecil Kimber, who had introduced his 18/80 M.G. in 1929—but the 18/80, though it retailed for a third of the price of a Bentley, and was only some 10 m.p.h. slower, was not particularly cheap at £545, or nearly £200 more than was asked for its prototype, the Morris Six. Swallows had to find a chassis which was compact, inexpensive, and in large-scale production. Lyons liked six-cylinder engines, but while his liking was tempered by a healthy distrust of the 'light sixes' of 1½-litre capacity which the slump had bred, he was anxious to combine the 'long, low look' with a higher degree of forward vision than had been possible with the unmodified Standards, Swifts, and FIATs of

1929–30. An underslung frame was therefore desirable, and this would mean a special chassis.

Standards were the obvious suppliers. Not only were they returning to prosperity in the teeth of the Depression, but excellent relations had been established with Captain J. P. Black through the agency of the Standard Swallow already in production. Further, the company had introduced a compact and simple two-litre 'six', the 16 h.p. 'Ensign', which was infinitely preferable for the Swallow concern's purposes than such machines as were made by their other chassis suppliers. Austin's 'Sixteen' was elephantine and indestructible, while Wolseley's overhead-camshaft 2-litre 'Viper' was ruled out, since it had been designed to take identical coachwork to that used on the big 21/60 h.p. 'County' model. And, the firm reasoned, if the 16 h.p. Swallow Standard saloon could be sold economically at only £275, a completely new car utilizing Standard components should be possible at a retail price of little over £300.

The recipe, as it turned out, was simple enough. The Standard's 65·5 × 101·6 mm. (2,054 cc) side-valve engine was adopted in untuned form, the stiff seven-bearing crankshaft lending itself to further development as required. The price paid for this was, of course, the high cost of a major overhaul when it was needed, hence the presence of later S.S. and Jaguar engines, and even Chevrolet Sixes, in some surviving S.S. Is. This was not, of course, a significant factor with later units, which were noted for their longevity. Standard's four-speed gearbox was blessed with reasonably close ratios and was likewise retained, though in the interests of fast cruising and durability the higher of the two optional top-gear ratios (4·66 : 1) was used in all the first S.S.s, whereas most Standard Sixteens were supplied with a 5·11 : 1 top gear. The Marles-Weller cam and lever steering gear and the front and rear axles were likewise stock Standard components.

Nonetheless, the Swallow Coachbuilding Co.'s claim that the chassis was 'specially manufactured by the Standard Motor Company', exclusively for them, held water, as more conventional packagers found to their cost. The double-drop frame was underslung and the wheelbase, at 9ft. 4ins., was three inches longer than the Standard's. The front semi-elliptic springs were mounted outside the chassis frame. The engine was set back seven inches to give a 'sports car' look. Lyons and Walmsley might adhere to Standard's Bendix-Perrot cable-operated brakes (they were not to adopt hydraulics of any kind till 1949), but they used Rudge-Whitworth 'racing-type' wire wheels in place of the plainer Magna type. Like all cars of the period in the 'sporty' class, the S.S. had a central remote-control gear lever. The centrally-mounted handbrake was oddly cranked to allow three-abreast seating, though, as *The Autocar* commented at the time, 'the passenger sitting in the middle must dispose his feet to miss the gear lever'.

On this inexpensive, robust and simple chassis Lyons designed a rakish coupé, with a very long bonnet, helmet-type cycle wings and a relatively deep windscreen, in spite of which the complete car stood a mere 4ft. 7ins. off the ground, as compared to the Standard's 5ft. 8ins. A new vee-radiator with vertical chromium bars, crowned by a Swallow motif, completed the *ensemble*. The famous S.S. hexagon, incidentally, did not appear on this grille, and the instruments were likewise oval, as they were to remain till the 1934 season. This attractive monogram did, however, figure prominently in the first S.S. catalogue, which gave customers a choice of six basic colour schemes.

Though the S.S. I was the principal offering, and was to remain so until the advent of the Jaguar in 1936, a pretty little coupé on similar lines, the S.S. II, was also listed. This used a modified 1,052 cc Standard 'Little Nine' chassis, and sold for £210. The major styling

The four-window S.S.I saloon, best-seller of the 1934 range, was less claustrophobic than the coupé. This example has been restored by the factory. The licence plate is for show only.

difference between the S.S. I and the S.S. II was the use of a painted radiator shell on the 9 h.p. model.

The S.S. monogram not only served to differentiate the new cars from their predecessors; it furnished a convenient mystery. Opinions differed as to the significance of the initials; some said that they stood for 'Standard Swallow', others opted for 'Swallow Special' or 'Swallow Sports', and the diehards translated them into picturesquely alliterative abuse. The fact is that no definition was intended, let alone published—translation was left to each individual's taste. Standards might, and probably did assert that the machines were Standard Swallows, but all cars built up to March 1945 are correctly referred to as S.S.'s, whether they were of the Jaguar series or not, and nobody would ever dream of regarding even an early Jaguar as a 'Standard Swallow'!

The new models took the motoring public by storm. The bright colour schemes, the elongated bonnets, the '£1,000 look', and the actual price asked astonished trade and public alike. The influence even spread to the doors of the nursery, almost the first 'Dinky Toy' produced by Meccano being a realistic scale model of the S.S. I coupé. Henlys, Swallows' distributors, cheerfully contracted to buy half the output, and, provided at least 1,000 a year could be made, the new car was a safe bet. In fact, 1932 deliveries amounted to 776 cars, but by 1932 standards this was excellent, and only a foretaste of what was to come. The use of well-tried components successfully circumvented the teething troubles that often accompany an entirely new model. Thus it mattered little that the S.S. had done hardly any motoring when it appeared at Olympia for the first time.

In January 1932, *The Autocar* published the first road test of the S.S. I. By the sports-car criteria of the day it could hardly be described as 'very fast', but it should be remembered that the average 2-litre family saloon of the period was distinctly breathless at 60 m.p.h., and the Standard Sixteen could only just better this figure. Lea-Francis' 'Ace of Spades' could carry four people at over 70 m.p.h., but it required an o.h.c. engine to do this, and at £495 it was not exactly cheap. In the circumstances a speed of 71 m.p.h., with 60 m.p.h. available on the close-ratio third, was a performance of which no one had any need to be ashamed. The Bendix brakes were evidently behaving themselves, for a stop from 30 m.p.h. was accomplished in twenty-nine feet, while the excellence of the forward vision was commented upon. 'Obviously,' *The Autocar* observed, 'the S.S. I makes its primary appeal on the question of smart appearance, but while that alone might satisfy a few, it would not be sufficient for those who desire a performance above the average.'

The road-holding likewise came in for praise, which is interesting in the light of later critics' views on the S.S.'s tendency to 'run out of road'.

'It holds the road admirably, being very steady on bends and corners and giving the driver a feeling of complete confidence in its stability. Coupled with this is steering which is light and positive, the driver knowing his course to a fraction of an inch.'

55 m.p.h. was deemed a comfortable cruising speed, but evidently Swallows were already questing more urge. Though they did not publicize the fact overmuch till the following year, they were already offering an optional power unit in the shape of the 2,552 cc Standard Twenty.

As yet the S.S. was not making its mark in competition, though three cars took part in the R.A.C.'s first National Rally to Torquay. The drivers were A. G. Douglas Clease of *The Autocar* (who earned praise for a solo drive), E. F. Huckvale, the Swallow company's Secretary, and Kathleen, Countess of Drogheda. No awards were won, either in the Rally proper or in the ensuing Coachwork Competition. The S.S.'s day was to come.

In the Bristol *Concours* that July, the prize in the appropriate class went to the car's principal competitor, the Avon Standard, but a S.S. II took a second place at the *Concours* run in conjunction with the Guy's Gala meeting at Brooklands, and at Ramsgate, then a major annual event, the class for small closed cars was a Swallow benefit, a S.S. II beating a Swift Swallow. Two months before, the firm acquired some useful publicity when J. A. Mollison, the aviator, was photographed with his new S.S. I coupé.

As always, Lyons hedged his bets. Production of the Austin and Standard Swallows was tapering off, but the sidecars remained in the picture, and in April 1932, the introduction of the new Wolseley 'Hornet Special' sports car sparked off Swallow two- and four-seater variants. The 'Hornet Special' was an extensively tuned and modified version of the touring 'Hornet', and was supplied in chassis form only at £180. The individualist could have open, convertible or closed bodies fitted by a diversity of bodybuilders, including Eustace Watkins, Maltby, Patrick, Corsica, Hardy, Jensen and Holbrook. The Swallow styles were virtually identical to the 1931 model, a two-seater costing £255, and the four-seater £5 more. These types remained current throughout the 1933 season, and were the

The functional rear aspect of the 1935 L-head S.S.90 speedster, forerunner of the overhead valve S.S.100 line current from 1936 through 1940.

last special bodies turned out on chassis of proprietary design.

In September, the new 1933 S.S. cars were announced. The S.S II was hardly altered, though it followed the latest Standard 'Little Nine' in acquiring four forward speeds. The S.S. I, however, came in for a major face-lift. Power was increased by the provision of an alloy head, improved manifolding, and the choice of a S.U. or R.A.G. carburetter, the latter being more frequently found—indeed, it was standardized for 1934. Output was not quoted, but was in fact around 60 b.h.p. for the 20 h.p. engine, and some 10 b.h.p. less for the Sixteen. To combat overheating, a weakness of the 1932 cars, a new and more efficient radiator block was fitted, and this was cloaked with a wider shell of attractive aspect. Trouble had also been experienced with engine fumes—a frequent headache with low bonnet lines and big power units—and the 1933 cars had an armoured dash. A new cruciform-braced frame of longer wheelbase (9ft. 11ins.) and 1in. wider track was adopted, but, though Standards offered a preselective gearbox on certain models, Swallows steered clear of this 'improvement'. In this context, however, it is interesting to quote a letter written by Miss Alice Fenton to that great S.S. and Jaguar enthusiast, Colonel Rixon Bucknall, in December 1932:

'As regards the pre-selective gearbox, we are now in a position to accept orders for the Wilson box, but deliveries will not commence until early in the New Year.'

I should add that neither I nor anyone of my acquaintance, including members of the S.S. staff, has seen a Wilson-equipped S.S. I, though experiments were later made with the Cotal electro-magnetic box. This was not adopted either.

It was, however, the coachwork that came in for the greatest improvements. Gone were the helmet-type wings, and a shallower windscreen gave the car a more balanced head-on aspect and a neater silhouette, albeit at the price of inferior forward vision. The new sweeping wings and full-size running-boards certainly improved the car's appearance, and the seating arrangements had been tackled in an original way. The 1932 cars had been occasional and uncomfortable three-seaters, and the Henly modification of a double dickey seat in the boot, well outside the wheelbase, smacked of mediaeval torture. The low build, however, entailed the intrusion of the propeller-shaft tunnel into the back of the car, and this inconvenience was neatly turned to good account by the provision of two separate 'armchair' rear seats. The story that these were designed on the lines of the office chairs at Foleshill is certainly apocryphal! The 1933 coupé cost £325 in 16 h.p. form, and £335 with the 20 h.p. engine.

A. G. Douglas Clease subjected one of these new cars to a tough test of 1,000 miles over Highland roads, even exploring the then-diabolical stretch leading to Mallaig, on which the car did not 'bottom', as might have been expected. Even *Motor Sport*, which catered for a more selective readership, could find little fault when it sampled a similar car in the following June. It is surprising to find the forward vision described as 'extraordinarily good'; less surprising is the praise accorded to the S.S. as a fast tourer:

'We found that normal driving with the S.S.I produced an average of 40 m.p.h. over main roads, a figure which could be raised by dint of a little effort on the part of the driver. On one occasion we covered 41 miles in 50 minutes. The low centre of gravity, the high-geared steering, the rigid suspension, and willing engine all contributed towards this ability to maintain high average speeds without effort.'

The 1935 S.S.I drophead coupé. It cost £40 more than the regular saloons.

This furnishes an interesting commentary on British motoring conditions in a more spacious age—nowadays, I think I should want a motorway to ensure putting forty miles into the hour on an E-type with more than double the S.S. I's maximum speed, while even such a hardened Jaguar enthusiast as myself would not describe their present-day steering as high-geared!

Nineteen thirty-three saw a strong challenge from another firm of packagers, the New Avon Body Co. of Warwick. The Avons stemmed from a rakish sports two-seater designed by the youthful Jensen brothers in 1928, and fitted to an Austin Seven chassis. This style was put into series production on the Standard Big Nine chassis in 1930, and was followed shortly afterwards by two- and four-seater fixed-head coupés, which were available both on the 'Big Nine' and on the 16 h.p. 'Ensign' model. With their long, low bonnets, cycle-type wings, and fabric heads with dummy hood irons, they competed on fairly equal terms with the original Standard Swallows; but the advent of the S.S. saw Avons at a disadvantage, for the special under-slung chassis was not made available to them, and they had to simulate this effect by cunning body design. By the time the S.S. had entered upon its second year of life, the Jensens had set up their own firm in West Bromwich, and Avons were retaining another expert packager, C. F. Beauvais. Beauvais had just completed his ingenious transformation of the Singer 'Junior Special' (as the Nine was originally known) from a square box into the curvaceous 'Kaye

Ageless line: The original 2½-litre overhead valve Jaguar saloon of 1936 set the fashion for the British high-performance touring cars as well as being a yardstick on price. Side mounts were dropped at the end of the '37 season.

Don' saloon, and he proceeded to operate energetically upon the Avon Standards. The coupés and saloons were drastically revised, and a four-seater tourer with airflow wings and wheel discs replaced the two-seater model. The Avons were available on the four-cylinder Standard 'Big Nine' chassis, on the unhappy six-cylinder 'Little Twelve' with preselective gearbox, and on the 16 and 20 h.p. cars. As they used the stock chassis, they could be sold cheaper than the S.S., a 16 h.p. tourer being available for £280, and a coupé with dickey seat at £305, but the saloon listed at £325, exactly the figure asked for the corresponding S.S. I.

In 1933 *The Autocar* tested the S.S. I in 16 h.p. and 20 h.p. forms, and the Standard Sixteen in four-door and Avon saloon guises. It is therefore instructive to compare figures. The Standard turned the scales at 23½cwt, and recorded 61·64 m.p.h., 24·6 seconds being required to reach 50 m.p.h. from a standstill. The Avon, thanks to a lower all-up weight of 22¼cwt, and engine modifications including a high-compression cylinder head and R.A.G. carburetter, managed 75 m.p.h., and took nearly two seconds less than the factory-bodied saloon to accelerate from 10 to 30 m.p.h. The 16 h.p. S.S. likewise attained 75 m.p.h., and its fuel consumption of 20 m.p.g. was identical with the Avon's, but a better cruising range was ensured by a fuel tank capacity of twelve gallons as against the nine carried by the Warwick company's product. Acceleration figures were fractionally better, despite a higher weight of 25½cwt. For all their pleasing and more restrained lines, the Avons could not compete with the S.S.; the momentary advantage gained by their shapely tourer was lost by March 1933, when an open model was added to the S.S. I range. Though fair numbers were turned out in the next few seasons, they were never to worry William Lyons again—as late as 1937 they were marketing a beautiful four-door saloon on the

Standard 'Flying 20' chassis, but this retained the old side-valve engine, and was thus no match for the less expensive 2½-litre Jaguar.

Sales climbed steadily to over 1,500 cars in 1933, aided by the energetic Henly organization, which ran 'sales circuses' of cars; these toured the country, introducing the range to provincial customers. As early as April 1930, a fleet of six Swallow saloons—Austins, Standards, and Swifts—had undertaken a 5,000-mile circular trip, and late in 1932 a second Henly convoy of S.S. Is and S.S. IIs centred its activities on the south of England. In February 1933, special S.S. display weeks were held in London, Manchester, and Bournemouth. By 1934, Henlys had dreamed up two more attractive ideas—the first of these was an ingenious raffle which anticipated one of Independent Television's programmes by a quarter of a century. An S.S. I saloon was locked in a garage, six keys to which were mixed up with several thousand useless ones, and dropped into a bag. The first person to draw a key that would open the garage won the car. The second gimmick was a gymkhana at Hanworth Air Park, open to owners of the three *marques* which Henlys distributed—Alvis, Rover, and S.S. The judging of the *Concours d'Elégance* was simplified by making the S.S. owners judge the Rovers and so on!

Performance was improving. A 20 h.p. coupé tried by *The Autocar* in April 1933 was found to be 13 lb. lighter than its lower-powered sister, and recorded 81·82 m.p.h., took fifteen seconds to accelerate from a standing start to 60 m.p.h., and cruised comfortably all day at 70 m.p.h. The testers, however, reported that it felt rougher than the Sixteen. No statistical breakdown is available for those early years, but it would seem that the 16 h.p. car was fractionally more popular, the British public being alarmingly horsepower-conscious, and preferring to sacrifice 5 m.p.h. in top speed for an annual saving

Beauty: the 'one-off' 3½-litre S.S.100 fixed-head coupé exhibited at the
1938 Earls Court Show.

of £4 in taxation. Nobody seems to have worried about testing the
S.S. II, already something of a Cinderella, but owners spoke of 65
m.p.h. on the 5·43 top gear, 50 m.p.h. on the close-ratio third, and
fuel consumptions of the order of 32 m.p.g. Directional stability was
a little suspect, and sharp turns of the wheel were apt to result in
skids.

The company, having produced a car which surpassed all its
rivals for looks, and a good many of them on performance, now
decided to try their hand at something more sporting. The spring of
1933 saw the introduction of a sports four-seater, at the same price
as the coupé. The first one off the line went, appositely enough, to
Captain Black of Standards, who had helped to make the S.S.'s
success possible. Later Walmsley had built a sports two-seater
derived from the production two-seater, with a long tail and hori-
zontally-mounted spare wheel, quite unlike the later S.S. 90 and
S.S. 100. This model was never put into production, and I have been
unable to trace what happened to the prototype.

The 1933 season saw the beginning of serious competition work.
As yet, most of the successes came from the *Concours d'Elégance*;
though the Avon Standards took the class honours in the R.A.C.

Baby Jaguar: The 1938 1½-litre was in fact a 1¾-litre with overhead valve
65 horsepower Standard-built engine. Body work was as roomy as on
the six-cylinder cars, but acceleration suffered in the cause of m.p.g. The
price tag (£318) dates the photograph more than does the automobile.

The Beast: the prototype 'VB' model for airborne operations 1944. It
had a Ford Ten engine.

Rally, Douglas Clease's S.S. I tourer was successful in the Scottish event, S.S. Is scored a 1-2-3 victory at Eastbourne, and a private owner, Mrs Olive, took first place at Ramsgate, beating a factory entry. The cars even featured in the J.C.C. Caravan Rally held in September of that year, Miss Constance Carpenter's *ensemble* of S.S. I and Car Cruiser winning the award for the 'caravan equipped by its owner in the most useful and ingenious way'. Towing a large caravan behind the elongated S.S. I must have been no joke, though Standard's gear ratios undoubtedly helped on awkward gradients!

The 1934 edition of the S.S. catalogue devoted a page to 'competition successes', but could find little to report beyond victories in Continental *Concours d'Elégance* (be it said, against far costlier *salon* items), and the use of a S.S. I tourer as the Official Course Car at the Manx Grand Prix—a tribute, no doubt, to Lyons' and Walmsley's motorcycling connections! It was also reported that Major E. M. Harvey's S.S. I had 'delighted the crowds' at Shelsley Walsh 'by its fast and silent ascent in the excellent time of $61\frac{2}{5}$ seconds, gaining the third position in its class'. The same kind of remark was to be made fourteen years later, about the twin-camshaft Jaguar, but at Le Mans as well as Shelsley.

Outside the *Concours d'Elégance*, the cars made little impression in the big events, V. A. Budge managing only fifty-eighth place out of seventy-one finishers in the Monte Carlo Rally, and Douglas Clease's entry in the R.A.C. Rally occasioning comment solely on account of the excellent reception afforded by its Philco radio set! But members of *The Autocar* and *The Motor*'s staffs continued to use these cars extensively, no doubt seeking, as did many members of the public, the reasons behind the meteoric success of Lyons and Walmsley. Brian Twist of *The Autocar* broke new ground when he tried for a Triple Award in the three classic M.C.C. long-distance trials, using different variations on a theme by Standard in the 'Exeter', the 'Edinburgh', and the 'Lands End'. For the 'Edinburgh' his mount was a 20 h.p. S.S. I tourer—admittedly in those days trials were not the mud-plugging affairs, conducted on vertical timber-strewn Cotswold slopes, that they are today, but I am not surprised that Twist told Lyons that the car was 'much too good to take in for a trial'. But low build, excessive length, and poor ground clearance notwithstanding, the S.S. collected its premier award. No criticism could be made of either the handling or of the remote-control gear change, but the steering was considered overgeared, this fault being accentuated by too small a wheel.

But in July 1933, Lyons took a courageous step, He entered a Trade Team of three S.S. Is for the International Alpine Trial.

The Alpine was, and is, the toughest of all the rallies. For a firm as young as Swallows to tackle it was a brave venture, though this particular event saw some other unlikely starters, including a Daimler Fifteen, a Humber Twelve tourer entered by Lionel Martin, and a team of three Vauxhall 'Light Sixes' with American drivers, sponsored by the General Motors organization. To handle his entries, Lyons chose the late Humfrey Symons, later famous for his trans-African record runs on Rolls-Royce, Morris and Wolseley cars; Miss Margaret Allan, well known at Brooklands for her exploits with Bentleys; and C. M. Needham, who had won a *Coupe des Alpes* in the 1932 event on a $4\frac{1}{2}$-litre Invicta.

As it happened, this attempt was not crowned with success. Needham recalls that he was concerned about the steering, which tended to stiffen up on full lock, and required frequent greasing— a potential loss of valuable time in such a trial. More disconcerting was the model's inclination to overheat. The 1933 improvements to the cooling system had alleviated this failing in normal road work, but in the Alps it was to prove the cars' Waterloo, both Miss Allan and Symons succumbing to blown head gaskets. The latter struggled on, changing one gasket in forty minutes, but he ended up on a tow-rope behind Leschallas' A.C., and all hopes of the Team Prize were lost. Needham, on the sole surviving 'works' car, after a solo drive with a leaking radiator, finished eighth in the 3-litre class for individual entries, Koch on a privately-owned S.S. taking sixth place in the same class.

In 1934, however, Lyons was back in the Alps, the three 'works' cars being assigned to Douglas Clease, Needham and S. H. Light. As in 1933, they were 20 h.p. four-seaters, and all three were barely run-in when they were delivered. Two of the cars suffered, as might have been expected, from distortion of the cylinder heads, but Needham managed to keep out of trouble by using a 25% Benzole mixture, and devoting his practice time to ordinary running-in rather than to preliminary onslaughts on the passes. In spite of these handicaps, the S.S. team took third place in their class in the Team event, for which achievement they won a silver plaque. The works Talbots and Adlers tied for first place, but in fairness to Lyons, it should be conceded that the former were specially modified '105s', conforming far more closely to the racing version than to the stock Vanden Plas tourers. It is also no disrespect to M. Roesch's masterpiece to comment that it sold in untuned form for more than double the list price of a S.S. I! The 'Alpine' was not run in 1935, and next time a S.S. figured in the entry list, it was to have the pushrod o.h.v. engine, and appreciably more horses.

Meanwhile, the cars were becoming popular with stars of the stage and screen, an attribute which was to earn them the nickname of 'Wardour Street Bentleys'. The late George Formby bought a S.S. I in 1933—a pleasing gesture of support for a Lancashire-born firm by a Lancashire-born comedian. There is also a delightful tale told of a well-known radio personality who bought a coupé, had it painted white, and sent it back to Foleshill for a respray after every *concours* victory! There may be some truth in this story, as by 1937 a footnote in the Jaguar catalogue warned customers that it would cost them £10 extra to specify white cellulose on their cars.

The firm was also reaping the rewards of its progressive export policy in the sidecar days. A press release of December 1933 claimed that export business for the year was up 227% on 1932. This may not have meant much, since all the company's energies in the first year of production must have been centred on selling the S.S. at home; but it is fatal to judge Britain's motor industry in the early

1930s by the 'Export or Bust' standards of, say, 1948. There was no export quota enforced by the Government, and no steel allocation to worry manufacturers. The home market, emerging from the dark years, was becoming increasingly healthy, helped on its way by the numerous casualties among the specialist manufacturers. Features such as sliding roofs, opening windscreens and leather upholstery were universal, and nobody cared a whit for the American who liked neither, or the wretched client in Africa with his pleas for dust sealing and rain-proof coachwork. British car exports subsisted precariously on one-make loyalties going back to 1914, and such loyalties could not possibly obtain in the case of a *marque* not two years old. In spite of this, and a total export sale for the year of well under one hundred cars, there were S.S. agencies in France, Switzerland, Austria, Portugal, Spain, Sweden, Holland, Egypt, Morocco, Palestine, India, Australia, Czechoslovakia, and Belgium, while individual cars had been shipped to clients in Madeira, Jamaica, and Poland. Spain, surprisingly enough, was quite a good market for the S.S. in pre-Civil War days, the agent being Don Carlos Salamanca, who had given his name to a cabriolet style much favoured on Rolls-Royce chassis in the early 1920s.

Standards lengthened the stroke of their six-cylinder engines to 106 mm. for 1934, and the S.S. followed suit, capacities being enlarged to 2,143 cc in the case of the Sixteen, and 2,663·7 cc for the Twenty. Though Bendix brakes were retained, they now worked in larger 12½-inch drums, and the four-speed gearbox acquired synchromesh on second, third and top gears. Other improvements included a stronger cruciform-braced frame, Silentbloc spring shackles requiring no lubrication, self-cancelling trafficators (an optional extra in 1933), reversing lights, a quick-action fuel filler cap, a chromium-plated spare wheel cover, and what contemporary advertising described as 'devastating new acceleration and speed'. The 16 h.p. engine developed 53 b.h.p., and the Twenty some 15 b.h.p. more. In addition to the four-seater coupé and the tourer, a four-light saloon was now offered, and the hitherto sceptical *Scribe*, writing in *The Autocar*, had to confess that this was another stylistic triumph:

'When the S.S. was first introduced two or three years ago, I would not have owned it, even had it been given to me. It was too bizarre for a man of my retiring disposition, but the 1934 saloon is all the first coupé was not—a real gem of a car.'

He went on to bracket the car with the Avon Standards, which cannot have pleased Foleshill overmuch.

Nineteen thirty-four was the year of the hexagons—the actual badge was designed by an Iliffe employee named Reavesby—and the instruments of the new cars were set in an attractive dull chromium facia. As standard equipment on a S.S. I coupé costing a mere £335, one got a speedometer, electric clock, ammeter, oil pressure gauge (no cheap warning light!), fuel gauge, and water thermometer, not to mention such a forgotten luxury as an opening rear window with a remotely controlled blind. What is more, these models came in fifteen different basic colours, and nineteen possible combinations of exterior and interior finish. The most expensive variant was the 20 h.p. saloon at £345.

Meanwhile the S.S. II, which had survived two seasons virtually unchanged, also came in for major revision. Always eclipsed by the S.S. I, and suffering from fierce competition from such makers as Hillman, Triumph, and Riley, the little car was still regarded as a special-bodied Standard rather than as a make in its own right, *The Autocar* carrying this concept to extremes by dividing its report on the S.S. display at the 1933 Show into two halves, the small cars, of course, being relegated for this purpose to the coachwork section! For 1934, they were brought into line with the S.S. I, the cycle-type wings being discarded, and all the main alterations, including the synchromesh gearboxes, being incorporated. Saloon and coupé styles only were listed, but buyers had the choice of the full range of colour options. Engines available were Standard's 63·5 × 106 mm. (1,343 cc) Ten and 69·5 × 106 mm. (1,608 cc) Twelve. Gear ratios were 5·29, 7·68, 12·84 and 20·85 to 1, and outputs from the lightly tuned engines were 32 b.h.p. and 38 b.h.p. respectively, at 4,000 r.p.m. Prices ranged from £260 to £270, and in 1934 the S.S. II had its brief moment of glory, when three 'Standards' collected the Team Award in the Austrian Alpine Trials. Two of them were in fact Canley productions, but the third was a S.S. II saloon driven by Prince Ernst Windisch-Graetz.

A well-proportioned 1935 S.S.II sports touring in a North Country rally. Though these cars faithfully reproduced the sixes' style in miniature, not even the British horsepower tax (£1 per unit of R.A.C. rating) could prevent their eclipse by the big S.S.Is.

The additional power had its effects, and the S.S. I began to win competitive events, C. M. Needham pulling off a class win in the Scottish Rally, as well as climbing Shelsey Walsh in 50·2 seconds, a marked improvement on Major Harvey's 1933 figure. The '£251 to £300' price class at *Concours d'Elégance* was fast resolving itself into a S.S. preserve—Eastbourne saw four class wins (three of them going to Captain Plugge's S.S. I saloon), Ramsgate two, and Bexhill four, not to mention four second places. Another car collected an award at Dieppe, while S. H. Light's tourer won its class in the *Concours de Confort* run in conjunction with the Monte Carlo Rally.

But the days of the 'promenade sports car' were nearly over, and in the M.C.C.'s one-hour High-speed Trial at Brooklands in September, T. Leather's S.S. I tourer lapped at a creditable 79·05 m.p.h. Both *The Autocar* and *The Motor* were covering large mileages on 20 h.p. open cars, the former reporting on KV7570 over 20,000 miles, and the latter's AYY940 being observed over half that distance. *The Motor*'s S.S. I was kept in standard trim (though it seems to have had the higher-ratio rear axle standardized on 1935 cars), and recorded 84·5 m.p.h. on top gear, and 65 m.p.h. on third, a gallon of fuel lasting eighteen miles when the car was fully extended. The ground clearance was good enough to cope with Hard Knott and Wrynose Passes, and road holding was considered outstandingly good, 'provided that the shock absorber adjustment is correct'. Clutch and brake pedals were a little heavy for woman drivers, and the testers had this to say of the steering:

'The . . . ratio represents an excellent compromise . . . . An idealist might wish for a slightly more direct, higher-geared feel when the car is going fast on a gusty day, but most drivers would find nothing to criticize in this direction.'

The Autocar's machine was A. G. Douglas Clease's personal transport, and was modified to the extent of twin carburetters (also found on the 1935 cars) fed by a S.U. electric pump. It was noted that in 20,000 miles of hard driving the only stoppage was caused by a broken fan belt.

The Light Car tested the 10 h.p. S.S II saloon in August 1934. Appointments were much appreciated, especially the manual ignition control mounted on the steering wheel boss: 'An item which will certainly appeal to those skilled drivers who believe that experience always counts for more than mere automaticity'.

An all-up weight of just over 21 cwt. did not make for brisk performance, only 61·23 m.p.h. being recorded over the flying quarter-mile, while a standing 'quarter' occupied 27·4 seconds. The fuel consumption was fair, at 27 m.p.g.

Writing many years later, F. J. Eric Findon, the magazine's then Editor, recalls that he liked the S.S. II, though he did not consider it in any way outstanding in its class, as was the S.S. I.

'Comparing the S.S. II with contemporary light cars, I would say that it showed up badly on performance, but held its own in equipment and appearance. The "Aero-Minx" could make rings round it on the road, and so could the Triumph.'

S.S.100 at Speed: this stubby classic's reputation far outstripped its modest production. This is the post-war ex-Ian Appleyard 3½-litre as restored.

Not the best medium for the '100', but in Britain the best-selling sports cars of the 1930's were expected to be good all-rounders, and models like the Jaguar speedsters and B.M.W.'s '328' were to be seen in the traditional British reliability trials.

The organization, now controlled by a subsidiary company of Swallow, S.S. Cars Ltd., was growing fast, and occupied the entire thirteen-acre site at Foleshill. A S.S. Car Club was formed in the summer of 1934, and the inaugural Rally at Hanworth produced not only the inevitable Autogiro demonstration, but a hundred-odd entrants. September saw the Bolton Police purchase a S.S. II tourer, this firm's first link with the guardians of law and order. There was still a long way to go to the days when the sight of a badge-less black Jaguar in the mirror would automatically lop 20 m.p.h. off a driver's speed.

Output was verging on 1,800 cars a year, and the time had come to place the firm's publicity on a regular basis. This was done in 1934 with the appointment of E. W. Rankin as Publicity Manager and Public Relations Officer. Rankin, a Londoner, had started in the motor industry in 1924 as an advertising representative for General Motors, in the days when their Hendon factory (now making refrigerators) was seeking to flood the market with British-assembled Buicks and Chevrolets. It was also becoming apparent that something would have to be done about the S.S. I engine if development were to pursue its successful course. The faithful old side-valve Standard could not readily be made to develop more than 80–85 b.h.p., and in touring form it was giving a lot less. It could propel a four-seater saloon at 75–80 m.p.h., but more was shortly going to be needed, and Lyons had set his sights at 90 m.p.h. Now that the cars were selling on performance as well as looks, something new was needed urgently, and to this end W. M. Heynes was appointed Chief Engineer.

Heynes had joined Humber Ltd. as a pupil in 1922, and had risen in their service to Head of the Technical Department Design Office, a post he held from 1930 to 1934. During this period the Rootes Group had built up such successful designs as the 'Snipe' and 'Pullman'. From now onwards, S.S. Cars were to design their own engines, instead of persuading others to adapt them to their requirements.

As if to emphasize the break with the old days, William Walmsley (who died only in May 1961) severed his connection with the company at the beginning of 1935. In the past sixteen years he had seen the firm he had jointly founded grow from a tiny shop building a handful of sidecars a week to one of the major producers of specialist cars in Great Britain. The company purchased all his holdings, and he went on to organize Coventry Steel Caravans, pioneers of the use of aluminum in mobile homes. The day of the packagers was over, and S.S. Cars Ltd. became a public company. With this formation, Arthur Whittaker, who had joined Swallows before he was nineteen, was appointed General Manager—a position he held well into the 1960s, in addition to the post of Deputy Chairman.

Meanwhile the 1935 S.S. range was announced. The cars were unchanged externally, though two new models appeared, one of them an open four-seater on the S.S. II chassis, listing at £260 in 10 h.p. form. An extra £5 was charged for the 12 h.p. unit. The second innovation was a pretty four-seater swept-tail saloon known as the 'Airline', and available only on the S.S. I chassis. Unlike the standard saloons, it carried two spare wheels in cellulose-finished covers, one in each front wing, leaving the boot free for luggage. The impression of speed was accentuated by horizontal bonnet louvres, and it cost £360 as a Sixteen, and £365 with the 20 h.p. engine. Alas, an American journal might call it 'the most beautiful thing on wheels', but nobody liked the 'Airline' much, heat and

fumes rendering it signally uninhabitable. It cannot have been as black as it was painted, though, because one or two of this model—the most attractive-looking of the old S.S.'s—still survive.

Mechanically, the 1935 cars were considerably improved, with a high-compression head, evolved in consultation with Harry Weslake, a higher-lift camshaft, a bigger sump, twin R.A.G. carburetters in place of the single instrument used in 1934, and revised cooling arrangements—it had been found that the 1934 cars, by contrast with their predecessors, were over-cooled. Despite the experiments with electric pumps in 1934, A.C. mechanical pumps were still used, but higher axle ratios were standardized on the S.S. Is to give better top-end performance, a 4·5:1 top gear being used on the 16 h.p. cars, and a ratio of 4·25:1 on the Twenties. The beautifully produced 1935 catalogue devoted a whole page to optional extras, which included 'Dunlop competition Tractor-Type tyres' at £5 1s. each (the controversial 'comps.', later banned by the R.A.C.), and a S.U. electric pump (specified for high altitudes). Metallic colour schemes featured in the catalogue at £5 extra, and D.W.S. four-wheel permanent jacks could be had on any model for the same cost, but only if they were ordered with the car. Heaters did not figure in any shape or form, nor did demisters or screenwashers, but a Philco car radio, 'a scientifically designed, permanent wireless installation, not a portable set', could be specified on any S.S. model for as little as sixteen guineas, plus a fitting charge of £3. It was claimed that current consumption was less than for one headlamp, but as yet the retractable aerial was not standardized, and I remember seeing early S.S. saloons with a curved chromium aerial ex-

The works' S.S. 100s in the 1937 Welsh Rally, in which they won the Team Prize. *Left to right*, E. H. Jacob, E. W. Rankin (P.R.O. of Jaguar for thirty years until his death), The Hon. Brian Lewis, and Mr. and Mrs. T. H. Wisdom. The cars are 2½-litre models: the '3½' did not reach the catalogue until the 1938 model year.

A 1938 3½-litre saloon outside the Foleshill Factory used until the beginning of the 1950's. The hexagonal motif is much in evidence, while a wider body and bigger boot distinguished the 1938-48 models from the earlier 1936-37 type.

tending from the top of the windscreen to the rear window.

They were also the first cars from Foleshill to make any impression on the American market, where foreign car sales had slumped to a miserable trickle after the 1929 Stock Market collapse. Though one or two of the oldest established concerns, like Mercedes-Benz, retained showrooms in New York, the rest had given the United States up as a dead loss, and the foreign-car dealers had retired to fifth-floor warehouses on the East Side. One character used to demonstrate his wares down his gangway. Once, when the brakes of a Bugatti failed during such tortures, passers-by looking skywards could discern the immortal horseshoe radiator protruding through a wall. British Motors of New York, however, had ideas ahead of their time when they took on the S.S. agency in 1934, and set their sights straight at the snob element by signing on H.R.H. The Prince of the Asturias, heir to the Spanish Throne, as a salesman. The Prince, they told the world, came into their showroom to buy a S.S., and was so impressed that he stayed to sell them! An 'Airline' saloon was exhibited at the 1935 New York Show, the only other British representative being a PA-type M.G. 'Midget' two-seater. Neither *marque* made a very deep impression, though more than fifteen years later, by which time the TD M.G. and XK120 Jaguar were household words in the States, the collectors were to hunt feverishly for survivors of this earlier export drive. A curious facet of this early American sales campaign is that the side-valve cars were never made available with left-hand drive—this in spite of the far-sighted policy pursued with the sidecars a decade earlier.

We hear no more of British Motors, but the classified advertisement section of *The New York Times* for 14 February 1936 carried this passage of alliterative ballyhoo:

Foleshill just after the war, with a batch of six-cylinder saloons ready for delivery – to a long waiting list.

Smartest and costliest of the regular pre-war range was this four-passenger convertible, costing £465 on the 3½-litre chassis. Some were made after the war but generally speaking soft tops were reserved for clients with dollars.

'ANNOUNCEMENT: Thirty-three of the Sensational British Standard Swallow Sport Cars will arrive in a shipment from England. These cars are in various body types and are the latest models available. Above cars will be on display at our showroom not later than 19 February and can be purchased at a considerable saving.'

The advertisers were Hilton Motors of 151st Street, and it is indicative of the low valuation set on the American market that these cars were not, as might have been expected in 1936, the new pushrod o.h.v. Jaguar saloons and tourers, but genuine 'Standard Swallow's, unsold S.S. Is left over from the previous season. Had anyone questioned S.S. Cars on the subject, they would have asserted quite truthfully that the S.S. I was still in limited production, but it is unlikely that anyone worried. Nearly all the cars thus shipped were 20 h.p. models, in the same way that America later took 3½-litre Jaguars, leaving the less powerful '2½' to the home market.

The Motor tested a 20 h.p. 'Airline' saloon with the revised gear ratios in April 1935—the higher top gave 80 m.p.h.—only 3 m.p.h. faster than the saloon tested by the same magazine a year earlier, but the use of a closer-ratio third pushed the maximum on this gear up from 57 m.p.h. to a useful 65 m.p.h. Weight was up nearly 3 cwt. on 1934, but acceleration was very little affected, except by an expected improvement at the top end. *The Motor* liked this new high top gear, claiming that 'one can cruise at 70 m.p.h. without feeling that the car is travelling fast'. (Evidently the 'Airline's' reputation for directional instability was not always justified.) *The Autocar*, however, commenting on a 20 h.p. saloon tried as late as August

1935, felt that this 4·25:1 ratio was rather high, and found the engagement of first and second gears tricky. Vision was cited (as always) as excellent, so evidently journalists still liked lowering themselves into a kind of cavern. . . . Incidentally, the younger generation of writers from the middle thirties would still be testing cars in the 1950s and 1960s, and slating Sir William Lyons for the thick pillars on his early 3·4-litre models!

The usual *Concours* wins were chalked up in 1935, Bexhill alone netting three first places. While the standards of style and finish kept pace with the cars' competitors, there is no doubt that the method of adjudication then adopted kept the S.S.'s in the forefront. Cars were judged according to catalogue price, one of the class divisions occurring at £350: hitherto all the S.S. I.s had run in the '£251–£350' class, but with the advent of the 'Airline', listing from £360 upward, the Foleshill concern could make inroads into a higher price group.

In March 1935, the S.S. 90 two-seater was announced—in effect a halfway house between the old S.S. and the Jaguar models. The 2·7-litre side-valve engine was retained, basically in its twin-carburetter 1935 form, but the compression ratio was raised to 7:1. The four-speed gearbox had the close ratios of 4·5, 5·83, 8·98, and 15·3 to 1, though alternative top gears of 4·25:1 and even 3·75:1 were available to order. This unit was mounted in a special 8ft. 8ins. wheelbase chassis, André telecontrol shock absorbers and Bendix brakes being used as on the touring types. The prototype had a two-seater body with sloping tail and recessed spare wheel, but production cars followed the 'Le Mans' layout, with an 18-gallon slab tank and vertically-mounted spare. One chassis was fitted experimentally with a fixed-head coupé body, but this was not proceeded with. The simple radiator and stoneguard, big Lucas headlamps, and vee-braced tie-bar suggested the later overhead-valve '100' model. A 100 m.p.h. speedometer was standard equipment, but the maximum speed was nearer the 90 mark, as the name implied. All this was excellent value for £395, but only about fifty were made, and not more than four or five survive, of which at least one now has a 2½-litre Jaguar engine installed. The Hon. Brian Lewis drove one through the 1935 rally season, without any signal success, though a S.S. I won its class in the M.C.C.'s Torquay event, and eight cars collected first-class awards in the R.A.C. Rally, their drivers including Douglas Clease, Mrs Wisdom, and S. H. Newsome, the Coventry S.S. agent. Several S.S.'s ran in the M.C.C.'s High-Speed Trial at Brooklands in September, perhaps the most remarkable performance being A. Goldman's lap at 60·32 m.p.h. in his S.S. II tourer.

At the same time as the S.S. 90, there was introduced a drophead coupé on the standard S.S. I chassis, which made up for the discontinuation of the fixed-head coupé at the end of the 1934 season. The price was £380 or £385, according to which engine was used, and the hood folded neatly away into the top of the luggage locker lid. Though a reproduction of one of these cars appeared on the badge of the abortive National Motorists' Association, I understand that only a few hundred were made.

As yet the factory, though it was capable of turning out over a thousand cars a year, had no moving assembly line, but service seems to have been dispensed with dispatch and courtesy. A Welsh enthusiast recalls a visit he paid to the service department at Foleshill around this time. As he was leaving the factory, having collected his car, he found that the dynamo was not charging. The head of the department promptly took the dynamo off another car, fitted it, entertained the client to tea at his home while the work was being carried out, convoyed him out of Coventry (always a navigational hazard) and adjusted the car's brakes by the roadside *en route*—all this on a Sunday.

As the 1935 Motor Show approached, it became apparent that some interesting new designs were brewing, and it was known that an indecently rapid S.S. I tourer was on test. It was not known what lay beneath the bonnet, but William Lyons, as usual, could not resist telling the man in the street a little about it. In the first week of September, S.S. advertisements carried the following tantalizing passage, heralding 'an entirely new S.S. for 1936':

'. . . characterized by an outstanding mechanical specification, magnificent coachwork, and truly astounding performance, the details of this wonderful new S.S. will provide material for the most sensational new car announcement of the year.'

As it was further known that something interesting was coming from the drawing-board of E. G. Grinham at Standard, and that Cecil Kimber, frustrated in his efforts to 'improve the breed' by racing, was planning a new line of sports-touring M.G.s to compete with the S.S., speculation was rife. What was more important, the customers once again had money to burn.

How does the S.S. rate in history? Is it merely a link between the side-carriages and the Jaguar? It is too easy to judge the S.S. I by the standards of 1965 and to lay undue stress on the shallow windscreen, the exaggerated styling, the unpredictable Bendix brakes, the occasional tendency to run out of road in the wet, and the overheating troubles. The S.S. was bedevilled by two circumstances which were not its fault—first, its flamboyant lines attracted a flamboyant type of customer, who was often rather free and easy with his average speed stories: and second, Lyons and Walmsley contrived to offer a remarkable combination of finish and performance at a price which defeated comprehension. For every one who asked 'How do they do it?', there were two or three wiseacres who insisted that there had to be a snag somewhere, and who were for ever trying to find out where the quality was skimped. Hence the S.S.'s failings were ventilated more than were those of its competitors. By contrast, this is what the late John Cobb wrote of the S.S. I in 1934:

'I am amazed at the wonderful performance. . . . Its acceleration, its roadholding, its maintenance of high speeds without effort, and its powerful brakes, compel my admiration.'

And I hardly imagine that such an eminent driver would have written that of a car simply because it was a little less tricky to handle than the 10½-litre Delage or the Napier-Railton.

CHAPTER 4

The Big Cat

1936–40

'*The new 2½-litre S.S. Jaguar is a car with many excellent qualities and an outstanding road performance. To produce it at so modest a price is an engineering achievement of which the makers should feel proud.*'

The Motor, May 1936

'*A Jaguar is a somewhat rare thing over here*' [Belgium].

Paul Frère, *The Autocar*, May 1938

LYONS' preliminary announcement of September 1935 was part of a plan which was to transform the structure of S.S. completely. To begin with, Walmsley's retirement was followed by the flotation of S.S. Cars Ltd. as a public company. The Swallow Coachbuilding Co. Ltd. went into voluntary (and purely formal) liquidation, and a new concern, the Swallow Coachbuilding Co. (1935) Ltd. was formed as a subsidiary of S.S. Cars Ltd, to continue sidecar manufacture. Thus the wheel had come full circle.

Meanwhile the company, in collaboration with Harry Weslake (then, as now, England's great expert in cylinder head design,) was evolving a re-designed cylinder head with pushrod operated overhead valves to power the 1936 model S.S. The result transcended all the firm's hopes. They needed to boost the output of their 2½-litre unit from 70 to 90 b.h.p. in order to raise the effective maximum speed of their saloon models from 80 m.p.h. to the region of 90 m.p.h. In fact 104 b.h.p. was given at 4,500 r.p.m. without deviating from the original side-valve unit's dimensions of 73 × 106 mm. The bottom end followed previous practice, with a seven-bearing counterbalanced crankshaft of notable stiffness, and light-alloy connecting-rods. These were eyed with some distrust by the purists. True, they did tend to expand, resulting in a lower oil pressure, and few old Jaguars will now hold more than 35–40 lbs. pressure under normal running conditions. Steel rods undoubtedly do boost oil pressure to a minimum of 60-odd lbs., but the original dural ones will take 4,700 r.p.m. even in quite elderly engines. Invar-strut aluminium pistons were used in a chromium iron block. The combustion chambers were of lozenge shape, and the twin S.U. car-buretters were fed by an electric pump of the same make from a twelve-gallon tank at the rear. This basic specification was to cover all Jaguar engines in production up to the end of 1948, and the design was to survive for three years after this, alongside the twin-overhead-camshaft XK unit. Though conceived entirely by Weslake in the S.S. works, it was manufactured by Standards at Canley, as had been the earlier side-valve engines.

Standards also made the four-speed synchromesh gearbox, which had a delightfully positive central change and ratios of 15·3, 8·98, 5·83 and 4·25 to 1, an arrangement typical of Jaguar touring-car design for the next twelve years. A single dry-plate clutch was used, as hitherto. The box-section, cruciform-braced frame, however, was now built by Rubery Owen, and had no affinity with Standard designs; it was underslung at the rear only. Wheelbase was 9ft. 11ins., and the complete car measured a compact 14ft. 10ins. from stem to stern, as contrasted with the 15ft. 8ins. (without bumpers) of the rival 2-litre M.G.

For this chassis Lyons evolved an elegant and beautifully proportioned four-door close-coupled sports saloon affording far more comfortable accommodation than had its predecessors. Whereas the S.S. I retained a bizarre look to the end of its days, the new 2½-litre model had that balanced elegance normally associated with cars such as the £1,500 Park Ward Bentley. Unkind critics even said that Lyons copied his Jaguar from the Bentley, and adduced as evidence the presence of one of these cars at Holbrook Lane in 1935. It is high time that this *canard* was disposed of. S.S. Cars Ltd. did not buy a Bentley, let alone dissect it. Jaguars, along with all manufacturers worthy of their salt, do, of course, procure samples of their competitors' products, and nobody makes any secret of this. But they were not doing so in 1935.

Centre-lock wire wheels wearing 5·50 × 18 tyres and an entirely new radiator rounded off the car's lines. The chromium-plated grille with vertical bars derived directly from the original 1931 design, but its agelessness is illustrated by its far closer affinity with present-day Jaguar styling. This was forcefully brought home to me when I visited the Jaguar factory, and saw a splendidly restored 1937 2½-litre saloon standing in the showroom alongside the latest Mk. IX with automatic transmission and power steering.

A distinctive car must have a distinctive name. The S.S. hexagon alone would not suffice, and William Lyons decided to cash in on the current craze for zoological names. Wolseley were then favouring venomous insects, while Alvis, Riley, and Rolls-Royce preferred birds of prey, though the latter confined them to their range of aero-engines. Legend claims that Lyons and his Publicity Manager, 'Bill' Rankin, waded through interminable pages of zoological dictionaries, but, charming as this story is, it is not true. A short list of possible names was, however, drawn up, and 'Jaguar' figured prominently in this, until somebody remembered that another Coventry firm, Armstrong Siddeley Motors, had named a long series of aero-engines, starting with the 'Puma' of the First World War, after the more predatory members of the cat family. Worse still, these cats already included a Jaguar—a fourteen-cylinder radial—which had been supplied in some quantity to Service and civilian customers throughout the world. A telephone call to Parkside, however, soon laid this ghost. The aeronautical 'Jaguar' was obsolete, Armstrong's having passed on to a 'Tiger' which even then was being built for the 'Whitley' bomber. By a strange coincidence, the men at S.S. were to become familiar with this aircraft in the near future, though by that time it would be 'Merlin' powered.

So Jaguar it was. And such was the success of the car and the name alike that many people now associate the name of this South American relative of the leopard with a fast touring car, and are puzzled by the ferocious animal which forms the background to so many of Jaguar advertisements!

Not that the 1936 cars bore the insignia of the 'Big Cat', which was reserved for colour advertisements. The word 'Jaguar' appeared under the winged 'S.S.' emblem on the radiator, and that was all. By 1937, however, an accessory firm had sought to rectify the deficiency by producing a proprietary 'Jaguar' mascot which Rankin described as resembling 'a cat shot off a fence'. Lyons was appalled, and Rankin, who was an enthusiastic amateur sculptor, promptly designed an anatomically correct reproduction of a jaguar; this was 'stylized' into its present form by the late F. Gordon-Crosby, *The Autocar*'s artist, and remains to this day. The resemblance to the M.G. 'Tigresse' mascot produced by Smith's in 1930 is probably coincidental, though Gordon-Crosby was closely associated with the late Cecil Kimber at that time, and actually ran a '18/80' M.G. saloon himself. In any case, only five 'Tigresses' were made, though rumour had it that mascot production was considerably in excess of this amount, and probably a few of these eventually found their way on to Jaguars. The 'Big Cat' mascot, incidentally, was always an optional extra, the price in 1937 being £2 2s.; the first Jaguar to fit it as standard was the Mk. VIII of 1957.

The car was introduced at a special lunch at the May Fair Hotel on 21 September 1935, a fortnight before the Motor Show, and those present were invited to guess the price. By now, of course, they were wise to Lyons and his team, and the average of the guesses submitted was a mere £632, as contrasted with the '£1,000' expected of the S.S. I four years before. Even then the true answer staggered them—£385.

Also in the 2½-litre Jaguar range were a tourer, conforming to the saloon's mechanical specification, but resembling the previous S.S. I model closely in appearance, at £375, and a '100' sports two-seater model on an 8ft. 8in. wheelbase, at £395. This followed the superseded '90' closely in external line, but in the excitement caused by the saloon, both these models were rather overlooked at this stage. As, however, rumour credited the prototype Jaguar-powered open S.S. I with a top speed of 90 m.p.h., and an 0–60 m.p.h. acceleration figure of sixteen seconds, the knowledgeable took good note of this new sports car.

To keep his finger on the small car market, Lyons also offered a 1½-litre Jaguar saloon at £285. This was in appearance a scaled-down version of the 'six', and, like its bigger stablemate, it used Girling mechanical brakes with large drums—twelve-inch as against fifteen-inch on the 2½-litre. Unfortunately, it adhered to the side-valve 1,608 cc Standard 'Twelve' engine, and used a single down-draught carburetter. Though Standards themselves had flirted in 1935 with a twin-carburetter 'Ten-Twelve' saloon (10 h.p. chassis, 12 h.p. engine), and had found it capable of a genuine 70 m.p.h., the little Jaguar was terribly underpowered, and sold on its refine-

Unitary construction and independent rear suspension in 1944—but final drive by chain and a big-twin J.A.P. motorcycle power unit give the game away. The VA-type S.S. for airborne use.

ment and luxurious appointments alone. Only about 240 were turned out in two seasons. To round off the range, the S.S. I was continued in saloon and 'Airline' versions, virtually unchanged except for a Jaguar-type grille, the same modification obtaining with the S.S. II saloons. Prices were reduced, and ranged from £235 for the 10 h.p. saloon to £350 for the 20 h.p. 'Airline'. Only a few of these cars were made during 1936, and production tapered off as demand for the Jaguars grew. A S.S. advertisement issued in October 1935 also mentioned the availability of a 2-litre o.h.v. pushrod unit as an alternative engine for the 2½-litre Jaguar, but the impression made by the new model was such that for once the British public forgot about the horsepower tax. At any rate, nothing more was heard of this type.

Meanwhile, Cecil Kimber had produced his competing model, and the 'Two-Litre' SA-type M.G. saloon appeared at the same Olympia Show, priced at £389. *The Autocar* bracketed it with the Jaguar, commenting that the two contestants were 'outstandingly fine cars, quite new in conception, and thoroughly British in type'. Kimber, like Lyons, favoured a long-stroke six-cylinder o.h.v. engine, but decided to use a slightly smaller bore to bring his offerings within the 18 h.p. taxation class. At 2·3 litres it developed less power, though it certainly possessed pretty lines, and the copper-plated

instrument panel was a thing of beauty. Its instrumentation was even more comprehensive than the Jaguar's, but it never constituted a serious menace to the Coventry-made car's sales. From personal experience of both models, I should say that the M.G.'s accurate steering and powerful Lockheed hydraulic brakes gave it an advantage over the Jaguar, but unfortunately the M.G. gearbox had peculiar and inept ratios—50 m.p.h. was an absolute maximum on third and even this was not very comfortable. Further, Abingdon attained its superb lines by perpetuating the long, low look, and the elongated M.G. was difficult to manoeuvre. Neither car was much fun on ice! A year later the SA was joined by a companion 1½-litre VA-type: while this had appreciably more performance than the side-valve 1½-litre Jaguar, and was quite a match for its o.h.v. successor, it did not compete in price at £325 for a saloon. Finally for the 1939 season M.G. came up with a very pleasant car in the shape of the 2·6-litre WA. This retained the 2-litre's lovely coachwork, but was, at last, blessed with a close-ratio gearbox, and its performance stood halfway between the 2½-litre and 3½-litre Jaguars, with an honest 90 m.p.h. available. Alas, Abingdon had already decided to withdraw from the unequal struggle by 1938, and even if Hitler had not intervened, 1940 would have been the last season for the big M.G.s. Already the citizens of Oxford were noticing a neat little saloon with

The first production batch of XK120s ready to leave Foleshill for the docks, 1949.

independent front suspension, which was to emerge in 1947 as the YA M.G. I need not add that M.G. went on from strength to strength with their 1,250 cc two-seater.

In any case, Lyons was able to get his Jaguar into production some four months before the 2-litre M.G. I remember seeing Jaguars on the road very early in 1936. The Hon. Brian Lewis drove one in the Monte Carlo Rally of that year, and upheld the firm's honour by taking second place in his class in the Coachwork Competition, and another second place in the 'Engine Appearance Contest'—a tribute to the remarkable way in which Jaguar engines keep clean. As late as May 1936 the Nuffield Organization was admitting that it had 500 unfulfilled orders on hand for the M.G., which (an unusual point, this!) was being promoted under the slogan 'For space . . . for grace . . . for pace'. The Jaguar Publicity Department was completely unaware of this when they adopted their now-famous slogan—'Grace . . . Space . . . Pace' ten years later.

As yet, Lyons was not much interested in competition as such, though members of the organization entered the cars privately for rallies, W. M. Heynes driving in the S.S. Car Club's Scarborough Rally in June. The Welsh Rally, however, proved to be something of a triumph for the cars from Coventry, and those who had hitherto treated them as mere *concours* pieces were surprised to see S.S. take home the awards for the best performances in the large and small closed car classes alike, the victorious machines being D. S. Hand's $2\frac{1}{2}$-litre and R. E. Sandland's $1\frac{1}{2}$-litre, the latter following up its win with a class win in the *Concours*.

In the meanwhile, the '100' two-seater was beginning to make an impression. Deliveries did not start until March 1936, but it soon became apparent that S.S. had a winner, especially at the astonishing price of £395. The forecast of 100 m.p.h. was not quite true, the car tested by *The Autocar* in July 1937 recording a two-way maximum of 91·84 m.p.h. The 0–60 m.p.h. time, hitherto estimated as 11 sec., was in fact $13\frac{1}{2}$ sec. But these slight shortcomings should not detract from the '100''s very real merit. There is a tendency among enthusiasts to laugh the '100' off as yet another nasty confection from the 1930s, and no good whatever was done to its reputation by the exaggerated claims made on its behalf during the War. But it had great merits—it was light, at $23\frac{1}{2}$cwt. ready for the road; it was simple, and possessed of an entirely untemperamental push-rod engine; it could out-perform any of its competitors, with the possible exception of the Type 328 B.M.W., which scored by virtue of its independent front wheel suspension, but set the purchaser back a crippling £695. It possessed neither a fastidious palate for fuel nor an excessive thirst, *The Autocar* recording 18–21 m.p.g. Its failings were skittishness at high speeds, a fearsome tyre consumption, hard suspension, and poor lock in relation to its compact size, the turning circle being thirty-six feet for an overall length of 12ft. 6ins. Engines were tuned to give extra output, at least 115 b.h.p. being obtainable from the $2\frac{1}{2}$-litre unit. Incidentally, the '100' was by no means flimsy, by any standards: in 1960, one was motored through Allard's Gap at Prescott Hill in practice, was re-passed by the scrutineers, and went on to make a couple of outstanding ascents.

The '100''s reputation and popularity far exceeds the number built. Various estimates of this have been published in the past, but the actual total was only just over 300 units. Of these, the Jaguar Drivers' Club currently records forty-two—thirty-one of them the $3\frac{1}{2}$-litre model—and a large number have been exported to America since the War. There they are prized collectors' items, and a really sound one may set a buyer back $40,000 when new. Despite the strictures of the diehard element in the Vintage Sports Car Club, the S.S. 100 is a force to be reckoned with in Post-Vintage Thoroughbred circles, F. M. Wilcock winning the Montagu Challenge Trophy at the V.S.C.C.'s Beaulieu Rally in May 1960 on a $3\frac{1}{2}$-litre car, against some pretty fierce opposition. Commented the Monthly News Bulletin of the Jaguar Drivers' Club: 'The judges felt relieved at getting away without being pelted.'

Despite the reluctance of S.S. to support racing, S. H. Newsome managed to obtain the firm's blessing, and ran an early '100' at Shelsley Walsh in September 1936, modifications including a higher compression ratio and a lower axle ratio: 4:1 was standard. The car ran perfectly, climbing in 53·09 seconds, or nearly a second faster than the Hon. Brian Lewis's best with the side-valve '90'. Though beaten by two sports Bugattis, Newsome's was the fastest unsupercharged car in its class, and the time compares quite favourably with the 47·85 seconds taken by Cholmondeley-Tapper in a Grand Prix Maserati. T. H. Wisdom, the well-known driver-journalist, lapped Brooklands at 104·41 m.p.h. that October, in what William Boddy described as 'a rather prepared' car, but the M.C.C.'s High-Speed Trial a month earlier had shown the potentialities of untuned examples of the breed running with full road equipment. 'As a make,' *The Autocar* commented, 'the S.S. Jaguars stood out.' H. Bolton's $2\frac{1}{2}$-litre '100' lapped at 87·91 m.p.h., which is remarkable when one considers that an 8-litre Bentley did no better than 82·59 m.p.h., and Scribbans on a $4\frac{1}{2}$-litre Lagonda 89·73 m.p.h. F. H. Snell's Jaguar saloon circulated at 77·74 m.p.h.

There were also some Continental appearances, of which the most important took place on the *marque*'s old stamping-ground—the International Alpine Trial. The 'Alpine' had fallen out of favour with British manufacturers (perhaps it was too inclined to show up the propensity of the native product for boiling on hills?); whereas the 1934 event had attracted forty-five starters from across the Channel, 1936 was to see only eight, including Derby and Cricklewood Bentleys, and a prototype 1937 model 14 h.p. Triumph 'Vitesse' driven by the redoubtable Donald Healey. S.S. was represented by a standard model '100' (BWK77), entered and driven by Mr and Mrs T. H. Wisdom, and it came through with flying colours, winning its class, making the best individual performance irrespective of class, and bringing home one of only four Glacier Cups awarded—the others went to Healey's Triumph, an Adler, and a Lago-Darracq. One Cornet drove a Jaguar in the Belgian 24-hour Race at Spa in June, but failed to figure in the results. Among the other entrants incidentally, was an unknown young Frenchman by the name of Maurice Trintignant, driving a 'souped up' Hudson Eight.

Meanwhile, the French, disgruntled at their lack of success in *Grandes Epreuves*, had turned most of their major races into sports-car events, among them the Marne Grand Prix, which was dominated by the tank-like 3·3-litre Bugattis. A 2½-litre Jaguar, however driven by the Australian F. J. McEvoy, won the 3-litre class (in which the bigger French manufacturers were not interested) at 69·98 m.p.h., from two Amilcars—presumably the abortive 2½-litre 'fours' with which the moribund Boulogne-Sur-Seine firm was toying at the time. A year later Delage, under Delahaye control, were making their usually over-bodied D.6–70 go very fast, and any Jaguars running in this class would have come up against worthier opposition.

Both *The Autocar* and *The Motor* tried the 2½-litre saloon and found it to their liking.

The Autocar said:

'The synchromesh goes through well for all but the fastest of lightning gear changes such as few people want to use. . . . It is steady in the sports car manner on corners, can be put fast with complete confidence into an open road curve, yet is not harsh on the springing.'
The steering, they said, 'achieves an excellent balance between the firmness and accuracy desirable for a car capable of so good a performance, and lightness of control at low speeds.'

Two-and-a-half turns from lock to lock, indeed, represented a far cry from the Mk. VII and Mk. VIII saloons of a later era.
The Motor enthused over the flexibility of the car:

'The pick-up on top gear . . . is immediate and consistent, right down from 10 m.p.h., from which speed the car will reach 70 m.p.h. in just over half a minute—all on the direct drive . . . . A Girling braking system is provided which gives the powerful yet smooth control required in a high-speed car.'

Both periodicals also approved such pleasing touches as the provision of a comprehensive tool kit housed on the inside of the luggage locker lid—a Jaguar feature for many years, though it must be confessed that this installation was relatively uncomplicated on the early saloons, which still had those side-mounted spare wheels— a feature of unaccountable snob value to the present-day American 'classic-fancier'. The vital statistics, too, justified the Press's approval, for the 2½-litre Jaguar saloon, turning the scales at 30½ cwt. unladen, recorded 86 m.p.h. on top gear, 70 m.p.h. on third, reached 50 m.p.h. from a standstill through the gears in just under twelve seconds, took thirty-one feet to stop from 30 m.p.h., and averaged

Records at Jabbeke. Major A.T.G. Gardner with the four-cylinder, XJ-engined M.G. before his successful run, 1948.

Variations and gyrations: Pycroft's 2½-litre Pycroft-Jaguar in the Bally-clare Handicap Race, Ulster, 1947.

Elegance for export: the 1949 Mk.V drophead coupé.

Speed trim: the late R.M.V. Sutton in the XK120 with which he attained 132.596 mph at Jabbeke in May 1949.

21 m.p.g. Incidentally, *The Autocar* did a 'recap.' with one of these cars in April 1941, when a 1936 saloon with 68,000 miles on the clock was found to be capable of cruising at a comfortable 65 m.p.h. on that depressing fluid, Pool petrol, and did 20 m.p.g., not to mention 2,000 m.p.g. on oil. This one had never had a major overhaul—only periodic decokes having been carried out. Incidentally, these pushrod engines were astonishingly durable, and returned very low oil consumption if normally driven, though energetic use of third gear was apt to bring about an alarming rise. The power units almost always outlasted the bodies and chassis—some time ago I drove a very tired 1938 $\frac{1}{2}$-litre saloon, which was, so its owner assured me, 'not long for this world'. Years of street parking had wrought havoc with the rear part of the body, and I would not vouch for the chassis being crack-free, but the performance was still impressive, and the engine ran happily up to an indicated 4,200 r.p.m. The Girling brakes, too, were well up to their job.

Fortified by a good Press, S.S. Cars Ltd. came out with an attractively presented little book of 'Opinions', which included testimonials from Sir Malcolm Campbell ('I was so impressed with the sterling qualities of the new S.S. that I decided to buy one myself'), the Earl of Cardigan ('Probably no car caught on so rapidly'), and a cross-section of journalists and private owners. One of these latter wrote what must have been the most gratifying passage of all:

> 'By taking out owners of sports cars in the £700 region I have already broken several hearts on telling them the price, and also, I believe, made not a few converts.'

Lyons had succeeded in marketing a quality car at a mass-production price.

Still, all manner of excuses were being found for the Jaguar; but the detractors had yet to find the fly in the ointment. It was useless to dismiss the car as 'cheap tin' after a privately-entered example had turned in the best performance in the Alpine Trial, so now they started to question Lyons' economics. They asserted that he deliberately built his smaller models at a loss, to publicize his bigger cars—an allegation levelled in particular at the 1938 o.h.v. 1$\frac{1}{2}$-litre, which, (or so the wiseacres insisted) could not be an economic proposition at a list price of £298. After all, the equally well-equipped 1$\frac{1}{2}$-litre M.G. listed at £325, and this had all the gigantic resources of the Nuffield Organization behind it. What they conveniently forgot was that Lyons costed his cars for long production runs and relatively infrequent design changes—and in this case he was able to turn a very low profit margin to good advantage. Whereas 2,407 M.G.s were turned out between April 1937 and September 1939—a creditable run for a specialist car, be it said—Lyons kept the 1$\frac{1}{2}$-litre Jaguar in production from late 1937 to March 1949—the War years excepted; and during this period over 12,000 left the works.

No major changes were deemed necessary for 1937, though the 2$\frac{1}{2}$-litre cars emerged with a larger radiator and shock absorbers, while a new type of Girling brake was used, with fourteen-inch drums. The provision of a S.U. starting carburetter put paid to complaints of erratic starting on some of the first models, and Lucas P.100 lamps became standard equipment. The frame was widened at the rear, and the interior appointments rearranged to give more leg-room for rear-seat passengers. The 1½-litre saloon continued unaltered, prices remained as for 1936, but the S.S. I and S.S. II were dropped. The cars were on show at Paris, as well as at Olympia.

By this time, S.S. Jaguar production was in full swing, and early in 1937 we are vouchsafed a further glimpse into the way Lyons ran his factory. In the words of *The Motor:* 'The centre of the factory is like a railway junction, with endless trains of chassis and bodies.'

Demand, we are told, still exceeded supply, but modern assembly-lines were now used, and, (a characteristic Lyons touch, this!) notices were posted everywhere advising employees of the week's production targets, the hourly totals actually achieved, and warnings of the deleterious effects of careless handling. This is still true: to the windscreen of every Jaguar that goes out on test is affixed a label reading: 'Avoid Damage'. As might be expected of a firm whose roots lay in coachbuilding, the standards in the body shop were of the highest. To quote *The Motor* again:

'A feature of this car is the amazing finish of the coachwork, the outer surface of which carries four priming coats, three colour coats, and a final lacquer, technically known as "mist".'

Every car was subjected to a twenty-eight-mile road test, during which the headlamps were not worn, to avoid scratches to the chrome when bonnets were opened. It is reassuring to note that everything that was said in 1937 applies today, only seven times the number of Jaguars now leave the works each week.

S.S. cars did well in the big rallies of 1937, now that the '100' model was in series production. Not that it ever had much of a chance in the 'Monte Carlo', for 1937 was the last year in which open cars were permitted. In past years, some very odd variations on the Ford V8 theme had figured in the awards list, and Lebègue's victorious Delahaye in 1937 was nothing more nor less than one of the 1936 sports-racing models with more adequate hooding and the usual complement of chains and shovels. Highest-placed S.S. was Harrop's, which finished twenty-ninth.

A works-entered team of '100's driven by T. H. Wisdom, E. W. Rankin and E. H. Jacob, and the Hon. Brian Lewis ran in the R.A.C. event, but were beaten by J. Harrop's privately entered car of the same type, which, it was said, was his everyday business mount. Nonetheless, the Jaguars had a field day, Harrop winning the Rally outright, not to mention the class for open cars over 15 h.p. and the Buxton starting control prize. Wisdom, on one of the 'works'

XKs in action for the first time, Production Car Race, Silverstone, 1949. The winner, Leslie Johnson (No. 7), and Peter Walker (No. 8) at Abbey Curve.

cars, was placed second in class and Rally alike, and took the prize for the best Leamington starter. The Jaguars of Rankin/Jacob and Lewis were fourth and fifth overall, only Flint's Type 55 Frazer-Nash B.M.W. intervening. This two-litre car, incidentally, ran in the same class as the 2·7-litre Jaguars, its R.A.C. rating being 15·7 h.p. The manufacturers' team prize, of course, went home to Coventry, and it is doubtful in the circumstances if anyone cared much that the *marque* could manage nothing better than a third place in the *Concours d'Elégance*. Harrop, incidentally, was able to ensure his first place in the tests by an ingenious electrical device which automatically switched on the engine and released the handbrake when the door was opened. There was nothing in the regulations to prohibit this, though most people would surely have forgotten, and vaulted neatly over the S.S. 100's low side.

The Welsh Rally was won by E. H. Jacob's '100', which also won its class. S.S. collected the manufacturers' team prize; as E. W. Rankin had also nominated his entries in his capacity of secretary of the S.S. Car Club, they brought home the Club Team prize as well.

Mr Rankin had other reasons to be proud. In this Coronation year, with promise of new hope in a new reign, the slogan 'Born of this Day and Age' was coined, and a Jaguar advertisement published in November 1936, at the end of the new model's first season, shed some light on the boom in S.S. cars. Total orders over the past twelve months were up 124·7% on 1935, which, translated into solid figures, meant a potential production of 4,000-odd cars a year: further, one in every three of these new orders had been placed by previous S.S. customers, which meant that the firm had now built up a faithful following. Most important of all, the 2½-litre S.S. Jaguars delivered in the month of September 1936 accounted for 89·8% of all new registrations in the 20 h.p. taxation class. None of the Jaguar's direct competitors were thus rated, nor was it a rating favoured by the mass-producers. Austin made an Eighteen, Morris an Eighteen and a Twenty-One, Hillman's popular 'Hawk' was likewise rated at 21 h.p., while Vauxhall's had recently discontinued their 20 h.p. 'Big-Six' in favour of a Twenty-five. In terms of cold statistics, S.S. were gaining favour at the expense of the 'Flying 20' made by Standards, their engine suppliers—and this particular car used the unit but recently discarded by S.S. Cars Ltd.!

Throughout the summer of 1937, rumours were circulating on the subject of a 'new 100 m.p.h. S.S.', and those who peered under the bonnet of S. H. Newsome's Shelsley Walsh entry at the September meeting obtained a preview of this new 3½-litre car. Outwardly an ordinary 2½-litre '100' running *sans* lamps, it rocketed up the hill in 45·52 seconds, being beaten in its class only by Skinner's Morris Special, a lightened 1934 'Minor' chassis into which had been infiltrated a 4,168 cc Hudson engine!

The 1938 programme, when it was announced, was found to embrace two entirely new models, only the 2½-litre being continued. Standardized bodywork of identical size was adopted for all three types. These bodies were appreciably bigger, with five inches more interior length, greater overall width, wider doors, and, most important of all, they were the firm's first attempt at all-metal construction. Gone were the composite structures inherited from Swallow days. The spare wheels were removed from the wings, being transferred first to the boot lids, and then, when this proved an awkward arrangement, to a separate tray under the boot. The 2½-litre acquired two separate exhaust manifolds, one per three cylinders, and twin exhaust pipes. Of the two new models, the 1½-litre had a 73 × 106 mm. (1,776 cc) four-cylinder o.h.v. pushrod engine derived from the Standard Fourteen. Output was 65 b.h.p. at 4,500 r.p.m., and it differed from the six-cylinder cars in that its S.U. carburetter, now of down-draught type, was fed by a mechanical pump. The 3½-litre was, however, a new departure: but the head conformed basically to the original Weslake recipe, it was not merely a bored-out version of the smaller 'six'. The 82 × 110 mm. (3,485 cc) engine developed 125 b.h.p. at 4,250 r.p.m. The twin S.U. carburetters were fed by twin S.U. electric pumps from a fourteen-gallon tank at the rear, while an automatic choke was fitted on this model, though the 1½-litre and 2½-litre cars retained the irritating manual 'screw-on' type. While the standardization of coachwork undoubtedly made for lower production costs and better proportioned lines, it left the wretched 1½-litre with a formidable weight to cart around. The 2½-litre '100' was continued, being joined by the promised 100 m.p.h. model—a 3½-litre '100' costing a mere £445. Attractive foursome drophead coupés were now available on all three chassis, and prices ranged from £298 for the 1½-litre saloon to £465 for the 3½-litre drophead coupé.

The 3½-litre '100' was a very fast car indeed. Newsome's experimental machine had been evolved by fitting a prototype 3½-litre engine into his 1936 2½-litre '100'. By raising the compression ratio to 12½:1, 160 b.h.p. was obtainable, running on 'dope'. No other modifications were found necessary. This car staggered the public at the last Brooklands meeting of 1937, when T. H. Wisdom drove it to victory in a Long Handicap at an average speed of 111·85 m.p.h., his fastest lap being accomplished at 118 m.p.h. The car, of course, ran stripped, but apart from a compression ratio of 11:1, and the substitution of magneto ignition for the usual coil, it was completely standard. A special 3:1 axle ratio was used for track work, enabling the car to cruise at 4,500 r.p.m.: the object of the exercise was to prove that the car's ordinary road performance of over 100 m.p.h. was well within its compass.

On test by *The Autocar* in September 1938 the 3½-litre '100' attained a mean maximum speed of 98·1 m.p.h., its best time topping the century. It recorded a fuel consumption of 16-18 m.p.g., and could attain 31, 52, and 82 m.p.h. on its three indirect gears. The car would run at 10 m.p.h. without snatch in top gear, but:

'third is a wonderful gear. A burst in this ratio for overtaking purposes sends the car shooting forward, and it is up in the 60 to 70 m.p.h. range extremely rapidly.'

0–30 m.p.h., incidentally, occupied a mere 3·8 seconds, and 60 m.p.h. could be reached in 10·4 seconds. The handling escaped criticism, the high-geared steering met with the usual approval, and even the suspension more than passed muster.

'The right degree of damping is afforded by the shock absorbers—hydraulic and friction in combination at the front, and hydraulic only at the rear. But the riding is not harsh by sports car standards. Movement of the road wheels caused by surface variations is quickly dealt with, no acute reactions being felt.'

The car tested seems to have been a little slower than standard, for Cyril Mann's car, running with screen removed, recorded 106 m.p.h. and covered a *standing* lap of the Brooklands Outer Circuit at 86 m.p.h. The cars were, however, 'much too fast for chassis', and were apt to perform alarming gyrations on tricky circuits such as the Crystal Palace, on which top gear could never be used.

Export business was booming, and 1937 saw an increase of 25% in the number of cars sent abroad. Jaguars might, as Paul Frère observed, be rare in Belgium, but distributorships now operated in France, Germany, Austria, Holland, Switzerland, Denmark, Portugal, Hungary, Rumania, and Yugoslavia. A French-language catalogue was issued in 1938. It is hard to associate the now rigorously democratic Balkans with luxury cars, but references to the motoring press of those far-off days reveals that two S.S. Jaguars won first and second prizes at the Belgrade Motor Show in April 1939, and that one of the first people to take delivery of a 3½-litre '100' was H.R.H. Crown Prince Michael of Rumania (as he then was). The Rumanian Ministry of Air and Marine gave him one to celebrate his promotion to second lieutenant in the Mountain *Chasseurs*. Shades of Ruritania!

Meanwhile, production delays at home had been occasioned by the change-over to all-metal body construction. Soon, however, the factory had settled down into the new routine, and by April 1938 production was running at 85–100 cars a week. *The Autocar* considered the new 1½-litre to be 'certainly a car worth waiting for', but it seems that any misgivings the S.S. directorate may have had were unfounded, for by July 150 cars were leaving the works every week, and in November the trading profit for the financial year was declared as an impressive £29,159.

The rally season was generally successful, despite energetic challenges not only from the B.M.W.s but from Walter Grant-Norton's 'Jabberwock' Ford team, which used 1933 Model 18 cabriolets of hot-rod-like aspect. Such cars could be procured for about £20 even in 1938, and, as they used the old 14·9 h.p. Model BF chassis and an 80 b.h.p. engine, their power-to-weight ratio was impressive. Nor as yet could the closed Jaguars compete with the Delahayes, Hotchkisses and Ford V8s in the Monte Carlo Rally, and the 1938 event was won by Bakker Schut's Ford. Willing on one of the new 3½-litre saloons finished well down in forty-second place; though it was quite something for a saloon costing a mere £445 to win the *Grand Prix d'Honneur* in the Comfort Competition, a privilege all too often reserved for rolling three-ton limousines with fitted washbasins and other domestic appurtenances. The R.A.C. Rally saw another victory for Harrop, whose 3½-litre '100' beat the Type 328 B.M.W.s of Hugh Hunter and Leslie Johnson to win the Unlimited Open Car Class; but in the Scottish event, run this year in conjunction with the Glasgow Exhibition, Newsome and Mathews had to give best to Lord Waleran's vee-twelve Lagonda and G. M. Denton's Ford. Mrs Hetherington won her class in the Welsh Rally.

Meanwhile the '100s' were making a considerable impression in sprints and hill-climbs, where their skittishness was not so great a handicap. At Wetherby, Bradley's S.S. was only fractionally slower than Sydney Allard on one of the first Allard Specials, who set a new sports-car record for the course. At the M.C.C. meeting at Donington in June, the S.S. 100s again performed impressively, Bradley's cornering being described as 'most spectacular', and in July the *marque* had another good day on the same circuit at the Junior Car Club meeting. Newsome was doing better and better at Shelsley: in June, he recorded 43·98 seconds, the fourteenth fastest ascent, beating such formidable machinery as Hugh Hunter's *monoposto* Alta (44·5 sec.), Kay Petre's supercharged side-valve 1935-type Austin (46·08 sec.), and a Type 328 B.M.W. (47·01 sec.). He also beat an E.R.A., but even E.R.A.s have their off-days! In September, he was beaten by sixteen other cars, but his best time was faster still, at 43·65 seconds, or only six seconds slower than Raymond Mays' latest record for the hill with the 2-litre E.R.A. The cars could manage nothing better than ninth place overall in the Paris-Nice Rally, but Pycroft and Wisdom made the fastest times in their class for the flying lap test at Montlhéry, and repeated this performance at the La Turbie hill-climb. Pycroft, incidentally, used his everyday car, purchased new in October 1936—it had, at the time, covered 31,000 trouble-free miles on the road.

In July 1938, the Light Car Club ran a three-hour sports-car race at Brooklands. G. E. Matthews and J. D. Firth entered '100's, Firth finishing sixth at an average speed of 59·7 m.p.h. Matthews drove spectacularly, but was forced to retire after he had worn out all his spare tyres. The racing season closed with an impressive performance by H. E. Bradley in the Phoenix Park Races. Though unplaced in the main event, his 3½-litre '100' set up a new lap record for unsupercharged cars at 93 m.p.h., the best previous performance in this category being 88·2 m.p.h., by one of the then-new 2-litre Aston Martins in 1936. In the circumstances, critics might fairly be asked to overlook the fact that the *marque's* first T.T. entry—a 2½-litre nominated for A. Cuddon-Fletcher and Arthur Dobson to drive—quietly non-started.

The cars were unchanged for 1939, though a last-minute surprise at Earls Court was a two-seater fixed-head coupé of most attractive appearance on the 3½-litre '100' chassis. A price of £595 was quoted, but only the one prototype was made. Maltby, the Folkestone coachbuilder, showed a 2½-litre car with one of their own drophead coupé bodies. The wheel had come full circle, and the S.S., the erstwhile non-standard Standard, was now being supplied as a chassis for other bespoke *carrossiers*! For some time now, Swiss coach-builders had been making pretty cabriolet bodies on the 2½-litre chassis, and at the Ramsgate *Concours d'Elégance* in July 1938 one of the entries had been a 3½-litre with a razor-edge saloon body on Bentley lines by Freestone and Webb. Another interesting special-bodied S.S. was to appear in the summer of 1939, when Mrs J. P. Black, wife of the Managing Director of Standards, took delivery of a chauffeur-driven limousine, also on the 3½-litre chassis. This body was executed by Mulliners of Birmingham.

All the three 1939 models came up for test during the year, the 3½-litre showing itself capable of 88·24 m.p.h., accelerating through the gears to 30 m.p.h. in 4·7 seconds, and to 70 m.p.h. in just under twenty seconds. Weight had gone up slightly to 32¾ cwt., and *The Autocar* considered that it was 'a driver's car', the rev. range being 'usable comfortably in top gear', by which was meant anything up to 4,700 r.p.m. The manual ignition control was appreciated, as was the relative softness of the suspension, while the steering, at 2¾ turns from lock to lock, was commendably high-geared. *The Motor*, reporting upon a slightly earlier model in May 1938, commented:

'The S.S. designers popularized an almost vertical position for the steering wheel, and this fact, combined with a driving seat offering support in exactly the right places, adds materially to the ease with which the Jaguar is controlled. The difficult task of providing high-geared steering which is also light in operation on so large a car, has been successfully achieved so that on the open road, while cruising at 70 m.p.h., the car is directed more by the action of the wrists than anything else. Castor action is fairly definite, and the car would, no doubt, be found suitable for the purpose of tackling Alpine passes.'

The 2½-litre, tried by *The Motor* in June 1939, took 4·7 seconds (exactly the same as its bigger sister) to reach 30 m.p.h., but appreciably longer (25 seconds) to attain 70 m.p.h. Top gear maximum was 87 m.p.h., 60 m.p.h. being available on third. The 1½-litre's comprehensive equipment, which included the usual manual ignition control, a water thermometer and a rev. counter, came in for praise, and *The Autocar* considered that it felt 'a safe, taut car'. The rod-operated Girling brakes 'needed only mild pedal pressure for good results in either ordinary slowing down or rapid emergency stopping'. Alas, pleasant road manners and luxurious appointments could not compensate for a lack of urge, as is indicated by a maximum speed of 71·71 m.p.h., and the 25·1 seconds taken to reach 60 m.p.h. The small Jaguar did, however, inherit several good features from its bigger sisters, including a close-ratio third gear, giving 57 m.p.h., while the fuel consumption of 25–27 m.p.g. was satisfactory for a 1·8-litre saloon weighing nearly 27 cwt., and a great deal better when allied to the useful cruising range conferred by a fourteen-gallon petrol tank. The 1939 Jaguar gearboxes were considered by all the testers to be quick in action.

1939 was, of necessity, a short competition season, but it was an excellent one for the Jaguars. At the United Hospitals and University of London M.C. meeting at Donington in May, there were only seven races, yet the '100s' mopped up two firsts, two seconds,

and two third places. A month later, at the Cambridge University A.C.'s Donington meeting, the S.S. team (Truett, Goldman, and Gibson) won the relay race at an average speed of 67·39 m.p.h., and when the M.C.C. staged a day's racing at the same circuit, the Jaguars were out in force once more, winning the relay race, and three out of the four handicaps on the programme. The J.C.C. Members' Day at Brooklands netted them one win and seven places, Mann's 3½-litre emerging victorious in the Test Hill Sweepstake, and becoming airborne in the process—all in the the very best tradition! Not to be outdone, the enthusiastic private owner of a 1½-litre saloon celebrated this last year of peace by covering 32,000 miles on the road in four and a half months.

Harrop took a 3½-litre saloon through the Monte Carlo Rally that January: he chose Athens as a starting-point, but carefully specified Palermo as an alternative, should the perilous (and high-scoring) Balkan route prove quite impassable. As it happened, road conditions were relatively easy, and Harrop came through from Athens to finish equal tenth, with good times to his credit in both the tests and the timed hill-climb at Eze. Honours that year were divided between Delahaye and Hotchkiss, the two *marques* tying for first place.

In the R.A.C. Rally, the B.M.W. team of Murray, Fane, and Johnson beat the S.S. Car Club's '100s' (Gibson, Gordon, and Mann) for the Club Team Prize, the B.M.W.s also winning their class, though S.S. cars came second, fourth, sixth, seventh, ninth and eleventh. Drophead coupés on the 1½-litre and 2½-litre chassis won their classes in the Coachwork Competition. Fords took the honours in the Scottish Rally, but Jaguar had a double vengeance in the Blackpool and Welsh events, scoring an outright victory in the first, and a class win in the second. What was more interesting, the driver in each case was Grant-Norton, who had deserted his faithful 'Jabberwock' Ford for a S.S. 100.

The 1940 models were announced in July 1939. No major mechanical improvements were made, though the six-cylinder models came equipped with hydraulic piston-type shock absorbers all round. Folding tables were provided, and a system of 'air-conditioning' was standard equipment on the 2½-litre and 3½-litre saloons. Nowadays we grudge paying extra for a heater in any model, however inexpensive, but in 1939 such a luxury was confined to bespoke bodies in the £2,000 price bracket, and to a few American cars such as the Nash, an example of which had been tested in the Royal Borough of Kensington's gas chamber during the Munich crisis the preceding autumn. The S.S. heater used hot water from the car's cooling system, and incorporated a demister and a defroster. Such luxuries were not available on the standard 1½-litre saloon at £298, but a 'special equipment model' was now listed at £318, for which price the customer got not only the air conditioning, but 'large super-beam headlamps, universally adjustable front seats, F.T.58 foglamps, and specially finished luggage locker'. Approved extras for all models included Ace wheel discs, fabric-covered luggage trunks styled to fit Jaguar luggage boots and Philco radio, now cheaper than hitherto at £15 15s. plus a fitting charge of £3.

Twelve basic exterior colour schemes were available.

The '100' fixed-head coupé did not reappear in the 1940 catalogue, but for those who wanted something more sybaritic on the short chassis, S. H. Newsome had introduced a two-seater drophead coupé with swept tail, selling at £475 in 2½-litre form, and £535 with the 3½-litre engine. Only three were made before the outbreak of war.

S.S., like almost all car manufacturers, went straight over to war work in September 1939, but car production was allowed to work itself out. The T.T. was cancelled, among the entries in this 'race that never was' being a '100' to have been driven by J. M. S. Alexander. By February 1940, a supplement to the Jaguar catalogue advised customers that the drophead coupés and the 1½-litre special-equipment saloon were no longer available. As late as May, with the war situation worsening hourly, *The Autocar* was reporting that cars were still being turned out from materials on hand at Holbrook Lane, and published a photograph showing 1½-litre saloons in the despatch bay. By that time, at any rate, the few customers remaining were subject to the impost of purchase tax, and would soon have to obtain a Ministry of War Transport permit before they could take delivery.

Thus Jaguar went to war. William Lyons had plans for rebuilding his factory, which were to go on through the War years. He had had the satisfaction, four years before, of having his product described as an 'engineering achievement' where hitherto he would have been content with recognition as a packager alone. At the age of thirty-eight, he commanded a factory employing over a thousand with a potential output of 200 cars a week. In the curtailed 1939 season, he had achieved a record production figure of 5,378 cars. He had achieved marvels by producing and selling a genuine 100 m.p.h. car—the 3½-litre S.S. 100—at £445. Lyons, however, was a General, and not merely a clever selection board, and even during the war years he was laying plans for cars that would eclipse the S.S. Jaguars, even as in their turn they had eclipsed the old S.S. I.

Engineered for export: a 1967 4.2-litre E-type roadster, conforming to U.S. safety regulations, seen at the Canadian Expo.

CHAPTER 5

Goodbye to S.S.

1941–48

'*Under the able direction of Mr W. Lyons, the Jaguar company faces the post-war period with considerable additional manufacturing capacity, an excellent engineering department, and a very fine record, not only in product on but also on the part of the cars, which have built up immense mileages with great reliability. The company is now . . . one of the major producers of British high-performance cars.*'

The Motor, September 1945

'*Stocks of solid fuel are so low and allocations so erratic that production may be held up for further indefinite periods as a result of coal shortage . . . It cannot be said, in the light of such uncertainty, that there is any prospect yet of making up the lost leeway.*'

W. Lyons, February 1947

THROUGH the war years, S.S. Cars Ltd. continued the expansion of their plant. The Alvis, Daimler and Rover works apart, Coventry's motor industry suffered more from the complete disorganization of the city's life than from physical damage to their own premises. However, the Germans had not overlooked S.S., for after the War an aerial photograph of the Holbrook Lane works was found in the Luftwaffe's files. It was dated 8 June 1939. In November 1940 six shops at the works were destroyed.

Much of the company's activity, of course, centred round the manufacture of box sidecars, while 700 assorted trailers a week were turned out for the War Department. On the aircraft side, S.S. produced main components for the wings of Short 'Stirling' bombers, and undertook all repairs on 'Whitley' bombers that had hitherto been handled by Armstrong-Whitworths, the manufacturers of this type. When the 'Whitley' was taken out of service, S.S. switched to repair work on 'Wellingtons'. Components were made for other aircraft, notably the Supermarine 'Spitfire', Avro 'Lancaster', De Havilland 'Mosquito', and Airspeed 'Oxford', while the firm acted as sub-contractors to Armstrong-Siddeley's aero-engine division, making parts for another 'Big Cat'—the 'Cheetah' seven-cylinder radial. Towards the end of hostilities, S.S. Cars were selected to make complete centre-sections for Britain's first operational jet-propelled fighter, the Gloster 'Meteor III'.

Some very interesting experiments with W.D. vehicles were also conducted under the direction of C. W. L. Baily and Walter Hassan. The latter, famed for his work in Bentleys' experimental department, with E.R.A. Ltd. and with Thomson and Taylor at Brooklands, where he had been responsible for such interesting track cars as the 8-litre Bentley-based Barnato-Hassan and the 4·9-litre B.H.W. (Bugatti-Hassan-Wilkins), had joined Lyons in 1938, and had played a big part in the development of the S.S. 100 design. Their efforts were directed largely towards the evolution of lightweight transport for the airborne forces, and much work was done on two-wheeled trailers. Far more important technically, though, were a pair of intriguing prototypes made in 1944—these are often mis-called 'baby Jeeps', but were in fact intended as airborne alternatives to the heavy motorcycle combination. They anticipated the 2·4-litre car of 1956 having unitary construction of chassis and body, and the E-type of 1961 in possessing independent suspension all round—the rear springing was not dissimilar to the E-type's, though it lacked the lower suspension links, and there were, of course, no inboard disc brakes! The two cars made differed as to engine and transmission. The original 'VA' used an engine familiar to pre-war owners of Swallow 'chairs'—the 1,096 cc vee-twin J.A.P. This was mounted at the rear of the structure on the off-side, and drive from the gearbox to the lockable differential was by chain. Type 'VB', its successor, used a more conventional power unit in the shape of the Ford Ten, power being transmitted *via* a Ford three-speed gearbox and short propeller shaft to a conventional back end. An auxiliary box gave a choice of six forward ratios, ranging from 5·375:1 to 34·38:1. The concentration of weight over Type 'VA's back end gave it excellent traction—and the front could be lifted easily by one man. Unfortunately, both cooling and transmission gave trouble. Type 'VB' worked very well, but was rendered redundant by the rapid development of transport aircraft designed to carry greater loads. Thus both the little Jaguar and its contemporary, an attractive miniature 'Jeep' designed by Standards, and powered by their 8 h.p. engine, were discarded.

In March 1945, an Extraordinary General Meeting of the Company was called, at which it was decided to rename the firm 'Jaguar Cars Ltd.', and drop the 'S.S.' for good. At a time when the War was breeding endless organizations designated by incomprehensible initials, Lyons rebelled against the trend. For one thing, a name sounded better than mere initials: for another, the company was now associated in the public's mind with the successful Jaguar series, and no longer with the 'non-standard Standards' of an earlier era. In 1945, too, everyone was uncomfortably aware of what the initials 'S.S.' signified to the people under Nazi domination. Henceforward a monogrammed 'J' would replace the S.S. hexagon on the rear bumper, though the old name took quite a long time to die, and a preliminary 'post-war' catalogue issued in 1945 still bore the winged S.S. badge.

Lyons had not only renamed his company; he had also taken a further step towards independence. Hitherto, it had suited his book to have Standards build engines to his design. Before the end of the war, however, all machinery used in the manufacture of the 2½-litre and 3½-litre units had been transferred from Canley to the S.S. factory. This was a wise step, as it enabled him to speed up the reconversion of his plant to peacetime conditions. The manufacture of the post-war cars was put in hand in July 1945, and the first car rolled off the line in October. Gearboxes for the six-cylinder cars were made by Moss, but manufacture of the 1,767 cc four-cylinder power units was still entrusted to Standards, for while Captain Black had dropped the six-cylinder 'Twenty' at the outbreak of War, he had found a new use for the o.h.v. 'four'. This was destined not for a Standard, but for the Triumph '1800', the first post-war product of a company Black had but recently purchased. Toward the end of 1945, another link with the past was severed with the sale of the Swallow sidecar interests to Helliwells of Walsall.

Wisely, Lyons did not immediately introduce a new model. Heynes was working on two new types of car, and the knowledgeable saw in his promotion to the Jaguar board in 1946 a tacit recognition of his Chief's confidence in his ability to produce something interesting when the time was ripe. Jaguars were not deceived by the fool's paradise that followed immediately upon VE-day, and they preferred to consolidate, and re-equip their factory against the return of competitive trading conditions. Over £100,000 was expended on machine tools alone in 1947. In the meantime, the 1940 range was put back into production (minus such luxuries as folding tables), though only the four saloon models were listed—the three basic types, and the 'special equipment' 1½-litre introduced for the 1940 season. The first catalogue, it is true, depicted the drophead coupés and the '100' as well, but customers were warned that these would not be available in the immediate future. Major changes embraced the adoption of hypoid final drive throughout the range, while the 'sixes' benefited by the use of a Metalastik crankshaft torsional vibration damper and the latest type of Girling 2 LS brakes, still mechanically operated. The inlet manifolding was modified

Mille Miglia, 1950: crowds line the road out of Brescia as Biondetti's XK120 shoots by in the rain.

Manoeuvrability at Cannes. The Appleyards in the driving tests, Alpine Rally, 1950. The car is now in the National Motor Museum, Beaulieu.

on the 1½-litre, and a minor, but thoughtful, improvement was the provision of black-face dials on instruments throughout the range; these, incidentally, were to be found on some of the last pre-war models. 'Air conditioning' remained standard equipment on all cars except the cheaper 1½-litre saloon. Purchase tax and higher production costs had affected prices, but nonetheless these remained competitive, at £684 for the 1½-litre (£535 basic), £729 for the 'special equipment' 1½-litre (£570 basic), £889 for the 2½-litre (£695 basic), and £991 for the 3½-litre (£775 basic). Needless to say, these figures were of academic interest to the vast majority of British Jaguar enthusiasts, and many people who placed their orders in 1946 had to wait eight years for delivery! True, there were second-hand models to be found, but Lyons' policy in continuing his pre-war designs helped keep their value up, and in January 1947, customers were parting with £825 for a 1939 1½-litre, £495 for a 1936 2½-litre, and £385 for even a 1935 S.S. I.

The fortunate purchasers of new Jaguars also got something which was sadly lacking in 1946—colour. The general rule in those days was 'black with brown leather upholstery', and the car-starved public did not cavil at this. Citroën of France, indeed, were still issuing their cars in a uniform black as late as 1953, and Austins introduced the then new A.40 (which offered a choice of five different finishes) in October 1947, under the slogan 'Colour comes back to motoring'. A journalist might describe the Jaguar display at the 1947 Geneva Show—the first of the post-war exhibitions—as 'a refreshing example of British asceticism', but Lyons offered buyers a choice of seven exterior colour schemes, and hardly anyone else did.

Export, of course, bulked large, the six-cylinder cars being specially popular. As a corollary, the 1½-litre acquired a new lease of life in the days of petrol rationing on the home market, for its uninspired performance was forgotten, and it was in demand for its moderate thirst of 27 m.p.g., allied with Jaguar good looks. Belgium was, in those days, the best foreign market, thanks to her African possessions. She had emerged from the War with a good international credit balance, and in pre-war days both the Jaguar and its then rival, the 2-litre M.G., had established a foothold on her roads. She was, further, the first country to adopt the Jaguar as executive wear. In March 1946, Madame Bourgeois, the energetic distributor in Brussels, took an order for five 3½-litre saloons to be used officially by Belgium's ambassadors to Turkey, Yugoslavia, Persia, Czechoslovakia, and Chile, and by November 1947, an increase of 500% in Belgian Jaguar sales was reported. By contrast, the overall rise in European sales was a niggardly 300%! At this juncture, the Belgian Government stepped in and placed a ban on the import of all cars valued at over £600, whereupon Lyons arranged to assemble his cars on the spot, at the Vanden Plas works. A staff was trained at Coventry, and, two days before the opening of the 1948 Brussels Show, the first 'Belgian' Jaguar was driven off the assembly line by Lyons in person. The result of this adroit measure was a 20% reduction in Jaguar prices, to the detriment of French luxury-car sales in that country. The idea was that an increasing proportion of

Belgian-made components should be incorporated as time went on, but in 1949 the Belgian Government relented, and the plant became redundant. To the end, the only Belgian contributions, the labour apart, were plugs, tyres, and batteries. Most of the Jaguars assembled were drophead coupés, the convertible style having rejoined the range late in 1947—'for export only', of course.

The Jaguars appeared at all the post-war Continental shows, and attracted some rather odd special coachwork. Vanden Plas brought out a flamboyant two-seater cabriolet on what looked like a '100' chassis at Brussels in 1948, and two months later at Geneva there were shown two 3½-litre drophead coupés by Swiss coachbuilders, neither of them readily recognizable as Jaguars—the full-width effect by Langenthal was reminiscent of an overblown Lancia 'Astura', but Reinbolt and Christé fielded a much prettier version with a grille which anticipated Mk. VII by three years. A Vanden Plas coupé won an award at the Brussels *Concours d'Elégance* in June 1948.

The Cripps era of austerity was now at its height, and the compulsory export quota for British cars was creeping up to 75%. Indirectly, I was one of the beneficiaries of this, for while on leave in Lebanon and Syria in June 1947, with my cousin Michael Pitt-Rivers, I used one of the first post-war 1½-litre saloons. I could not have laid my hands on such a machine in England, nor, in the normal course of events, could Michael have done so in the Middle East. At the time, however, his brother Julian was tutor to the late King Feisal of Iraq, and the car was purchased second-hand from a diplomat in Baghdad. He persuaded an oil company official to drive it down to Amman, and it coped manfully with very difficult road conditions. Despite its great weight and rather limited output, it gave no real trouble, though we lost the exhaust system once, and thereafter were careful to remake the 'road' in front of us when negotiating rocky sections. It created a *furore* among the locals, who had never seen anything like it before, and one small boy was **so**

A familiar shot of Ian Appleyard and his immortal XK120, NUB120, getting down to the serious business of a best overall performance in the 1950 International Alpine Rally.

mesmerised by the gleaming black saloon that he ran slap into it while we were crawling through a village!

The Central Office of Information exhorted Britain *via* its gloomy posters to sell to hard-currency areas, and William Lyons was quick to seek a foothold in markets hitherto never seriously explored. True, his cars were known in the U.S.A., and '100s' had run in the rather amateurish sports car races of the late 1930s and early 1940s, but so far British cars had sold on their 'cuteness'—even the M.G. was still looked upon as merely 'cute', and such everday articles as the Austin and Standard Eights had become quite popular as town runabouts. Lyons shipped his first consignment of 3½-litre cars to America in January 1947, distributing them through Hoffman of New York, and thereafter sales built up rapidly. Left-hand drive became available for the first time—American parking habits demanded strong bumpers, so the 'dollar export' 3½-litres acquired overriders. Later, of course, with the advent of Mk. V, the cars were to be endowed with massive and virtually indestructible protection from the chromium-plated excrescences which cluttered up the products of Detroit. Nine out of ten American customers wanted convertibles, so Lyons gave them convertibles.

It must have been a little embarrassing to him to see the 3½-litre in stock form advertised as 'a 100 m.p.h. car'—a claim never made by Coventry, but he recognized from earliest days the need for an efficient service organization behind the sales drive. In March 1947, Roger Barlow, *The Autocar*'s American correspondent, was observing that there were 'no Jaguar spares this side of the Atlantic', but a year later Lyons himself was in New York, signing up agencies left and right. With every agency, as might have been expected, went a clause stipulating that an adequate stock of spares must be carried. 'You cannot get any volume of export business,' he informed the Press, 'by long-range correspondence. The only effective way to secure business is to go and get it. Only by maintaining a very high standard of quality in workmanship and finish can we hope to establish a permanent market.' For his pains, he returned with a full order-book worth over a million dollars. The energetic young Lancastrian—he was still only forty-six—was to make a habit of personally inspecting his export markets in future. In June 1948, he carried the export drive into the heart of the custom-car country by staging a special Jaguar show in Hollywood. Sixteen cars were sold on the opening day, the late Clark Gable acquiring a 3½-litre drophead coupé. This was to be the first of many Jaguars, mostly XKs, to be owned by the star.

The new factory worked flat out on cars for export. Flywheel and clutch assemblies were balanced statically and dynamically, and bodies still hand-rubbed. The factory remained faithful to its 'Clapham Junction' method of assembly, whereby all chassis and bodies, irrespective of type, were offered up to each other at a single point. Though this entailed a closer control, it saved space, and it obtained until recently. Incidentally, when the assembly line was first laid down for the original Jaguars in 1936, all its components, with the exception of electric motors and reduction gear, were made in the

factory. The labour force now numbered 1,500, but Jaguars were not over-officered. Arthur Whittaker, the general manager, who had been with Swallows in the earliest days at Blackpool, told *The Autocar* that only two directors were needed for every 500 workers. To this day, every executive at Jaguar has at least two jobs, and they thrive on it. In 1947, Jaguar was the only major firm to run without a sales director, the functions of this official being discharged by the Managing Director—William Lyons—and his office staff. Output was running at 200 cars a week, when conditions permitted.

The motor industry was going through difficult times in the late 1940s. Admittedly, there were no sales headaches at home, even for the specialist manufacturers whose products must of necessity have a limited sale. Many of these were to find to their cost, when the buyers' market returned, that they had to sell a vehicle whch had nothing that the Jaguar did not offer, and retailed for at least 20% more than Jaguar's corresponding model. But for the moment both Jaguar Cars Ltd. and their rivals were in the same boat, with home orders so far in arrears that even the temporary abolition of pleasure motoring in 1947 could not have an adverse effect; while the problem of selling a thirsty car like the 3½-litre, which would achieve 20 m.p.g. only with tediously careful driving, could be laughed off. The Americans preferred the biggest model, and home customers were quite content to take the more frugal 1½-litre and 2½-litre saloons. The headache was not selling cars—it was producing them. Rumour even credited Jaguars with a refusal to accept any more orders—and rumour was quickly scotched. Steel shortages, coal shortages, and power cuts followed one upon the other. Labour troubles were circumvented largely by Lyons' dynamic approach and firm belief in incentive bonuses, but enlightened management could not conjure up coal that simply was not there.

Worse was to follow. In February 1947, fire broke out in the stores, destroying all the company's stocks of soft trim and interior hardware and furnishings, to the value of £100,000. As luck would have it, disaster struck on a Friday, but twelve hours later architects, structural engineers and builders were swarming over the gutted block. Over the weekend, replacement supplies were brought in, and the factory was back to normal working on Monday. And then, by a cruel stroke of ill-fortune, a week later Jaguars had to close down completely because of power cuts. At the beginning of March, *The Autocar* quoted Lyons as saying: 'Production is going ahead at pre-crisis level, and we are hoping that some order will come out of chaos.' Jaguar prices rose, however, and the cheapest model, the 1½-litre saloon, now cost £865.

There were also broad hints that the industry might be nationalized, or forcibly rationalized by limitation of the number of models produced, a method adopted by Adolf Hitler in Germany in 1939. Nothing happened, but in February 1948, Jaguars found it necessary to deny rumours that they were 'earmarked for extinction as motorcar makers'. Though they did not say as much to the press, they already had good reason to suppose that they had a sensational dollar-earner on the stocks.

It is a tribute to the design that even after eleven years the big Jaguars had dated relatively little, and were still capable of competing with their rivals in world markets. At that time, of course, the only really fast touring cars of non-British origin were France's Delahayes, Delages, Hotchkisses and Lago-Talbots, and Italy's 6C–2500 Alfa-Romeo, all of which were costly—Italy was still in a poor way economically, and the French Government's attitude to *automobiles de luxe* was, if anything, more obstructive than our own. Not content with niggardly steel allocations, they adopted the view that nobody should own anything bigger than a 2·8-litre Citroën Six, and taxed vehicles accordingly. *The Autocar* tested a 3½-litre Jaguar saloon in March 1948, and found it to be 'a mile-eater in luxurious form'. The big car did 91 m.p.h. uncomplainingly on a diet of Pool petrol, but the abandonment of the manual ignition control was lamented: this had been discarded at the end of 1947, even skilled customers being evidently content with 'mere automaticity'. A month or two earlier, Laurence Pomeroy had commented upon a similar car in *The Motor*. A firm believer in independent suspension, he nonetheless approved of the Jaguar:

'The designer ... has obviously sought to combine transatlantic top gear performance with European road-holding and appearance ... the first time for ten years I had done any Continental motoring on semi-elliptic front springs, and I was admittedly astonished to find that at high cruising speeds they swallowed the inequalities of French *pavé* with no apparent difficulty. The steering wheel betrays perhaps more kick-back than one would have had with i.f.s. ... but the ride was good by any standards, and we were able to average 46 m.p.h., heavily laden, with no difficulty at all.'

During the immediate post-war period, it was constantly being rumoured that the '100' would be reintroduced. Heynes told *The Autocar* that he considered the company's reputation had been built up upon competition. However, all the 'new' cars reported, including LNW100, better known of the two 100s rallied by Jaguar's Yorkshire distributor Ian Appleyard, were leftover 1940 models from factory stock. All the same, the breed had three very successful post-war seasons.

The nature of the competition calendar in those days certainly helped the '100'. Restrictions on both fuel and foreign travel ruled out long-distance races and rallies, and the motoring organizations wisely confined their efforts to hill-climbs, sprints, and short races on airfield circuits, all of these being forms of competition for which the '100s' were eminently suited. Further, the cars which supported such events in the months immediately following the War were an extraordinary assortment. Anything could, and did, take part, and entry lists of the period read like museum catalogues. At Elstree Races in April 1946, the new generation of Allards was out in force,

The new S.S.I Airline Saloon.

as were the '100s' and 328 B.M.W.s, but there was also a sprinkling of '30/98' Vauxhalls (this was *not* a V.S.C.C. event), Anthony Heal had brought along the 1910 10½-litre FIAT, and John Morris, not to be outdone, ran his Series-J Duesenberg. The engine of this car, incidentally, later found its way into Brian Morgan's exotic B.D.M. *coupé de ville*.

There is also no doubt that the S.S. 100s and the B.M.W.s were the fastest sports cars readily available. As yet the trickle of classic-car exports had not yet started, and several hundred S.S.'s must have been in circulation. Further, the more powerful sports car could not be bought new, though as time went by Sydney Allard's little factory at Putney produced ever-increasing numbers of the Ford V8-powered J and K two-seaters. The Allard, however, cost £1,125 in its cheapest form at the end of 1946, and the 2·4-litre Healey roadster, then the fastest four-seater purchasable anywhere, a formidable £1,566. Those who wanted more urge than the S.S. offered in standard form built Jaguar-based specials, the immediate post-war period producing some intriguing variants. Newsome was

still competing with the famous 3½-litre prototype, now with a 6·5 : 1 axle ratio for hill-climbs, and figuring in the entry lists as a 'Jaguar Special'; and Gordon Parker devised an attractive little machine called the 'Jaguette', which, as its name implied, consisted of a 1939 2½-litre Jaguar engine and S.S. I gearbox installed in a NA-type M.G. 'Magnette' chassis. Pycroft, whose car we have already met competing in the Paris-Nice Rally before the War, had rebuilt it in 1946 with a delightful aerodynamic two-seater body. In this form it boasted a detachable hardtop, and the twenty-gallon fuel tank was now carried forward of the rear axle, thus conferring greater stability and less drag. In its revised state, the car would accelerate to 60 m.p.h. from a standing start in 10·8 seconds, or nearly three seconds faster than the stock version tested in 1937—and it would achieve 24 m.p.g. on the road. It also won the first race at the first meeting ever held at Goodwood. Finally, the Jerseyman Frank Le Gallais concocted an ingenious rear-engined machine on Auto Union lines, powered by a 3½-litre engine; it distinguished itself for many years both on the mainland and in Channel Island events, and

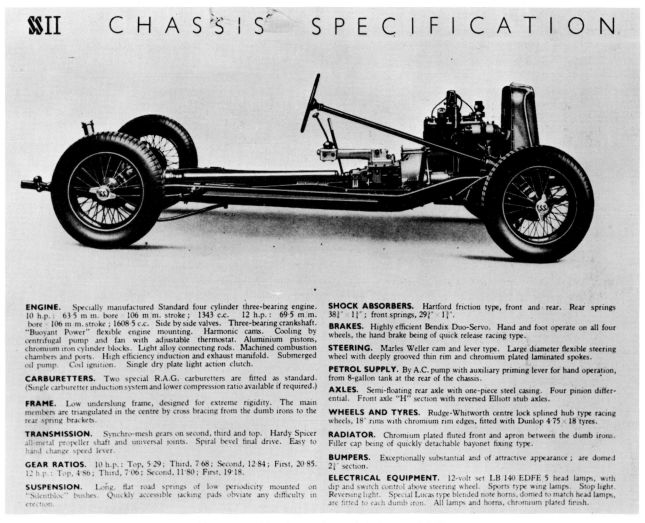

SS II CHASSIS SPECIFICATION

ENGINE. Specially manufactured Standard four cylinder three-bearing engine. 10 h.p.: 63·5 m.m. bore × 106 m.m. stroke; 1343 c.c. 12 h.p.: 69·5 m.m. bore × 106 m.m. stroke; 1608·5 c.c. Side by side valves. Three-bearing crankshaft. "Buoyant Power" flexible engine mounting. Harmonic cams. Cooling by centrifugal pump and fan with adjustable thermostat. Aluminium pistons, chromium iron cylinder blocks. Light alloy connecting rods. Machined combustion chambers and ports. High efficiency induction and exhaust manifold. Submerged oil pump. Coil ignition. Single dry plate light action clutch.

CARBURETTERS. Two special R.A.G. carburetters are fitted as standard. (Single carburetter induction system and lower compression ratio available if required.)

FRAME. Low underslung frame, designed for extreme rigidity. The main members are triangulated in the centre by cross bracing from the dumb irons to the rear spring brackets.

TRANSMISSION. Synchro-mesh gears on second, third and top. Hardy Spicer all-metal propeller shaft and universal joints. Spiral bevel final drive. Easy to hand change speed lever.

GEAR RATIOS. 10 h.p.: Top, 5·29; Third, 7·68; Second, 12·84; First, 20·85. 12 h.p.: Top, 4·86; Third, 7·06; Second, 11·80; First, 19·18.

SUSPENSION. Long, flat road springs of low periodicity mounted on "Silentbloc" bushes. Quickly accessible jacking pads obviate any difficulty in erection.

SHOCK ABSORBERS. Hartford friction type, front and rear. Rear springs 38¼" × 1¾"; front springs, 29¾" × 1¾".

BRAKES. Highly efficient Bendix Duo-Servo. Hand and foot operate on all four wheels, the hand brake being of quick release racing type.

STEERING. Marles Weller cam and lever type. Large diameter flexible steering wheel with deeply grooved thin rim and chromium plated laminated spokes.

PETROL SUPPLY. By A.C. pump with auxiliary priming lever for hand operation, from 8-gallon tank at the rear of the chassis.

AXLES. Semi-floating rear axle with one-piece steel casing. Four pinion differential. Front axle "H" section with reversed Elliott stub axles.

WHEELS AND TYRES. Rudge-Whitworth centre lock splined hub type racing wheels, 18" rims with chromium rim edges, fitted with Dunlop 4·75 × 18 tyres.

RADIATOR. Chromium plated fluted front and apron between the dumb irons. Filler cap being of quickly detachable bayonet fixing type.

BUMPERS. Exceptionally substantial and of attractive appearance; are domed 2¼" section.

ELECTRICAL EQUIPMENT. 12-volt set LB 140 EDFE 5 head lamps, with dip and switch control above steering wheel. Sports type wing lamps. Stop light. Reversing light. Special Lucas type blended note horns, domed to match head lamps, are fitted to each dumb iron. All lamps and horns, chromium plated finish.

Chassis specifications of the little-known S.S.II.

later in its career it acquired a twin-camshaft XK engine.

At the first post-war event in England—the Bristol M.C. and L.C.C.'s hill-climb on the rough drive of Naish House, Portishead, Parker's S.S. finished second to Baillie-Hill's H.R.G. in the 'large sports car class'. Mann, driving the same car as he had used pre-war, took second place in his class at Elstree in April 1946 behind the late K. W. Bear's Type 50 Bugatti, and at Bo'ness N.A. Bean made fastest time of the day in forty seconds with a 3½-litre car, beating Thorne's Allard and the Ford V8 specials of Watson and Clarkson. Bean and his '100' were to distinguish themselves on this course several times in the future, but competition grew steadily fiercer. In 1947 he won his class, but his time of 43·4 seconds was only fourteenth fastest, f.t.d. going to George Abecassis with a 3·3-litre Bugatti with a time of 38·2 seconds. By 1950, Bean had to be content with a second place in his class; the victor on this occasion was Warburton's Allard.

At the Cambridge University Automobile Club's Gransden Lodge races in June 1947, 2½-litre '100s' finished second and third in the 3-litre class, and Mann was placed second in the 5-litre class, sandwiched between two 4½-litre Bentleys. R. M. Dryden, then an eminent exponent of Formula 3, regularly drove his S.S. 100 at Prescott and was rewarded with a class win in June 1948: his time was 53·62 seconds. The '100s' short wheelbase probably cancelled out its tail-happiness on this tortuous hill, as the late Tom Cole

COLOUR SCHEMES

SSI AND SSII SALOON

BODY	UPHOLSTERY	WHEELS	WINGS	HEAD and TRUNK
Black.	Brown, Silver-Black, Red or Green.	Black.	Black.	Black.
Apple Green.	Green.	Apple Green.	Olive Green or Black.	Olive Green or Black.
Carnation Red.	Red.	Black or Carnation.	Lake, Black or Carnation.	Lake or Black.
Birch Grey.	Blue or Red.	Birch Grey or Red.	Birch Grey.	Birch Grey.
Lavender Grey.	Blue or Red.	Lavender Grey or Red.	Lavender Grey.	Lavender Grey.
Dark Blue.	Blue.	Dark Blue or Grey.	Dark Blue.	Birch Grey.
Ivory.	Green, Red, Brown or Beige.	Ivory.	Ivory.	Ivory.
Cream.	Green, Red, Brown or Beige.	Cream.	Cream.	Cream.
Nile Blue.	Blue.	Nile Blue.	Black.	Black.
Crimson Lake.	Crimson Lake.	Crimson Lake.	Crimson Lake.	Crimson Lake.
Beige.	Beige or Red.	Beige or Red.	Beige.	Beige.
Olive Green.	Green.	Olive Green.	Olive Green.	Olive Green.
*Silver.	*Light Blue.	*Silver.	*Light Blue.	*Light Blue.

SSI AND SSII OPEN FOUR SEATER

BODY	UPHOLSTERY	WHEELS	WINGS and TRUNK
Black.	Green, Red or Brown.	Black.	Black.
Apple Green.	Green.	Apple Green.	Apple Green.
Carnation Red.	Red.	Carnation Red.	Carnation Red.
Birch Grey.	Blue or Red.	Birch Grey or Red.	Birch Grey.
Lavender Grey.	Blue or Red.	Lavender Grey or Red.	Lavender Grey.
Ivory.	Green or Red.	Ivory or Red.	Ivory.
Cream.	Green or Red.	Cream or Red.	Cream.
Nile Blue.	Blue.	Nile Blue.	Nile Blue.
Crimson Lake.	Crimson Lake.	Crimson Lake.	Crimson Lake.
Beige.	Brown or Red.	Beige.	Beige.
Olive Green.	Green.	Olive Green.	Olive Green.

SSI AIRLINE SALOON

BODY	UPHOLSTERY	WHEELS	WINGS
Black.	Green, Red, Brown or Silver-Black.	Black.	Black.
Apple Green.	Green.	Apple Green.	Apple Green.
Carnation Red.	Red.	Carnation Red.	Carnation Red.
Birch Grey.	Blue or Red.	Birch Grey or Red.	Birch Grey.
Lavender Grey.	Blue or Red.	Lavender Grey or Red.	Lavender Grey.
Dark Blue.	Blue.	Dark Blue.	Dark Blue.
Ivory.	Green, Red, Blue or Brown.	Ivory.	Ivory.
Cream.	Green, Red, Blue or Brown.	Cream.	Cream.
Nile Blue.	Blue.	Nile Blue.	Nile Blue.
Crimson Lake.	Crimson Lake.	Crimson Lake.	Crimson Lake.
Beige.	Beige or Red.	Beige.	Beige.
Olive Green.	Green.	Olive Green.	Olive Green.
*Silver.	*Light Blue.	*Silver.	*Silver.

Wheels on all Models have Chromium Plated edges.

*This colour scheme is £5 · 0 · 0 extra.

The above standard colour schemes offer an extremely wide field of choice only made possible by a system of production which, though highly organised, is of necessity complicated when so many variations are possible. For this reason, any deviation from the standard order of finish entails dislocation of routine involving extra production cost for which a nominal charge of £2. 10. 0. has to be made.

Colour options for the S.S.I and the S.S.II.

logged another class victory there a year later, on a car he subsequently raced in America. At Bouley Bay in July 1947 Mrs Wisdom drove a stripped 3½-litre '100' with twin rear wheels, which she had flown out by 'Aerovan' freighter; in spite of this she was beaten by the J-type Allards, though she had the satisfaction of making the fastest climb by a member of her sex. Pycroft's special '100' finished eighth in the Ulster Trophy Race, and Tom Cole did well in the Brighton Speed Trials, taking second place in the Unlimited Sports Car Class to no less a vehicle than R. R. C. Walker's 3½-litre Delahaye. It is of interest to note that this machine was victorious in that controversial race run at Brooklands in 1939 to determine 'The World's Fastest Production Sports Car'. The 1949 season saw the '100s' fading from the picture at long last, largely thanks to Sydney Allard, whose highly accelerative V8s grew faster and faster as their ingenious designer first bored out their engines, and then converted them to o.h.v. A year later, no one would have thought of matching any '100' against an Allard, but by that time the XKs were beginning to reach home buyers. What was more, the XK's superior stamina and handling would ultimately oust the Allard, not only from serious competition work, but from the market as well; though not before the London-built cars had adopted the Jaguar power unit in place of American vee-eights.

Long-distance rallies simply did not exist. Petrol restrictions were one cause; as far as would-be British participants were concerned,

Extras for the S.S.I and the S.S.II.

there was the additional snag of a foreign travel allowance which dwindled from £75 to £25 per annum, and was finally abolished altogether. In any case, there were no 'foreign parts' whither to rally—France and the Low Countries had been ravaged by war, Germany, Austria, and, to a lesser extent, Italy, were in the hands of Allied Control Commissions and therefore not rallyable terrain, while the Balkans, Greece excepted, had disappeared behind the Iron Curtain. Such romantic places as Jassy and Tallinn, once favoured starting-points in the Monte-Carlo Rally, were cut off from the Western world. Rodney Walkerley and W. M. Couper, however, decided to run their own two-man 'Monte' in January 1947, and persuaded William Lyons to lend them a 3½-litre Jaguar for this exploit. Their choice of route was from John O'Groats, via Calais, Le Mans, Tours, Bordeaux, Lyon and Grenoble, and they made it, in the coldest winter for years, despite battling with food and petrol coupons, acorn coffee, unhelpful signposts, the French aversion to double-dipping headlamps, and, of course, snow. Average speed for the total distance of 1,310 miles was 25·1 m.p.h., and the entire Rally Committee, headed by M. Noghès in person, gave them a right royal welcome at the finish. Neither Mr Walkerley nor Jaguars claimed it as a victory, but the former wrote in *The Motor*: 'Only a very good car could have got through under the really bad conditions we encountered.'

Five years later, long after the model was obsolete, another of the 'cart-sprung' 3½-litre saloons was to figure in a marathon tour. In 1952 an enterprising caravan manufacturer, Mr Sam Alper, decided to test his Alperson 'Sprite' model by towing it 10,000 miles over a very tough route which circled the Mediterranean, taking in such countries as the Lebanon and Turkey. He chose the Jaguar as the most suitable towing vehicle, and both car and caravan came through with flying colours, though the former's exhaust manifold disintegrated from the bumping over rough roads, and the latter shed one wheel and buckled the other, when the outfit started to snake. Ten thousand and ninety-six miles were covered in 33½ days, the average speed, excluding stops, working out at 29·8 m.p.h., and the Jaguar's fuel consumption came to a moderate 15·92 m.p.g., or not much more than it would use driven solo. Mr Alper was most impressed with the behaviour of his car, especially its ability to tow the caravan at 60/65 m.p.h. on good roads. Jaguars, it would seem, did not approve—at any rate, their publicity made no mention of this venture.

Nineteen forty-seven saw the return of the 'Alpine' to the Calendar, but the only *Coupe des Alpes* won that year went to a *Vintage* car—Descollas' type 43 Bugatti. Appleyard on LNW 100 finished third in his class, but in 1948 he was back again, as were a number of other British cars, notably the Allards and a works team of the new o.h.v. Sunbeam-Talbots. The Jaguar performed with distinction, winning a *Coupe* and taking first place in its litre class. In addition, Appleyard made the best performance in the timed hillclimb on the Col d'Izoard, and was placed first in the braking and acceleration tests. In May 1949 he ran this car for the last time in

the Dutch Tulip Rally, winning the over 1,500 cc class. As the XKs were not ready for the 1949 'Alpine', he shared the wheel of a Healey 'Silverstone' with its manufacturer, Donald Healey, and added a second class victory to his score. Yet Appleyard's greatest days were to come.

Prices rose again in the spring of 1948, and the 1½-litre now retailed in England at £953, while the 3½-litre cost £310 more. It was, however, apparent that the new and long-awaited Jaguar models were imminent, and in August 1948 a pointer was given when Major A. T. G. Gardner successfully attacked 2-litre world's records on the Jabbeke-Aeltre motorway. As always, he used his aerodynamic M.G., but under the bonnet was a 142 b.h.p. engine of Jaguar manufacture, which sounded like a component part of the '100''s rumoured successor. Further, another link with the past was about to be broken—the 1½-litre was going out of production. From 1945 to 1948, the reorganized Triumph concern, under Standard control, had been making many friends with its unusually-styled '1800' models—a razor-edged saloon and a roadster with dickey seat, and radiator set well back, almost in the old S.S. I tradition. These used the 1,776 cc engine evolved for the 1½-litre Jaguar, though the complementary Standard Fourteen adhered to side valves. Emboldened, however, by the demise of the horsepower tax at the end of 1946, Standards embarked upon a one-model policy, and in 1947 the 1,800 cc 'Vanguard' prototype with short-stroke engine was announced. The capacity was increased to 2,088 cc before production commenced, and late in 1948 the Triumph Roadster discarded its Jaguar-type engine and four-speed gearbox in favour of the new 'Vanguard' with three-speed box. The saloon followed suit shortly afterwards. As Standards were no longer making the 14 h.p. o.h.v. engine for their own use, Jaguar decided to discontinue small cars, and early in 1949 the 12,713th and last 1½-litre left the works. A long and amicable relationship had come to an end. Henceforward every Jaguar was to be powered by a Jaguar-built engine.

In September 1948 Jaguars at last announced the initial half of their new programme—the Mk. V saloon and coupé. It is of interest to note that it is incorrect to refer to the 1945–48 cars as Mk. IVs, though many people do. This is merely 'dealer's parlance' for the model that immediately preceded the Mk. V, in the same way that the Jaguar factory now term (unofficially) the original style of 2·4-litre and 3·4-litre saloon Mk. I, just because it came before Mk. II. Nor was there a Mk. VI, this designation having been adopted by Bentley to describe their first post-war model introduced in 1946. Bentleys, incidentally, repaid the courtesy later on—when Mk. VI gave way to the R-type in 1953, the new model was referred to as B7 to avoid confusion with Jaguar's well-established Mk. VII model.

Mk. V was a transitional model which bridged the gap between the old 1938 type and the overhead-camshaft saloons already taking shape in the experimental shops. It lasted three seasons, being discontinued in the summer of 1951, and it successfully tided the firm over the early years of the new series. Nearly 11,500 were made, and the impact of flat rate tax and export drive alike is shown by the fact that 8,787 of these were 3½-litres. In this new design, Heynes used the same engines as hitherto, the outputs being unchanged at 102 b.h.p. at 4,600 r.p.m. for the 2½-litre, and 125 b.h.p. at 4,250 r.p.m. for the bigger unit. Gear ratios were likewise virtually unchanged, the 3½-litre having a 4·3:1 top gear and a 5·87:1 third; the 2½-litre box was similarly stepped but had slightly lower overall ratios. The chassis was however, entirely new.

A deep box-section frame was used, with the side members arched over the rear axle. This improved ground clearance, but also gave Mk. V its characteristic 'down by the bows' attitude. The front suspension was independent, by wishbones and torsion bars, damped by Girling telescopic hydraulic shock absorbers, and sixteen-inch disc wheels replaced the eighteen-inch wire type that had characterized every previous S.S. and Jaguar model. Gone, too, were the mechanical brakes, which gave way to very efficient 2LS Girling full hydraulics working in twelve-inch drums. Alas, these were supplemented by a cable-operated handbrake operating on the rear wheels only, and actuated by an unpleasing umbrella-handle affair under the dashboard. Nobody liked it, and it never reappeared in this form on subsequent Jaguar models. The body followed previous Jaguar lines, with thinner screen pillars and detachable spats over the rear wheels to distinguish it from earlier models.

Saloon and drophead coupé models were catalogued, prices being £930 basic with the 2½-litre engine, and £998 when the 3½-litre unit was specified. Purchase tax inflated these figures by about £260 on the home market, but this was at the time academic, for home customers were still receiving examples of the older type.

The contemporary press was appreciative, Joseph Lowrey reporting as follows in *The Motor* (March, 1950):

'.... A standard of riding comfort which is outstandingly high, a standard which has not been bettered in any car of any nationality which it has been our good fortune to test.'

The car was largely tested in Sweden, and was found to be readily controllable on icy roads. Top speed was 91 m.p.h., 67 m.p.h. being available on third gear. Fuel consumption averaged out at 18·2 m.p.g., and the car would accelerate to 30 m.p.h. in 4·9 seconds, another 9·8 seconds being needed to attain 60 m.p.h. The comprehensive instrumentation, including a 'blue' panel light for night driving, was liberally praised, but the unlovable handbrake incurred criticism. Steering was lower-geared than hitherto, at 3¼ turns from lock to lock. The earlier example of the breed tested by *The Autocar*, incidentally, took a good 4½ turns, which squares far more closely with my recollections of the Mk. V. Understandably, *The Autocar*'s team found the car very light to control, and felt that to 'put fifty miles or more into the hour' was untiring.

Personally I do not agree with this last sentiment. A Monsieur Luis de Ortuzar evidently did, for in January 1950 he claimed that he had driven his 1949 3½-litre saloon 488 miles from Paris to Biarritz at an average speed of just over 58 m.p.h., and offered a prize of £1,000 to anyone able to beat this figure in a production saloon car made before 1950. As far as is known, there were no takers.

Mk. V was a remarkably long-lived machine. It was the first Jaguar model to become really popular with police forces, and I have been told that some patrol cars remained in service for more than 200,000 miles. Certain it is that the only Jaguar taxi I have ever seen was a 3½-litre Mk. V encountered in Crawley New Town. Incidentally, most of the motoring involved in the research for this book—and *Lost Causes of Motoring*—was done on Michael Sedgwick's 1950 2½-litre saloon, which also played in one film, and made 'rude noises' for a long-playing record. His own comments show a devotion to his oft-maligned Jaguar model:

'Reliability is astonishing. Performance is nothing spectacular, and a genuine 90 m.p.h. requires a following wind. I reckon on an average consumption of 22 m.p.g. over 17,000 miles, with 24 on long runs, and 26 if one resists the urge to use the delightful gearbox and keeps below 60 m.p.h. The box is slow, but sweet in operation so that this is readily forgivable. Fast cornering requires fairly brutal techniques, and I do not recommend Mk. V for rally driving tests, though it is surprising how quickly one can be wound round a tight corner. All my passengers praise the back-seat ride unreservedly.'

Though the XKs were to have the lion's share of competition successes, it is worth remembering that the Irish driver Cecil Vard took third place in the 1951 Monte Carlo Rally on a 3½-litre Mk. V saloon.

I feel that the story of the 'cross-bred' Jaguar saloons needs clarifying. It has been stated that during the transitional period, some Mk. VIIs appeared with pushrod engines, and that there were also Mk. Vs with XK power units. The former never existed, and though one Mk. V saloon was fitted with the twin o.h.c. engine, Jaguars are emphatic that this was not a serious experimental car. It was done just out of interest, and the result is not remembered with any affection.

Mk. V was clearly capable of satisfying the staider customers, but the gap left by the abandonment of the '100' still had to be filled. On October 27 1948 the doors of Earls Court opened on the first Motor Show to be held for ten years, the official ceremony being performed by H.R.H. The Duke of Gloucester. For a few days petrol rationing, the 'export only' labels, the gloomy posters and all the trappings of austerity could be forgotten, while covetous Britons tried the seats of cars that would probably be obsolete by the time they reached the top of the waiting list. Nuffields had a galaxy of new types headed by the Issigonis-designed Morris 'Minor', Rootes a new six-seater Hillman 'Minx' and a restyled Humber 'Hawk', Austin the controversial 'Atlantic' convertible, and Singers the slab-sided SM.1500. For most people, the restyled Mk. V Jaguar was sufficient draw in itself, but among the dignified saloons and drophead coupés there stood a long, low, sleek bronze roadster, protected from sticky fingers by a guard rail.

The XK120 Jaguar had arrived.

CHAPTER 6

XK

1949–50

' . . . The outstanding impression left by this wonderful car is its combination of extravagant performance, and silent, effortless functioning, exhaust sound vanishing at about 2,500 r.p.m.'

William Boddy, *Motor Sport*, February 1951

'I just couldn't find anything wrong with this superb speedster, world's fastest production car, which does 130 m.p.h. in top gear and 90 in third.'

Courtenay Edwards, *The Daily Mail*, February 1950

IN my museum at Beaulieu there are relatively few cars made since the end of the Second World War, but there is always a Jaguar, and one from the family which sprang from the elegant bronze roadster first seen at the 1948 Earls Court Show.

One can design a car of outstanding elegance, outstanding speed and outstanding durability, and endow it with an engine developing a remarkable number of brake horses per litre—but somebody has to foot the bill, and it is generally the customer. With their XK120, Jaguar offered a combination of virtues that had never hitherto been furnished, let alone at such a competitive price.

True, 120 m.p.h. performance was purchasable in 1939, and cars of this calibre were in production. These included the Type 57SC Bugatti, victorious at Le Mans in 1937 and 1939, the Type 135M Delahaye which had won the same race in 1938, and the 2·9-litre Alfa-Romeo, which had encountered no dangerous opposition in the last two Mille Miglie before the War. Of these, the Bugatti disposed of some 200 b.h.p. from 3·3 litres, and the Alfa's output was 180 b.h.p., but both made use of eight-cylinder engines, with twin o.h.c. as on the Jaguar, and both used forced induction. The Alfa-Romeo, in fact, had two superchargers. The Delahaye, by contrast, was a less exotic vehicle, using a long-stroke 3½-litre six-cylinder engine with conventional pushrod-operated o.h.v., said to derive from the unit installed in the firm's medium-capacity trucks—in spite of which mundane origin it disposed of 160 b.h.p. in its most highly developed form. It must be conceded that the Bugatti, at any rate, could outpace a standard XK120 Jaguar in 1949 form,

as is instanced by Wimille's hour record at 135·42 m.p.h. in 1936 with an *unblown* sports-racing version, but there were not, and never have been, Bugatti agents in every town, and the late Ettore Bugatti would have blenched at the thought. In any case, these splendid machines of 1939 were not for the man in the street. The Delahaye cost £1,085 as an open tourer, the Bugatti around £1,400 (helped by a favourable rate of exchange), and the Alfa-Romeo a resounding £1,950. Double these prices, and one can assess fairly accurately just how much Lyons was offering for the beggarly £998 (£1,275 with purchase tax added) at which the original XK120 listed.

Further, the XK120 used a twin-overhead-camshaft engine, and hitherto such complexity had not been entrusted very readily to the ordinary customer. The average garage could not be expected to service such a unit. Indeed, in England, there had been a marked reluctance on the part of makers of less expensive vehicles to put the valves upstairs, let alone the camshaft. It had been left to another former manufacturer of sidecars, F. W. Mead, to pioneer the use of o.h.c. in 'bread-and-butter' cars, with his 9·5 h.p. Rhode of 1921, though Wolseleys were also early in the field, and Lord Nuffield developed their design for use in Morris, Wolseley and M.G. cars right up to 1936. Thereafter, however, this layout had been dropped, and the Nuffield Organization were to revert to o.h.c. only at the same Show as saw the introduction of the XK Jaguars. Singers admittedly remained loyal to an 'upstairs' camshaft to the end of their independent existence, and indeed for several years beyond, but their cars were never best-sellers. Overhead camshafts were noisy, and this stricture was undoubtedly justified in the case of the original Rhode, excellent performer though it was. As for twin o.h.c., such a layout was acceptable and indeed desirable on a racing car, but it introduced elements of noise and complexity ill-suited to the general public. There is no doubt that the splendid sound-effects provided by the 2·3-litre Alfa-Romeo and the Type 51 Bugatti lent force to this argument, but the later 3·3-litre Bugattis were un-

64

commonly quiet in action—too gentlemanly for some adherents of *Le Pur Sang!*

Nor was aerodynamic sports-car bodywork anything new. For several years before the War, Italian specialist coachbuilders had been turning out some attractive open and closed styles on Alfa-Romeo, Lancia, and FIAT chassis, and the abridged 1940 Mille Miglia had been won by a 328 B.M.W. with full-width two-seater body by Carrozzria Touring. All of these cars, even the 1100S FIAT coupé, had, however, been made in relatively small numbers and their price was out of all proportion to the standard article. Probably the first aerodynamic sports car of this type to be made in Italy in any real quantity was the Alfa-Romeo 'Giulietta' of 1954.

It would hardly be fair, either, to claim for the 30,000 XKs made overall that they changed the motoring habits of a generation as did the Model-T Ford and the Austin Seven before them. It would be nearer the truth to assert that the XK120 served to modify the concept of a sports car as it is generally understood. If we agree that a 'sports car' should be defined as a vehicle intended to be driven for sheer enjoyment, we must also concede that up to 1949 certain penalties were accepted in return for such *joie de vivre* at the wheel. Permitted (and, indeed, expected) failings included hard suspension, noise, vibration, a tricky gear-change or clutch (more often both!), overgeared steering, and a finicky palate for petrol, plugs, and traffic conditions. To this must be added all-weather equipment innocent of protection and prejudicial to vision, the erection of which might involve the crew in a nightmare game of cats' cradle with sticks and pieces of canvas, by which time they were wet through. The XK was quiet, it gave a boulevard ride, its gear-change was perilously easy, the steering was within the compass of the slightest women drivers, and it survived on the miserably low octane value furnished by Pool petrol during the first four years of its life. Weather protection was taken care of by ample mudguarding, and the hood, though it conferred a minimum of visibility in its original 1949 form, did at least keep the elements out. The result widened the appeal of the sports-car vastly, though it promoted some nostalgia among the diehards, as witness this imaginary dialogue by the late Laurence Pomeroy in *The Motor* (January 1952):

THE TYPE XK JAGUAR "120" IN TOURING TRIM

Whilst the Type XK Jaguar "120" Super Sports Model has been designed with every consideration directed to performance, its appearance and comfort are of the highest order. Perfect streamlining combined with sweeping contours endow this car with a beauty and distinction seldom found in high performance sports models. The generous width of the cockpit (52 inches) and the deep, resilient upholstery afford perfect comfort, whilst complete weather protection is provided by hood and side curtains which are stowed out of sight when not in use.

A capacious luggage compartment is provided in the tail which also carries the spare wheel in a separate compartment.

The London Show folder of the XK120, 1949. Considerable space is devoted to the four-cylinder XK100 variant which was still listed in 1950, though it never existed in the form described here.

'Has the production model Jaguar the performance of a racing car?'
'Yes.'
'Does it behave like a racing car?'
'No.'
'Would you, Pomeroy, prefer it if it did so behave?'
'Yes.'

The conservative element, however, constituted a minority, and the measure of success attained by Lyons and Heynes can be assessed when one considers the versatility of their XK engine. True, it never attained quite the compass of the Standard 'Vanguard', which has powered everything from tractors to 100 m.p.h. sports cars like the Triumph TR series and the Morgan 'Plus Four'. But outstanding performance has been extracted from a unit that will burn normal fuels, run up to and beyond six-figure mileages without the need for major overhauls, potter happily through rush-hour traffic, and combine the roles of week-day hack and week-end Club racing mount. Not only has this engine powered the XK series, but it has also served in fast saloons from 1951's Mk.VII to the XJs of 1980. In the competition field, it has stood behind every international competition victory won by Jaguar since the end of 1949, not to mention laurels won by Jaguar-powered H.W.H., Cooper, and Lister cars. It has been adapted to take international speedboat records. Its original output of a formidable 160 b.h.p. in 1949 has been boosted to

Specifications for the XK100 and XK120 models.

S P E C I F I C A T I O N S

2 LITRE TYPE XK "100" MODEL

ENGINE. Four cylinder 70° twin overhead camshaft ; 2 litre Jaguar engine; 80.5 mm. bore × 98 mm. stroke; 1,995 c.c. developing 105 b.h.p. at 5,000 r.p.m. ; compression ratio, 7 to 1 ; highest grade cast iron block ; cylinder head of high tensile aluminium alloy with spherical combustion chambers ; aluminium alloy pistons ; light alloy connecting rods ; forced lubrication throughout by submerged pump through Tecalemit full flow floating suction filter ; twin S.U. horizontal carburetters with electrically controlled choke ; counterweighted crankshaft, 2⅜" diameter in three steel backed bearings.

TRANSMISSION. Four-speed single helical gearbox with synchromesh on 2nd, 3rd and top ; remote control centrally positioned gear lever ; Borg & Beck 10" diameter single dry plate clutch ; Hardy Spicer propeller shaft in needle roller bearings ; hypoid bevel rear axle ; overall gear ratios : 1st 13.79, 2nd 8.1, 3rd 5.59, top 4.09.

SUSPENSION. Independent front suspension by wishbones and torsion bar ; telescopic hydraulic dampers ; half elliptic rear springs with Girling P.V.7 dampers.

STEERING. Burman re-circulating ball type, positive and accurate at all speeds ; 18" diameter steering wheel.

BRAKES. Girling full hydraulic two leading shoe brakes ; 12" diameter Millenite drums fitted with cooling ducts ; friction lining area, 184 sq. ins.

ELECTRICAL EQUIPMENT. Lucas 12 volt de luxe with 64 ampere-hour battery ; constant voltage control dynamo ; vacuum and centrifugal automatic ignition advance ; flush fitting head lamps and wing lamps.

INSTRUMENTS. 120 m.p.h. speedometer ; revolution counter ; petrol gauge ; oil pressure gauge ; water temperature thermometer ; ammeter ; clock ; twin bladed screen wipers ; electric petrol reserve tap with warning light.

FUEL SUPPLY. From 15 gallon rear tank with reserve supply ; twin S.U. electric pumps.

WHEELS AND TYRES. Pressed steel, bolt-on disc wheels with wide base rims ; fitted with Dunlop 6.00" × 16" tyres.

BODY. Aerodynamic two-seater body of aluminium on laminated frame; capacious luggage locker in tail with separate spare wheel compartment ; individually adjustable bucket seats.

DATA. Piston area sq. ins. per ton, 30.1 ; top gear m.p.h. per 1,000 r.p.m., 19.7 ; top gear m.p.h. at 2,500 ft. per min. piston speed, 76.23 ; litres per ton-mile, dry, 2903.

PRINCIPAL DIMENSIONS. Wheel base, 8' 6" ; track front, 4' 3" ; track rear, 4' 2" ; overall length, 14' 0" ; overall width, 5' 1" ; overall height, 4' 2" ; ground clearance, 7½" ; dry weight, 21½ cwt. approx.

3½ LITRE TYPE XK "120" MODEL

ENGINE. Six cylinder 70° twin overhead camshaft 3½ litre Jaguar engine ; 83 mm. bore × 106 mm. stroke ; 3,442 c.c. developing 160 b.h.p. at 5,000 r.p.m. ; compression ratio, 7 to 1 ; highest grade cast iron block ; cylinder head of high tensile aluminium alloy with spherical combustion chambers ; aluminium alloy pistons ; light alloy connecting rods ; forced lubrication throughout by submerged pump through Tecalemit full flow floating suction filter ; twin S.U. horizontal carburetters with electrically controlled choke ; counterweighted crankshaft, 2⅜" diameter in seven steel backed bearings.

TRANSMISSION. Four-speed single helical gearbox with synchromesh on 2nd, 3rd and top ; remote control centrally positioned gear lever ; Borg & Beck 10" diameter single dry plate clutch ; Hardy Spicer propeller shaft in needle roller bearings ; hypoid bevel rear axle ; overall gear ratios : 1st 12.3, 2nd 7.23, 3rd 4.98, top 3.643.

SUSPENSION. Independent front suspension by wishbones and torsion bar ; telescopic hydraulic dampers ; half elliptic rear springs with Girling P.V.7 dampers.

STEERING. Burman re-circulating ball type, positive and accurate at all speeds ; 18" diameter steering wheel.

BRAKES. Girling full hydraulic two leading shoe brakes ; 12" diameter Millenite drums fitted with cooling ducts ; friction lining area, 184 sq. ins.

ELECTRICAL EQUIPMENT. Lucas 12 volt de luxe with 64 ampere-hour battery ; constant voltage control dynamo ; vacuum and centrifugal automatic ignition advance ; flush fitting head lamps and wing lamps.

INSTRUMENTS. 120 m.p.h. speedometer ; revolution counter ; petrol gauge ; oil pressure gauge ; water temperature thermometer ; ammeter ; clock ; twin bladed screen wipers ; electric petrol reserve tap with warning light.

FUEL SUPPLY. From 15 gallon rear tank with reserve supply ; twin S.U. electric pumps.

WHEELS AND TYRES. Pressed steel, bolt-on disc wheels with wide base rims ; fitted with Dunlop 6.00" × 16" tyres.

BODY. Aerodynamic two-seater body of aluminium on laminated frame ; capacious luggage locker in tail with *separate* spare wheel compartment ; individually adjustable bucket seats.

DATA. Piston area sq. ins. per ton, 45.48 ; top gear m.p.h. per 1,000 r.p.m., 22.1 ; top gear m.p.h. at 2,500 ft. per min. piston speed, 80 ; litres per ton-mile, dry, 4250.

PRINCIPAL DIMENSIONS. Wheel base, 8' 6" ; track front, 4' 3" ; track rear, 4' 2" ; overall length, 14' 0" ; overall width, 5' 1" ; overall height, 4' 2" ; ground clearance, 7½" ; dry weight, 22½ cwt. approx.

J A G U A R   C A R S   L T D   C O V E N T R Y   E N G L A N D

close on double this amount without drastic redesigning, and David Murray, whose *Ecurie Ecosse* was one of the most successful independent Jaguar 'operators', comments:

> 'One must remember that this engine was tuned for reliability, and not for maximum speed. It is certain that more horsepower could be obtained from this engine if it was tuned for short periods and not for the longer-distance races *Ecurie Ecosse* had been competing in.'

The XK story, however, goes back to the War years, when Lyons, Heynes and Baily first mooted the idea while fire-watching. Their idea was an extension of their original plan in 1935—to evolve a higher-performance engine for post-war cars generally. The XK120 was, in fact, to be a test-bed for the engine destined to power this new model, and it proved such a successful test-bed that plans were laid to put it into production. The Mk. VII of 1951 was not just a development of the XK120, but the consummation of the programme that had fathered the earlier type *en route*. There is also no doubt that the pre-war and immediate post-war competition successes of the S.S. 100 encouraged Lyons to stage a come-back in the sports car market.

The XK engine, now so famous, was designed and developed by Heynes and his team, C. W. L. Baily and Walter Hassan, while Harry Weslake was again retained to take care of cylinder-head design. The team started with the proverbial clean sheet of paper, only very few provisos being made. As Heynes put it, the company's basic aim was 'to produce a series of engines with a higher basic performance than is normally obtainable which would not call for constant revision of design to keep abreast of competition'. Another, and unusual consideration concerned the unit's external appearance, and this was summarized as follows:

> ' . . .Designed . . . so that it looks the high-speed efficiency unit that it is, and conveys to the layman some idea of the thought and care which has been expended on the design and construction of the unseen functional parts.'

There was thus no intention on the part of Jaguars to lay themselves open to such gibes as Ettore Bugatti had levelled at Sir Henry Royce, whose work he stigmatized as 'a triumph of workmanship over design'. Ettore himself did not live to see the XK engines, but his son-in-law and successor at Molsheim, M. René Bolloré, is on record as having expressed his approval of the Mk. VII on a visit to England late in 1951.

Also, in common with other manufacturers in the immediate post-war period, Jaguars decided to hedge their bets by designing two alternative types of engine—an 'economy' unit for the home market, where the R.A.C. taxation formula was giving way to an equally tiresome method of assessing duty by cubic capacity, and a high-performance type for world markets. Jowetts, it will be recalled, tested a 1·2-litre unit for their 'Javelin' alongside the 1½-litre version they eventually adopted. The two different engines were to follow the same basic design principles, and had to utilize a large proportion of interchangeable parts, in the interests of cost-cutting.

Advance particulars of the new Jaguar.

Various layouts were considered, including a 'four' and a vee-eight, and a 'six' and a vee-twelve, but once again the Jaguar preference for six-cylinders in line won through. The companion 'economy' unit was to have four cylinders, and it was on this model that most of the initial testing was done. It is of interest to note that all the variations tried out used a relatively long stroke, and this has been a feature likewise of every series-production Jaguar engine made since, with the exception of the 2·4-litre of 1956; this despite the fact that the original specification called for speeds of up to 5,000 r.p.m., and since then the XK-type has been made to turn faster still.

In the immediate post-war years, a series of engines with 'X' (experimental) designations were evolved. The original four-cylinder test unit, the XF, had a bore of 66·5 mm., a stroke of 98 mm., and a capacity of 1,360 cc. Its twin-camshaft head had a close affinity with the final XK design, but the crankshaft was not up to the high rates of revolution demanded, and Heynes next tried a cross-pushrod o.h.v. layout, reminiscent of the 2-litre B.M.W., on the Standard-based 1,776 cc 1½-litre Jaguar block. This version (Type XG) suffered from noisy valve gear, and gave way to the 80·5 × 98 mm. (1,999 cc) XJ unit on which most of the experiments in port and head design were tried out. This was a twin o.h.c. unit, like the original XF, and it was one of these engines, and not the later four-cylinder XK, which was loaned to Major Gardner for his successful record attempts in Belgium in August 1948. The first six-cylinder engine in the experimental series was a development of this type, with the bore enlarged to 83 mm., the resultant capacity being 3·2 litres. At this stage, Heynes was considering a power plant of 'in-between' size to replace the existing pushrod 2½-litre and 3½-litre models. But it was found that the XJ 'six' gave inadequate low-speed torque. The cure for this was to lengthen the piston stroke to

ADVANCE PARTICULARS
OF THE NEW

JAGUAR

Type XK

"100" AND "120" SUPER SPORTS MODELS

FITTED WITH TWIN OVERHEAD CAMSHAFT ENGINES OF 2 LITRE OR 3½ LITRE CAPACITY

JAGUAR CARS LTD COVENTRY ENGLAND

106 mm., and thus was the final XK120 engine attained.

This very brief summary cannot possibly take acount of the years of painstaking research behind the evolution of one of the most consistently successful power plants of all time. The intention was to market the XK engine in its final form in the two basic types—the four-cylinder 1,996 cc version with similar dimensions to the XJ, and the six-cylinder 83 × 106 mm. (3,442 cc) model. In the best Jaguar tradition, the bottom end was massive, the counter-balanced crankshaft being forged from 65-ton steel; six-cylinder units had seven-bearing crankshafts, as hitherto, and a four-bearing type was used in the four-cylinder model. The guiding hand of Harry Weslake was generously acknowledged in the cylinder head design, and his finished product, in aluminium, weighed a mere 50 lbs, as against approximately 110 lbs for a comparable cast-iron head. The overhead valves were set at 70 degrees to the vertical, and operated by twin chain-driven overhead camshafts. Combustion chambers were of hemispherical shape, this design being not only more efficient, but giving a better flow of cooling water to the valve seats. Furthermore, they made for simpler machining and easier servicing. Intensive research was undertaken in the evolution of a camshaft drive that combined efficiency and silence, the original single-chain method being discarded owing to a high-pitched whine, audible only at some distance from the engine. Heynes used a conventional system of lubrication by a gear-type pump, the dry-sump type not being adopted until 1954, and even then only on competition engines. Ignition was by coil, and carburation by a pair of horizontal S.U.s. Output of the six-cylinder engine was 160 b.h.p. at 5,000 r.p.m., and the 2-litre unit gave 105 b.h.p. at 5,400 r.p.m., the latter representing more than 50 b.h.p. per litre—quite an improvement on the old '100'. Cylinder blocks for production engines were made by Leyland Motors, and still are.

Sceptical journalists at the 1948 Show wondered whether the XK120 had ever run on the road. It is unlikely that the Show car itself had more than 'works mileage' on it, but in the twelve months preceding the announcement three prototypes, all differing slightly in detail but all with the six-cylinder engine, had been subjected to intensive testing, mainly in the hands of R. M. V. Sutton, well known in the late 1920s for his competition successes with Lea-Francis cars. Writing in *Motor Sport* some years later, Sutton admitted to having had some misgivings when he was told that the car would be publicized under a '120 m.p.h.' slogan, but he decided to put the matter to the test, and took one of the prototypes out in the small hours of the morning. On a deserted five-mile stretch not far from Coventry, he tried for 120 m.p.h., and attained it without difficulty. 'The car itself,' he observed, 'put my mind to rest, as I found it delightful to handle.'

Less intensive testing was undertaken on the four-cylinder prototypes, though one of these took the road with an experimental form of air-strut suspension, which was not proceeded with. But to the four-cylinder engine belongs the honour of making the twin-camshaft design's first public appearance, for in August 1948, one of the XJ engines was lent to Major A. T. G. Gardner for insertion into that indefatigable record-breaker, EX.135, which had started life in 1933 as a K3-type M.G. 'Magnette'. Not only did it provide Jaguars with some valuable high-speed testing, but it also enabled the Major to extend his record-shattering activities into the 2-litre class. The Jaguar-M.G. hybrid attained 176·7 m.p.h. over the kilometre and 173·7 m.p.h. over the mile. Despite tuning which yielded the impressive output of 146 b.h.p. at 6,100 r.p.m., the engine note was described as 'not specially loud, and somehow irrelevant'.

Though the four-cylinder car was listed through 1949 and 1950 as the XK100, using a chassis identical to that of the six-cylinder XK120, it never went into production, and no cars were built to the catalogue specification. The tremendous demand for the XK120, allied to the well-known Jaguar preference for six cylinders, had its effect. When the 2·4-litre saloon was introduced for the 1956 season, rumours circulated to the effect that this first unitary-construction Jaguar had been designed round the XK100 power unit. This is not so, for the development programme on the twin-camshaft 'four' was completed by 1949, and the 2·4-litre was not put in hand till 1953.

The XK120's 3,442 cc engine was fitted into a box-section frame of great torsional rigidity, with large box-section cross-members. The springing followed a layout similar to that used on Mk. V, with torsion-bar front suspension and semi-elliptics at the rear. Steering was of Burman recirculating ball type, and the Lockheed full hydraulic brakes worked in twelve-inch drums. A proper central fly-off handbrake supplemented these, but, like Mk. V's umbrella handle, it operated on the rear wheels only. The four-speed gearbox had synchromesh on second, third and top, and standard ratios were 3·64, 4·98, 7·22, and 12·29 to 1, with the option of a 3·27:1 rear axle which was said to endow the car with a top speed in the region of 140 m.p.h. A Borg and Beck single-dry-plate clutch was used, and final drive was by hypoid bevel.

This chassis was cloaked with an aerodynamic two-seater body of typical Jaguar elegance—it won William Lyons the honour of a Royal Designer for Industry later on—a narrow oval grille replacing the full-width Jaguar vee-radiator current since 1936. The narrow top panel of the bonnet opened upwards, alligator-fashion, prompting William Boddy to enquire apprehensively in *Motor Sport* whether the makers suggested that:

'its plugs will not require constant attention, that oil will not be flung on to hot surfaces, and that the noise is not such that the manufacturers' one desire is not to let it escape at all costs.'

Not that there was any cause for alarm. The XK engine would stand untold abuse, and I know of one Mk. VII saloon which survived a heavy dose of Derv, administered in the wilds of Greece at the only petrol pump within miles. It made the Yugoslav border, and five years later it was still running well, without a major overhaul in the intervening period.

A vee windscreen was fitted, but this was interchangeable with one of aero type for competition work. The rear wheels were partially concealed by detachable spats, and the sloping tail housed a luggage locker of generous proportions, though owners with more sporting proclivities could specify a twenty-five gallon fuel tank if they were willing to sacrifice some baggage space. Standard cars had a fifteen-gallon tank. All this was available for £1,273 including tax, or approximately $4,000 in the U.S.A.

There were still the scoffers, of course, who insisted that such a car was too good to be true. Either it was a shameless gimmick to boost the sales of Mk. V, or it would be found, when the car did go into production, that retail price and the weight of 22cwt. as well would have increased drastically. Lyons was quite unworried. The 1948-9 financial year was to show him a profit of £124,577, and Mk. V was selling very well without any help from the XK120. In February 1949, his agents in New York booked sales for 200 saloons and drophead coupés at the European Car Show.

Meanwhile, America was also waking up to the XK120. Lyons's dynamic efforts in the past two years had borne fruit, and, thanks largely to the spadework done by the Nuffield Organization with their 'TC' M.G., the American public was aware of the sports car as a serious proposition. I have always been unable to comprehend the American passion for sports cars, in a country where even before the energy crisis it was illegal to exceed 80 m.p.h. on *every* public road—in many states, indeed, one collected a 'ticket' for doing more than 60! Sheer snob appeal must account for a large proportion of sales, though such an appeal depends greatly on a European styling, as Austins found to their cost when they produced the Americanized A.90 'Atlantic' convertible in 1949. Despite the backing of a much-publicized series of long-distance stock-car records at Indianapolis, the Austin was too ugly for the sports-car *clientèle*, and even an outstanding performance and an indestructible engine could not sell it. With speed out of the question, the transatlantic buyer set a premium on standing-start acceleration, a virtue which Detroit products offered. Fortunately for British luxury-car manufacturers, they obtained this extra output by increasing the size of their engines, a permissible practice where petrol was cheap and plentiful. In 1949, a typical 'big' American car, the Cadillac '62', had a 5,420 cc engine developing 180 b.h.p.; by 1961, the corresponding model had a capacity of 6,370 cc, from which some 325 b.h.p. was extracted. As this latter unit lived in a vehicle measuring 18ft. 6ins. from stem to stern, there is perhaps some justification for buying a European sporting car even if one only wants acceleration! Eventually the Americans took to making sports cars themselves. I once asked Bill Rankin if Jaguars were worried by such offerings in this class as the Chevrolet 'Corvette' and Ford 'Thunderbird'. 'Good heavens, no!' was the retort; 'To an American, a sports car must be an imported car, and nothing else.'

The XK might still be an unknown quantity, but even at that first post-war London show, over 80% of the year's estimated output was sold to dollar customers. The Hoffman Motor Company, the then American distributors, announced in January 1949 that they had made over ninety sales on the brochure alone, though they did not add that that year's edition was something of a catalogue collector's item in its own right, with its Spirax binding and full-page colour illustrations. They waxed lyrical on the car:

> 'The Jaguar sells itself because it's exactly what the American enthusiast has wanted for a long time. It has the power to outspeed, outperform, and outmanoeuvre anything built over here, and the price is right.'

Meanwhile, there were no XKs for sale anywhere. Home customers were receiving the last of the beam-axle 1948 saloons and export purchasers the first of the Mk. Vs, but the first of the new o.h.c. models was not delivered till July 1949, and none were to be released to the home market until March 1950, eighteen months after the car's announcement. I saw the first one I had encountered outside a showroom about that time, parked in the Brompton Road, near Harrods. There was a crowd around it. It is of interest to note in passing that, out of 7,713 XK120s produced between 1950 and 1953, only 571—or a bare 8%—were sold for use in Britain. But while the critics waited, Lyons was planning an exploit that was to spark off editorials in *The Motor* and *Motor Sport*.

In May 1949, R. M. V. Sutton took one of the first production cars to the Jabbeke-Aeltre motorway for tests officially observed by the Royal Automobile Club of Belgium, and succeeded in covering a flying mile at the electrifying speed of 132·596 m.p.h. The car ran minus hood and screen, with the optional extra undershield in position: the higher axle ratio of 3·27:1 was used. Dunlop Roadspeed tyres of the type recommended for competition work were fitted, and locally-purchased 74-octane fuel was in the tank. As tested, the car turned the scales at the catalogue figure of 22 cwt., but afterwards full touring equipment was donned, and a second run was accomplished at no less than 126·448 m.p.h. As if to drive the lesson home, Sutton then motored back past the assembled journalists at 10 m.p.h. in top gear.

The motoring world was staggered, to put it mildly. Mr G. R. Strauss, the Minister of Supply, sent a telegram of congratulation to Lyons, and more orders poured in, from Uruguay and Egypt among other countries. *Motor Sport* commented that 'it is possible to bestow the highest praise on the 3½-litre XK Jaguar, *sans peur et sans reproche*'.

There were, of course, a few sceptics left. They conceded that the car was fast enough, quiet enough, and remarkably docile. They did, however, draw a careful parallel between a planned demonstration arranged by the manufacturers' test staff, and a serious race. How would the car fare in the Mille Miglia, for instance, or at Le Mans?

The first post-war Le Mans of 1949 came and went. A 2-litre Ferrari, driven by Luigi Chinetti and Lord Selsdon, won from Louveau and Jover's 3-litre D.6 Delage. Britain's honour was upheld by Culpan's 2-litre Frazer-Nash, a lineal descendant of the B.M.W. 328, once the S.S. 100's great rival, and even the illustrious name of Bentley figured in the results, Hay's 1939 4¼-litre aerodynamic saloon gliding silently in sixth. But there were no Jaguars. Nor were there any in the 'Alpine', Appleyard having forsaken his '100' for a Healey. The XK120, some people opined, was a 'promenade roadster' like the old S.S. I.

JAGUAR 2½ LITRE MODELS
Specification

ENGINE. Six-cylinder, 73 m/m. bore × 106 m/m. stroke; 2663·7 c.c. Treasury rating 19 h.p., £15 Tax. Overhead valves, push rod operated. Exceptionally stiff seven-bearing counter-weighted crankshaft. Aluminium invar strut pistons. Chromium iron cylinder block with exceptionally long water jackets. Light alloy connecting rods. All-machined combustion chambers and ports. Detachable head. Cooling by centrifugal pump and automatic bye-pass thermostat. Completely submerged high volume oil pump. Single dry plate light action clutch. Large capacity heavily-finned aluminium sump.

FRAME. Low underslung frame, cross braced for extreme rigidity. Main members are box section fore and aft of cruciform members and are outswept to take full width of body without overhang.

TRANSMISSION. Four-speed gear box with synchro-mesh on second, third and top. Improved method of engagement ensures "finger tip" control by easy-to-hand change speed lever. Hardy Spicer all-metal propeller shaft and universal joints. Spiral bevel final drive.

GEAR RATIOS. First, 15·30 ; Second, 8·98 ; Third, 5·83 ; Top, 4·25.

SUSPENSION. Long flat road springs of low periodicity with extremely wide front and rear spring track. Luvax double-action hydraulic shock absorbers front and rear.

BRAKES. Large diameter Girling brakes, 13" × 1½" effective surface, fully compensated with rod operation throughout. Heavily-finned special alloy brake drums, 15" diameter. Hand brake lever of quick-release racing type.

STEERING. Burman Douglas worm and nut steering. Light yet positive at all speeds and incorporating Bluemel Douglas spring-blade steering wheel adjustable for height and rake.

PETROL SUPPLY. From 12-gallon rear tank. S.U. electric petrol pump. Twin carburetters.

WHEELS AND TYRES. Dunlop centre-lock splined hub type racing wheels. 18" diameter rims with chromium plated edges. Fitted with Dunlop 5·50 × 18 tyres.

ELECTRICAL EQUIPMENT. 12 volt set, 17 amp. charging rate, ensuring instantaneous starting. Large type head lamps with dip and switch control above steering wheel. Streamlined wing lamps. Stop light. Reverse light. Two interior lights. Special diffused illumination for instrument panel. Lucas blended note horns.

BODY. All panelled body of extreme strength on frame of first quality selected ash.

DOORS. Four wide doors, flush fitting and of generous width, with self-aligning chromium plated hinges incorporating Enots grease nipples. Positive action silent travel locks. Two doors on Tourer and "100" models—those on the Tourer being extra wide to permit easy access to rear seats.

SLIDING ROOF. Quick action, self-aligning, single control operation. Perfectly flush fitting, preserving an unbroken roof line. Very large opening.

WINDOW LIGHTS. Safety glass winding type.

WINDSCREEN. Special screen of new and improved design. Positively leak proof, opening from bottom by single-action winder which can be operated with one hand whilst driving.

UPHOLSTERY AND CARPETING. Finest quality Vaumol leather hide throughout in a range of colours to tone with exterior colour scheme. Floors thickly carpeted in colours to harmonize with general colour scheme. Open models upholstered in Celstra hide.

SEATING. Comfort of the most luxurious order is provided by deeply-sprung seats with form fitting back rests. The one-piece rear seat in closed model may be divided by heavily-padded folding arm rest which, when not required, can be folded back into recess in back rest, thus affording accommodation for three passengers in rear compartment. Foot-wells of greatly increased width provide ample leg room. Both front seats are quickly adjustable by means of special slide rails.

WINGS. One-piece pressings with deep valances affording maximum protection. Front wings on closed model are of high domed helmet type.

INSTRUMENTS. 100 m.p.h. 5" trip speedometer, 5" rev. counter, incorporating 8-day clock, ammeter, electric petrol gauge, oil pressure gauge, radiator thermometer, self-cancelling built-in trafficators. All instruments with white dials.

SPARE WHEEL AND COVER. Spare wheel with metal cover is carried, on closed model, on rigidly-mounted bracket and is recessed into well on near side front wings. On open models, no cover is provided and wheel is carried at the rear.

LUGGAGE ACCOMMODATION. Ample accommodation for luggage is provided in the capacious compartment in the tail of the closed model. A large trunk is provided on the Tourer. On the "100" model accommodation for small suit cases is provided within the body at rear of seats.

DIMENSIONS. SALOON AND TOURER.
Wheelbase, 9' 11" ; Track, 4' 6" ; Overall length, 14' 10" (Tourer, 15' 0") ; Overall width, 5' 7" (Tourer, 5' 6") ; Overall height, 4' 10" ; Ground clearance, 7½" ; Turning circle, 38'.
SS "100" Model. Wheelbase, 8' 8" ; Track, 4' 6" ; Overall length, 12' 6" ; Overall width, 5' 3" ; Ground clearance, 7" ; Turning circle, 36' 0" ; Weight, 19¼ cwt.

A soberer elegance makes for soberer print. A page from the '37 catalog showing the specifications for the 2½-liter S.S. Jaguar.

American publicity for Mk.VII. In 1954, Borg Warner transmission was optional, but for this market it had been standardized two years later. The situation in Mk.X days had changed so far that even those who wanted to shift for themselves had to wait.

THE *Superlative* MARK VII

Distinguished for its classic modern styling, the Jaguar Mark VII perfectly combines continental lines and Old World craftsmanship in garnishments with matchless performance. Exteriors are clean and simple — free of the garishness of excess chrome; new deluxe finishes range through a wide variety of distinctive colors, with matching or contrasting genuine leather upholstery. The sunshine roof offers the fun of open car motoring. The trunk has more usable space than any car on the market.

Exclusively designed for Jaguar, and a perfect complement to the high-performance Jaguar engine, the Borg-Warner automatic transmission is optional equipment on the Mark VII.

THE S.S.I.

RADIATOR. A special feature, entirely redesigned, conforming with the graceful body lines ; fitted with chromium plated fluted front, futuristic emblem and filler cap under the bonnet. The ensemble is completed with apron between the dumb irons. Cooling system incorporates new high efficiency impeller and special film block to prevent over-heating.

BUMPERS. Exceptionally substantial and of attractive appearance, are domed 3½ section. Those at the rear protect the spare wheel and trunk.

COACHWORK. Coachbuilt, with leather grained head and large travelling trunk ; the body represents the finest example of craftsmanship. The body is constructed on the soundest lines and is of extreme strength. Everything possible has been done to ensure lasting and trouble-free quality. The frame is of prime quality selected ash throughout, reinforced by aluminium and metal brackets.

THE DOORS. Flush fitting, and exceptionally wide, ensuring ease of access ; the doors are hinged on double-strength standing pillars from bottom side to cantrail by means of special self-aligning chromium plated hinges, incorporating Enots' grease nipples. Spring loaded all-steel door checks are fitted to the bottom of the doors secured to the chassis frame. Entirely new type slam locks of positive action are fitted. Each door is fitted with adjustable Bedford buffers.

THE HEAD. Leather grained, with chromium plated dummy head joints. Chromium weather mould protecting door, and chromium bead down hinge pillar and waistline.

Catalogues down through the years reveal the evolution of the Lyons theme. The '33 folder emphasized the front view, and bodywork was still the principal interest of a firm who in this season was also building custom coachwork on Wolseley chassis and exhibiting at Olympia among the purveyors of bodies rather than among the manufacturers proper.

Specifications for the Jaguar Mark VII.

the Jaguar Mark VII

The stately four door MARK VII SEDAN represents a pinnacle of automotive craftsmanship. Among its many virtues is the ability to carry six people swiftly over great distances . . . in supreme luxury.

The MARK VII is at home on any road . . . in town or country. Throughout the world it is frequently seen proudly bearing license plates marked *Corps Diplomatique*.

The MARK VII is available with automatic transmission and standard equipment includes such amenities as a sliding sun roof, double fuel tanks to allow tremendous luggage capacity . . . lavish yet tasteful use of hand-rubbed walnut panelling and glove leather upholstery.

It is a car that gives its passengers as much pleasure as the owner behind the wheel.

SPECIFICATIONS

- **Engine:** Six cylinder 3½ litre twin overhead camshaft Jaguar XK engine developing 190 H.P. Twin S.U. horizontal carburetors.
- **Transmission:** Borg Warner automatic transmission. Four speed synchromesh gearbox with optional overdrive available on special order.
- **Suspension:** Independent front suspension; transverse wishbones, torsion bars and telescopic shock absorbers. Rear: Half elliptic springs controlled by telescopic shock absorbers.
- **Brakes:** Vacuum servo-assisted hydraulic. Friction lining area 179 sq. ins.
- **Steering:** Recirculating ball. Adjustable steering wheel.
- **Wheels:** Steel disc wheels with Dunlop 6.70 x 16 in. tubeless tires.
- **Fuel Supply:** Twin S.U. electric pumps. Capacity 20½ gallons in two tanks of 9½ and 11 gallons. Turn-over switch on instrument panel.
- **Electrical:** 12 volt 64 amp/hour battery.
- **Instruments:** 120 mph speedometer, tachometer, ammeter, oil pressure, water temperature and fuel gauges, electric clock.
- **Body:** Four door all steel six seater with sliding roof. Built-in heater, defroster and windshield washers. Upholstered in finest quality leather over foam rubber. Polished walnut panels.
- **Luggage Accommodations:** Capacious 17 cubic foot trunk with spare wheel fitted inside.
- **Dimensions:** Wheelbase 10 ft.; overall length 16 ft. 4½ ins.; width 6 ft. 1 in.; height 5 ft. 3 ins.; dry weight 3696 lbs.

THE 2½ LITRE JAGUAR "100"

The 2½-litre Jaguar 100.

The 2½-litre Jaguar 4-Door Saloon.

THE 2½ LITRE JAGUAR 4-DOOR SALOON

THE 2½ LITRE JAGUAR OPEN TOURER

The 2½-litre Jaguar Open Tourer.

The 1½-litre Jaguar 4-Door Saloon.

THE 1½ LITRE JAGUAR 4-DOOR SALOON

132·6 M.P.H. ON PUMP PETROL · · ·

On May 30th, 1949, an entirely standard Jaguar 3½ litre XK 120 Sports Two-Seater, running on pump fuel, attained a speed of 132.6 m.p.h. over a flying mile on the Jabbeke-Aeltre Road in Belgium. This speed was officially timed by the Royal Automobile Club of Belgium and is the fastest ever recorded by a standard production unsupercharged car.

By 1950 Jaguar had something to shout about, and the XK120 catalogue contained this full-page boost.

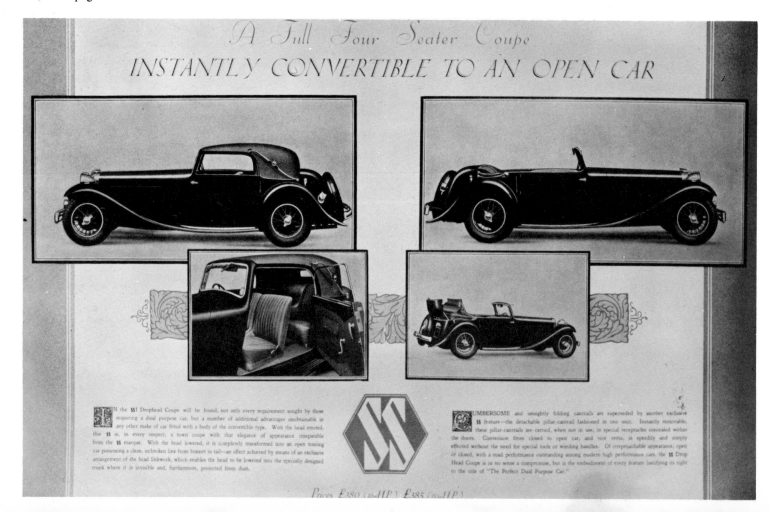

They were wrong. The Silverstone meeting in August 1949 included a novelty in the form of a Production Car Race, the forerunner of those present-day entertainments in which tinware squeals and rolls its way round circuits, stop-lights winking obediently *en route*. This pioneer race was quite well supported, Healeys contributing their new 'Silverstone' model, Allard the latest J-type, Frazer-Nash the 2-litre, and Riley their 2½-litre, 100 b.h.p. saloons. In the small-car classes, the new Jowett 'Javelins' fought it out with H.R.G.s, M.G.s and Morgans, and there was a sprinkling of pre-war machinery. There were also three of the new Jaguars.

Though the special 3½-litre '100' used in pre-war days by Newsome and Wisdom had been works-prepared, previous factory participation in competition had been confined to rallies and the Alpine Trial. For Silverstone, however, Lyons sent down three standard XK120s, patriotically cellulosed in red, white and blue respectively. These were assigned to Peter Walker, Leslie Johnson and 'Bira', and they dominated the race, 'setting the seal on prestige', as *Motor Sport* put it. Johnson won the one-hour event at an average speed of 82·8 m.p.h., and Walker was a good second. 'Bira' was unlucky—someone had inadvertently fitted a touring tube into one of his tyres, and this burst after sixty miles. The three cars did a *tour d'honneur* at the Shelsley Walsh meeting in September, the silence of their ascents occasioning comment—shades of Major Harvey and his S.S. I in 1933! Before the opening of the 1949 Earls Court Show, the Hoffman Motor Company let it be known that they had purchased the next six months' output of XK120s.

No changes were found necessary on the twin-camshaft cars for 1950, though Mk. V was given even tougher bumpers and a more efficient bonnet-locking device. Glowing reports came in from America, and in the XK's second year of life, John Bentley, a British journalist living in the U.S.A., thoughtfully recorded his impressions for the benefit of his less fortunate compatriots at home, whose dreams of a new Jaguar were no nearer fulfilment. He found the brakes temperamental, and their linings susceptible to dirt and water alike; too many road shocks, in his opinion, were transmitted to the steering wheel, and the vertical rear bumpers were useless as a defence against American parking techniques, but otherwise he was lyrical in his praises:

'Whether you play tunes on the gearbox ... or potter along in the lackadaisical style more appropriate to a lower-geared saloon, there is always that sensation of tremendous power, disciplined by superb design, never obtrusive yet instantly ready for use. Given the slightest chance the XK will murder anything on the road, on acceleration or maximum speed.'

Nineteen-fifty was a big year for Jaguar in America. The XK120 formed the centrepiece of their display at the British Car Show held in New York in April—this was the biggest publicity drive yet undertaken in the U.S.A. by Britain's motor industry, and twenty-one makers put their wares on show. The XK120, resplendent in white, stood on a velvet cloth, flanked by bronze statuettes of Jaguars designed by Bill Rankin. The velvet cloth, incidentally, is an essential for press showing of cars in America. This enterprising piece of show-business netted them $300,000 worth of orders. It was estimated at the time that some 50,000 British cars were circulating on U.S. roads, of which 14,000 were initially registered in 1949. Among the customers at New York was Clark Gable, who bought his first XK120.

Meanwhile *The Motor* had accorded the XK120 another editorial on the occasion of its road test of the model. The journal proudly proclaimed that it had become:

'The first instrument whereby such impartial figures could be attained, although testing of such a car is not wholly without embarrassment, since there are few places in the world where level road speeds of the order of two miles a minute can be sustained so as to be recorded with accuracy and safety.'

The Motor's example, despite an increase of 3½ cwt. in weight over the prototype, attained a two-way maximum speed of 124·5 m.p.h. third gear producing 90 m.p.h. and second 62 m.p.h. The car as tested had an 8:1 compression ratio and the lower 3·64:1 axle ratio. Weight of the car as tested was 25½cwt. From a standing start, 30 m.p.h. was attainable in 3·2 seconds, and 50 m.p.h. in 7·3 seconds. Only ten seconds—or fractionally more than the record figure attained by the 'Light Sports' Railton in 1935—were needed to reach mile-a-minute speeds, but the Jaguar could be accelerated up through the gears to 100 m.p.h. in just under half a minute, whereas the Railton could not quite make the century. Good performance throughout the range is indicated by the ability to accelerate on top gear from 10–30 m.p.h. in 6·7 seconds. Fuel consumption 'driven moderately hard' worked out at 19·8 m.p.g., and owners of the cars confirm this. It was found that the normal starting procedure with a warm engine was to engage second gear, change directly into top, and then brake sharply to bring the car back within the legal limit in built-up areas! The flexible suspension allowed 'a trace of roll to be felt during really fast cornering', but the small steering wheel movements required gave the car a precise controllability. Like Mk. V, it handled better than it felt. The brakes, a controversial subject among early XK owners, were behaving well on this occasion, light pedal pressures producing excellent results, though maximum energy was required to ensure stopping in 31 feet from 30 m.p.h.

'What is really creditable,' *The Motor* went on, 'is the way in which the car can be slowed or brought quickly to rest from speeds above 100 m.p.h. without fuss or misbehaviour on smooth or rough surfaces.' The headlamps 'were not really worthy of the car', a sustained 70 m.p.h. being the safe limit, in the tester's opinion, at night. No comments were passed on the standard of accessibility afforded by the alligator bonnet.

William Boddy, no mincer of words, tried an early XK120 for *Motor Sport* in April 1951, and found the engine 'like a bank clerk, quite devoid of temperament'. He also found that hitherto easy corners became acute, so deceptive was the impression of speed, or

A page from the special drophead coupé folder issued in 1935. Though only £5 extra was charged for the 2.7-litre, 20 hp motor, the horsepower tax was not forgotten by Britons, and most buyers opted for the lower impost and the loss of some acceleration.

absence of it, given by the Jaguar. Despite the tendency of the soft suspension to 'wallow', directional stability was little impaired, and the steering lock was taxi-like. The relative position of brake and accelerator pedals took some time to become familiar, but Mr Boddy was less happy with the brakes. Normally these worked well and progressively, but several times he encountered disconcerting and unaccountable fade. The engine was a first-touch starter from cold, and ran very cool, but the maximum two-way speed with the 3·64:1 axle was estimated at no more than 110 m.p.h., and this particular car would not habitually cover more than fourteen miles on a gallon of fuel. The presence of a cigar lighter occasioned ribald comment, but the locking flap on the fuel filler was considered unfunny—like the similar device on Mk. V, it sometimes played up.

I have dwelt at considerable length on these early press reports, as they help to show the XK120 in perspective against the standards of 1950. Its dual personality was something quite new; true, there had been other cars combining flexibility, docility, and out-and-out performance, like the open Railtons and the vee-twelve Lagonda. The Railton, however, was hampered by the limitations of the Hudson design from which it stemmed, and the gearbox was designed for emergency rather than regular use. The Lagonda undoubtedly combined the flexibility of a steam car with a remarkable urge when the gears were used energetically, but as sold to the public it turned the scales at some two tons, it was awkward and expensive to maintain, and it set the purchaser back £1,600 even before the War. There is no doubt, however, that the vee-twelve's rather hard torsion bar independent front suspension felt much more secure than did the Jaguar's softer system, and the Lagonda *felt* as directionally stable as it was. Jaguars tested in 1949 and 1950, incidentally, still adhered to a single exhaust pipe, hence the resultant subdued note. Later on, the adoption of twin exhausts was to produce a harsh staccato bark under violent acceleration.

But Jaguars still hung back from racing. They regarded the XK 120 as a fast roadster, and this function it fulfilled admirably. The story goes that Lyons was literally bullied into organizing a Competition Department after some clueless amateurs had put up most undignified performances with their XKs in a minor Belgian event, gyrating in the manner of the S.S. 100 at its worst. The infuriated 'Madame Jaguar' (Mme. Bourgeois) had so heckled him on the telephone that he gave in. Be that as it may, I suspect that the truth is that there were no cars to spare for this kind of amusement in 1949 and early 1950. There were certainly very few to be seen at Club events at Silverstone and Goodwood during 1950; Members' Day on the Sussex circuit that May produced a flock of the latest Allards, but their main competition came from Guy Gale's aged Darracq, which had won the 1938 T.T. No XKs were present. Even in August, the Bouley Bay Hill-Climb in Jersey attracted none of the twin-camshaft cars, though Le Gallais' 3½-litre pushrod-engined mock Auto-Union was defeated in ·the unlimited class only by Poore's 3·8-litre *monoposto* Alfa-Romeo and Sydney Allard on his latest J.2 model.

In the U.S.A., however, the situation was easier, and the XKs scored their first serious success at the Sports Car Club of America's Palm Beach races in January 1950. Bill Spear's car, resplendent in 'bridal white', succumbed to brake trouble, but Leslie Johnson took fourth place in general classification, and was second in his class to George Huntoon on an odd device known as a Ford-Duesenberg Special, which looked like a 1928 Indianapolis car with road equipment, and probably was! This success was widely advertised by Jaguars during the 1950 season—later, of course, they were to achieve far more than places in minor national events.

However, both the Targa Florio and the Mille Miglia saw private Jaguar entries. Neither of these events had ever produced an outright British victory, despite the distinguished efforts of M.G. and Aston Martin in the small car classes of the 1930s, and it seemed inevitable that the production-model Jaguars, as yet untried in long-distance racing, would be outclassed against the might of the costly and highly-tuned Ferraris. This in fact happened, but the Italians had a bad fright in the process, as the only Jaguar in the Targa Florio, driven by Clemente Biondetti, actually led for a while before retiring. Four cars were entered in the Mille Miglia, the drivers being Biondetti, Haines, Leslie Johnson and T. H. Wisdom. An attempt was made to run the cars in the International *Gran Turismo* class, but despite their 'cabriolet tops', they were forced to compete against the sports cars proper. Competition this year came not only from the Ferraris, but from Donald Healey on a prototype 3·8-litre Nash-Healey and the rising star J. M. Fangio on an Alfa-Romeo. Haines crashed, the veteran Biondetti broke a rear spring early on, and Wisdom was the unluckiest of all, as his transmission packed up a mere thirty miles from the finish at Brescia. Johnson, however, survived, taking fifth place in general classification—his time was less than an hour longer than Marzotto on the winning Ferrari, said to have cost the wealthy textile manufacturer £5,000. Franco Cortese on a 2-litre Frazer-Nash finished eighth.

In May, the XK120s took part in the race meeting at Westhampton, Long Island, but those were the days of the Cadillac-Allard's ascendancy in the U.S.A., and Erwin Goldschmidt could manage no better than third place in either his heat or the final—in the latter he gave best to Briggs Cunningham's Ferrari, and to Tom Cole, who had at last forsaken his S.S. 100 for a Cadillac-powered J.2 Allard.

June 1950, however, saw the second post-war 24-Hour Race at Le Mans, which attracted an interesting entry list. In addition to the Ferraris and the Frazer-Nash that had distinguished themselves in 1949, there were two Bentleys—Hay on the car that had done so well the year before, and E. R. Hall on the 4¼-litre with which he had finished second in the 1936 T.T. Further challenges came from the 5·4-litre Allard, from M. Lago's 4½-litre Talbots, which looked uncommonly like road-equipped Formula I machines, and from America's Briggs Cunningham, who was carrying out a preliminary reconnaissance with a brace of Cadillacs, one a more or less standard saloon, and the other '*Le Monstre*', a fearsome all-enveloping aero-dynamic two-seater. There were also three privately-entered XK 120s running in standard trim, though, one suspects, with moral if not financial support from the factory. Drivers were Leslie Johnson and H. L. Hadley, Clark and Haines, and Whitehead and Marshall.

In the event, Louis Rosier brought his Lago-Talbot home in first place, making a fastest lap at 102·84 m.p.h. The Johnson/Hadley Jaguar circulated for twenty hours in an uncanny silence which the older journalists present compared with the 2·3-litre Talbot '90' on its *début* twenty years before; thereafter the clutch declined to grip, and that was that. The Jaguar, however, had been deceptive, for it lapped at a surprising 96·98 m.p.h., and twenty hours at this sort of pace is no mean feat for a 'promenade sports car'. In fact, the press concentrated their invective on the unfortunate M. Lago, who, they asserted, had merely hung wings and lamps on his Grand Prix cars. Laurence Pomeroy, however, praised the French designer for evolv-ing a Grand Prix machine so readily adaptable to sports-car events, and it is likely that these sentiments were echoed by Jaguars, for, when they did enter international competition, they were to incor-porate a far larger number of stock components than did any of their major competitors. Clark and Haines went the whole distance, taking twelfth place and averaging 80·94 m.p.h. The third Jaguar finished fourteenth. Leslie Johnson submitted a lengthy report on the XK120's behaviour, which was carefully studied at Coventry.

Fortified by this experience, Jaguars not only entered for the Production Car Race at Silverstone in August, but cars were also prepared for the first post-war Tourist Trophy on the Dundrod Circuit in September. What is more, Tazio Nuvolari, who was in the country at the time, specially asked Lyons if he could drive one of the cars at Silverstone. Alas, though the *maestro* attended practice sessions, and expressed himself well pleased with the Coventry product, his health gave way and he did not drive in the race. Had he done so, it is possible that Jaguars might have returned home with more than a class win. As it was, Enzo Ferrari had also elected to support the event, and on the bumpy airfield circuit Ascari, taking advantage of the generous handicap accorded to his 2-litre Ferrari, led Walker's Jaguar home. In any case, the Italian's average speed was higher—83·72 m.p.h. as against the XK120's 81·88 m.p.h.

The Italians, however, did not contest the T.T., and the principal competition came from N. R. Culpan's 2-litre Frazer-Nash. Pouring rain, and brakes that were even then regarded as below par, might have produced a result adverse to Jaguar, but the young Stirling Moss never made a mistake, and led the race from start to finish, averaging 75·15 m.p.h. Whitehead on the second car followed him home, his average speed being only 1 m.p.h. slower. The feat was made even more memorable by the fact that this was Jaguar's first success in a long-distance race, and Moss's first serious sports-car race. Stirling Moss himself describes it as his first big success, and says that he owes it to the kindness of Tommy Wisdom, who allowed him to drive the XK on this occasion.

To revert for a moment to the summer: July was marked by Jaguar's re-entry into two totally different types of event. The Municipality of Eastbourne put the clock back fifteen years, and staged a midnight *Concours d'Elégance* at which the *Grand Prix d'Honneur* for an *ensemble* of car and lady was won by Mrs Haines and her white XK120. More important, however, Ian Appleyard had at last procured an XK120 (NUB 120) and had entered it for the International Alpine Rally—the word 'trial', with its muddy connotations, was no longer used! The event was, as usual, gruelling, and ruthless time penalties took as great a toll as did mechanical faults. Only five *Coupes* were awarded—four went to the 745 cc flat-twin Dyna-Panhards of Lapchin, Grosgogeat, Burgerhout and Signoret, and the fifth to Appleyard, who made Best Individual Performance, and collected almost every available trophy on the road section. Over the flying kilometre on the *autostrada* his 109·8 m.p.h. had no real challengers, and in the timed climb of the Stelvio Pass he was beaten only by a 2·5-litre Alfa-Romeo. On the Gross-glockner Pass, however, the northern descent was observed, and we may detect a slight weakness yet in Jaguar brakes by noting that Appleyard was placed fourth, behind a Sunbeam-Talbot, an Alfa-Romeo, and a M.G. *The Autocar* tried the car in the condition in which it returned to England after its alpine exploits. It was found that the right front wing and left wheel spat were working loose—the car at that time still wore disc wheels and spats—that oil fumes were seeping up through a loose floorboard, and that the brakes required a heavy pedal pressure and were badly out of adjustment. But they still did their job, and the steering showed no signs of wear. Appleyard, understandably enough, used the lower of the two avail-able axle ratios on NUB 120, but modifications were confined to air slots cut in the bonnet to counter vapour lock at altitude, a separate control overriding the automatic choke, and a duplicate horn button for the passenger.

Meanwhile, Jaguar were facing the need for expansion. Lyons' achievements had won further recognition in 1950, when he was elected to the Presidency of the Society of Motor Manufacturers and Traders, and in this capacity he delivered the annual show-time message. It was not an auspicious Show. The Korean War had played havoc with steel supplies, and chromium plate was again disappearing from radiator grilles and hub-caps. H.R.H. The Princess Elizabeth was billed to open the Show, but she was taken ill at the last moment, and her sister, H.R.H. The Princess Margaret, had to deputize for her. A printers' strike prevented anything like the usual press coverage. Lyons, however, sounded a quietly confi-dent note, stressing the steady increase in exports, and promising more and better cars for the world, 'including soon, I hope, our own car-starved motoring public'. He also could not resist commenting on the small number of new models unveiled at this Show. For William Lyons had stolen the Exhibition again—this time with the Mk. VII saloon.

This was the 100 m.p.h. saloon that had occupied the design department's energies for the past six years. Finished in pale metallic blue, it revolved upon a turntable. It represented the consummation of the development programme of which the XK120 had been but a stepping-stone.

The new 'Prima Ballerina', as *The Autocar* described Mk. VII, indeed derived closely from its sports-car predecessor, having the same type of massive frame, and similar steering and suspension arrangements. The hydraulic brakes were, however, of Girling design and manufacture, and had Dewandre vacuum servo assistance in view of Mk. VII's much higher weight of 34½cwt. Gone also was Mk. V's umbrella-handle handbrake, which had been replaced by a fly-off lever similar to that used on the XK120. Power was provided by a standard XK engine, developing 160 b.h.p. at 5,200 r.p.m., but mounted five inches further forward in the frame; and the four-speed gearbox was controlled by a stubby central lever of sporting aspect and delightfully positive action. Ratios were 4·27, 5·84, 8·56, and 14·4 to 1. The twin S.U. carburetters were fed by twin electric pumps, but on Mk. VII the fuel was divided between two saddle tanks of nine and eight gallons respectively, one in each rear wing. This duplicated system met with approval in unlikely places, a Lebanese 'coachbuilder' introducing an entirely unauthorized modification designed to render the cars eminently suitable for international smuggling. A grille more closely related to the older design was used, and the graceful if bulky saloon body not only provided enormous luggage capacity, but its excellent leather upholstery, interior woodwork, and sliding roof derived from the old days of the pushrod models. The Mk. VII was a really big car, of the type to appeal to Americans, with a ten-foot wheelbase and an overall length of 16ft. 4½ins. List price, including purchase tax, was a mere £1,276, but the entire production was reserved for export, and the show car was shipped direct from Earls Court to the Waldorf-Astoria Hotel in New York, where the American dealers were eagerly waiting. Orders for 500 Mk. VIIs, worth seven million dollars, were booked on the spot for the Eastern States alone, the value of total orders from the U.S.A. being estimated at $20,000,000. By the end of November, a further $7,000,000-worth of cars had been reserved.

Participation in international events seemed likely for 1951, for F. R. W. 'Lofty' England, the company's Service Manager since 1946, was made Competition Manager as well. England was an ideal choice, for he had had a long career as a racing mechanic, and between 1932 and 1938 had worked for Sir Henry Birkin, Whitney Straight, the E.R.A. organization, Richard Seaman and 'Bira'.

The year was rounded off neatly by two most impressive performances. With the de-rationing of petrol in the spring of 1950, the R.A.C. Rally had returned to the calendar, and that November Appleyard duly won his class, and collected a starting control award, though first place in general classification went to Holt and Asbury's TD M.G. Stirling Moss and Leslie Johnson took the latter's Palm Beach and Le Mans car (JWK 651) to Montlhéry, and averaged 107 m.p.h. for twenty-four hours without any trouble.

But a weekly production of 250 cars was not enough for John Silver, Jaguar's Production Manager, and already negotiations were in hand to take over another works, the former Daimler No. 2 Shadow Factory in Browns Lane, Allesley, on the outskirts of Coventry. This had been built in 1939 as part of the re-armament programme, and had served Daimlers well, not only boosting their output of munitions, but also furnishing a temporary headquarters during the 'blitzes' of 1940 and 1941. Since the end of hostilities, however, this factory had been used for Daimler's peacetime production of cars and buses. Between the end of 1950 and November 1952 the entire equipment of Jaguar Cars Ltd. was gradually shifted from Holbrook Lane, production being steadily maintained, and even increased, during the transfer. With a million square feet of space, Jaguars now had room to breathe and production rose sensationally. Further, though a prospect of green fields was obscured by the housing on the other side of Browns Lane, the new factory was less than a mile from rural Warwickshire.

With the XK120 vindicated, and Mk. VII already launched in America, Lyons was looking for other fields to conquer.

1951 was to bring a foretaste of the future.

Trying the rival firm's wares: Rudolf Uhlenhaut of Daimler-Benz in an early XK120.

Alpine scene: the Appleyard XK NUB 120 and a J.2 Allard halt in the mountains.

Salient features of the Jaguar type XK engines.

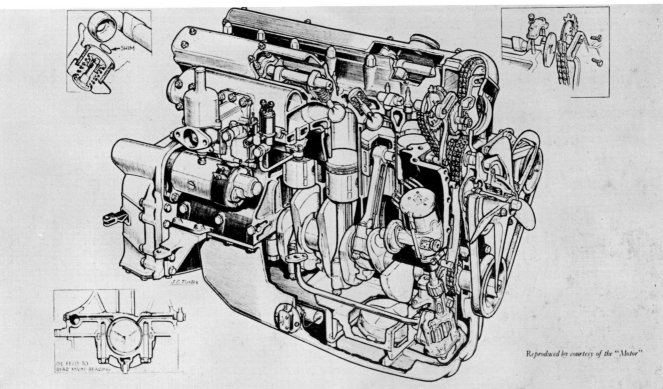

Reproduced by courtesy of the "Motor"

SALIENT FEATURES OF THE JAGUAR TYPE XK ENGINES

In this new range of Jaguar engines all compromise in design has been eliminated. Each engine can be truthfully stated to incorporate all the most advanced technical knowledge available to-day on naturally aspirated petrol engines. Tests carried out on the completed units have shown the wisdom of the decision taken by the Jaguar Company nearly nine years ago to develop an engine on these lines.

In addition to bench tests, totalling many thousands of hours, extensive road tests at home and abroad have been carried out and it is significant that the 2 litre engine, loaned to Colonel Gardner when he broke the world speed record in the 2 litre class at 176 miles per hour, is a completely standard unit with the exception of modified pistons to give a higher compression ratio.

From the following condensed resume of the more important features of the Type XK engine, it will be seen that no reliance has been placed upon the use of new or untried inventions. Instead, a blend of known and proved detail designs of the highest efficiency has resulted in the creation of a production engine of unparalleled quality and performance.

The following are some of the more important points :—(1) *Hemispherical head of high strength aluminium alloy.* (2) *Valve seatings of special high expansion cast iron alloy are shrunk into the combustion head.* (3) *Induction system, including the valve ports, were designed in collaboration with Mr. Harry Weslake, generally accepted as the foremost expert in this particular science.* (4) *Twin overhead camshafts, driven by a two-stage chain, act directly on the valves through floating tappets.* (5) *Oiling system— exceptionally large capacity oil pump with large diameter oil galleries, a feature which ensures an adequate supply of cool lubricant and eliminates frothing.* (6) *Exhaust valves of high grade austenitic steel immune from lead attack.* (7) *Water circulation—direct flow across the head from a high pressure pump. The head is fed by a gallery alongside the block which ensures equal distribution between all cylinders. The cooling to the block is controlled at a constant temperature by means of restricted circulation.* (8) *The crankshaft is a 65 ton steel forging, adequately counterweighted ; the main bearings in both four and six cylinder engines are 2¼" diameter. These bearings are larger than have ever been previously used on passenger car engines of similar capacity, and are responsible to a large degree for the exceptional smoothness with which these engines deliver their power, which is maintained up to the high maximum r.p.m. of which these engines are capable. The four cylinder has three bearings and the six cylinder has seven bearings. The bearings themselves are of the Vandervell thin shell type and have shown on test to have practically unlimited life.* (9) *Pistons—are Aerolite aluminium alloy, fitted with chromium plated top rings, which tests show give over 100 per cent. increase in life to the bores.*

CHAPTER 7

The C-Type

1951–52

'*The driving of the Jaguar XK120C on the motor roads of Europe is . . . a great and memorable experience, and tribute must be paid to the designers and executives who have made possible such a fine contribution to British automobile engineering.*'

The Motor, October 1952

'*Considered from any angle, the Mk. VII Jaguar is an outstanding car. It has extremely good performance, is very comfortable to drive and to ride in, is very completely equipped, has a modern yet dignified appearance, and is very good value—indeed, it is in that respect phenomenal.*'

The Autocar, April 1952

IN the two years that followed the introduction of Mk. VII, the Jaguar company occupied itself in two very different ways in the fields of commerce and competition. On the production line, a note of consolidation was struck, and up to the end of 1954 no entirely new touring models were introduced. The XK120 was made available in fixed-head and drophead coupé forms, and export customers were given the benefit of the factory's competition experience with a 'special equipment' series introduced in 1952. Mk. VII likewise benefited from racing experience, but the main improvements concerned the adoption of alternative transmissions better suited to the lazy driver—the inevitable consequence of a successful breakthrough into the carriage trade.

In the competition field, however, Jaguar made tremendous strides. No longer were they merely 'showing the flag', to reassure the more sporting clients that their cars were capable of competing with the best. For the next six years, a Competition Department, under the direction of 'Lofty' England, was to write the name of Jaguar in the boldest of capitals all over the world. When the *marque* retired from official participation at the end of the 1956 season, the cars would no longer be just 'amazing value for the money'; and a study of Jaguar's publicity slogans down the years shows a trend away from the sensational. In the summer of 1951, the Mk. VII was being advertised as 'the car that turned the head of the world', but a month or two later this had given way to the classically simple

'Grace . . . Space . . . Pace'. In 1959, even this was to play second fiddle to the sweeping, but justifiable assertion that the Jaguar furnished a 'Special Kind of Motoring which no other car in the world can offer' —and in this there was no price qualification.

But in the whole of Jaguar's approach to competition, one factor stands out. The twin-overhead-camshaft Jaguars must share with Bentley and Aston Martin the honour of doing more for British prestige in sports-car racing than any other makes have achieved, but William Lyons' objectives were far narrower than those of his competitors. Bentley's invasion of Grand Prix racing in 1930, admittedly, was the result of a *formule libre* which gave his cars an unexpected chance, and in any case Birkin's car was not works-sponsored, but W. O. Bentley, as long as his firm's finances permitted, would support any event of significance in the international calendar. He eschewed the Mille Miglia, but then so did the makers of all the bigger British cars before the War. Jaguar's outstanding rivals in the 1951–6 period were Ferrari, Aston Martin and Mercedes-Benz; but Enzo Ferrari, David Brown and Alfred Neubauer all set their sights on the Sports Car Constructors' Championship, and each, in turn, won it: William Lyons, with as good a record as any of them, never brought the Championship home to Britain in six years of consistent racing.

The reason is not hard to seek. The sole Jaguar objective in sports-car racing, as W. M. Heynes has since stated in print, was to win at Le Mans, in fact to run the fastest *scheduled* service over the Sarthe Circuit that could be envisaged. From this basic target stem both the splendours and the miseries of Jaguar's racing career. Given a well-surfaced course with good straights and tricky corners, which had to be circumnavigated around the clock, the Jaguar design staff had to evolve a car capable of going very fast, and performing consistently without mechanical weaknesses, allied with manoeuvrability and a high standard of retardation to combat driver-fatigue. Hence the uncanny durability of the XK unit, whether with wet- or dry-sump lubrication, and whether fed by carburetters or, as later, by fuel injection. The engines were seldom too fast for their gearboxes and back axles at Le Mans, troubles which dogged the Ferraris. Hence also the disc brakes. Jaguar reliability is reflected in the fact that until late in the firm's competition career the cars were always driven to and from the circuits, and the 'limited' trade-plates painted on their dark green coachwork became a familiar sight. Even in 1958, when the D-type now at Beaulieu was required for exhibition at Geneva, Bob Berry, then Assistant Public Relations Officer, drove it out. He had a cold run, but a much easier one, I suspect, than he would have had on a contemporary Ferrari. Nobody would go shopping in a sports-racing Ferrari unless it were unavoidable, and some of their bigger efforts, notably the 4·9-litre, were unmanageable brutes, demanding drivers of the calibre of Ascari and Hawthorn; but the wider scope of Enzo Ferrari's programme brought its advantages as well. Le Mans bred a race of superbly-braked Jaguars, but equally the faultless surface imposed limitations on Jaguar suspension, especially at the rear, and these placed them at a hopeless disadvantage to the Ferraris and Mercedes-Benz on the Nurburgring or the nastier stretches of the Mille Miglia, such as the Radicofani Pass. In events which suited the C- and D-types, especially the longer grinds, they were always a good bet. As all-round *motor-cars*, the Jaguars were a sounder proposition than the Ferraris but as all-round Championship contestants, the balance was always cast in favour of Maranello.

Further, Jaguar simply did not have the cars to support a full season's programme. A stable of six vehicles must be regarded as an irreducible minimum—three for the team, one for practice, one reserve, and one for experiments with new modifications—and Jaguars seldom, if ever, had any to spare. A car sent to Italy for the Mille Miglia, or to Sicily for the Targa Florio, meant a potential waste of valuable Le Mans material if anything went wrong. Admittedly Jaguar design attained a degree of standardization to which Ferrari never aspired, and most breakages could at a pinch be replaced from factory stores, but in the event of a complete write-off the odds were against there being a spare C- or D-type car on hand to fill the breach. Not that any of this detracts from the merit of their achievements. William Lyons set his sights at winning Le Mans, and did so five times, not to mention a second place in 1954. Enzo Ferrari wanted to win the Constructors' Championship, and did so seven times.

Meanwhile, Mk. VII had been establishing a niche in public favour. It was a very big car by European standards—I know this only too well, as my first Jaguar was a second-hand example of this model purchased in the summer of 1955. Within its limitations it handled amazingly well. It was certainly as good an all-rounder as any of its competitors from either side of the Atlantic, a fact that was recognized even in 1951. Christopher Jennings, writing in *The Motor* that October, compared it with the Cadillac, not only in view of its enormous capacity for luggage, but on price as well, for at $3,850 it was very cheap for an imported car. The contemporary Cadillac listed at $3,097. Jennings dropped a broad hint to Lyons in passing:

'I believe that if an alternative version of the Jaguar, complete with automatic transmission and power-operated steering, could be made available, a factory double the size of the present one would be needed to cope with the demand from a section of the American public hitherto untouched by the invasion of the European automobile.'

It is unlikely that Lyons needed the tip. A 'factory double the size of the present one' had, as we have seen, been underwritten, and the Americans were to be offered their favourite transmission in 1953. They were, however, to have to wait another six years before the low-geared Jaguar steering was given power assistance.

It is of interest to assess Mk. VII against its principal competitors of the period, the o.h.v. Cadillac vee-eight, the 'Fire Power'-engined Chrysler, also a vee-eight but a more advanced design with hemispherical heads, and Mercedes-Benz' '300' model, introduced in the spring of 1951. All three were to compete with Jaguar on the circuits as well as on the showroom floor, Sydney Allard fitting the Cadillac unit in his J.2s and JRs, the Chrysler vee-eight powering not only some Allards but Briggs Cunningham's 5½-litre Cunninghams, and the Mercedes-Benz forming the basis of the formidable 300SL coupés and 300SLR open two-seaters.

Of these three rivals in saloon form, the Chrysler was advanced in other respects, for power steering was offered as an option and was indeed fitted to the car tested by *The Motor* late in 1951. Purchasers could also have caliper disc brakes at extra cost, but the test vehicle did not have these, unfortunately. The Cadillac had neither of these amenities, and both were typical Detroit products in other respects, with automatic transmissions and 5½-litre short-stroke engines. The Mercedes-Benz had a 3-litre short-stroke single o.h.c. engine mounted in a typical Mercedes chassis, with swing-axle rear suspension. The car tried was a sedate six-seater saloon, but the firm also produced a model parallel with the XK series, the 300S roadster. But that was as far as the parallel went, for the 300S, though beautifully finished, and independently sprung all round, was an immensely heavy vehicle in the best Post-Vintage-Thoroughbred traditions. It was also murderously expensive, costing £5,529 in England at a time when an XK120 could be bought for a fraction over £1,600.

Accurate price comparisons between the four cars are impossible, but the price differential in a common market was not great. Engine outputs are, however, interesting—Mercedes extracted 115 b.h.p. from 3 litres, Jaguar 160 b.h.p. from 3½-litres, Cadillac needed two extra litres to obtain an identical output, and the more efficient Chrysler unit, though no bigger, disposed of some 180 b.h.p. Relating weight directly to road performance, the Mercedes, for all its smaller engine and conservative styling, emerges creditably, for, though it turned the scales at 35·4 cwt. as against the Jaguar's 34½ cwt, it gave an identical mean maximum speed of 101 m.p.h. on a fractionally lower top-gear ratio—4·44:1 against the Jaguar's 4·27:1. Thanks to lower indirect ratios, it was actually quicker from a standing start to 30 m.p.h., though it needed 14·9 seconds to reach 60 m.p.h., whereas the Mk. VII could attain mile-a-minute speeds in a mere 13·7 seconds, and by the time both cars were doing 90 m.p.h., the Jaguar was nearly four seconds ahead. The much-criticized Jaguar brakes actually achieved a brisker stop from 30 m.p.h., and the advantages of high gearing and aerodynamic body-work are reflected in an overall fuel consumption of 17·6 m.p.g. for the Jaguar, and only 16·2 m.p.g. for the smaller Mercedes. The later overdrive-equipped Mk. VIIs could in fact comfortably exceed 20 m.p.g. on long runs—though in mitigation of these comparative statistics it must be admitted that some of the differences are so marginal as to be accountable by the foibles of the individual cars tested. Jaguar steering—now requiring four-and-three-quarter turns from lock to lock—was clearly attuned to the needs of the American woman driver.

By contrast, the American figures are interesting, if only to show that Jaguar and, to a lesser extent, Mercedes-Benz, had evolved vehicles worthy of serious consideration as everyday transport in the United States. The Cadillac was remarkably light at only 38cwt., but the Chrysler turned the scales at well over two tons, in spite of which it could attain 101 m.p.h. I feel that the Cadillac must have been off form, for its 90 m.p.h. top speed was well below the *marque's* known capabilities. The advantage of well-chosen ratios, manually operated, is illustrated by the fact that both Cadillac and Chrysler were appreciably slower up to 30 m.p.h. than the Mercedes, and both needed over fifteen seconds to attain 60 m.p.h. Fuel consumption of both cars was a creditable 14 m.p.g., but unfortunately no comparative statistics are available for braking. The Chrysler's 2LS hydraulics were described as 'adequate' for general Continental touring, albeit the Cadillac suffered from 'a considerable amount of fade'. Fade was also encountered on both the Jaguar and the Mercedes-Benz under mountainous conditions, so this was apparently not an American peculiarity! As for styling, both the European products pleased the eye in entirely different ways, the German car possessing rigidly conservative lines and the Mk. VII an elegant simplicity, innocent of meaningless chrome ornamentation, even though it might be regarded as bulky nowadays. By contrast, the Cadillac's exaggerated lines were accentuated by air intakes in the rear wings which admitted no air anywhere, while the Chrysler, if perhaps a trifle more restrained, was far too old-fashioned for American tastes, and the company's sales, the advanced specification notwithstanding, plummeted down. This decline was not arrested until the cars were completely restyled in 1955. All four were big by British standards, both Jaguar and Mercedes-Benz measuring over sixteen feet from stem to stern; the Detroit offerings were nearly eighteen feet long.

The '300' Mercedes-Benz, be it said, did not long remain a competitor for the Jaguars. As the years went by, it grew more and more executive without losing any of its quality, and by 1960 automatic transmission was compulsory. The company, however, continued to compete worthily against Jaguar with their smaller '220' model, also with the overhead-camshaft engine. This was redesigned in 1954 and again in 1959, and as a 100 m.p.h. saloon with outstanding handling its sales were always watched with interest.

The first Mk. VII reached Australia as early as April 1951, when the first one to be shipped to the Dominion was delivered to Alderman J. B. Chandler, the Lord Mayor of Brisbane. Exports to South Africa, however, were not to start for another six months. American enthusiasm was reflected in the result of *Fortune's* survey of imported cars, published at the beginning of the year. This rated the Jaguar as 'the best-looking imported model', though the best dollar value was thought to be the Rolls-Royce, with Jaguar in second place. In November, a second public opinion poll established that the Jaguar was now 'the most desired imported car', the runner-up scoring only half the number of votes cast for the Coventry product. At home, this demand had to be satisfied, and a special plant was installed which reduced the time taken to dry wood facias from twelve hours to nine minutes, and also, it was asserted, rendered them immune from blistering in tropical climates. The scope of Jaguar sales was further widened by the introduction of a delight-fully-proportioned fixed-head coupé on the XK120 chassis, retailing at £1,276, which made its *debut* at the Geneva Show in March. Unlike its predecessor, the '100' coupé shown in 1938, it went into full production.

Mk. V continued quietly in production until July. Though only the 3½-litre version figured in the buyers' guides, both variants were made right up to the end. Among the most appreciative customers were the police, and by the end of the year seventeen city, borough, and county Forces were using Jaguars. Mk. V also accounted for the *marque's* first competition success of 1951, when Vard and Young drove a 3½-litre saloon into third place in the Monte Carlo Rally, a worthy upholding of the prestige gained for British cars by Gatsonides' second place in 1950 on a Humber 'Super Snipe'. At Sebring, John Fitch was unlucky in the six-hour race for the Sam Collier Memorial Trophy, for brake troubles beset him, and at the finish his XK120 'had nothing to stop on except compression'. It must have been excellent compression, for it netted him a class win though victory on formula went to Koster and Deshon's diminutive Crosley, and the distance prize to Fred Wacker's Cadillac-Allard.

The touring XK120 was fast being outclassed, or, more specifically, outbraked, in major events, though it was a force to be reckoned with at a less elevated level, and Wicken and Craig finished second and third in a handicap race at the Easter Monday Goodwood meeting. April saw further successes. At Castle Combe, L. Wood was placed third in the class for Unlimited Sports Cars, behind Oscar Moore's H.W.M. (really a Formula II racing car) and K. Watkins' Allard; and the Boreham Meeting was a good day for Jaguars, as Parker's Jaguette was the fastest sports car, W. B. Black's XK120 the fastest standard open car, and J. H. Craig's XK (presumably modified) the fastest open car over 3,000 cc. The cars, however, failed to distinguish themselves against Ferrari and Cadillac-Allard opposition in the Argentinian Sports Car Races, and even Palm Springs, scene of the breed's first foreign victory, brought in nothing better than a third and a fourth place, behind a Ferrari and a Cadillac-Allard again. By contrast, a race for Production

Sports Cars held at Silverstone in conjunction with the International Trophy produced an all-Jaguar field, in which circumstances Stirling Moss was a natural winner at 84·5 m.p.h. Jaguars also did well at the Gamston meeting. Johnnie Claes won the Belgian one-hour race for production cars, leading a field of *eighty-four* home at 81·22 m.p.h., and Scherrer was first in the production sports-car class of the Bremgarten Preis race at Berne. His average of 78·12 m.p.h. compares very well with the 86·78 m.p.h. of the outright winner, Willy Daetwyler, whose Alfa-Romeo was nothing more nor less than one of the 1937 4½-litre vee-twelves built for the 750 kg. Grand Prix Formula, running with road equipment on this occasion, of course! Finally, Leslie Johnson had again taken his faithful JWK 651 to Montlhéry. This time it was transported to the Autodrome by lorry, but modifications did not extend beyond those made for Sutton at Jabbeke in 1949. The 'flying start' hour was covered at a speed of 131·83 m.p.h., and to cap this, Johnson proceeded to put 131·2 miles into a second hour, from a standing start.

There were other, less serious episodes. Those who remembered the S.S. I days must have smiled when Mlle. Janine Vincent won a prize for 'la plus jolie toilette de jeune fille' at the Cannes *Concours d'Elégance*, partly, at any rate, on the strength of her XK120. Jaguars also invaded the Bentley Drivers' Club's August hill-climb at Firle in April. Officially the fastest time of the day went to H. J. Wilmshurst's 4½-litre Bentley, with a climb in 37·6 seconds, but it was

Anticipation of British-Leyland days was this Jaguar-M.G. hybrid which did over 175 mph at Jabbeke in August, 1948. Chassis was Major Goldie Gardner's famous streamliner, EX135. The motor was a twin-cam, four-cylinder XJ-type Jaguar prototype.

Mixed styling: disc wheels with spats at the rear, and thin pillars grafted onto the traditional Jaguar shape did not please everyone. But the tough and durable Mk.V of 1949-51 was more than a stopgap; it was a classic.

Mk.V convertible. This retained the traditional three-position top and most of them were exported.

Cecil Vard winning third place in the 1951 Monte Carlo Rally. Mk.V owners soon became accustomed to the curious angles assumed by the independent front end, and in skilled hands the car could be cornered very fast.

Mk.V dashboard.

whispered darkly that a very unofficial ascent by the caterer's XK120 was a good four seconds quicker! Perhaps the worst requited performance of all, though, fell to Leslie Taylor in August 1951. He drove his car the 965 miles from Darwin to Alice Springs, across the Australian outback, in 10 hours 32 minutes, or an average of something over 91 m.p.h. For his pains, he had his XK120 impounded, and was charged with exceeding the speed limit, driving without a Northern Territory licence, and driving a car not registered in the Northern Territory—and all this in spite of lopping 5½ hours off the previous record! By contrast Duncan Hamilton, who was booked for exceeding 100 m.p.h. in a built-up area with his C-type, escaped with a fine of forty shillings.

Already, however, rumours of improved Jaguars were on the horizon. Clemente Biondetti had appeared at Monza late in 1950 with an odd Jaguar Special of his own devising, consisting of an XK engine, gearbox and back axle in a Maserati frame, the whole camouflaged beneath a Ferrari two-seater racing body and radiator grille. It took eighth place in the 1951 Giro d'Italia, and duly lined up for the Mille Miglia of that year, along with three XK120s driven by Moss, Johnson and Gatti, a Covent Garden fruit importer, Cortese's Frazer-Nash, Donald and Geoffrey Healey in a Nash-Healey, and Wisdom and Hume in a DB.2 Aston Martin saloon (the legendary VMF64, which the Hon. Gerald Lascelles later owned and frequently used). This strong British contingent fared but patchily. The Aston Martin duly won its class, for closed cars over 2,000 cc, but brake troubles put Johnson and Moss out early on, while Biondetti's 'special', which proved much faster than the standard cars, packed up when the chassis flexed on a level-crossing and the fan cut through the radiator hose. Gatti retired when his car hit a road marker.

Jaguar hopes were, however, centred on Le Mans. The main challenge came from the 4·1-litre Ferraris of Chinetti, the 1949 winner, Chiron, and Spear; from the big Chrysler-engined 5·4-litre Cunninghams; from the 4½-litre Talbots, victorious in 1950; and from the Cadillac-Allards of Allard/Cole and Hitchings/Reece. The DB.2 Aston Martin saloons and the lone Nash-Healey coupé of Rolt and Hamilton could also be relied upon to give the heavy metal a good run for its money. Jaguars, however, had sprung a surprise with their new C-type. The engine was basically standard and retained the wet-sump lubrication and the two horizontal S.U. carburetters. Harry Weslake had effected modifications to both the inlet porting and the exhaust system, and the use of high-lift camshafts and a lighter flywheel had boosted output to an impressive 210 b.h.p. at 5,800 r.p.m. The four-speed gearbox had ratios of 3·31, 4·51, 6·59, and 11·2:1, though closer ratios, including a 3·99:1 third gear, were available, and when the model went into production after the race customers had a selection of axle ratios from 2·9:1 to 4·27:1. As this car was not designed for touring, it was found possible to utilize a smaller and lighter battery for the 12-volt lighting and starting system. While the engine was a logical development of the unit fitted to the XK120 and Mk. VII, the chassis was entirely new, use being made of a tubular frame with heavily-drilled channel-section side-members. The standard Jaguar front suspension layout was retained, but a new system of rear springing was adopted, the axle casing being located by underslung longitudinal links, the fulcrums of which were attached to a transverse torsion bar. Rack-and-pinion steering replaced the recirculating ball type, and braking was taken care of by Lockheed 2LS hydraulics, still with twelve-inch drums, but with a special system of automatic adjustment. The end-product was appreciably lighter than the touring model, at 18½cwt.,

First time out for the XK120: the late Leslie Johnson winning the One-Hour Production Car Race at Silverstone in 1949.

further weight having been pared by the substitution of knock-off wire wheels for the discs which had proved so slow and awkward to change at Le Mans in 1950. The body was of aerodynamic type, and incorporated a forty-gallon rear tank: the whole bonnet assembly hinged up to give access for servicing. The three works C-types were entrusted to Johnson/Biondetti, Whitehead/Walker, and Moss/Fairman. In addition, Lawrie and Waller had entered a standard XK120.

Jaguars dominated the race, despite vigorous opposition from the South Americans Fangio and Gonzales, who this year were driving for Talbot. The hefty Cunninghams also went well, and by 4 a.m. on the second day the Walters/Fitch machine had crept up to third place. Jaguars had their casualties: five hours from the start, when the cars were lying first, second, and third, Biondetti lost all his oil pressure; at midnight a further blow was to come when Moss, in the lead, was greeted by a resounding bang as he emerged from Arnage—a connecting-rod had broken. Thereafter the Whitehead/Walker combination was left to uphold the honour of the Big Cat. This they did to good effect, winning at an average speed of 93·49 m.p.h., seventy-seven miles ahead of the second car, Meyrat and Mairesse's Talbot. On Index of Performance they took third place only, behind two French miniatures, a Monopole (alias Panhard) and a Dyna-Panhard. As the fastest lap of the race was credited to Stirling Moss before his retirement, designers, drivers and builders had every reason to be satisfied. The Lawrie/Waller XK120, incidentally, lasted the whole distance as well, averaging 82·52 m.p.h. The President of the Automobile Club de France sent a telegram of congratulation to Lyons, and the Malcolm Campbell Memorial Trophy went to a Jaguar for the second year in succession: in 1950 the award had been made to Ian Appleyard, in recognition of his Alpine victory. It was announced that the C-type would go into limited production, though *The Autocar* warned that 'it is not likely to be available for the home market in the foreseeable future'. Home customers were, however, allowed to benefit from the hard work of Heynes and Weslake, for a Jaguar service bulletin advised private owners that they, too, could buy high-lift camshafts (£15 each), high-compression pistons (£21 a set), and dual exhaust systems (£15).

While Jaguars were trouncing the Ferrari and Talbot opposition at Le Mans, *The Autocar* was testing a production Ferrari, the 2½-litre Tipo 212 Export two-seater. It proved to be remarkably tractable, the vee-twelve engine giving it a dual personality not unlike the Jaguar's, while its racing ancestry was reflected in an output of no less than 140 b.h.p. at 6,500 r.p.m. Weight as tested was 18 cwt. It possessed an extremely close-ratio five-speed gearbox, and would attain 120 m.p.h. on top (4·28:1), and 110 m.p.h. on the 4·66:1 fourth. A cigarette lighter was standard equipment, but hood, side curtains, and windscreen wipers alike were not. The price was the equivalent of £3,200 in its native Italy, and when the Ferraris came to Earls Court the following October, rumour spoke of a £10,000 price-tag on the big 4·1-litre 'Tipo America' saloon.

In America, John Fitch won his class in the Hampton Cup race at Bridgehampton on a modified 'Le Mans-type' car entered by Whitmore. This machine had high-lift camshafts of Winfield manufacture, Al-Fin brake drums, an aluminium competition body fabricated in America, and Borrani wire wheels, these latter being available as optional extra equipment in the U.S.A. In Northern Ireland, a young man named Mike Hawthorn was winning the Ulster Trophy race on a 1½-litre Riley built for the 1936 T.T.—the same car which he later restored, and which now forms part of his Memorial in my Museum at Beaulieu. Mike drove a splendid race, but the opposition which included Sydney Allard on one of his Cadillac-engined J.2s, and the great Louis Chiron on an XK120, was handicapped right out of the event.

New names were coming to the fore; one Ian Stewart took a third place at Winfield in July, while at Boreham in August a colourful figure came into Jaguar history, when Duncan Hamilton won the Lyons Trophy—a special race for XKs.

Jaguar supported the T.T. in September, and pulled off an easy win after Rolt, Johnson, and Moss had all shattered the Dundrod lap record in practice. Lance Macklin, however, was little slower in the new DB.3 Aston Martin, which circulated at 81·9 m.p.h. The T.T. this year was hardly an international event, non-British cars being represented solely by Trouis' little D.B.-Panhard and the Ferraris of Hall and Baird. Hall crashed early on and Baird had to be content with sixth place, his co-driver Mike Hawthorn missing a spell. Moss won, averaging 82·55 m.p.h., and Walker was second, close behind. Though a British car—Cortese's Frazer-Nash—won the Targa Florio for the first time in history, Jaguars did not enter. Nor did they manifest any interest in the Carrera Panamericana, the long-distance race held in Mexico in December. It was subsequently elevated to the status of a Championship event, and attracted serious entries from Gordini, Mercedes-Benz and Ferrari, but the Coventry firm attached little importance to it, their 1952 entry of a C-type being cancelled and the car sold to Duncan Hamilton. This car was prepared for Masten Gregory, but Stirling Moss's request to be allowed to drive was turned down. He and 'Lofty' England did, however, follow the race with a view to possible entry at a later date. One or two privately-owned Mk. VIIs ran in the touring-car section in 1951, but the regulations were revised the following year to exclude twin-carburetter engines in this category, and that was that. In any case, Lyons' abstention does not seem to have affected Mexican sales adversely, for later on an assembly plant was opened in Mexico City, and functioned for some time before the Mexican Government clamped down.

Appleyard, now partnered by his wife Patricia, William Lyons' daughter, had a good year's rallying, still on the famous NUB 120. In the Tulip Rally he had his revenge on Ken Wharton, who had been adjudged winner in 1950 after the Jaguar was penalized—this year Appleyard won the event, and the Swiss driver Habisreutinger, also on an XK120, took second place. In addition, Appleyard

Hollywood meets the XK120: Clark Gable specified a radio and wheel trims on his.

'From Paris with Love' — a still from the film of that name shows a '53 special equipment XK120 convertible with Elaine Labourdette at the wheel.

The XK120 coupé, second body style to be announced, lost none of the roadster's looks, the hardtop being an obvious part of the car and not an afterthought.

The Jabbeke records, 1949: R.M.V. Sutton with his XK120.

By modern standards, the Johnson-Hadley XK120 which performed so impressively at Le Mans in 1950 is very much a 'touring car'. But a lap at over 96 mph from a car 'the same as you can buy' was not lost on the world.

cleaned up another twenty-odd awards! He also made the best individual performance in the R.A.C. Rally, and won the Lancashire Automobile Club's Morcambe Rally outright. The Alpine successes of 1948 and 1950 were repeated once more, though this time it was a very close victory over Imhof on an Allard. Only ten *Coupes* were awarded, and seven of these went to British cars—Appleyard's and Habisreutinger's Jaguars, Imhof's Allard, Gott's H.R.G., Duff's Frazer-Nash, the Wisdoms' Aston Martin (VMF 64 again!), and Wadsworth's Healey. Eighth place in the big-car class, incidentally, went to Grant-Norton and Loader, who had once opposed the S.S. 100s with their 'Jabberwock' V8 Fords—but in 1951 they shared an XK120. For this performance the Appleyards were accorded a civic reception by Leeds Corporation. To cap an impressive season, Ian Appleyard not only won the London Rally, but emerged from the contest with the only clean sheet. His cars were privately entered, but Jaguars lent the fullest support, including preparation by the works service department.

The Appleyards were the outstanding Jaguar team in the rallies of the day, but other drivers were adding to the *marque*'s laurels as more and more XKs rolled off the lines. W. F. Mead won his class in the M.C.C.'s Edinburgh Rally in May, and Claes and Ickx won the Liège-Rome-Liège event in August, another XK taking second place. Ferrari and Porsche opposition defeated the cars in the Tour de France, but private owners Hache and Crespin did well to take fifth place in a rally in which British machines had not hitherto been prominent. The M.C.C.'s National Hastings Rally, held in November, recorded another class win, this time for Grounds and Hay, and in the coachwork competition Mrs Snow's white XK, complete with leopard-skin upholstery, was adjudged the best vehicle in its category.

No new models were announced for 1952. Towards the end of the year, export was accounting for 96% of all the cars produced, and of these an impressive 61% were earning sorely-needed dollars for Britain. The Show cars might not be new in design, but both the Mk. VII and the XK120 won coachwork awards in the competition run by the Coachbuilders' Association (I.B.C.A.M.) in connection with the Motor Show. Henceforward Jaguars were to be successful in this annual contest with almost monotonous regularity.

This was not to say that steady improvement was not being effected. The late John Cooper, then Sports Editor of *The Autocar*, used an XK120 roadster during the winter of 1951-2, and had this to say of it:

'It is a complete mystery to me, as I think it must be to most people, how these cars, with all their virtues, are produced and sold at the price charged for them.'

A 7:1 compression ratio was still necessitated at home by the continuance of Pool petrol, and this limited the top speed to around 110 m.p.h., but both brake fade and roll had been largely eliminated. The first production C-type was delivered to Duncan Hamilton, and among the other illustrious clients was Dr Giuseppe Farina, the

Alfa-Romeo and Ferrari driver. Unlike Hamilton, there is no record that he raced his Jaguar. Alberto Ascari preferred a Mk. VII saloon.

The Motor tested the C-type during 1952, and it was singled out for comment by the Editor, Christopher Jennings. During its sojourn with the test staff, it also made a profound impression upon Mrs Jennings, who, as Miss Margaret Allan had been a member of the first S.S. works team of all, in the 1933 Alpine Trial. To Jennings, the C-type was 'a great and memorable experience'. Weight as tested was 20 cwt., and in this form it attained 143.7 m.p.h. on top gear (the fastest Jaguar to be submitted to full road test till the advent of the E-type in March 1961) and 119 m.p.h. on third, the urge being such that 100 m.p.h. could be exceeded in top gear up a 1-in-10 hill. At a constant speed of 40 m.p.h., a gallon of fuel could be made to last for thirty miles, but the overall consumption was also moderate at 16 m.p.g. Acceleration was out of this world by touring-car standards, the C-type reaching 30 m.p.h. in 3.2 seconds, 60 m.p.h. in 8.1 seconds, and 100 m.p.h. in 20.1 seconds. At the other end of the scale, the car would potter quite happily in the crowded thoroughfares of Brussels, and it proved possible to record 10-30 m.p.h. acceleration figures in top gear—this on a design which won twice at Le Mans! The rack-and-pinion steering was 'not only light and responsive, but sufficiently high-geared for the driver to change direction more by wrist action rather than arm movement'. The hydraulic brakes gave no trouble, but after all this evidence of docility one is brought back to earth by the realization that goggles were required wear at above 50 m.p.h., weather protection was non-existent, and there was no provision for week-end baggage either, 'though the body sides . . . proved so commodious that all the impedimenta of a prolonged trans-Continental journey could be housed therein, leaving additional room for the quantity of water-proof clothing rendered necessary by the absence of a hood and windscreen'. All this performance cost no more than £2,327, even in England.

During 1952, likewise, all the modifications evolved during the XK's racing career were incorporated into a 'special equipment' model available with roadster or fixed-head coupé bodywork. For an extra £115 on the basic price the customer was rewarded with high-lift camshafts, a lightened flywheel, twin exhausts, and centre-lock wire wheels. Despite Pool petrol, an 8:1 compression ratio was standard on this series, but all production was reserved for export anyway. A coupé tested by *The Autocar* in October 1952 was, as might have been expected, heavier than the roadsters at 27 cwt., but this extra *avoirdupois* was compensated by an output of 180 b.h.p. from the modified engine, and the car did 120.5 m.p.h. on a 3.77:1 top gear. All the usual XK virtues were present, and acceleration was well up to standard, 60 m.p.h. being attainable in 9.9 seconds and 100 m.p.h. in 28.2 seconds. Steering was still satisfyingly high-geared at 2¾ turns from lock to lock, little more than the two-and-a-half required by the C-type. The XK, indeed, performed altogether too easily, and we can sense a warning note in the tester's summing-up: 'It is the driver, and the road, that are the limiting factors, and not the car'.

Jacques Ickx (left) and Johnny Claes after winning the Liège-Rome-Liège Rally, August 1951. Once again the car is HKV500, victor of Silverstone two years previously.

At the beginning of 1952, also, *Ecurie Ecosse* came into being. This organization, which was to do so much to keep the name of Jaguar before the race-going public even after the works had withdrawn from active competition, was the brain-child of David Murray, and its headquarters were in a small mews in Edinburgh. Its original ambitions did not extend beyond sports-car racing, and the original team consisted of Murray, Bill Dobson, Ian Stewart and Sir James Scott Douglas, Bt. Their cars were four XK120 roadsters and Ian Stewart's newly-acquired C-type, and they adopted dark blue as their colour. Maintenance was in the hands of W. E. ('Wilky') Wilkinson, a tuning expert of many years' standing.

In view of Jaguar's long association with the Scottish *équipe*, it is often claimed that Jaguar Cars Ltd. have, or had, a proprietary interest in *Ecurie Ecosse*, but this is not so. Jaguars have, however, always given Murray first refusal on the last season's works cars, when replacement machines have been on the stocks. In return, *Ecurie Ecosse* have covered, especially in the days of the D-type, far more events than the works could or would have compassed. Sometimes the Scottish cars have gone very fast indeed—in fact, at the International Charterhall meeting in October 1951 Ian Stewart's C-type far outstripped Stirling Moss on a works machine, and at the time it was estimated that Stewart's model could attain as much as 155 m.p.h. Both Murray and Wilkinson, however, are emphatic that they were helped most generously by Jaguar. As Murray told me himself:

> 'In cases, *Ecurie Ecosse* has been able to point out . . . certain suggested improvements, but on the other hand Jaguar developments and improvements passed on to *Ecurie Ecosse* greatly outnumbered the former.

In February 1952 the official works team for the year was announced, Moss, Whitehead and Walker being joined by Ian Stewart and Duncan Hamilton. A month later the R.A.C. announced the award of the Dewar Trophy to Jaguar Cars Ltd., a well-deserved recompense for a year that had included victories at Le Mans, in the Alpine Rally, and in the T.T., as well as Johnson's memorable high-speed run at Montlhéry.

An interesting season of sports-car racing was on the way. In addition to the Ferraris of Italy, the Talbots and Gordinis of France, the Jaguars, Aston-Martins and Healeys of Great Britain, and the blue-and-white Cunninghams from across the Atlantic, Mercedes-Benz were threatening a come-back with their 300 SL coupé. This had the single o.h.c. 85 × 88 mm. 3-litre engine first used in the '300' saloon, but with Bosch fuel-injection in place of the touring car's twin Solex carburetters, and aerodynamic fixed-head coupé coachwork incorporating gull-wing doors. Two Italian newcomers were a potent 2-litre vee-eight FIAT unveiled at the Geneva Show, and Alfa-Romeo's weird and wonderful 'Disco Volante' ('Flying Saucer') with 3½-litre six-cylinder twin o.h.c. power unit. As it happened, only the German car was to be a major force in sports-car competition—the FIATs confined their serious impact to minor Italian races, and the Alfa-Romeos were never fully developed, though while they were going they were very fast indeed.

The Sebring Race in Florida had now become a twelve-hour event, but Jaguars sent no works cars, and the Schott/Carroll XK120 did well to finish second behind Larry Kulok's Frazer-Nash. At the Silverstone International Trophy meeting, however, Jaguars entered for the two production-car races, and won both. Among the touring machinery, Moss in a Mk. VII had no bother against such opposition as Wharton's energetically-handled 1947-type

Appleyard's third Alpine Jaguar: the XK120 (RUB120) which won
the partnership their last Coupé des Alpes, 1953.

Healey saloon and Allard on his Mercury-powered P.1, and was victorious at an average speed of 75·22 m.p.h. The C-types, having attained production status, were allowed to run as production sports cars, and were expected to make mincemeat of the 2½-litre DB.3 Aston-Martins and the J.2 Allards. Admittedly Moss won, averaging 84·02 m.p.h. to the 83·47 m.p.h. of Parnell's Aston, but the seventeen laps saw the elimination of both his team mates, Walker succumbing to brake trouble. The so-called 'Race of the Champions' lined up Moss of Great Britain, 'Bira' of Siam, de Graffenried of Switzerland, Pietsch of Germany, Claes of Belgium, and Gaze of Australia in identical XK120s, and made them fight it out from scratch over five laps. Moss earned an easy hat-trick, leading from start to finish.

The British Empire Trophy, in 1952, was contested in the Isle of Man over a circuit ill-suited for the bigger cars, and hopeless for any Jaguar. The works, with Le Mans close at hand, sent no cars, but *Ecurie Ecosse* fielded Sir James Scott Douglas in an XK120, and Duncan Hamilton ran his own C-type. Axle trouble eliminated the latter after only five laps, but the Scottish car created a very favourable impression, Scott Douglas finishing sixth and winning the unlimited class.

Jaguar did not compete at Berne, but Mercedes-Benz did, Kling winning in the silver 300SL from his team-mate Lang, in front of the Aston Martins of Duke and Parnell, and Biondetti in his Jaguar Special. They also elected to support the Mille Miglia, where they were up against not only Ferrari and Aston-Martin, but also Leslie Johnson, now handling a 4·1-litre Nash-engined car for Donald Healey. Jaguar sent Stirling Moss in a lone C-type, its first appearance with Dunlop disc brakes. He was 'a likely third' at Bologna, in spite of a leaking fuel tank, but steering damage resulting from leaving the road put him out at this juncture, and Bracco's Ferrari was left to lead Kling, on the fastest of the 300SL Mercedes, home to the finish. It was fitting that Moss should be the first driver to race a disc-braked Jaguar, for he had helped them with the development testing, both at Silverstone and on an airfield near Coventry, and recalls many of the earlier headaches, such as boiling fluid, flexing calipers, and servo failures.

And then came Le Mans, and the long-awaited Jaguar-Mercedes duel. Cunninghams produced a lighter car whose 5½-litre Chrysler engine was said to develop 300 b.h.p. at 5,200 r.p.m. Allard likewise pinning his faith to the hemispherical-head Chrysler unit, the inevitable 4½-litre Lago-Talbots had acquired aerodynamic bodies,

A *coupe* and a coupé: Reg. and Joan Mansbridge with their XK120 in the 1953 Alpine Rally.

and Aston Martins had fitted a coupé top to one of their DB.3 team cars. The Ferrari effort was spearheaded by Ascari and Villoresi in a 2·9-litre saloon. Jaguars ran three 'improved' C-types, crews being Moss/Walker, Rolt/Hamilton, and Whitehead/Stewart.

The 1952 race was memorable and dramatic. The late Pierre Levegh, driving single-handed, staved off the full force of the Mercedes-Benz attack for twenty-three hours before sheer exhaustion took control, and he changed absent-mindedly from top to bottom gear, breaking the crankshaft. This left the 300SL of Lang/Reiss and Helfrich/Niedermayer in sole command of the situation, and they crossed the line, the most unpopular victors of all time. The French refused even to play *Deutschland über Alles* for them! But long before this, the race had ceased to have any interest for Jaguars.

The startling speed manifested by Mercedes-Benz in the Prix de Berne and the Mille Miglia had alarmed the Coventry concern, and, with the race only four weeks ahead, they had frantically restyled the cars, with longer noses and long sloping tails, reminiscent of the Talbot with which Levegh had so nearly won. The radiator grille, low-set, was tiny in relation to the one used on the 1951 cars, and all three cars succumbed to overheating in the first three hours of the race. True, the smaller radiators used in tests had been scrapped in favour of standard-size units, just before the race, but the grilles had not been enlarged. Laurence Pomeroy used this unhappy incident as a stick with which to beat the traducers of Brooklands in *The Motor*. Had the Motor Course still been in existence, he argued, high-speed testing on the track would have exposed this weakness.

Sportingly, Jaguars did not scratch their entries for either the Monaco sports car race or the Rheims event later that month. Monaco, was, however, a disappointment, as the exotic Spanish Pegasos, which figured in the entry list for the first time, did not appear, and Mercedes-Benz did not deign to enter at all. Nor were the Ferraris impressive in practice, but a spectacular pile-up, of the kind that only this circuit can provide, eliminated nearly all the worthwhile opposition, in the form of Moss's Jaguar, Manzon's Gordini and Parnell's Aston Martin, leaving the Italian *marque* to romp home to a 1–2–3 victory.

Rheims was slightly better, though as neither Mercedes-Benz nor Ferrari sent cars, it was hardly a great occasion for the Jaguars. Further, the race distance was a mere 224 miles. Moss, however, drove a good race to win at an average of 98·18 m.p.h. The main opposition came from Manzon's Gordini, but this crashed. Mairesse

Seven days and seven nights at over the 'ton': Hadley, Johnson, Fairman, and Moss with the XK120 coupé LWK 707 at Montlhery, August, 1952.

was second on a 4½-litre Talbot, and Sir James Scott-Douglas, still driving a standard XK120 for *Ecurie Ecosse*, third. Moss, incidentally, was driving T. H. Wisdom's production C-type, with 8:1 compression ratio, but equipped with disc brakes.

July saw the Jersey International Sports Car Race, which was not very international. *Ecurie Ecosse* sent Ian Stewart with a C-type and Bill Dobson with an XK120, Frank Le Gallais forsook his sprint special for a standard XK120, and Oscar Moore ran his H.W.M.-Jaguar, a 1950 Formula II car with the original 2-litre Alta engine replaced by a XK unit. Stewart put in a lap at over 90 m.p.h. to win easily, though Wharton drove his Frazer-Nash with consummate skill to deprive Dobson of a second place for the Scottish *equipe*.

Britain staged her first day-and-night race that year. This event, the Goodwood Nine Hours, started at 3 p.m. and ended at midnight. Support for a new date in the calendar was quite impressive, and included two 2·7-litre Ferraris (Cole/Graham Whitehead, and Baird/Salvadori), not to mention Levegh and Etancelin with the 4½-litre Talbot that had so nearly won at Le Mans. Drivers were limited to sixty-eight laps at a stretch, and misfortunes attended both Jaguar and Aston Martin. Parnell's Aston was incinerated in a spectacular fire at the pits, the Whitehead/Stewart Jaguar ran out of road after only two hours, and at 9.30 p.m. Rolt shed a wheel, leaving Stirling Moss on the surviving Jaguar to fight it out with the only remaining Aston Martin shared by Collins and Griffith. Two hours from the end the Jaguar's rear axle locating arm broke, and the Aston Martin had no difficulty in winning.

Some odd devices enlivened the sprint meetings of 1952. As well as Oscar Moore's Jaguar-powered H.W.M., there was E. P. Scragg's Alta-Jaguar, which had started life as a 1½-litre racing machine pre-war in the hands of George Abecassis. Le Gallais' rear-engined car now had an XK120 engine installed, and in consequence it was able to defeat Poore's 3·8-litre Alfa-Romeo this year at Bouley Bay. In contrast, an American firm offered some quite pretty fibreglass sports bodies, following the XK's lines very closely, for fitment to the Singer SM.1500 chassis.

The Rally season was as impressive as ever, and eleven Jaguars ran in the 1952 Monte Carlo Rally. It was a good year for Britain, Sydney Allard's Allard winning the event outright, with Stirling Moss second in a Sunbeam Talbot. Cotton's Mk. VII Jaguar finished fourth, Herteaux on a similar car sixth, and W. H. Waring took class honours in the coachwork competition. A. G. Douglas Clease used another Mk. VII to cover this event for *The Autocar*, remarking that 'it handled magnificently in the worst possible conditions'. He also found that 'in cruising there is less sensation of roll than with the XK120', but Mk. VII was clearly a handful on ice.

The R.A.C. British Rally saw a win for Godfrey Imhof in his big Cadillac-Allard, though Jaguars finished second, third and fourth in the big-car class, and Miss Mary Newton put up the best performance by a lady on her XK120. Jaguars likewise dominated the

big-car class in the *Rallye Soleil*, but positions were reversed once again in the 'Tulip', Wharton's Ford 'Consul' beating Appleyard and NUB 120 in general classification. Nonetheless, the inevitable combination of driver, navigator and car collected their inevitable *Coupe* in the Alpine Rally. True, Appleyard was only fourth in general classification, but Maurice Gatsonides took second place on a similar Jaguar, and the organizers presented Appleyard with the first Alpine Gold Cup ever awarded in the history of the event, on the strength of three successive clean sheets. Laroche and Radix took second place in the Liège-Rome-Liège Rally, and both the big-car classes in the M.C.C.'s national event also fell to Jaguar, one of the successful drivers being Stirling Moss at the wheel of his XK120 coupé.

The Jaguar's versatility also manifested itself in sprints and hill-climbs during the year. True, Neilson's class win at Rest-and-Be-Thankful in July proved nothing, in that the opposition came mainly from Bentleys and Melville's '30/98' Vauxhall, cars made before William Lyons had aspired to anything beyond a sidecar. At Shelsley in August, however, Peter Walker followed in the wheel-tracks of Newsome by taking a works C-type up the hill in 41·14 seconds—a creditable performance for a machine that was designed purely to win at Le Mans. The high spot of the Brighton Speed Trials was undoubtedly Lloyd-Jones's extraordinary 'Triangle Flying Saucer' with Rolls-Royce 'Kestrel' aero engine, but the sports-car classes saw an interesting duel between the ex-Parker supercharged 2½-litre Jaguette and its creator's latest device, the Jaguara, a machine of Lotus-like appearance with a twin-super-charged XK engine. The Jaguette, driven by its new owner, W. Coleman, won, adding to its laurels the fastest sports-car time of the day in 28·45 seconds. Mrs Sarginson was the meeting's fastest lady competitor: her XK120 recorded 30·76 seconds.

Leslie Johnson might be *racing* Healeys, but in August he took an XK120 'special equipment' fixed-head coupé to Montlhéry with an

Not a television stunt, but Jaguar's Norman Dewis with an XK120 'streamliner' at Jabbeke, October 1953. The bubble canopy helped to boost speed to over 170 mph. Standing behind the raised cockpit cover is the late Malcolm Sayer, Jaguar's aerodynamicist.

impressive team of drivers—Stirling Moss, H. L. Hadley of twin-camshaft Austin fame, who had partnered Johnson at Le Mans in 1950, and Jack Fairman, another old hand from Le Mans. Pitwork was in the hands of Mortimer Morris-Goodall, shortly to join the Jaguar competition department, and D. J. Scannell of the B.R.D.C. The team went after long-distance records, and the car (LWK 707) circulated for seven days and seven nights, abandoning the marathon only after 16,852 miles had been covered at an average speed of 100·31 m.p.h. The World's and International Class C 72-Hour Record fell at 105·5 m.p.h.—this incidentally, had stood since 1937 to the credit of an all-feminine crew on a Matford, a forgotten French relation of the Ford V8. Three other World's records and four more class records were collected at the same time, and a detailed examination in the Shell Company's laboratories after the run revealed that:

'Crankshaft wear was so low that, in spite of the car having covered nearly 17,000 miles on the record run, plus just under two thousand previously, the crankshaft was still within production tolerances and would have been passed by the inspection department for installation in a new car.'

The maximum bore wear was found to be 3–3½ thousandths; slight erosion was found on one piston crown, but the cylinder head was 'virtually free from deposit'. *Motor Sport* acclaimed the exploit as 'perhaps our finest post-War accomplishment', and LWK 707 formed the centre-piece of the Jaguar display at Earls Court in 1952.

This year William Lyons needed no new model with which to steal the Show: he had stolen it with the well-tried, and still undated, XK120 coupé.

What other competitors saw of the C-type in its heyday. Stirling Moss winning a 34-lap race at Boreham, August, 1952.

CHAPTER 8

A Year of Grace

1953

LYONS and his team had good reasons for facing 1953 with confidence. Failure at Le Mans had been offset by a good year in the club-racing field, and the versatility of the Jaguar engine had been admirably proven by the diversity of its successes—Rheims, the Alpine Rally, Shelsley Walsh, and even comic-opera events such as the *Formule Libre* 'Japanese Grand Prix' staged on an airfield near Tokyo, in which F. Anton's XK120 was victorious. Further, they had a surprise up their sleeve in the form of the Dunlop disc brakes which Stirling Moss had tried out in the Mille Miglia. That the car had failed to stay the course had been no fault of the braking system.

Disc brakes were no novelty. Dr F. W. Lanchester had used them on his cars as long ago as 1902, and the Vintage A.C.'s also incorporated such a device working on the transmission, though its presence was more of an interesting technical phenomenon than anything else, and Sydney Westall of the company's team asserted —not without some justification—that it was 'only good for making toast'. The enterprising Chrysler Corporation, which had pioneered hydraulics in 1924, offered disc brakes on their biggest Crown Imperials from 1949, but discarded it after a few seasons. There is no doubt, however, that we owe both the system's rapid development and Britain's present-day ascendancy in the field of retardation to the enterprise of Dunlop and Jaguar, and it is further to Jaguar's credit that they have always fitted disc brakes all round, or not at all. Half-measures were not good enough for Heynes.

Competition, however, was not all, and in the export market Heynes's original thesis of evolving an engine which 'would not call for constant revision of design' was paying off. At the party thrown in November 1952, to celebrate the completion of the transfer of manufacturing operations to Browns Lane, Rankin had published some interesting statistics covering Jaguar export sales. In 1938, 10% would have been an optimistic view of the percentage of cars sent overseas—not that this worried anyone at the time! In 1946, the proportion had risen to 26%, which was nearly doubled in the ensuing two years. The overall figure for 1951 was 84%, and the export quota was still increasing. In the past three years production had gone up by 118%, and even this had exceeded all expectations, as the new factory was expected only to double output. Jaguar, as a specialist firm, did not aspire to head the list of cars imported into America where *volume* was concerned, but the Coventry firm was earning more dollars than any other individual manufacturer. As yet, though, France, Germany and Italy were still busying themselves largely with European, African and Asiatic sales, while the average American was quite content with the saurians of Detroit. He was, in fact, keenly watching the horsepower rat-race.

In 1951, even Jaguar's 160 b.h.p. had been big business by American standards, rivalled only by the heaviest metal that Detroit could produce. By 1953, however, the crop of vee-eights was well under way, and Cadillac was offering 210 b.h.p., Lincoln 200, Buick 188, Chrysler and Packard 180, and Oldsmobile 165. Of these, only the conservative Packard company still offered an eight-in-line, and all the contestants in this 'race' were large-capacity units, Oldsmobile alone displacing less than 5 litres, and that by a very small margin. Jaguar's well-tried 3,442 cc engine could propel the Mk. VII·as rapidly as any of these monsters in a straight line, and the British car could walk away from them on winding roads. But the Jaguar still had a four-speed manual transmission, and the average American was tired of shifting gears. For years, the two lower ratios had served solely for starting, negotiating city traffic and descending steep hills, and since 1940 automatic transmissions had been on the upgrade. They were still a high-cost option on all but the most expensive cars, but every year more and more customers specified them, and by 1951 even Chevrolet was marketing a cheap 'automatic' in the shape of the 'Powerglide' system. Such a vehicle could be bought for the equivalent of £570; while admittedly these devices took a great deal of the fun out of driving, they also eliminated a lot of the chores as well, and were fast becoming an essential option for large touring cars. Mk. VII, unlike previous Jaguars, was selling to people who would not have looked at an XK120, a Healey, or a M.G. William Lyons, therefore, elected to take the hint dropped by Christopher Jennings some time back, and offer the car with an automatic transmission.

He was not a pioneer of this in England. While we may gloss over the odd Hayes 'self-selector' device fitted to a handful of Austin Sixteens in 1935, and the 'hydro-kinetic turbo-transmitter' used on the Invicta of 1946 (we may mention in passing that most of the survivors of this model now have Jaguar four-speed boxes!), there is no doubt that Rolls-Royce adapted the General Motors 'Hydromatic' system to their export models in October 1952, and so anticipated Lyons by four months. What is more, not only Rolls-Royce and Bentley, but Armstrong Siddeley as well, were offering automatic transmissions on the home market by October 1955, by which time the first Mk. VIIs so equipped were available in England. For this time-lag we have to thank the *marque*'s popularity in North America.

It has been asserted that automatic skims the cream off driving. I must confess that some of the earlier devices were depressing once the novelty had worn off, and the ascent of a long and traffic-encumbered hill was not enlivened by the frantic upward and downward shifts as engine speed rose and fell. Brisk acceleration was

The Jaguar team at Le Mans, 1951 — the C-type's debut.

impossible in these circumstances; no sooner had one found a gap in the traffic, and moved out, than the box shifted itself back into high range, and the whole process had to begin once more! I am, however, not only an unrepentant Jaguar owner, but an unrepentant supporter of Borg-Warner automatic transmission as well, especially the later type with an intermediate 'hold' which ensures the retention of 'second' gear when it is needed. I have had several automatic Jaguars from a Mk. VII to the current XJ, and I am grateful to automatic every time I settle down to the ninety-mile grind from London to Beaulieu. I probably save myself over five hundred gear changes on this first stretch alone! I was especially grateful to automatic selection in March 1957, when I was able to drive within a month of breaking my leg in a ski-ing accident, and indeed motored for the next four months in plaster up to my thigh.

The Borg-Warner transmission as applied initially to the Mk. VII in January 1953, however, offered only high and low ranges, the 'hold' in the latter being applicable only below 40 m.p.h. A steering column lever, illuminated at night, controlled the selection of the two ratios, plus reverse. The success of the automatic Jaguars was such that at the present time all Mk. IX saloons—the Mk. VII's successors—shipped to the U.S.A. are equipped with Borg-Warner transmissions unless otherwise specified by the customer, and some 80% of home orders for the biggest Jaguar model now incorporate it. These early Mk. VIIs did not bear the word 'automatic' in chrome script on the boot lid—this device was introduced with the Mk. VIII in 1957.

In May 1953, America voted the Jaguar 'the No. 1 sports car of the year', and, to cap this, the American sports car drivers' championship went to Sherwood Johnston, who had used an XK120 to build up a lead of 4,000 points over his nearest rival. In October, some U.S. prices were actually slashed, the XK roadster costing the equivalent of £1,193 instead of £1,440 as hitherto. The unhappy Englishman continued to pay £1,602. The American-produced Jaguar catalogue of the period, by the way, makes amusing reading, the Mk. VII being described as perfectly combining 'continental lines and Old World craftsmanship in garnishments with matchless performance', and the XK120 fixed-head coupé, Leslie Johnson's accomplishments notwithstanding, as 'a snug, sleek, package'. The only other innovation in the production Jaguar range was the introduction of a drophead coupé on the XK120 chassis. Also during the season, Salisbury rear axles replaced the E.N.V. type throughout the XK range.

The exploits of Ian Appleyard, as ever, highlighted Jaguar's performances in the international rallies during 1953. *The Autocar* might observe that Mk. VII was 'not the most suitable car' for the tests at the conclusion of the Monte Carlo Rally, but it was the only Jaguar model available on the home market that was eligible for the Rally, and with it the Appleyards took second place in general classification, behind Gatsonides' Ford 'Zephyr'—on this occasion they were, as usual, works-backed, the first time that Jaguars had interested themselves officially in the 'Monte'. Fifth place was taken

by Cecil Vard on the stalwart old Mk. V saloon which had finished third in 1951. Appleyard also won the R.A.C. Hastings Rally outright in March, with NUB 120, while Peignaux and Jacquin on an XK120 scored a victory in the Lyons-Charbonnières event. A Ferrari won the big-car class in the *Rallye Soleil*, but Jaguars were second and third, and Thirion's Mk. VII was successful in the Unlimited Touring-Car class—partly because Britain was now the only European country making 'unlimited tourers', and of these the Jaguar was the only one with sporting proclivities. For once neither Appleyard nor his erstwhile rival Wharton won the Tulip Rally, though the former collected fifth place and the inevitable class win.

May saw the famous combination of the Appleyards and NUB 120 win yet one more event outright—but the Morecambe Rally was to be her swansong, and she was at long last retired, with 50,000 competition miles behind her, not to mention a hard life as everyday business transport. Jaguar put her in the works museum, and for a while she lived at Beaulieu, between the W. 196 Mercedes-Benz with which Fangio won the 1954 and 1955 World Championships, and Lord Brabazon's 1908 Grand Prix Austin. To replace her, Appleyard bought another two-seater, RUB 120, with which he contested the Alpine Rally, collecting his sixth class win and *Coupe*. *Coupes* were also won by two other XKs, entered by the Mansbridges and by Fraikin/Gendebien, but the writing was on the wall, and the small cars, the Porsches especially, were beginning to figure prominently at the top of the awards list. The XK entered by Henson and Cooper was run in the Rally as part of a heavy testing programme undertaken by Ferodo Ltd.—a sporting gesture, this. November saw another Appleyard success—second place in the Lisbon Rally, with a drophead coupé body on his car. Thereafter he announced his retirement, returning to the family business—to sell and service Jaguars!

To round out the season, the Fraikin/Gendebien team finished second in the Liège-Rome-Liège, behind the Lancia of Claes and Trasenster, and Air Vice-Marshal D. C. T. Bennett, later to sponsor the Fairthorpe sports car, won the unlimited sports class in the Evian-Mont Blanc event.

The year things went wrong: a 1952 works C-type with the long streamlined nose that played havoc at Le Mans.

Second Victory on the Sarthe Circuit: the Rolt/Hamilton C-type leads
a Ferrari, 1953.

Jaguars had a full racing season in front of them, though one of their rivals, Mercedes-Benz, elected to rest on their laurels. They asserted that the 300SL had dominated the international events of 1952, but in fact they had only met the Jaguars face to face on two occasions—in the Mille Miglia, when they fielded three cars to Coventry's one (even if that one was conducted by Moss), and at Le Mans, where the cooling *débacle* had eliminated all three Jaguars before they could show their mettle. Undoubtedly the 300SL was capable of 150 m.p.h., but then so was the 1952 Jaguar, and it would be interesting to know what would have transpired had Jaguars been able to perfect their Le Mans cars, or had Mercedes-Benz elected to try their luck at Rheims. Stirling Moss inclines to the view that Le Mans, at any rate, might have turned out differently.

Jaguars were not at Sebring, though Aston Martin sent Parnell and Collins on a brace of 2·9-litre DB.3s, both of which retired. The Index of Performance award went to Bonnet on a DB of his own

design, and American-entered C-type Jaguars were placed third, fourth, and fifth on distance: the best of them managed seventh place on formula.

Nor were the 1953 cars ready for the Mille Miglia either, though three C-types started, the 'works' machines of Moss and Rolt having disc brakes, and Johnson's privately-entered example drum brakes, but an interesting modification in the form of a five-speed gearbox with geared-up top, in the Ferrari manner. The main opposition came from the works Ferraris of Ascari, Villoresi and Hawthorn, but Alfa-Romeo had at last brought the 3½-litre 'Disco Volante' models to a fair state of readiness, and these were handled by the formidable team of Fangio, Kling, and Sanesi, while Lancia made their *debut* in international sports car events with a team of 3-litre vee-six cars (Bonetto, Biondetti, Maglioli, Taruffi, and Borniglia). The Aston Martins were still the 2·9-litre DB.3 cars, and were driven by Abecassis and Collins, and a lone Nash-Healey was assigned to

Discs triumphant: The place: Rheims. The date: June, 1952. The car:
C-type Jaguar. The driver: Stirling Moss.

the American John Fitch. As the only cars in the race with disc brakes, Jaguars were considered to stand quite a chance of victory.

But it was not to be. Johnson's fuel tank split, and Moss had rear axle trouble. Even the Mk. VIIs which ran in the touring-car section were out-classed by Paul Frère's enormous and very rapid Chrysler. The International Trophy meeting, at Silverstone, usually a safe day for Jaguar, was likewise a slight setback, for the production sports car race brought out not only the Allards and Aston Martins, but two works-entered 4·1-litre Ferraris, driven by Hawthorn and Cole. On a short race over a bumpy airfield circuit, both these and the Astons had the legs of the Jaguars. Moss, of course, had no trouble with his Mk. VII in the touring-car event. 'Lofty' England and Mortimer Morris-Goodall were reserving their maximum effort for Le Mans.

Already three standard cars had been taken to Jabbeke by Norman Dewis, the firm's chief tester, and a standard XK120, with undershield and aero-screen, had been timed at 141·846 m.p.h.— 10 m.p.h. faster than Johnson's hour run at Montlhéry in 1951. The C-type in 1953 trim had recorded 148·435 m.p.h.—not sensational by the standards of the year, but encouraging, since Jaguars surely had something up their sleeve, and Le Mans was to be won on endurance and handling as much as on sheer speed. The Mk. VII was also tried, and turned in 121·704 m.p.h.

A week or two before Le Mans, Jaguar unveiled an aerodynamic prototype of exciting aspect. It was said to have a light-alloy tubular frame, and to weigh 15 cwt. dry, but it did not run in the race. Later writers have asserted that it was a D-type, but Jaguars assure me that it was not. It was in fact a halfway house between the C-type in its 1953 form, and the 1954 D-type. It had the 'D''s monocoque structure, but an altogether higher frontal area, and the engine was the wet-sump C-type. The machines they actually used on the Sarthe circuit were C-types, differing very little externally from the the victorious model of 1951. The substitution of triple Weber carburetters for the twin S.U.s had raised the output again to 220 b.h.p., and weight had been pared by 2cwt. by the use of light alloy radiators, smaller-diameter frame tubes, and lightweight bodies. Most important of all, the three cars, to be driven by Rolt/ Hamilton, Moss/Walker, and Whitehead/Stewart, all had Dunlop disc brakes on all four wheels. The Belgian pair, Laurent and de Tornaco, shared a standard production C-type with drum brakes. The Ferrari attack was as usual spearheaded by Ascari and Villoresi on a 4½-litre car, the other machines, of 4·1-litres capacity, being assigned to Farina/Hawthorn, the brothers Marzotto, and Chinetti/ Cole. Aston Martin had the new, lighter 2·9-litre DB.3S cars, drivers being Parnell/Collins, Abecassis/Salvadori, and Poore/Thompson. Allard had fitted his Cadillac-engined cars with aerodynamic bodies, and was sharing the wheel of one with Parker, the second one being entrusted to Arkus-Duntov and Merrick. Lancia had three Mille Miglia-type 3-litre vee-sixes, running supercharged—these were driven by Taruffi/Maglioli, Manzon/Chiron, and Bonetto/Valenzano. The 'Disco Volante' Alfa-Romeos now had closed bodywork, the team being led by the Fangio/Marimon combination, and the three 5,454 cc Chrysler-powered Cunninghams were the biggest and heaviest cars in the field. Drivers were Cunningham/Spear, Walters/ Fitch, and Moran/Benett. Among the relative outsiders were a pair of 2-litre Frazer-Nashes, two 2-litre Bristols with identical engines and bizarre aerodynamic coupé bodies, and two six-cylinder Gordinis with 2·3-litre and 2·5-litre engines. As always, the 4½-litre Talbots had possibilities in view of their known staying power, and four started, the attack being led by Levegh/Pozzi. Chambas' car was running supercharged. The entry list even included a brace of Pegasos, but they got no further than practice sessions.

It was anyone's race, as the speeds recorded down the Mulsanne straight indicated. Fastest was the Cunningham, at 154·81 m.p.h.; the Alfas managed 152·8 m.p.h., and Jaguars were very little slower at 151·9 m.p.h. The best Ferrari was timed at 150·44 m.p.h., the supercharged Talbot at 145·98 m.p.h., the Allard at 145·36 m.p.h.,

and the Lancia at 136·49 m.p.h. In the event, though, the real struggle was between Jaguar, Ferrari and Alfa-Romeo, with the Cunninghams intervening strongly, especially towards the end.

Sydney Allard led at the start, demonstrating the big car's astonishing acceleration, but his effort only lasted four laps, and at the end of the first hour Moss on the Jaguar led Villoresi on the fastest Ferrari. Fuel feed trouble caused the British driver to make two pit stops, which dropped him back to fifteenth, but the Rolt/ Hamilton Jaguar moved up into first place, followed by Villoresi, the smaller Ferrari of Chinetti and Cole, two Alfa-Romeos and the Walters/Fitch Cunningham. Hawthorn's Ferrari was soon out, disqualified for replenishing brake fluid before the statutory 235 miles were up, and Fangio's Alfa-Romeo likewise found the pace too hot, retiring early. Three hours from the start the Gordinis were moving up the field, Moss was still trying desperately to regain lost ground, and the 'reserve' Jaguar of Whitehead and Stewart, which had been set the task of shadowing the leaders, moved unobtrusively into fourth place, dislodging the two remaining Alfas without apparent effort. Already two Talbots were out, Chambas on the blown car with a seized engine, and by 8 p.m. both Bristols had caught fire on the circuit.

The Jaguars of Moss and Rolt came in to change drivers, and a tyre was changed on the leading car before Hamilton drew away again. Only the Ascari/Villoresi Ferrari was up among the leaders now, the second car having been delayed through a pit stop; the two Alfas were, however, running healthily enough in third and fourth places, and the Gordini of Behra/Mieres now lay fifth. At 8.30 Ascari managed to pass Hamilton and take the lead, where he stayed until a refuelling stop enabled the Jaguar to get ahead once more. The Lancias, which had never really been in the picture, dropped steadily back.

With night falling, Hamilton and Rolt still led at ten o'clock, but the Sanesi/Carini Alfa-Romeo had now passed the Ferrari, and Kling and Riess lay fourth with the second 'Disco Volante' in fifth place, the Walters/Fitch Cunningham was running like clockwork, shadowed, as ever, by the Whitehead/Stewart Jaguar. Shortly after

Ecurie Ecosse: Jimmy Stewart (elder brother of Formula 1 driver Jackie Stewart) in action in the rain at Aintree, May 1954. He finished second in the *Daily Telegraph* Sports Car Race with the C-type.

eleven o'clock, the Ascari/Villoresi Ferrari snarled out of the dark to take the lead for the last time; the superior braking power of the Jaguar forced the Ferrari to maintain a cracking pace, and sooner or later this pace had to tell. Eight hours from the start, Hamilton had resumed the lead once more, never to be seriously challenged. He was lapping steadily at 105 m.p.h., and over a circuit nearly 8½

miles round his times varied by little more than four seconds! Behind him, the order was as before—Ferrari, Alfa-Romeo, Alfa-Romeo, Cunningham, Jaguar.

At 4 a.m.—the half-time mark—matters had largely sorted themselves out. The Alfa-Romeos had retired, and two of the Ferraris were in sixth and seventh places, leaving only the Ascari/Villoresi

The big one. Mk.VII's proportions were outstanding in 1951, and so was the performance from 3.5 litres and 160 horsepower.

The rolling fortresses. Mk.VII was still winning saloon races in Britain as late as 1956, but earlier it had had things all its own way in the big-car class. Here Ian Appleyard is seen winning the 1954 Production Touring Car Race at Silverstone.

Seat of government on the original r.d.h. Mk.VII. As yet only straight manual gearbox was available. The selector for the twin petrol tanks can be seen in the centre of the facia.

A development model takes the air. The 'C/D' prototype at Jabbeke, 1953.

Jaguar victorious at Monte Carlo, 1956. *Left to right,* Frank Bigger, Derek Johnston, and Ronnie Adams with their Mk.VII sedan.

car as a serious threat to a Jaguar victory. The only other potential danger came from the blue-and-white Cunningham, and the Jaguars held first, fourth, and fifth places, the Moss/Walker car having made up almost all its lost time. At 5 a.m., as the dawn mist cleared, Rolt, who had again taken over the leading car, received a 'slower' signal, and Ascari made another desperate bid. Rolt, however, was only playing cat-and-mouse, for when the Ferrari came uncomfortably close, the green car speeded up again, and was soon widening the distance between the two cars at a rate of ten seconds a lap. The problem for Ascari was no longer to catch the Jaguar, but to avoid being caught by the Cunningham, which churned unfalteringly on. Two hundred and ninety-nine laps and nearly nineteen hours from the start, it was all over when the Ferrari gave up on the circuit. The rest of the race was almost a procession, with the Rolt/Hamilton car some thirty miles ahead of its nearest rival, the sister machine of Moss and Walker, while Fitch and Walters on the Cunningham managed to stave off a 1–2–3 victory by keeping ahead of Whitehead and Stewart. Behind came the sur-

vivors of the gruelling pace set by the Jaguars—the Marzotto Ferrari, the Trintignant/Schell Gordini, the Cunningham/Spear Cunningham, Levegh's' always-game Talbot, the privately-entered C-type of Laurent and de Tornaco, and the third Cunningham of Moran and Benett. Only the Jaguar and Cunningham teams had finished intact, the winner's average was a record 105·85 m.p.h. and, though this was the first occasion on which the race had been won at a three-figure speed, the first seven cars across the line—all three works Jaguars, two Cunninghams, a Ferrari, and a Gordini—had averaged more than 100 m.p.h. for twenty-four hours.

It was a remarkable achievement, even with disc brakes. As Duncan Hamilton pointed out, the Jaguars were giving away a litre to the Ascari/Villoresi Ferrari, 'which had been beautifully driven by a very fine driver'. Laurence Pomeroy in one of his erudite summaries in *The Motor* stated that the race had been won on a combination of speed, endurance, and stopping power. Overall, the Ferrari was potentially the fastest car on the course, and the Alfa-Romeos could have been dangerous had they attained a better state

Duncan Hamilton's D-type pulls away from the pits in the rain at Le Mans, 1954.

of readiness. It was also noticed that the most successful performers, the Jaguars and the Cunninghams, were conservative as to suspension arrangements, Briggs Cunningham having even reverted to a beam front axle—shades of the Bentleys! The Jaguar team returned to a civic reception at Coventry, still wearing the familiar limited trade plates, and Duncan Hamilton departed to drive his own C-type in Oporto. He was unlucky enough to run it into a pylon, injuring himself and depriving the city of electricity for some hours!

Nor was he any luckier at Pescara, whither he and Peter Whitehead had repaired to run the former's C-type in the 12-hour Race. After various vicissitudes including encounters with suicidal old ladies, equally suicidal cows, and irresponsible Italians stoking bonfires in gardens adjoining the course, the car sheared a chassis cross-member after eight hours, when well up among the leaders.

The Rheims race, which had saved the *marque*'s reputation in 1952, again furnished Moss and Whitehead with a victory for the works C-type. Opposition was provided by Fitch on the Le Mans Cunningham, Maglioli on a 4·1-litre Ferrari, Rosier's Lago-Talbot, and Abecassis at the wheel of a new Jaguar-powered H.W.M sports-car. A crash eliminated Fitch, and Maglioli was disqualified for driving on his lights before the permitted hour and receiving a push-start. After that, it was a Jaguar benefit.

Ferrari, anxious to make up for their failure at Le Mans, sent three 4½-litre cars to Spa for the Belgian 24-hour Race, but no works Jaguars were there to oppose them. Instead, the flag was flown by three *Ecurie Ecosse* C-types, and Scott Douglas and Gale did well to finish second behind the Farina/Hawthorn Ferrari. At the International Charterhall meeting, Parnell's DB.3S Aston Martin beat the Scottish-entered Jaguars, and the Goodwood Nine Hours again proved to be unlucky for the Coventry *marque*, albeit the Moss/Walker and Rolt/Hamilton cars were faster than the Aston Martins. Both Jaguars disappeared during the last hour with lubrication troubles due to oil surge. *Ecurie Ecosse* sent Stewart and Salvadori with a C-type to the Nurburgring, and it did well to finish second behind the Ascari/Farina Ferrari, though the result would doubtless have been different had not the Lancias, running well for once, found themselves in the pits with flat batteries.

In August, H.R.H. The Duke of Edinburgh inspected some of the successful British competition cars of 1953 at Goodwood, including the Jaguars and their rivals the Aston Martins. Had Jaguar won the T.T., it is likely that they would have won the Sports Car Constructors' Championship as well, in spite of the avowed

Second at Le Mans (on a first outing) was speedily followed by a win at Rheims. The Whitehead/Wharton D-type takes the checkered flag, July 1954.

limitations of their racing programme. Alas! the more powerful multiplate clutches used on this occasion gave trouble—the gears, it transpired, had been over-hardened, and Rolt and Whitehead retired, leaving the Collins/Griffith and Parnell/Thompson Aston Martins in command of the situation. Moss, however, managed to hold out until two laps from the end. Calmly he waited, and then pushed the dead Jaguar across the line to take fourth place, and to put Jaguar one point ahead in the Championship. Twenty-seven points to twenty-six—and only the Carrera Panamericana to round off the season. Jaguars had no intention of entering, but Ferrari, who had entered, might fail in that unpredictable event, a 'Grand National' of motoring.

In the meantime, the Jaguar engine had been quietly building up a sound reputation for itself on water, thanks to the efforts of Norman Buckley. In this respect it followed in the wheel tracks of another illustrious twin-overhead-camshaft sports car engine, the Type 57 Bugatti, which had been used quite extensively in racing boats before the War. In 1947, Buckley was competing with 'Miss Windermere II', an American Ventnor hull powered by a 4-litre six-cylinder side-valve Lycoming engine, which gave it a top speed of around 65 m.p.h. In this form it collected a number of awards including the formidable Challenge Trophy presented by the Lowestoft and Oulton Broad Club—a solid block of marble surmounted with an onyx slab, on which rested two miniature speedboats in silver. 'The total weight', Buckley recalls, 'amounted to no less than two and a half hundredweight'.

Buckley decided in 1949 to attack class speed records on Lake Windermere, and sought a more potent and reliable unit than the Lycoming. In October 1949, he persuaded Jaguars to supply him with an XK120 engine, which he adapted for marine work by scrapping the coil in favour of a Lucas magneto, thus eliminating the need for a battery, fitting oil coolers, and substituting direct water cooling for the conventional radiator. Otherwise no modifications were made, and the compression ratio remained at 8:1.

In this form, still using the original Ventnor hull, the boat was used to attack three records in the 800 kg. class: the one-hour record, held at the time by the former Auto-Union driver Hans Von Stuck, and the three-hour and twenty-four-nautical-mile records, which stood to the the credit of the Italian Rancoroni. The one-hour record duly fell in September 1950 at a speed of 55·55 m.p.h., but Buckley had a narrow escape when settling down for the longer grind. He felt what he thought was water lapping around his feet, and pulled

Improved shape: the revised 1955 D-type with long nose and separate
sub-frame in test at the M.I.R.A. Proving Ground.

The Hawthorn-Fangio duel at Le Mans in 1955, with the D-type in the lead.

in alongside his tender boat. The 'water' turned out to be some thirty gallons of high-octane petrol, the tank having split from buffeting in the lake. Had he continued with the attempt, the petrol would probably have made violent contact with the hot exhaust pipes. After a new tank had been fitted, 'Miss Windermere II' went on to take the three-hour record at 51·58 m.p.h., and the twenty-four-mile record fell at 63·49 m.p.h., despite a broken propeller-shaft which put paid to the first run. The Jaguar engine gave no trouble at all, and it was also found that the boat, which together with its trailer, cradle and equipment, turned the scales at two tons, could easily be towed to meetings behind Buckley's Mk. V saloon. At the Lake Garda meeting in 1951, 'Miss Windermere' finished second in the Oltranza Cup race, also coming in first in the special event for boats in the 800-kg. class. By the end of the season Buckley was using a modified Jaguar engine, with high-lift camshafts and a 9:1 compression ratio, and made the fastest two-way run at the Windermere meeting. His mean speed was 79 m.p.h.

No records were taken in 1952, but Buckley was able to attain 100 m.p.h. by using a new C-type engine in a Canadian 'prop-riding' hull. In 1954, this unit was modified to 1953 Le Mans specification, triple Webers replacing the twin S.U. carburetters. Others, notably the German Von Mayenburg, fitted their speedboats with Jaguar engines, and similar boats are in use in Australia and New Zealand.

Back at Coventry, the quest for efficiency continued, and towards the end of the year short-wave radio sets were installed in the company's fork-lift trucks to make for a quicker turn-around. Norman Dewis, too, was off on another of his jaunts to Belgium. Early in October, an unusual vehicle had been seen on the Jabbeke road—it was one of the fantastic vee-eight supercharged Pegasos, and it proceeded to motor down the measured mile at 151 m.p.h., 10 m.p.h. faster than the standard XK tested in April, showing an appreciable margin even over the C-type. This could not be allowed to happen, and in a matter of days Dewis was at Jabbeke on an XK120 with 'full optional equipment', plus a cockpit hood and the usual undershield. This time he brought pump fuel with him from England, but his 172·412 m.p.h. left no doubts as to the Jaguar's pre-eminence. At the same time, the experimental C/D-type cross-breed was given another airing, and turned in 178·383 m.p.h., just to remind the sporting fraternity that Messrs. Heynes and England had no intention of resting on their laurels. Jaguars insisted that the Pegaso's little excursion was purest coincidence, and no doubt it was—be that as it may, the Spanish car disappeared even from the entry lists, and by 1958 its makers had reverted to the construction of vast diesel lorries of superb quality.

Nineteen fifty-three drew to a close. The XK120 was still contributing its quota of grace, Mk. VII combined space with automatic transmission, and the C-type, even in its third year of operational life, had enough pace to worry its opponents. Jaguars did not enter the Carrera Panamericana, but Ferraris did—and won it, together with the Constructors' Championship. Whitehead and Gaze shipped a C-type to Australia with the intention of running it in the Australian 24-hour Race early in the New Year, which they did, only to retire after ten hours with a familiar Jaguar fault, a broken rear radius arm. Not that this could snatch victory from the *marque*, for an Australian lady enthusiast, Mrs Anderson, brought her XK120 coupé with C-type engine across the line in first place, having averaged 53·8 m.p.h. round the clock—this in spite of a carburetter which detached itself *en route*, obliging the pit staff to rob a spectator's car in order to keep the wheels turning! The 1953 team cars, disc brakes and all, were sold to David Murray at *Ecurie Ecosse*, a sure indication that Heynes had something entirely new for 1954.

And the forty-fourth and last C-type, full of honour, was delivered to a satisfied customer.

The year of the Big Cat: Le Mans, 1957. The first and second-place D-types of Flockhart/Bueb and Sanderson/Lawrence.

CHAPTER 9

D for Discs

1954–55

'Like all Jaguars, the D-type has a wonderfully smooth engine. It has, in fact, perfect traffic manners and can be used for shopping without any thought of its potential performance.'

John Bolster, *Autosport*, February 1955

'I do not approve of the possession of very fast cars by inexperienced drivers, but I feel that this is one of the easiest of the real flyers to handle.'

Ibid.

In 1954 Mercedes-Benz as yet showed no sign of re-entering racing, though Lancias were displaying a keen and unwonted interest in international competition. No changes were announced in the personnel of the Jaguar team for the new year. The main news was thus provided by Mk. VII, which became available with Laycock de Normanville electrically-selected overdrive.

This modification, which, like the automatic transmission, was an optional extra, gave the car a fifth geared-up ratio of 3·54:1. This did not substantially increase the maximum speed, the car tested by *The Autocar* attaining only 102·1 m.p.h. Where the advantage did show clearly was in an overall fuel consumption of 20 m.p.g., and during the Suez crisis of 1956–7 a Mk. VIIM known to me habitually exceeded this figure. According to the tester, the overdrive unit offered a 'smooth, clutchless down change with a complete absence of jerk', but this was obtainable only if the direct drive was engaged with great care. It was not unknown to encounter a jerk on the upward shift, either. Sensibly, Jaguars offered overdrive on top gear only, as it was evidently felt that the urge and flexibility of the XK engine demanded no more than five speeds. They also recognized that such systems commended themselves largely to the lazy driver, who would not know what to do with six or seven forward ratios if he were given them.

The whole distribution system in the United States underwent a complete overhaul, and in 1954 an American subsidiary company, Jaguar Cars North American Incorporated, was set up in New York.

This development was preceded (not followed!) by the institution of Jaguar service classes for agents' engineering staffs. More than 14,000 Jaguars were now in service in the U.S.A., and the New York Sports Car Show in February had as its centre-piece an XK140 special equipment roadster in white with gold-plated fittings—hardly the correct wear for Earls Court, but a perfect gimmick on the other side of the Atlantic.

The effects of this reorganization in America were impressive, and statistics subsequently released showed that no fewer than 1,822 Jaguars were sold in this market in the first six months of 1954, and it was found possible to reduce the prices of certain models that October, despite the advent of the revised Mk. VIIM and XK140 types. Jaguar even achieved the biggest *volume* sale of all imported cars, selling a hundred more vehicles than Volkswagen. During the year, the Mk. VII automatic transmission model became so popular with Americans that the progressive hire firm of Victor Britain Ltd. persuaded the Board of Trade to let them buy a fleet of these 'export-only' cars for use by visitors to this country—it was, however, made clear that only dollar customers need apply.

Meanwhile, the American motor industry was a little worried by the high sales of imported sports cars, in the same way as it was later to be stampeded into launching its 'compacts' by the booming sales of Volkswagen and Renault 'Dauphines'. 1953 had seen the advent of the glass fibre-bodied Chevrolet 'Corvette', and during 1954 Ford followed suit with the big eight-cylinder 'Thunderbird'. Henry Ford II had, however, no illusions whatever about the sports-car market; he called his new creation a 'personal car', and sold it on exclusiveness, one of his customers being the Ferrari driver Umberto Maglioli. The Chevrolet was a more serious contender; but pretty as it was, it suffered from a lack of horses, and the 150 b.h.p. of its 1954 'Blue Flame Six' was no match for the 190 b.h.p. of the 'special equipment' XKs. Original plans to produce 1,000 a month were hurriedly slashed by two-thirds, and it was not until 1955 that the 'Corvette' established itself as a potent if over-ornamented sporting machine,

Scottish Jaguar: the late Ron Flockhart, who won for *Ecurie Ecosse*
at Le Mans in 1956.

by which time there was a low-cost vee-eight engine to power it, and the services of John Fitch and Zora Arkus-Duntov, late of Allard, to run the development programme. American enthusiasts, nonetheless, wanted an imported car, and neither 'Corvette' nor 'Thunderbird' had any noticeable effect on Jaguar's trans-Atlantic sales.

Jaguar had also been recruiting for their apprentice scheme, launched in 1948. They asked for 'the best type of apprentice', and procured them, as witness *The Autocar*'s comments way back in 1952, when the journal's roving camera noted, at Earls Court:

'the Jaguar apprentice, smartly overalled, who *never* gets mixed up between XK120s, Type Cs, and Mk.VIIs . . .'

In June 1954, William Lyons became the first member of Britain's motor industry to be honoured by the Royal Society for Arts with the rank of R.D.I. (Royal Designer for Industry)—a tribute to a man who not only knew what he wanted, but knew how to plan it, and to market the finished article. The citation recognized 'his considerable experience of motor-car design work at all levels, and his responsibility for the general design and conception of the Jaguar car, the reputation of which stands so high today'. Honoured at the same time was Italy's (and the world's) foremost stylist, Signor Pinin Farina. Though as yet the Italian's influence had not spread to the British presswork industry, the bracketing of their names was a compliment to both. The following year, Farina was to show his appreciation of Lyons' styling when he evolved a one-off XK140 coupé for an American client, and left the standard radiator grille untouched, because the *maestro* liked 'the Jaguar primitive line which has always been very beautiful'.

The year also saw the genesis of still more Jaguar-engined 'specials'. Shattock's all-independently-sprung R.G.S.-Atalanta, which was sold to amateurs in 'kit-of-parts' form, acquired a C-type unit in place of the Lea-Francis and Ford V8 engines hitherto worn, and

Coopers evolved a successor to their Cooper-Bristol, also using the XK engine in its C-type form. A small number of H.W.M. sports cars was also made, with a 1953 type Formula II frame, De Dion rear axle, and the choice of the 3·4-litre Jaguar or 5·4-litre Cadillac engines. Later on, the sole surviving E-type E.R.A. was to appear at a Crystal Palace meeting, running with full road equipment and an XK power unit in place of the original Riley-based 1½-litre 'six'. Even this drastic rebuild, however, could not dislodge the unhappy machine's hoodoo. When Kieft Cars built a one-off sports car for the American driver Erwin Goldschmidt, power was transmitted from the big De Soto 'Firedome' vee-eight engine *via* a Jaguar four-speed box. Generally speaking, though, Jaguars did not supply engines or components to other constructors. They were on occasions willing to sell individual engines to special customers for installation in specific cars, as witness the Cooper-Jaguars and Brian Lister's later Cambridge-built machines—but with one exception, the Allard Motor Co., they never permitted series production of Jaguar-

Sebring, 1955: Mike Hawthorn's winning D-type passed the burnt-out remains of a Ferrari.

powered cars by other constructors. In this they were not alone—Colin Chapman of Lotus was to have considerable difficulty in procuring even one Ford 'Consul' engine from official sources.

The 1954 racing season started off with the Australian '24', which was, as we have seen, won by a privately-owned XK120. On the other side of the world, *Ecurie Ecosse* ran two cars in the Buenos Aires sports-car race. James Stewart retired when lying fifth, but the second C-type—the standard XK120s had by now been pensioned off—was brought home in fourth place by Sir James Scott Douglas and Ninian Sanderson, behind two Ferraris and the rival Aston Martin of Collins/Griffith. As light relief, the B.B.C. staged a 'pit-stop competition' on television, in which Aston Martin again vanquished Jaguar, represented by Duncan Hamilton, Peter Walker and a C-type.

The British season started well at Castle Combe, where James Stewart, driving for *Ecurie Ecosse*, finished second in the unlimited sports-car class behind Sidney Greene's very rapid A6GCS 2-litre Maserati, driven by Roy Salvadori. Less successful from the Jaguar viewpoint was the British Empire Trophy Race, now transferred to another twisty circuit, Oulton Park in Cheshire. Hamilton, driving his own C-type, could manage no better than fourth place behind

Alan Brown's Cooper-Bristol, Salvadori on the Maserati, and Gammon's amazingly rapid 1½-litre Lotus, which had even passed one of the other Jaguars *en route*, handicap or no handicap! The Scottish *équipe* sent James Stewart to Ibsley for the *Formule Libre* event in May, and he had the satisfaction of finishing second to that fantastic machine, the V-16 B.R.M., driven on this occasion by Ron Flockhart.

The International Trophy Race meeting at Silverstone highlighted two facts—first, that Jaguars were unbeatable in the saloon-car class, and second, that they had at the moment no production sports car capable of coping with the big Ferraris. The D-types, though their existence had been revealed, were not yet ready to race, while David Brown's new car, the 4½-litre V-12 Lagonda, was not particularly impressive either. Walker had to be content with third place on the C-type, behind Gonzalez' Ferrari and Abecassis on the new H.W.M.-Jaguar. In the production car event, the Mk. VIIs sailed through in line ahead, Appleyard making his *debut* on the circuits, and beating Rolt and Moss in the process. Fourth place, to everyone's surprise, fell to Parnell on the new Daimler 2½-litre 'Conquest Century' saloon. This vehicle's orthodox pushrod engine was to prove capable of a high degree of development, and was

A backward glance from Mike Hawthorn at Sebring, 1956. Brake trouble put him out after ten gallant hours, though Sweikert's D-type managed third place.

eventually persuaded to run up to 5,800 r.p.m., at which rate of rotation it developed 116 b.h.p. Daimlers, however, underwent a change of direction at this point, in more senses than one, and the 'Century' was dropped.

In May, Jaguars unveiled the D-type—their bid to keep the schedule service at Le Mans running to time in 1954. This bore very little relation to anything that had preceded it, though Norman Dewis's Jabbeke machine had given some indication of the way the wind was blowing. For the first time chassis-less construction was adopted: the structure was a monocoque, built around a centre-section of immense strength. An integral front section supported the engine and front suspension units, and a tail assembly, bolted to the centre-section, housed the spare wheel and tankage. A typically Jaguar front suspension system—upper and lower wishbones and longitudinal torsion bars—was used, and the rear suspension featured a live axle, trailing arms and torsion bars. The C-type's rack-and-pinion steering gear was retained, as were the four-wheel Dunlop disc brakes of the 1953 model. The engine was basically the same XK unit, but the lessons of the Nine-Hour Race at Goodwood had been learnt, and dry-sump lubrication, with an additional oil pump, had been adopted. This change brought with it other advantages, for it resulted in a lower engine mounting and consequently a lower centre of gravity. The compression ratio remained at 9:1, carburation was by three twin-choke Webers, and 250 b.h.p. was developed at 6,000 r.p.m. The four-speed synchromesh gearbox had very high ratios—2·79, 3·57, 4·58, and 5·98:1—but these were altered according to circuit, and on the hilly Agadir course Duncan Hamilton used a 4·09:1 rear axle. With the highest ratio ever used—2·53:1—the car in its original form would do close on 200 m.p.h. The Hardy-Spicer propeller shaft and the Salisbury rear axle, as well as the cylinder block and head castings, were standard Jaguar components.

With an oval air intake at the front, a streamlined fairing behind the driver, and a small, curved Perspex windscreen, the D-type had little of the sports-car look about it, but the cars were always driven to the circuits when time permitted—they arrived by road under their own power for the preliminary trials at Rheims and Le Mans, and Duncan Hamilton drove his D-type from Casablanca to Agadir during the Moroccan races. It gave far less trouble on the road than did his borrowed tender car! The bonnet lifted up in one piece, as had the earlier C-type's, and overall it was a far more compact machine, the wheelbase being six inches shorter at 7ft. 6ins., and the overall length seven inches shorter at 12ft. 6ins. Frontal area and drag were drastically reduced. Its tractability was emphasized when Harold Hastings of *The Motor* had a ride with Norman Dewis, Jaguar's chief tester, on the M.I.R.A. proving-ground at Lindley before the cars went to France. Little more than 150 m.p.h. was attained on this occasion, but crash helmets had to be firmly held on, as the wind tended to force these off on the banked track. The Jaguar, however, never forgot its good manners, and Hastings recorded: 'The clutch and gear-change . . . must be above reproach, because the overall impression was one of a smooth, continuous surge forward'.

Royal visit: the newly knighted Sir William Lyons with Queen Elizabeth II and a D-type at the factory, March, 1956.

Before Le Mans, comparative tests were carried out on three cars—the D-type, still in bare aluminium, the cross-bred 1953 experimental prototype, and another experimental C-type with fuel injection. The results were impressive, and encouraging. At Le Mans, Rolt on the new D-type did a standing lap at 107 m.p.h., and his best flying lap at 115·6 m.p.h. was faster than Ascari's fastest lap in the 1953 race, as well as being eight seconds better than the C-type's best effort in that event. Down the Mulsanne straight he was timed at 169 m.p.h., or 14 m.p.h. quicker than the fastest car in the 1953 race, Fitch's Cunningham. It should be said that widening and resurfacing operations at Mulsanne had made greater speeds possible since the previous June, but the tests seemed to indicate that the cars now had assets even greater than their disc brakes. Certain it was that this period of testing was more profitable than participation in the Mille Miglia, which the firm ignored this year. Of the private entries, the H.W.M.-Jaguar retired at Ravenna, and Gendebien's XK120 coupé did not figure in the awards list.

Le Mans, however, furnished an interesting field. The Cunninghams were back again, supported this year by the Walters/Fitch combination on a Cunningham-modified 4½-litre Ferrari. Aston Martin, though relying in the main on their well-established DB.3S, had two interesting newcomers, a supercharged coupé variant of the basic type, and the vee-twelve Lagonda that Parnell had tried at Silverstone. Gordini was running a team of three twin-overhead-camshaft 'sixes', one of them 2·9-litres capacity. Maserati ran three cars, and though Alfa-Romeo were absentees, having abandoned the 'Disco Volante', Talbots were back again, the big 4½-litre engines being credited with 260 b.h.p.—quite an output for an engine of basically 1936 design. Ferraris were trying everything from 'small' 3-litres to an immense 4,954 cc vee-twelve said to develop 340 b.h.p. The slightly smaller 4½-litre variant was good for 290 b.h.p., or 40 b.h.p. more than the Jaguar's advertised output.

The works Jaguars were entrusted to Moss/Walker, Hamilton/Rolt, and Whitehead/Wharton.

The 1953 race was won by Jaguar, on brakes. The 1954 event fell to Ferrari, largely on acceleration, a fact which was proved by the superior straight-line speed of the D-types, Moss's Mulsanne time of 172·76 m.p.h. being 10 m.p.h. in excess of anything recorded by any Ferrari, even the 5-litre car. Not that Ferrari had everything their way. By midnight the 4½-litre car of Maglioli and Marzotto was out, after lying second and lapping at 118·5 m.p.h. The rain was pelting down, and Gonzalez and Trintignant were in the lead on a Ferrari, separated from their team-mates Rosier and Manzon by the Whitehead/Wharton Jaguar in second place. All three Jaguars suffered from misfiring, traced, after plug changes had been tried, to blockages in their fuel filters. A wet dawn came up. Though the Rolt/Hamilton car was now free of trouble and running lustily, Moss had been forced up the escape road, and out of the race, by a complete and sudden absence of brakes, and the Whitehead/Wharton car went out from cylinder head trouble after it had been running for some time with only top gear left in the box. Gearbox troubles had, however, also eliminated the Rosier/Manzon Ferrari, and the blown Aston Martin, hitherto a steady performer, retired shortly

after noon. This left Gonzalez and Trintignant on the only remaining big Ferrari to fight it out against the surviving D-type of Rolt and Hamilton. The Jaguar very nearly did it, for when Gonzalez crossed the line he was only three miles ahead of Hamilton, who had been lapping at 117 m.p.h. The race averages were 105·1 m.p.h. for the Ferrari, and 105 m.p.h. for the Jaguar. Spear and Johnston drove consistently to bring their Cunningham home third, and Laurent, partnered this year by Swaters, was fourth on his privately-entered C-type.

Meanwhile Cooper's Jaguar-powered sports-racing car had appeared. It utilized a multi-tubular space-frame, independent suspension of both front and rear wheels was by transverse leaf and wishbones, and the engine was a standard C-type. The car weighed 16½ cwt. Whitehead drove one in the 1954 Hyères 12-hour Race, but it retired.

Jaguars scored a 1–2–3 win at Rheims, the works D-types of Whitehead/Wharton and Rolt/Hamilton leading the Laurent/Swaters C-type home. They did not have the competition they deserved, since Ferrari sent no works cars, and Aston Martin no cars at all. In the absence of these, the fastest cars apart from the Jaguars were the Cunninghams and Maglioli's new 3-litre four-cylinder

'Monzanapolis, 1957'. The Jaguars look incongruous alongside the Offenhauser-powered habitués of the Brickyard.

750S Ferrari. Moss set a killing pace, making the fastest lap at 110·87 m.p.h. before gearbox trouble put him out—the strain also told on Maglioli's car, and after the Ferrari's retirement it was a foregone conclusion for the Jaguars. Of the July events, neither the Leinster Trophy nor the sports-car race held in conjunction with the British Grand Prix at Silverstone attracted the D-types, understandably enough, but in the Irish race Joe Kelly came through from scratch to finish second in his C-type. At Silverstone, the Aston Martins emerged on top, accounting for first place and the fastest lap alike, and even Parnell's Lagonda finished in front of the C-types. Among the also-rans, incidentally, was an example of the Swallow Coachbuilding Co.'s 2-litre Doretti, making its first appearance on a circuit.

Whitehead won the Wakefield Trophy Race on the Curragh circuit with his Cooper-Jaguar, by now running well, and the C-types of Hamilton and Kelly were second and third respectively. A further sports-car event figured temporarily in the calendar, when the Dutch substituted a race for sports machines for their normal Grand Prix over the Zandvoort course—the reason for the change being the failure of Mercedes-Benz to enter their W.196 cars. Alan Brown was the outright winner on a Cooper-Bristol, but Ninian Sanderson's

C-type took the big-car class for *Ecurie Ecosse*.

Almost everyone turned out for the T.T. on the Dundrod Circuit, Jaguar, Aston Martin, Ferrari, Lancia, Maserati and H.W.M. being represented. It was, however, an 'index of performance' race and a victory for one of the smaller cars was inevitable. The actual winners were Laureau and Armagnac with a D.B.-Panhard, second place going to the works-entered Ferrari of Hawthorn and Trintignant. Jaguars had a bad day—not only did all their three cars retire, but during the unloading at Belfast someone dropped a crate on William Lyons' personal Mk. VII, modifying it almost beyond recall. The works entries were interesting, however, as while the Rolt/Hamilton and Whitehead/Wharton machines were standard D-types, the car driven by Moss and Walker had a 2½-litre engine, and later it was to be asserted that this was a prototype of the unit to be installed in the 1956 2·4-litre saloon. As regards engine dimensions, the two were identical, but the smaller T.T. car was a standard D-type, the power unit apart, and the object of the exercise was not so much to test the new engine, as to work to a capacity better favoured by the handicapping system in force at Dundrod that year. Jaguars were in fact deviating from their usual practice of making special modifications for Le Mans only. This 2½-litre engine

XK140 convertible, 1955. The restyled grille is in evidence here, but the most important improvement—rack and pinion steering—is an invisible one.

Hardtop XK140 – showing the roomier body to advantage. By this
time wire wheels, though normally a special equipment item, were the
rule rather than the exception on sports models.

had the normal car's dry-sump lubrication, a special crankshaft, standard connecting rods, and pistons with taller crowns.

The season closed with a race for unlimited sports cars at Goodwood, won by Salvadori driving a C-type for *Ecurie Ecosse* after the back axle of Hawthorn's 750S Ferrari had packed up. The American Masten Gregory took second place on a Ferrari, Abecassis' H.W.M.-Jaguar was third, and Titterington fourth on the second *Ecurie Ecosse* C-type. The Scottish *équipe* also sent two cars to Barcelona in October, but they were beaten by Picard's 3-litre Ferrari.

With Appleyard out of regular competition, the rally season was less spectacular than in 1953. Again Ronnie Adams led a works-supported team of Mk. VIIs in the Monte Carlo Rally, and Adams himself, partnered by Desmond Titterington, put up the best performance by a British car, finishing sixth. Cecil Vard, also on a Mk. VII this year, was eighth, but the team missed their chance to win the Charles Faroux Trophy awarded for nominated teams, as the third car was well down the list, in 156th place. Adams, too, was unlucky, for he led on the road section, but was defeated in the tests over the Monaco Circuit by a handicapping system which favoured the smaller cars.

Another Mk. VII, driven by Boardman and Duckworth, pulled off a class win and fourth place in general classification in the Dutch Tulip Rally; and Haddon and Vivian won their class in the 'Alpine', though they lost marks and thus missed the coveted *Coupe*. Parsons and Mrs Vann did very well, however, to win the M.C.C. event outright in November, on another of the big Mk. VIIs. Norman Dewis took one of the works D-types to Brighton for the Speed Trials on the front in September, but short sprints were not the car's *forte*, and he was beaten by Cyril Wick's Allard. Nor were any medals awarded to the driver who entered an XK120 for the Cheltenham Motor Club's Economy Run, and recorded an astonishing 58·7 m.p.g.

On the water, Buckley acquired no more records in 1954, but the German Christof Von Mayenburg took his XK-powered speedboat to the Austrian Lakes, and captured the World's eight-hour record for craft in the 800-kg. class with a speed of 76·5 m.p.h.

For the first time since 1950, Jaguars had something new on show at Earls Court. The fruits of racing experience were now being harvested, and output of the standard engine was raised from 160 b.h.p. to 190 b.h.p. at 5,600 r.p.m., high-lift camshafts being standardized throughout the range, as was an oil-insulated ignition coil. The improved Mk. VII (the M-type) had stiffer suspension, and closer gear ratios of 4·27, 5·17, 7·47, and 12·73 to 1. It was, of course,

Tamed D-type: the XK-SS. It did over 140 mph, but nobody reckoned at the time that four years later even more straight-line performance could be combined with civilized amenities on the E-type.

available in three forms: with a four-speed manual gearbox, with this box and Laycock de Normanville overdrive, and with the Borg-Warner automatic transmission. Minor detail improvements included headlamps with 'special Le Mans type diffuser glasses', wrap-around bumpers, full-length Dunlopillo front and rear seats, and flashing indicators instead of the semaphore type.

The XK120, of which over 12,000 had been built, gave way to a new XK140. The 190 b.h.p. engine was, of course, standard, and the ordinary model retained the disc wheels and rear-wheel spats, but 'special equipment' cars had wire wheels, twin exhausts and the 210 b.h.p. C-type engine. Overdrive was now an optional extra, the coupé models had roomier bodywork allowing space for two children or extra baggage behind the rear seats, and a new and somehow fussier radiator grille replaced the original XK120 type. Most important of all, the superb rack-and-pinion steering of the competition cars was adopted. A small medallion on the luggage boot lid reminded owners of the *marque*'s illustrious record at Le Mans: by the time the XK140 was withdrawn in favour of the disc-braked XK150 in the summer of 1957, two more dates were to be inscribed thereon. Prices ranged from £1,598 for the XK140 roadster to £1,644 for the drophead coupé, these figures including purchase tax

and applied to the cars in basic form. Certain selected customers with £2,686 to burn could now purchase a D-type, though production did not start till early 1955, and the cars sold to private clients were of the revised 1955 Le Mans type.

Incidentally, it is only fair to sort out the complexities of Jaguar nomenclature. Though the C-type was on occasions referred to as the XK120C, I have used the former designation, as the factory always has. In any case, the D-type was never called the XK120D, quite simply because it was entirely dissimilar to the XK series except as regards its engine. In America, the designations XK120MC and XK140MC are frequently used: these never appeared in the Jaguar catalogue, and in fact refer to modified ('M') cars—in other words, 'special equipment' XK touring chassis with the C-type engine.

These new models came up for test during 1955. In February of that year, John Bolster had a run in Duncan Hamilton's D-type, which he duly recorded in *Autosport*. He found the car capable of working up to 120 m.p.h. on any short straight, such performance being attainable with complete confidence thanks to the disc brakes. Speed was on this occasion limited by road conditions, and by the owner's injunction not to drive 'at much over 165 m.p.h., because she's got the low cog in at the moment'. *The Autocar* tried the XK140

An early 2.4-litre photographed alongside the Shakespeare Memorial Theatre at Stratford-upon-Avon.

'special equipment' fixed-head coupé in November, and found that it would do 129 m.p.h. in overdrive top, direct top gear offering 111 m.p.h. and third 80 m.p.h. Weight had gone up still further, to 31 cwt., as tested, as against the 27½ cwt. of a similarly-bodied 1952 XK120, and acceleration was actually inferior, though only fractionally so, the 0–90 m.p.h. time having increased from 22·1 seconds to 22·7 seconds. Like all the fiercer Jaguars, it was completely devoid of temperament, handling was much improved, and even the gear change, which some testers found too slow, was 'satisfactory'. The journal was able to reproduce an untouched photograph of the dashboard, showing the rev. counter needle at 4,800 r.p.m. and the slightly optimistic speedometer at 135 m.p.h., thus illustrating both the smoothness of the engine and the advantages of an overdrive top gear. Further, unlike some other very rapid closed cars, the Jaguar was habitable throughout its speed range:

'The car cruises very happily with the speedometer needle hovering between the 100 and 110 m.p.h. marks, and the crew is able to converse in normal tones. . . . The improved weight distribution, achieved mainly by repositioning the engine, has eliminated the oversteer noticeable in the earlier XK120 and the suspension is firm without being harsh.'

The Autocar also by way of contrast, tried the production version of Mercedes-Benz 300SL, which became available in Great Britain at the end of 1954. Stuttgart had produced a very fine car, and its four-speed gearbox, without overdrive, gave a maximum speed of 128·5 m.p.h., with 98, 70, and 44 m.p.h. available respectively on the three indirect ratios. It was lighter than the Jaguar at 28½ cwt. and reached 60 m.p.h. in 8·8 seconds, 2·2 seconds less than the British car. It was, however, a little thirstier at 18·4 m.p.g., as against the Jaguars' overall consumption of 21·7 m.p.g., achieved thanks to the overdrive. Over 90% of the German car's production was earmarked for export, and the thousandth 300SL had been completed by November, 1955. Though Jaguars did not disclose breakdown figures for individual models over the years, 8,933 XK140s were turned out between late 1954 and the middle of 1957. Even after due allowance had been made for import duty, the Mercedes was expensive at £4,393. The Jaguar with full optional equipment as tested cost £1,938.

American sales remained steady. William Lyons flew out in January 1955 to address a congress of three hundred of his dealers in New York, and at the same time to open the American subsidiary's new showrooms on Park Avenue—a far cry from shipment

of 'last year's model' S.S. I's in 1936! The transatlantic customer now had priority, and well he knew it. Profit for the financial year 1954–5 was £525,282—not a record, for the previous year had netted some £22,000 more—but tremendous strides beyond the mere £27,960 made in 1935, the firm's first year as a public company. More important, Jaguar had made a loss once, and once only—in the difficult reconstruction year of 1946. E. F. Huckvale, for twenty-five years company secretary, was made a director in 1955.

The international acceptance of the Jaguar as an everyday motor-car was highlighted by two remarkable performances during the year. A Mr and Mrs Thonning drove a 1952 Mk. VII saloon overland from Calcutta to London—the only modifications deemed necessary were steel plates under the sump, the car's 7½-inch ground clearance being on the low side for the really rough stuff, the fitting of Girling heavy-duty shock absorbers, and an insurance against limited refuelling facilities in the shape of an extra twenty-four-gallon fuel tank. In the event this leaked furiously, but no other trouble was encountered. Then Lucio Bollaert, an Argentinian enthusiast, drove his XK120 roadster with C-type modifications across the Andes, to disprove the commonly-held notion that such a trip was possible only with a jeep or with one of the heavier American sedans. Trouble was experienced with dust sealing, but the Jaguar went perfectly, despite the deplorable Chilean petrol, said to be 76 octane but probably much worse. Señor Bollaert considered the trip 'a good advertisement for Coventry', and lamented the fact that there were only seven Jaguars in the whole of Chile, which was probably as much due to currency restrictions as to anything else. The poor fuel was the worst snag, it would seem, for 1960 saw two crossings of the Andes in slightly improbable vehicles—John Coleman on his 1925 Austin Seven, and a party of Argentine firemen on a superannuated Brockway fire truck, also of 1925 vintage!

Two-Point-Four from the front: the smaller grille and neatly recessed lamps gave it a tidy look.

The Jaguar-engined sports-racing 'specials' were beginning to appear in some numbers, and enthusiasts in 1955 had the choice of three species: the H.W.M., using a D-type engine and gearbox in a tubular ladder-type frame, with De Dion rear axle and Girling drum brakes, weighing 17cwt.; the Cooper-Jaguar Mk. II, six of which were actually made, also with the D-type engine but this time inclined eight degrees in the space-frame, independent transverse leaf suspension front and rear, and Dunlop disc brakes, turning the scales at 17 cwt.; and the R.G.S.-Atalanta, likewise independently-sprung all round, but using a C-type power unit and Lockheed 2LS drum brakes. This car weighed 19 cwt. 'wet'. Jaguar-powered cars of one type and another seemed likely to dominate the Club event as well as the *Grandes Epreuves*.

Club successes came thick and fast. A book twice the length of this one would be needed to enumerate every win and place scored by the XK and its derivatives, but in 1955 any sports-car or *formule libre* race would attract its quota of tuned XK120s, C-types, D-types, and Jaguar-based 'specials'; any event for production sports cars would draw the more or less standard XK120s and XK140s; and the saloon car races, now growing in popularity, would be swamped by the vast Mk. VIIs, rolling over at alarming angles, yet always under control, and always winning, though Daimler 'Conquests' and later tuned Ford 'Zephyrs' and Austin A.105s would make them work for their living. To illustrate this, let us look at a typical long weekend in the season—Whitsun, 1955.

The West Essex Car Club were holding a meeting on the Snetterton airfield circuit in Norfolk, and here W. T. Smith's C-type won a five-lap race for unlimited sports cars. Goodwood attracted drivers of international calibre, notably Duncan Hamilton, whose week included a victory in the over 2,000 cc class at Chimay. He was in great form on the Sussex airfield: 'What he does,' to quote a contemporary report, 'is throw a car into a corner with tremendous courage and then nurse it through in a drift, correcting it with remarkable skill as he comes out of the bend.' All of which he did to excellent purpose on his D-type to win a ten-lap race for cars of over 2-litres capacity from Bob Berry on another 'D', and Protheroe's C-type. He also lapped at over 86 m.p.h. to beat Berry in the twenty-one-lap Johnson Challenge Trophy Race. Neither Brands Hatch—at that time, of course, still the old and very short circuit—nor the Crystal Palace, the S.S. 100's Waterloo in pre-war days, were good Jaguar country, and added nothing to the score, but Cornwall's bleak airfield circuit at Davidstow was a more promising venue, and here Shattock's R.G.S.-Atalanta and G. Tyrer's C-type finished second and third in the race for unlimited sports cars, behind J. F. Dalton's Austin-Healey 100S. Tyrer, indeed, had a good day, as he also won the production-car race and took second place in the *formule libre*, which also attracted, among other vehicles, a Mk. VII saloon, 'lapping silently, surprisingly fast, and with a great deal of tyre squeal.' At the Eifelrennen in Germany, Margulies' C-type managed to finish seventh, despite a slipping clutch, behind the works Mercedes-Benz and Ferraris. Even this catalogue of success does not take into consideration the myriad minor-league weekend events in America.

A cutaway drawing of the original Mk.I 2.4-litre showing the unitary construction.

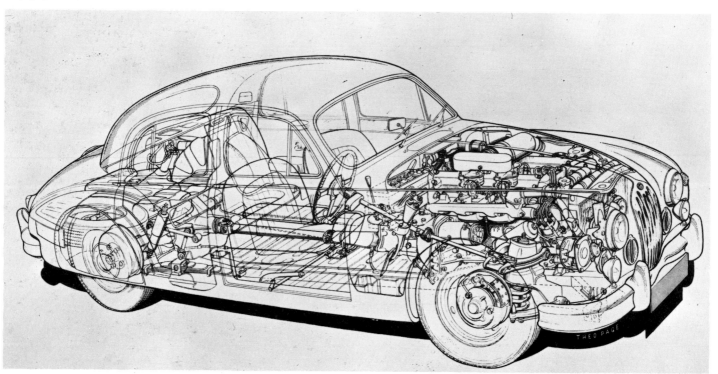

The big-time season started in 1955 with the African races, but Duncan Hamilton retired at Agadir and was only third at Dakar on his D-type. Racing, however, promised to be interesting, for Mercedes-Benz were back.

Sebring saw the first gathering of the clans. The new straight-eight 300SLR Mercedes-Benz were not there, but there were ten Ferraris, ranging in size from a 2-litre 'Mondial' to Jim Kimberly's big 4·9-litre car. Two 3-litre Maseratis were entrusted to Spear/Johnston and Valenzano/Perdisa. The works Jaguars were absent too, but Briggs Cunningham was pinning his principal hope on his newly-acquired D-type which ran, incidentally, in British Racing Green, and not in the American national colours of blue and white which it was to wear at Le Mans in the summer. He also entered his second Le Mans car—the Cunningham C-6, powered by a 3-litre four-cylinder Meyer-Drake engine of the type that had been standard wear for many years at Indianapolis. His Jaguar was shared by Hawthorn and Walters, and it won at 79·5 m.p.h., though the race was marred by an unhappy dispute between the Cunningham pit and Allen Guiberson, the entrant of Phil Hill's Ferrari. Walters on the Jaguar was alleged to have passed the Ferrari in defiance of a yellow flag waved by a marshal. The protest, however, was over-ruled, and Jaguar gained some valuable points towards the Constructors' Championship.

The British Empire Trophy Race went to Archie Scott-Brown's Lister-Bristol, the Monza-type Ferraris being off-form. Surprisingly enough, Shattock in the R.G.S.-Atalanta managed to stave off C- and D-type opposition in the final, though admittedly no works Jaguars were running. The Coventry firm gave the Mille Miglia a miss, even private entrants abstaining, and the Aston Martins came out on top in the race for large sports cars run at the *Daily Express* Silverstone meeting in May. Jaguars, of course, monopolized the biggest class—literally, as all the competitors were either Jaguars, or cars fitted with the twin-camshaft Jaguar engine. Despite some harrying from Ken Wharton's Ford, fastest car in the smaller classes, the saloon-car event was the inevitable Jaguar benefit, Hawthorn leading the Mk. VIIs home this time. No D-types went to Spa that May, and Frère's Aston Martin had a relatively easy time, but even the older cars could still perform with credit, and to everyone's surprise Scheid's XK120 not only finished fifth, but did so a bare three laps behind the winner.

The Ulster Trophy meeting was, by contrast, an excellent day for the Coventry *marque*. In the scratch race, Titterington on an

Mk.VIII, 1957. The Mk.VII Jaguar shape was retained with detail changes.
The single panel windscreen and two-toning can be seen.

Ecurie Ecosse D-type was the winner, his fastest lap of the Dundrod circuit at 91·43 m.p.h. being only 3 seconds slower than Hawthorn's record performance in the 1954 T.T. The handicap race fell to a promising young driver from Lincoln, W. T. Smith, on a C-type—he was later to die on the same course in that year's T.T.

Then came that tragic Le Mans. Mercedes-Benz produced the eight-cylinder 300SLRs, complete with air-brake flaps behind the cockpits—these were assigned to Moss/Fangio, Fitch/Kling, and Levegh/Simon. Maserati had two of the promising 3-litre cars; and the two Ferraris were to be driven by Maglioli/Farina and the French pair Trintignant/Schell. Though Enzo Ferrari was experimenting with disc brakes at Monza, they were not so far proving a great success, and they did not figure on his Le Mans cars. Cunninghams fielded both the Meyer-Drake-powered C-6, which had proved neither fast nor reliable at Sebring, and his D-type, which had won there. The Aston Martin team was supported by Parnell and Poore on the unhappy vee-twelve Lagonda, and Peter and Graham Whitehead shared a Cooper-Jaguar of the latest type. The works Jaguars were to be driven by Rolt/Hamilton, Hawthorn/Bueb, and Beauman/Dewis.

These 1955 cars had abandoned unit construction to some extent by using a separate steel-tube sub-frame in place of the welded-up alloy unit of the 1954 models. This was cheaper to repair in the event of a crash. The rear suspension was slightly modified, an extra oil pump was provided to take care of gearbox lubrication—had not the gearbox of the Whitehead/Wharton car caused its elimination in 1954?—and the use of a wider screen made it possible for the cars to be driven at speeds of up to 150 m.p.h. without goggles. Two hundred and eighty-five b.h.p. were now available; all the production D-types sold to the public conformed to this general specification, but retained the short nose, head-rest, and 250 b.h.p. engine of the original type. An even higher axle ratio of 2·53:1 was used.

The race will, of course, be remembered for the appalling tragedy which struck at 6.20 p.m. when Levegh's Mercedes-Benz rammed Macklin's Austin-Healey and spun into the crowds, literally exploding. Not only the unfortunate driver, but over eighty spectators were killed, and more than a hundred injured. Early in the morning, Mercedes-Benz withdrew their two surviving cars, as a gesture of respect and mourning, when the formidable Moss/Fangio combination was in the lead. In the event, Hawthorn and Bueb went on to win at 107 m.p.h., having made the fastest lap—a record for the course—at 122·387 m.p.h. Collins and Frère were second in a

Power-assisted steering was featured on Mk.IX, which could better 110 mph on 220 horsepower. It was the last of the Jaguar line to retain a separate chassis.

DB.3S Aston Martin, and Claes and Swaters on a privately-owned D-type third. Gearbox trouble eliminated Rolt and Hamilton, who retired after staggering round on the top two gears alone. Beauman ran the third car into a sandbank at Arnage, whence he was unable to extricate it. In the general air of disaster, personal tragedy struck, for John Lyons, William Lyons's only son, was killed in a road accident on his way to Le Mans. He was only twenty-five and had recently joined his father's firm after serving his apprenticeship with Leylands.

This catastrophic race produced the natural reactions and inquiries, and inevitably many postponements; cancellations followed as nation after nation abandoned races, either permanently, or until such time as the safety regulations could be rigorously overhauled. Among the events that did not take place in 1955 were the Rheims sports-car race and the Alpine Rally. On this tragic June evening, too, were sown the seeds which were to spell the death of the Mille Miglia. But in the meantime, the closed-circuit races remained on the calendar.

Jaguars sent only one car to Aintree in July, and even Hawthorn could not beat the Aston-Martins on a short circuit. He finished fifth behind the whole DB.3S team on his D-type, Ninian Sanderson's *Ecurie Ecosse* D-type being sixth. Nor were the major events of that August very encouraging. Mercedes-Benz turned out for the Swedish Sports Car Race, and Fangio won it for them; Michael Head's privately-entered C-type came in fifth, five laps behind the winner. At the 'international' Charterhall meeting there was no foreign participation, but Titterington won the Unlimited Sports Car event for *Ecurie Ecosse*, and took second place to Parnell's Aston Martin in the race for the John Brown Trophy. The Goodwood Nine Hours was also a victory for Aston Martins, but it broke the Jaguar hoodoo in this miniature Le Mans, for Titterington and Sanderson on the *Ecurie Ecosse* D-type finished second. On this occasion, the failures, be it said, were the 750S Ferraris, led by Portago and Hawthorn—they were very fast in practice, and very unreliable on the day. The Ferrari were triumphant in the International Trophy Race at Oulton Park, but Berry's D-type went well to finish fourth.

The Tourist Trophy was a triumph for Stirling Moss and Mercedes-Benz, who scored a classic 1–2–3 victory, and a glorious defeat for Mike Hawthorn and his D-type. Though his engine blew up on the penultimate lap, when he was lying second to Moss and ahead of Fangio, he had given the German *marque* a tremendous battle, and had never been lower than third in the field while he was

Holocaust: 2.4-litres and Mk.VIIIs after the fire at Browns Lane, February, 1957.

running. Much of the time he had led. In America, however, Sherwood Johnston, winner of his country's Sports Car Drivers' Championship in 1953, was doing great things with Briggs Cunningham's D-type, which had now finally supplanted the Cunningham C-6. In the America Road Race at Elkhart Lake, he was only just beaten by Phil Hill's Ferrari—tit for tat, perhaps, after Sebring!—but at Watkins Glen he made no mistake, led from start to finish, and showed a clean set of wheels to his nearest challengers, Spear and Lloyd on 300S Maseratis. He also had his revenge on Hill in the President's Cup Race at Hagerstown, leading the Ferrari in at an average of 87·9 m.p.h.

Nineteen fifty-five had been a year of triumph and tragedy. Jaguar had won again at Le Mans, but in such circumstances that this further proof of the car's stamina and speed would happily have been forgone by everyone. As yet the rallies, the 'Alpine' excepted, had not fallen beneath the shadow of the Le Mans disaster, and Jaguars had quite a good year. Adams, Vard and Appleyard ran a team of 'works' Mk. VII saloons in the Monte Carlo Rally. Individual results were not spectacular, for Adams finished eighth, Vard twenty-seventh after incurring heavy penalties at an entirely new and secret time-check, and Appleyard had to be content with eighty-fourth place; a core plug dropped out during the Mountain Regularity Circuit, and he retired from this test, with plumes of steam wafting up to mountain-top level. Though victory in the Rally went to the more compact Sunbeam '90' of Malling and Fadum, Jaguars won the Charles Faroux Team Trophy. It was noticeable that Mercedes-Benz cars finished in fifth and seventh places—rallies were henceforward to engage Stuttgart's attentions more and more, Stross and Pointing won the class for Grand Touring cars of over 2,600 cc in the R.A.C. Rally with a Mk. VII, and this same partnership of drivers helped to make up the R.A.C. entry which won the Team Prize in the Liège-Rome-Liège event, though this year a Mercedes-Benz 300SL was first in general classification. Le

Gallais put a C-type engine into his ageless 'special' and was rewarded with a third fastest time at Bouley Bay in July 1955, while the suitability of Jaguars for short sprints—hitherto in doubt—was clinched by the remarkable speed put up by Phil Walters on Briggs Cunningham's D-type during the N.A.S.C.A.R. Speed Week at Daytona Beach during March—164·136 m.p.h., or 14 m.p.h. quicker than the fastest Ferrari present. As an indication of the straight-line capabilities of the new type of American 'sports car', a Ford 'Thunderbird' managed over 118 m.p.h., or faster than the touring Jaguars. The best of the XKs must, I feel, have been otherwise engaged, for three years previously J. Bird's XK 120—technically a stock car—had recorded 119·8 m.p.h., and 'Uncle Tom' McCahill, one of the most outspoken of American motoring journalists, had turned in nearly 101 m.p.h. on a standard Mk. VII.

The 1955 Show came round: automatic Jaguars were now available on the home market, and Allards were offering their K.3, 'Monte Carlo', and 'Safari' models with Jaguar engines as an alternative to the 5·4-litre Cadillac. Briggs Cunningham signed up as a Jaguar distributor, and announced his intention of supporting the British firm by intensifying his racing activities on their behalf in America. Leslie Marr departed to New Zealand, his Connaught powered by a twin-camshaft Jaguar engine, and the Sports Car Constructors' Championship saw Jaguars slip down to third place, behind Mercedes-Benz and Ferrari.

Nobody, however, was really worrying about Jaguar-Allards, or even the availability of Borg-Warner's aid to the lazy motorist. William Lyons and his team had expended three years—not to mention £1,000,000 worth of tooling costs—on a completely new model, and this car, the 2·4-litre saloon, was on display at Earls Court. The 1956 edition of Jaguar's American catalogue highlighted the smaller car's ability to 'travel thirty miles on a gallon of gas at 45 m.p.h.'.

Nothing so mundane worried the general public.

E-types in production, 1967. Hardtops predominate.

CHAPTER 10

Accolade and Acclaim

1956

To those motorists whose desire for a car of compact dimensions is a matter of personal preference the opportunity is at last presented, not only for satisfying that desire, but for gratifying a natural wish to own a car the mere possession of which indicates insistence on owning nothing but the best—a Jaguar.'

Jaguar 2.4-litre catalogue, 1956

'The Jaguar changed the sports motoring scene suddenly, for we were presented with a car, at a price which many could afford, that equalled in performance the monoposto Grand Prix cars of a few years earlier. Moreover, such were the improvements in braking and road-holding which accompanied this new conception of a sports car that it could be handled safely by relatively inexperienced drivers.'

The Autocar, October 1955

THIS quotation from *The Autocar* summarizes perfectly the achievements of William Lyons and his team, who were to reap the benefit of twenty years of Jaguar development in 1956. For Lyons himself, it was a great year, for he was created a Knight Bachelor in the New Year's Honours List. This recognition of his vital contribution to British prestige and the export drive in the dark years when the country was fighting for economic survival was followed by another gesture of Royal interest and appreciation; a visit to the works in March. The new 'compact' 2·4-litre saloon kept Browns Lane working to capacity throughout a year, the latter part of which was to be overshadowed by the re-imposition of petrol rationing as a result of the Suez crisis. Further, Jaguar won a triple victory—not only were they triumphant on both their favourite circuits, Le Mans and Rheims, but a Mk. VII won the Monte Carlo Rally outright.

Of all the events in the international motoring calendar, the Monte Carlo Rally and *Les Vingt-Quatre Heures du Mans* are perhaps the most significant in the eyes of the British public. Of the other races, Sebring is too remote, the Mille Miglia too much an Italian preserve, while Silverstone has the functional qualities of an airfield which provides all the excitement, yet somehow lacks the glamour that once surrounded the Brooklands Motor Course. The associations of Rheims are primarily historical, with a flavour of jackdaws and Champagne, and Goodwood and Aintree, those two excellent circuits, are indelibly associated in the lay mind with horse-racing.

When it comes to rallies, the man in the street is hopelessly confused and cannot disentangle one long-distance event from another—in fact it is doubtful whether he realizes that the RAC British Rally now takes place shortly before Christmas, whereas it used to be run in the spring. But in the 1960s, the B.B.C. coverage of Le Mans, and the reporting of the Monte Carlo Rally by B.B.C. and I.T.N. alike, reached so high a standard that many people who look upon the motor car as transportation pure and simple were to be seen every January and June, with their ears glued to the car radio, listening to John Bolster or Raymond Baxter. Their minds were glued only to the progress of Jaguars, Aston Martins and other wearers of the green snarling down the Mulsanne Straight and through Arnage. Many a wife cursed her car-minded husband on such occasions—especially for those broadcasts in the small hours of the Sunday morning!

Victory in the 1956 Monte Carlo Rally was, indeed, a fitting start to Jaguar's competition year. A works-supported team again ran, the drivers being Adams, partnered this year by Biggar, Vard, and Mansbridge, all on Mk. VIIs. Adams' car was the Mk. VII saloon he had used in the 1955 event, and his win was therefore all the more creditable, though the road section was relatively easy this year. All the same, it was only the fourth ever scored by a British driver on a British car, previous triumphs being those of the Hon. Victor Bruce on an A.C. in 1926, Donald Healey on an Invicta in 1931, and Sydney Allard on an Allard in 1952. This year Jaguars did not win the Charles Faroux team Trophy, for though Mansbridge finished forty-fifth in general classification, the unlucky Vard was involved in a collision with a non-competing car, which mishap dropped him back to 153rd place. However, if the weather in the *Alpes Maritimes* was mild, that in Southern England was anything but, and John Bolster borrowed Adams' winning Mk. VII and tested it for *Autosport* amid the snows of Kent. He was unable to detect any roughness in the engine, or even any brake fade. Though Appleyard did not participate in the Monte Carlo Rally, he returned to the fray for the R.A.C. Rally in March. Now at the wheel of an XK140 with the registration VUB 140, he took second place in general classification. W. D. Bleakley did well to finish fourth on the new 2·4-litre car's first competition appearance.

The new 'compact' Jaguar had appeared at the 1955 Earls Court Show. News of its impending introduction had sparked off the usual flood of speculation. Some people asserted that the four-cylinder XK100 engine was to be revived; others hinted that Heynes would follow B.M.W.'s lead, and replace a successful 'six' with a compact vee-eight; and others still remembered the interesting car that had run in the 1954 T.T., and had since disappeared from sight, at any rate in its Dundrod form. These last were right—the days of the big four-cylinder unit in luxury cars were numbered, as Armstrong-Siddeleys were to find out to their cost when they sought to attack Jaguar's markets with the 2·3-litre 'Sapphire 234'. The little Armstrong was rapid enough, 95 m.p.h. being readily obtainable in standard form, but by contrast with the 2·4-litre Jaguar it was rough-running, and it was dropped from the range after only two seasons. The vee-eight rumours, however, had some foundation, for Jaguars had built such a unit in 1954. Not that it was either intended for a private car or suitable for installation in one: it was, in fact, a 9-litre tank engine with two overhead camshafts per bank of cylinders, which developed 320 b.h.p. at 3,750 r.p.m. Six prototypes were made and tested, one being tried on the road; development continued till 1958, when defence cuts caused the shelving of the programme. So far no Jaguar-designed vee-eight has been produced for a touring car.

Instead, Heynes adhered to a six-cylinder unit of 83 mm. bore, but with oversquare dimensions attained by shortening the stroke of the existing XK engine to 76·5 mm., giving a capacity of 2,483 cc. The engine followed the basic design in having a seven-bearing crankshaft; output was 112 b.h.p. at 5,750 r.p.m. The Borg and Beck single-dry-plate clutch and four-speed synchromesh gearbox, with ratios of 4·27, 6·21, 9·01, and 15·35 to 1, followed standard Jaguar practice, as did the Burman recirculating ball steering gear. But everything else was new.

Jaguars had long since ceased to make their own bodies; and frames, from the earliest days of the 'Big Cats', had been made to their design and order by Rubery Owen. But up to now every car except the first D-types had had a separate chassis. The 2·4-litre, however, featured unitary construction of chassis and body, with special stiffening at front and rear, and these shells were made in their entirety at the Pressed Steel Co.'s Oxford Works, and delivered to Coventry 'in the white'—in other words, unpainted and untrimmed. The new 'body' made use of smooth curves, and for the first time a curved windscreen was found on a Jaguar. The suspension, likewise, was entirely new, the torsion bars on the front giving way to a coil-and-wishbone arrangement. Rear suspension was of trailing-link type with cantilever semi-elliptic springs. The radius arm was located by a Panhard rod, and the suspension was insulated by

The rally winner: the Morley brothers with their 3.4-litre in the Tulip Rally, 1959. A Jaguar also won the touring category of that year's Tour de France.

rubber blocks, to circumvent the drumming often set up by unitary construction cars on uneven surfaces. The four-wheel hydraulic brakes were of the new Lockheed 'Brakemaster' type with servo assistance, and a central floor-mounted handbrake operated on the rear wheels only, in the usual Jaguar fashion. A feature of the new body was that the tools were now housed in the spare wheel compartment under the boot, and not in the boot lid. The standard model sold at £895 basic, but the vast majority of customers preferred the 'special equipment' model, which offered a heater (usually standard equipment on closed Jaguars), a central armrest in the rear compartment, an electric clock, twin vitreous-enamelled manifolds and the famous Jaguar mascot, all for £916, or £1,299 with purchase tax added. Laycock-De Normanville overdrive, operating on top gear only, was an optional extra—on cars so equipped the direct top-gear ratio was lowered to 4·55:1.

The Motor tested the car in this latter form during 1956, and found that the new short-stroke engine would run happily up into the 'red

zone' above 5,000 r.p.m. The gear lever was 'a little disappointing: it suffers from a combination of flexibility and pronounced cranking to the rear which bring it slightly nearer the reach of a tall driver, but make the angle awkward.' The location of the overdrive switch was also criticized, but of the gear ratios it was said that 'it is refreshing to return to a vehicle which is essentially meant to be driven'. The riding comfort and handling characteristics vindicated the retention of a conventional rear axle; the suspension was supple enough to damp out the effects of hump-backs, but firm enough to allow a degree of roll without any wallowing. Drumming was absent; the servo-assisted brakes were admirable on the open road, but less pleasing in traffic, where the time-lag associated with servo systems made itself felt on occasions. The little Jaguar's performance was not appreciably inferior to the bigger saloon models, and by virtue of its lower weight of 27 cwt., was able to attain 101·5 m.p.h. in overdrive, 93 m.p.h. in direct top, and 68 m.p.h.—or quite a lot more than was comfortably attainable on the old 2½-litre Mk. V— in third. The car took 4·6 seconds to reach 30 m.p.h., 14·4 seconds to reach 60 m.p.h., and 90 m.p.h. came up in 39·1 seconds from a standing start, an identical figure to that recorded on a 1956 model Mk. VIIM with overdrive tested by *The Motor* in September 1955. 10–30 m.p.h. acceleration figures could be recorded in the three highest ratios, overdrive included, but this latter practice was not recommended. The overall fuel consumption was rather high at 18·25 m.p.g., but more moderate driving could produce excellent results, and the American estimate of 30 m.p.g. at a constant 45 m.p.h. was found to have erred on the side of pessimism. Even the critical Joseph Lowrey, summarizing the car later in the year for the benefit of *The Motor*'s readers, could find no worse objections than these:

> 'The Jaguar gearbox continues to use a rather outmoded form of synchromesh, in contrast to the modernity of most other Jaguar design features; but no doubt the automatic transmission will eventually replace this box on all cars, instead of only some. For an Englishman of sporting tastes, rather firmer damping of the suspension might be preferable, but since Americans look like claiming most of the production for a good while to come, that is perhaps a pointless comment.'

In defence of Jaguars, it should be said that the average owner seems to like the gearbox, as is instanced by the fact that in February 1961 less than 20% of all 2·4-litre buyers specified automatic, while the suspension of the Mk. II models introduced for the 1960 season was improved out of all recognition.

As a contrast to the 2·4-litre in its original form, *The Autocar* tried a Mk. VIIM with the latest version of the Borg-Warner transmission in May 1956. This still had the steering column selector lever, but an intermediate ratio was now provided, and downward changes into this could be effected rapidly by means of a 'kickdown' switch linked to the accelerator pedal. The result blended the simplicity of automatic with the extra measure of control hitherto reserved for the manual systems. This car weighed 35 cwt. as tested, and would

Export sales mean resistance to all conditions of road and weather. An XK150 drophead coupé undergoes the water torture at Britain's M.I.R.A. Proving Grounds, Lindley.

attain 100·1 m.p.h. in high range: maxima in low and intermediate 'holds' were 39 m.p.h. and 72 m.p.h. respectively. Acceleration figures on the lower speed ranges were slightly inferior to those recorded on the 2·4-litre, 4·8 seconds being needed to reach 30 m.p.h., and the 0–60 m.p.h. time was only one-tenth of a second shorter than the smaller car's 14·4 seconds. The extra power told at the top end, and the automatic Mk. VIIM could reach 90 m.p.h. in 38·6 seconds. Overall fuel consumptions of the two cars were identical, but it was not considered likely that the big saloon could improve on 23 m.p.g. without freak driving, though manually-equipped cars on test had returned nearly 28 m.p.g. at a constant 40 m.p.h.

That the 2·4-litre could be made to go very fast is evidenced by the works-prepared machine which Paul Frère drove in the Spa Production Touring Car Race in May 1956. With a C-type head, two large-bore S.U. carburetters and a close-ratio gearbox, 125 m.p.h. was possible, Alas, this gearbox gave trouble and the delights of unitary construction were experienced when the pit staff tried to extract the box without removing the engine. Finally, part of the body shell was cut away—only herculean efforts by the Jaguar mechanics got it ready in time, and it ran by the courtesy of the track officials, who waived all rules and allowed Frère to start without having completed a single practice lap. In spite of this he won his class, put up the best performance irrespective of class, and lapped at 97 m.p.h. The 'compact' Jaguars were to do well in future saloon-car races, and would soon relegate the bulky members of the Mk. VII family to the public roads.

Meanwhile Leslie Marr had distinguished himself in New Zealand with the Connaught-Jaguar, taking fourth place at Ard-more and third place in the Lady Wigram Trophy Race at Christchurch, though he was unlucky enough to retire at Dunedin. This car was a standard 1955-type Formula I Connaught, with a D-type unit installed in place of the original 2,470 cc four-cylinder Alta-Connaught. The Armstrong-Siddeley preselector gearbox, however, was retained, and proved very well matched to the torque characteristics of the Jaguar engine. Rodney Clarke admits that he had suspected that the car might be nose-heavy, but in fact it handled better than it had in its original form. Jaguars also did well in the Ardmore sports-car race, Gaze's H.W.M.-Jaguar winning from the XK120s of Archibald and Moffatt. Elsewhere in the Commonwealth, the *marque* was distinguishing itself. Mrs Anderson, the winner of the 1954 'Australian 24' race, had a D-type shipped out early in 1956, and at the Uganda Motor Club's Kajasi Hill-Climb, f.t.d. was made by F. Brown's XK120, the fastest of the big touring cars being F. Singh's Mk. VII.

In March 1956, the newly-knighted Sir William Lyons received an official visit from H.M. Queen Elizabeth II and the Duke of Edinburgh, the Duke taking a keen interest in the Jaguar drawing office. This was the first state visit by Royalty, though the Duke of Kent, himself a Jaguar owner, had previously toured Browns Lane, and H.M. Queen Elizabeth the Queen Mother was the owner of a Mk. VII. The City of Coventry marked the occasion by presenting Prince Charles with a one-tenth scale model of a D-type, executed by that famous artist Rex Hays, perhaps best known for his superb series of models depicting the evolution of the Grand Prix car which I am happy to have in the Montagu Motor Museum at Beaulieu. Other illustrious clients bought Jaguars in 1956: H.R.H. Prince Georg of Denmark took delivery of a new 2·4-litre saloon, while ten

XK150 sports car: it came out nearly a year after the closed and drophead coupé models, and also launched a 250 horsepower version of the celebrated twin-cam six.

Mk. VIIs were shipped to New Zealand in April as Ministerial transport.

The American sales picture continued bright, and the dynamic Briggs Cunningham took a D-type to Journalists' Trial Day—the equivalent of our Guild of Motoring Writers' Test Day at Goodwood —in June. Such a potent machine was not entrusted to the press, though, and they had to be content with rides in the passenger seat. An odd stunt was laid on in October, when an XK coupé raced a flock of five hundred homing pigeons the 380 miles from Berea, Kentucky to Cleveland, Ohio. It is not clear what, if anything, this was supposed to prove, but the car finished forty minutes ahead of the birds! In November, XK140 roadsters carried off the Team Prize in the Great American Mountain Rally, making a clean sweep of their class, and 1956 was considered to be a record year for Jaguar North American Inc. Two thousand more cars were ordered in the first quarter of 1957, but even the 1956 U.S. catalogue specified automatic transmission as standard equipment on Mk. VII, manual boxes being available only to special order.

The Jaguar-powered specials were still to be seen on the circuits during 1956, but only H.W.M. were now offering new cars. Privately-owned D-types were about in fair numbers, and the outmoded C-types were still giving a good account of themselves. Max Trimble, the young Walsall driver, received, as a twenty-first birthday present, MVC 630, *alias* 'The Old War Horse', the ex-*Ecurie Ecosse* car in which Scott Douglas and Gale had finished second at Spa in 1953. Its reliability can be assessed by the fact that it only encountered trouble on three occasions in the season—a slipping clutch and low oil pressure which caused it to retire on its first outing in Trimble's hands at Brands Hatch on Boxing Day, 1955; bottom-end trouble in a twelve-lap scratch race at Goodwood, in spite of which it continued to take second place before an expensive overhaul became necessary; and a half-shaft which fractured, also at Goodwood, and converted the C-type very rapidly into an undriveable three-wheeler. At the height of the season it was raced once, and often twice, every week-end, never finishing lower than sixth at a Silverstone Club meeting, making f.t.d. at the Bentley Drivers' Club Firle hill-climb, winning a race at Oulton, and collecting class wins at Prescott and Staverton. Its best performance was, however, a second place behind Kyffin's DB.3S Aston Martin at the August Bank Holiday meeting at the Crystal Palace, no circuit for any Jaguar. Trimble modestly ascribes this to 'car and driver feeling like it', but it was no mean feat for a car that had done two seasons

The XK150s more rounded lines are shown off to best advantage on the coupé model.

with *Ecurie Ecosse* and one in the hands of Berwyn Baxter before he took over.

On the scores of reliability and cornering capacity, the Jaguar rated high in Trimble's estimation. The rack-and-pinion steering was heavy at low speeds, and alarmingly light higher up the range, while the car appeared to 'float' at speeds above 120 m.p.h. Replacements needed during the season were amazingly few, the most expensive items being tyres, for which the C-type had a voracious appetite. 'The Old War Horse' was always driven to meetings under its own power. When Trimble exchanged this car at the end of 1956 for an ex-*Ecurie Ecosse* D-type, he started to use a transporter, but only, as he puts it 'to avoid the risk of accident', for his new acquisition's road behaviour was 'superb, even in traffic, with its excellent gearbox and good visibility'. Fuel consumptions for the two cars are interesting, the C-type averaging 10–12 m.p.g. on a circuit, and 15–18 m.p.g. on the road, while the D-type, thanks to better aerodynamics and a lower frontal area, would do 12–15 m.p.g. when racing, and as much as 20 m.p.g. on the road. This latter car was the one used by Desmond Titterington during the 1956 racing season.

Trimble's experiences shed an interesting light on the flow of letters which enlivened the correspondence columns of *Autosport* in the spring of 1956. The relative merits of the four-cylinder sports-racing Ferraris and the C- and D-type Jaguars were discussed with vigour, the French driver Jonneret asserting that he had driven his C-type to no fewer than fourteen meetings during 1954. Much play was also made of the fact that *Ecurie Ecosse*'s *production* C-types had done a great deal towards securing second place for Jaguar in the 1954 Constructors' Championship. Very little was proved by all this as it was generally known that the term 'production' now specified that a given number of cars of the relevant type had been made, whereas in pre-war days it was possible to qualify for this category by inserting a half-tone block of one of last year's team cars in the catalogue, and putting a price on the machine.

The 1956 racing calendar proper opened in the sunshine of Sebring, where this year's 12-Hour Race boiled down to a straight fight between the 3·4-litre 'Monza' Ferraris and the D-type Jaguars. Boiled, regrettably, was the operative word; for though no trouble was experienced with either the new engines, said to develop 300 b.h.p., or with the fuel injection system, aimed at defeating the new fuel consumption rules at Le Mans, the brakes succumbed to the tropical climate of Florida. All four cars, sponsored by Briggs Cunningham and driven by Hawthorn/Titterington, Hamilton/Bueb, Spear/Johnston and Cunningham himself with Benett, retired. In some cases the pads wore away, in others they welded themselves to the discs, and the unfortunate Ivor Bueb found himself first unable to leave the pits because his brakes would not free, and then reduced to cross-country motoring when they refused to go on. Hawthorn drove a splendid race, duelling with Fangio on the leading Ferrari, until he, too, was beset by the prevailing malady. After eight hours he was still holding on, albeit in fourth place, but two hours from

Back at Monza, but with a saloon, and after long-distance records, March, 1963. This 3.8-litre Mk.II saloon averaged 106.62 mph for four days and four nights.

the finish he had no brakes left at all, and the car was regretfully withdrawn. The Ferraris of Fangio/Castellotti and Musso/Schell finished first and second, and third place went to the privately-owned D-type driven by Bob Sweikert, winner of the 1955 Indianapolis Race. This car, as the heated correspondents in *Autosport* were quick to point out, was a standard production model. The Chevrolet 'Corvettes' appeared for the first time at an international event, but signally failed to distinguish themselves.

Graham Whitehead brought one of Duncan Hamilton's D-types home in fifth place at Dakar, now billed as 'The World's Fastest Sports Car Race', and, as might have been expected, the handicappers of the British Empire Trophy Race at Oulton Park made a Jaguar victory impossible. Ron Flockhart finished well down in seventh place on his *Ecurie Ecosse* D-type, but in the process he had raised the sports-car lap record to 84·95 m.p.h. This record was equalled in the same race by Benoit Musy's Maserati, but the

Italian car blew up shortly afterwards. Aintree was no better, for the Aston Martins beat the Jaguars in the sports-car event, and even in the saloon-car race a Mercedes-Benz 300SL was victorious. In the Mille Miglia, however, Guyot's Jaguar was first in the category for 'cars of limited price', by which, one suspects, the Italians meant production saloons. Further, Duncan Hamilton had his revenge on the Grand Prix 2½-litre Gordini in the Coupe de Paris. He had finished second to this car in 1955, but in 1956 he averaged 97·46 m.p.h. over the Montlhéry circuit, beating not only the French Formula I car but a G.P. Maserati as well.

Whitsun 1956 brought as many Jaguar successes as had Whitsun 1955. Lawrence's C-type won a ten-lap handicap at Snetterton, Hamilton's D-type took second place in the big car class of the Grand Prix des Frontières at Chimay, and Bueb's Mk. VII won the production touring-car event at Silverstone from Ken Wharton's Austin 'Westminster', after Hawthorn had retired and John Coombs' 2·4-litre had succumbed to overheating. At Spa, as we have seen, Paul Frère distinguished himself with another 2·4-litre, and Ninian Sanderson beat Parnell's DB.3S Aston Martin in the 100-Mile Race for sports-racing cars of over 2-litres' capacity. In the same event, Desmond Titterington set up an absolute lap record for sports cars with a speed of 114·86 m.p.h. on MWS 303, the car which Trimble was to write-off on the same course a year later. Goodwood saw a procession of D-types in the race for big sports machines, Berry beating the *Ecurie Ecosse* cars of Flockhart and Titterington, while the latter won the twenty-six-lap Whitsun Trophy from Hawthorn's Lotus-Climax. It is interesting to note that the overhead-camshaft engine fitted in the latter came from the drawing-board of Walter Hassan, who had assisted in the evolution of the XK unit in the immediate post-war years.

Then came Rheims, Le Mans having been postponed till August to allow for alterations intended to prevent the recurrence of the 1955 disaster. Jaguars finished first, second, third and fourth, led by the works car of Hamilton and Bueb. The second works machine, driven by Hawthorn and Frère, was second, and to *Ecurie Ecosse* (Titterington/Fairman and Flockhart/Sanderson) fell the two remaining places. Triple Weber carburetters were used on all but the winning car, which had the Lucas port-type fuel injection tried out at Sebring. Transmission trouble eliminated the major opposition, in the shape of the 'Monza' Ferrari of Schell/Lucas and the 350S Maserati of Villoresi/Maglioli.

No capacity limit was imposed at Le Mans. Instead, some attempt at restraint was made, cars having to use full-width windscreens. This was not a particularly tricky rule—the horrors of Appendix C were yet to come!—but the new fuel consumption regulations gave food for thought, especially for entrants of big cars. This meant Jaguar alone, as nobody else was running a car of over 3,000 cc. For 1956, tank capacity was limited to twenty-nine gallons instead of the previous 44½ gallons, and every competitor had to complete thirty-four laps before his first refuelling stop. Hitherto, it had been permissible to take on fuel after only thirty-two laps. Reduced to simple figures, this meant that all cars had to average at least 11–12 m.p.g.

Aston Martin were running two DB.3S models, and a new 2½-litre DBR.1 prototype to be handled by team-leader Parnell. Ferrari had the equally new 2½-litre 'Testa Rossa' cars, and Gordini a brace of 2½-litre machines, one the well-known 'six' and the other a straight-eight derived from the French designer's Formula I engine. Anthony Lago was now pinning his faith on the 2½-litre six-cylinder short-stroke Maserati engine, said to be good for 215 b.h.p. at 6,000 r.p.m. and his two works entries were so equipped.

Jaguar were saving weight by utilizing smaller-diameter frame tubes, while a few more pounds were pruned off by the smaller tankage which the regulations demanded. All the works cars, driven

Saloons at speed, or the Tour de France was a happy hunting ground for the Mk.II. In the 1960 event, competitors had to run in a one-and-one-half hour race at Montlhery. Here are Consten (78), Jopp (79), and Behra (80).

this year by Hawthorn/Bueb, Frère/Titterington and Fairman/Wharton, had the Lucas fuel injection, which was found to give better all-out speed, but, unfortunately, an inferior fuel consumption. *Ecurie Ecosse*, however, adhered to conventional carburation on their solitary entry, entrusted to Flockhart and Sanderson. In addition to the D-types, there was a very touring-looking XK140 coupé, privately entered by Walshaw and Bolton.

The works cars were unlucky. A minute hair crack, virtually invisible to the naked eye, developed in one of the fuel feed pipes on Hawthorn's car which, for the first three hours, was in and out of the pits with such frequency that it dropped back twenty laps behind the leaders. Hawthorn's efforts to catch up, when once the faulty pipe had been detected and changed, were magnificent and he did, in fact, finish sixth against impossible odds. His two team-mates were eliminated in a matter of seconds on the second lap. Rain had made the surface slippery, and Frère had just passed Fairman on the approach to Les Esses. In the bend he spun. Though

Fairman was able to avoid him, he, in his turn, was rammed by Portago's Ferrari approaching from astern, and suffered a burst tyre. This he attempted to change, but accident-conscious officials hustled him away onto the soft verge, and here all his endeavours with the jack proved unavailing. Finally he limped back to the pits on a flat tyre, only to find that his steering-gear was hopelessly damaged. Frère, who had made violent contact with the sandbank, also damaged his car too badly to continue.

This left only two D-types in circulation, and of these only the *Ecurie Ecosse* car was in the running. By 10 p.m., it was lying second behind the Moss/Collins Aston Martin, both cars being on their seventy-third lap. A lap astern was the Gendebien/Trintignant Ferrari in third place. The Jaguar took the lead when Moss came in to refuel shortly after dawn, and with only six hours to go it was still there, though Hawthorn, his earlier troubles rectified, was bringing the D-type up through the field at a fine rate of knots, and lapping some four seconds faster than the leaders. The race remained a close

Nocker leads Lindner on the two German-entered Mk.IIs, to win the final round of the 1963 European Touring Challenge. The venue, surprisingly, is Budapest.

struggle right up to the moment that Ron Flockhart received the chequered flag, and brought Jaguar their fourth victory at Le Mans. It was 1954 all over again, only this time Aston Martin, and not Ferrari, had been the opponents, and this time Jaguar had won. The *Ecurie Ecosse* car had averaged 104·46 m.p.h. to the 104·04 m.p.h. of the Moss/Collins Aston Martin. Gendebien and Trintignant drove a consistent race to finish third in the Ferrari at 101·95 m.p.h. The *Ecurie Nationale Belge* D-type of Swaters and Rousselle was fourth, and Hawthorn and Bueb on the sole surviving works car sixth. For the first time in many years, a small car finished well up among the leaders, for Von Frankenburg and Von Trips were fifth in a 1,498 cc Porsche. Nonetheless, this was a great day for Jaguar.

No works Jaguars ran in the International Trophy Race at Oulton Park in August. Nor did the *Ecurie Ecosse* machines, though they entered and practised, and David Murray and 'Wilkie' Wilkinson did a lap of honour in the Le Mans winner. This, however, revealed the appalling state of the course in the pouring rain, and after consultation with Reg. Tanner of Esso and Norman Freeman of Dunlops, Murray decided that conditions were impossible, and that the cars must be withdrawn. He was much criticized for this decision, but it should be remembered that he forfeited all his starting money, and this on top of the expense of flying the whole *équipe* back from the Swedish Sports Car Races in order to take part in the Oulton Park event. The result was a walk-over for Aston-Martin, who also took first and second places in the Goodwood Trophy Race the following month. Sanderson made the fastest lap, though, for *Ecurie Ecosse* and Jaguar. It is possible to get some indication of the killing pace of this event from the fact that 'The Old War Horse'—Trimble's still very lively C-type—was lapped by the leaders within four laps of the start! Nor was the Alpine Rally encouraging—for the first time since 1949, no Jaguars figured in the awards list.

Norman Buckley brought the engine of his speedboat 'Miss Windermere III' up to D-type standard, with three Weber carburetters, and in this form the boat took the one-hour unlimited-class record at 79·6 m.p.h.

In October, Jaguar announced their retirement from racing. It was clear to them that new regulations would sooner or later demand a team of entirely new cars, and the expense of running a competition department was formidable. 'Lofty' England returned to his main duties as Service Director, but *Ecurie Ecosse* remained loyal to Jaguar, and duly bought the 1956 works cars. The association between this *équipe* and Browns Lane was to continue for three more racing seasons, and win still more laurels. The D-type remained in production.

For the ordinary motorist, too, life was becoming rather bleak. In November, as a result of the Suez crisis, he suddenly found himself issued with a book of petrol coupons thoughtfully preserved from the last dose of rationing in 1950, and big cars were at a discount for the time being. Indeed, when I ordered a new Mk. VIII saloon, I could get no better offer than £350 for my old Mk. VII from the firm that had sold it to me for £1,100 some fourteen months before! Had this state of affairs continued beyond May 1957, the results might have been damaging to Jaguars, but, as it happened, it merely absorbed a great deal of the accumulated backlog of home-market orders.

For 1957, the Mk. VIIM and 2·4-litre were continued unchanged. During the past year, the XK140 had become available with automatic transmission, and, surprisingly enough, 827 cars so equipped were built and sold. Mk. VII was, however, supplemented (and later supplanted) by Mk. VIII, an improved version aimed directly at the executive market. The principal mechanical change was the adoption of a 210-b.h.p. engine with C-type head and twin S.U. HD.6 carburetters, which, it was claimed, gave a better performance in the middle and lower speed ranges. A re-styled radiator grille was used, and a single-panel curved windscreen replaced the vee-type found on all the Mk. VII series. The three standard transmission options were available—four-speed manual, four-speed manual with overdrive, and automatic, the latter having the intermediate range of ratios introduced on the later Mk. VIIM cars. A heater was, of course, standard, as were folding tables, an electric clock, *three* cigar

Six hours at Brands Hatch, 1962: two 3.8's battle it out. Winners were the Parkes/Blumer combination at 75.37 mph.

lighters ('a feature that should be appreciated by some owners', commented *The Autocar*), deep pile carpets, and a nylon rug in the rear compartment. Customers who specified automatic transmission had a bench-type front seat in their cars, and recessed into the back of this were a newspaper holder and a boudoir clock. Radio, however, was extra, at £45, and the automatic model followed the later automatic Mk. VIIMs in having a species of umbrella-handle handbrake under the facia, albeit not such an irritating one as Mk. V's. Not that this mattered, for one of the blessings of automatic transmission is that it renders the handbrake redundant except when the footbrake fails, and this has never happened to me on a Jaguar. The 'Park' position on the gear selector takes care of normal parking. 6,226 Mk. VIIIs were produced between the model's introduction and 1959.

The Autocar tried a Borg-Warner-equipped version in February 1957, observing that 'the standard of finish and range of equipment place it firmly in the executive class'. The suspension was a good compromise between a boulevard ride and roll-free cornering, the steering was light for a two-tonner (it weighed 39 cwt.) without any form of power assistance, and the only fault to be found with the comprehensive instrumentation lay in the positioning of the rev. counter in front of the passenger. 106·5 m.p.h. was obtainable, with 72 m.p.h. on intermediate gear. The car would accelerate to 30 m.p.h. in 4·4 seconds; 0–60 m.p.h. took 11·6 seconds, and 0–90 m.p.h. 26·7 seconds. The handbrake had 'an indefinite, spongy feel about it'. Opponents of automatic transmission were surprised to find that for all its weight the Jaguar averaged 17·9 m.p.g. over 42 miles, and was therefore not too hard on standard-ration coupons.

I had been so impressed by the performance of my second-hand Mk. VII that I put my name down for one of these new models at Earls Court in 1956, and, thanks to rationing, was lucky enough to obtain delivery the following January. As a non-smoker I was not influenced by the profusion of cigar lighters, and the handbrake cannot have been unduly inefficient, as I cannot recall any trouble with it. I did several continental tours in this car, taking it down as far as Naples on one occasion. My Borg-Warner automatic Mk. VIII might have an executive air about her, but she was no sluggard, and I recall a very fast run from Villefranche to Paris—about 650 miles. I left at 6.30 a.m. and arrived at my destination shortly after 9 p.m. This may not seem to represent a very impressive average, but I stopped for a hearty breakfast at Aix, and took a two-hour stop for lunch at a 'three-star' restaurant outside Lyons. On the last leg of the journey I was pursued by a Frenchman in an XK120, and had no difficulty in keeping ahead of him, much to his dismay. When he eventually drew up alongside the Mk. VIII at a traffic intersection in Paris, he muttered to me: 'I never thought I should see the day when I couldn't catch one of the saloons. I must get myself an XK140.' My car was certainly good for 110 m.p.h., and probably more, and I only sold her in October, 1958 because she was a little big and awkward in London traffic.

Also at the 1956 Show was to be seen Sydney Allard's latest effort. The old range, dating from 1953, had been dropped, and in its place there was announced a new sports two-three-seater on a tubular frame, with independent front suspension by wishbones and torsion bars. The standard power unit was a 2,553 cc Ford 'Zephyr', but the 190 b.h.p. Jaguar engine was available as an option, and, with a dry weight of only 21 cwt., the car sounded a promising contender. At £1,951, however, it was £258 more expensive than the open XK140 Jaguar, and not even Allard's avowed intention of tailoring each car to the customer's specification could re-establish the London firm in the sports-car market. Allard concentrated increasingly on double reduction drives for ambulance chassis, though the 'Palm Beach Mk. II' continued to be available till the end of the 1960 season, and a handful of these Jaguar-powered cars were constructed.

The year ended with the announcement that there was to be no Monte Carlo Rally in 1957. Down at Weybridge, Louis Giron worked out an economy conversion for Mk. VII which utilized the existing carburation arrangements plus a third S.U. of smaller choke diameter and a separate linkage. This took care of the fuel supply until a 'second pressure' was applied to the accelerator pedal, whereupon full power was once more made available. Gentle boot-craft could return 24–30 m.p.g. at cruising speeds of 45–55 m.p.h., while a staggering 35 m.p.g. could be attained at a steady 35 m.p.h. —all much more interesting than the alternatives of coasting, driving in one's stockinged feet, or laying up the Jaguar and buying one of the bubble-cars that were then enjoying a brief but widespread vogue.

In the Cotswolds and the South Midlands, however, 2·4-litre saloons with rather unusual grilles were seen going indecently fast, and the observant were asking themselves what would happen if Heynes were to put his 3·4-litre C-type engine into the standard 2·4-litre structure.

This question was soon to be answered, but not before a sudden disaster had imperilled the entire Jaguar concern.

CHAPTER 11

Jaguar Phoenix

1957-58

'We'll do the job all right—the fire makes it a little harder, that's all.'
Sir William Lyons, February 1957

'The latest of Jaguar's "sports sedans" should be the answer to those who objected to the massiveness and conservatism of the Marks VII and VIII, as well as those who complained of the lack of sizzle in the earlier 2.4.'
3.4-litre road test, Sports Car Illustrated, September 1957

'The American recession just does not exist as far as we are concerned.'
Jaguar press release, April 1958

THE works Jaguar team had gone from the circuits, but they had left a heritage behind, and the new models introduced early in 1957 reflected the result of seven years' experience with the twin-camshaft engines.

The season, however, began badly, with a disappointing performance by the *Ecurie Ecosse* cars in the Buenos Aires 1,000-Km. race. A Ferrari won, a Maserati was second, and a second Ferrari third, while Sanderson, sharing a D-type with Mieres, could manage no higher than fourth place. Already it was known that the Jaguar range would shortly be augmented by a new super-sports model, of which the first pictures were released in January 1957. But before production of this could start, disaster struck at Browns Lane. At about 5.45 on the evening of Tuesday, 12 February, fire broke out in the tyre stores and spread rapidly to the assembly lines. The extent of the damage was estimated at £3½ million, including a number of cars which were utterly destroyed, and at least two hundred more which were gutted. Bob Berry and a number of the other members of the Jaguar staff made several trips into the burning building, driving completed cars out, but were obliged to give up after one of the rescued machines was brought out with the head-lining alight. Sir William Lyons himself led the Chief of the Coventry Fire Brigade to a point where the fire could be arrested, and the moment the firemen had departed, bulldozers were rushed to Browns Lane, leaky roofs were patched, and the ruined portions of the factory sealed off by the erection of walls. The Queen sent a telegram of sympathy to Sir William.

In one respect, Jaguars were lucky. The damage was grave enough, but the blaze had started at the right end, and the wrecked buildings were concerned only with the assembly and test of cars, and not with their basic manufacture. Had the fire started in the machine and engine assembly shops, the whole future of the company would have been jeopardized, and production disrupted for so long that resumption would have been very difficult indeed. As it was, a new, shortened assembly line had to be set up, while for the time being a new home had to be found for the final testing and rectification departments. Here the Dunlop Rim and Wheel Co. came to the rescue, and Jaguars were allowed to overflow into a corner of their own old Foleshill works, which Dunlops now occupied. But with a quarter of their main building destroyed or damaged, they still had their hands full.

For the first week, the workers were on short time, everyone working three-day shifts, but a mere thirty-six hours after the fire, cars were again coming off the line, and ninety-three were actually produced in that first full working week. By the beginning of April, Jaguars were able to announce that they were back to normal; over 1,000 cars had been made since the fire, and of these 70% had been exported. Even more amazing was the fact that 1957 turned out to be a record year, the 12,952 cars delivered representing an increase of 800 on the best previous performance; in 1956. All the damaged cars were broken up for scrap—while this may seem a lamentable waste, it was an essential move, for untold harm could have been done to the company's reputation had the damaged parts been sold at a salvage sale and put on the market as new.

As the bulldozers took over to clear the site, Jaguars were launching their new model, the 3·4-litre. This was, in effect, a 2·4-litre hull with the bigger engine—not the standard type, but the B-type variant with high-lift camshafts, twin S.U. HD.6 carburetters, and a dual exhaust system. Output was 210 b.h.p. at 5,500 r.p.m. The main styling alterations were cut-away rear wheel spats and a larger radiator grille, but mechanical differences went beyond a mere change of engine, and included engine-bearers modified to take the extra weight of the bigger unit, stiffer suspension, and a larger radiator block. The three standard variations of transmission were again available, ratios of the standard car being 3·54, 4·54, 6·58, and 11·95 to 1, the wide gap between bottom and second being noticeable The ratio of the overdrive top gear was 2·93:1, using a 3·77:1 axle, and with Borg-Warner transmission, 'high' was 3·54:1, while the intermediate range offered a selection of ratios from 5·3:1 to 10·95:1. On the automatic model, also, the selector lever on the steering column was moved to the centre of the dashboard. The makers, for once, issued definite claims of performance, quoting a top speed of 120 m.p.h., a fuel consumption of 24–26 m.p.g., the ability to accelerate from a standstill to 60 m.p.h. through the gears

in 11·7 seconds, and a standing quarter-mile in 17·9 seconds. Nor were these claims exaggerated.

The Motor tested a car with automatic transmission, and *The Autocar* the model with overdrive. Both cars managed mean maxima of 120 m.p.h., and the overdrive-equipped machine would attain 119 m.p.h. in direct top gear as well, 97 m.p.h. coming up in third, and 57 m.p.h. in second. Thirty-six m.p.h. was the maximum in bottom gear, as might have been expected with the ratios available. With automatic transmission, the car would accelerate from a standing start to 60 m.p.h. in 11·2 seconds, manual being much quicker at 9·1 seconds, while this latter car reached 100 m.p.h. in a staggering 26 seconds—something which would have been unthinkable on a full four-seater touring saloon even five years previously. The automatic car was slower, but still very impressive,

Creator and masterpiece: Sir William Lyons with 4.2-litre E-type coupé.

taking 30·3 seconds to reach the 'ton'. It also failed—though only by one-tenth of a second—to match the makers' claims for the standing quarter-mile—to compensate for this, however, the car with overdrive comfortably exceeded the target. Neither car recorded an *overall* fuel consumption figure commensurate with the original claim, the automatic 3·4-litre being, surprisingly enough, the more frugal of the two at 19 m.p.g. but both could return 24 m.p.g. when driven at steady speeds of 60–70 m.p.h.

The Motor considered the new 'compact' from Coventry as more than a match for the souped-up versions of popular American cars then available—their manufacturers referred to the tuned engines, be it said, as 'power packs'. It was 'comparable in roominess, refinement and ease of driving with the latest and lowest American cars'. The intermediate hold in the automatic gearbox provided 80 m.p.h. if extra acceleration was required for overtaking. Cornering was a little untidy, but this criticism stemmed mainly from a tendency to treat the Jaguar as the sports car it was never intended to be. Habitual crash stops produced an annoying judder from the hydraulic brakes, too, but this latest design was recognized as a very fine all-rounder.

Alongside this was announced the sensational XK-SS super-sports model. This was in reality only a D-type equipped for road use; the characteristic dorsal fin had gone, and a hood, a full-width touring screen and side windows had been added, as well as touring silencers and instruments, a luggage grid, and, in deference to United States customers, vestigial bumpers. The idea was not new, for OKV 1, one of the first D-types, had ended its career, after successful service for the works team and for Duncan Hamilton, as a fast touring car in the hands of J. L. Goddard, and another 'road-equipped' D-type was to be seen in Bournemouth a year or two ago. Production of the XK-SS was not directly disrupted by the fire, as none were made for sale until afterwards, but indirectly its demise was due to the February disaster, in which body panels and jigs were lost. No price was quoted on the home market, but the XK-SS retailed in New York for the equivalent of £1,570. H. C. F. Haywood of *The Autocar* had a short run in one in May 1957, and found that with a 3·54:1 rear axle, 144, 109, 85 and 66 m.p.h. were available on the four forward ratios. This, added to the D-type's Dunlop disc brakes, added up to an exciting motor car, to put it mildly:

'On the open road, driving in comfort and without haste, 100 to 120 m.p.h. showed on the speedometer on each clear straight, and yet the braking power was such that the car nosed into successive bends at 60 to 70 m.p.h., without apparent braking effort after the bursts of speed.'

With 250 b.h.p. under the bonnet—the standard D-type's three Weber carburetters were used—acceleration was equally startling. To quote Haywood again:

'At about 4,000 r.p.m. the power comes in so hard that a driver or passenger not accustomed to the car feels that he is perhaps in some rocket-propelled sledge.'

... which, translated into cold statistics, signifies a standing quarter-mile in 14·3 seconds, 0–70 m.p.h. in 7·5 seconds, and 0–100 m.p.h. in 14·4 seconds (or the time taken by a Mk. VII to reach 60 m.p.h.), and 0–120 m.p.h. in 19·7 seconds! The penalty paid for all this was very limited legroom in the passenger seat, and a clutch appreciably fiercer than that of the average XK. Very few people had the chance to drive this car, let alone own one. The Duke of Edinburgh tried it at Lindley, but only sixteen were made, deliveries ending in September 1957. The last D-type left the works a few months earlier. Jaguar clients whose taste ran to 150 m.p.h. would have another four years to wait before they had anything to order, and even then they would be on a long waiting-list. Not that Jaguar's competitors, real or merely aspiring, were standing still. Mercedes-Benz, after withdrawing the 300SL from production for a while, re-introduced it with a roadster body in place of the original fixed-head coupé with gull-wing doors, and the Chevrolet Division of General Motors announced that it was training a special public-relations staff to make the customers 'Corvette-conscious'. The Ford 'Thunderbird', however, grew bigger and bigger, and had blossomed out into a gargantuan four-seater convertible by 1958.

The export drive continued, and Sir William Lyons went over to Brussels in May 1957, when the indefatigable Madame Bourgeois—now 'Madame Jaguar' to everyone—opened her new showrooms in Brussels, in the presence also of M. Van Acker, her country's Prime Minister. *Ecurie Nationale Belge*'s successful yellow D-type was on show, as was the factory's latest design, the XK150 coupé. This latter was introduced to the American public on the Press Test Day at Lime Rock, Connecticut, sponsored by the U.S. branch of the Society of Motor Manufacturers and Traders. The magazine *American Artist* presented Jaguar Cars Ltd. with their Medal of Honour 'for excellence', the first time that such an honour had been accorded to an industrial design.

Nineteen fifty-seven also saw the formation of the Jaguar Drivers' Club. The original S.S. Car Club had lapsed during the war, and had not been revived. The new organization, however, had no connections whatever with the past, and in the past four years has blossomed into an energetic and successful club, holding race meetings and rallies. It is also sympathetically disposed to the older cars, and its S.S. section has helped preserve survivors from the pre-Jaguar days.

William Boddy visited the works in June 1957 on behalf of *Motor Sport*, and was impressed by what he saw, not least of all by the astonishing recovery that had been made since the fire, though the quality of Jaguar workmanship also came in for a bouquet. Crankshafts were dynamically balanced, and engines did one-and-a-half to two hours' running at speeds up to 2,000 r.p.m., to ensure that they were properly run-in before installation. Production was running at seventy cars a day, or approximately 345 a week, 60% of which were saloons and the remainder XKs. At the time, Jaguar were machining crankshafts for outside firms—a tribute to the high standards of their precision work—but this activity has now been dropped, at Jaguars' own request. They are too busy on their own work! In addition, the company was entrusted with the task of producing 'Merlin' aero engines, which included complete tooling-up; over a hundred engines were built and tested before defence economies brought about the suspension of the project.

In May 1957 the revised range was rounded off when the XK140 gave way to the new XK150. Enthusiasts were disappointed to find that only coupé bodies were available, and that these had a bulbous look which detracted from their lines—though the wider bonnet certainly made routine maintenance easier. 190 b.h.p. or 210 h.p. engines were available, the latter being the 'Blue Top' version evolved for the 3·4-litre. Gear ratios were 3·54, 4·28, 6·2, and 10·55 to 1, a 4·09:1 direct top gear being used on overdrive versions. The usual three transmission options were available. Standard cars had disc wheels (hardly ever fitted) and 2LS Lockheed hydraulic brakes working in twelve-inch drums, but the 'special equipment' models, in addition to such usual improvements as wire wheels, twin exhausts, twin fog lamps and screenwashers, boasted a major departure in the form of Dunlop disc brakes, available for the first time on a touring Jaguar. These had been exhaustively tested, a pre-production XK150 being subjected to thirty consecutive stops from 100 m.p.h., with only a minute's pause between each. The cheapest model in this new series was the standard fixed-head coupé at £1,764, and the costliest the 'special equipment' drophead coupé with automatic transmission, at £2,161.

The racing season began with Sebring, where Cunningham ran a D-type with the engine bored out to 87 mm., giving a capacity of 3,781 cc. It was driven by Hawthorn and Bueb, and finished third behind the Fangio/Behra 4½-litre Maserati and the Moss/Menditeguy 3-litre of the same make. Henceforward, a number of variations on the original 3·4-litre Jaguar theme were to appear. These had been sparked off by the 2½-litre cars raced in the 1954 T.T., and in 1956, Jaguar's last official racing season, a 3-litre car had been run at Rouen. All these modified engines, incidentally, were the work of the factory, with the exception of a 3-litre engine evolved by 'boring and stroking' a 2·4-litre unit, which *Ecurie Ecosse* raced during 1960. The 3·8-litre engine was to be used in production cars from September 1958 onwards, powering the Mk. IX and Mk. II saloons, and the XK150S and E-type Grand Touring cars.

In April 1957, an exciting machine appeared for the first time in the British Empire Trophy Race at Oulton Park. This was the Lister-Jaguar, a product of Brian Lister's Cambridge engineering firm. For some years, Lister's competition cars, powered by M.G., Bristol, Maserati, and even Rover engines, had been a familiar sight on the circuits, and Archie Scott-Brown, the one-armed driver, had risen to fame by his spirited driving of the Lister-Bristol, giving the powerful Jaguars an excellent run for their money on occasions. For the next year, until his tragic death in May 1958, Scott-Brown, driving Lister's 'works' car with Jaguar engine, was to make a great impression on national racing. Lister used a twin-tube frame, and front suspension was by coil and equal-length wishbones. A De Dion rear axle featured in the specification, steering was Morris-type rack-and-pinion made in the Lister factory, and the brakes were Girling discs, the rear ones being mounted inboard. Engine specification varied from car to car, since Lister supplied only chassis

and body, and customers fitted their own engines. Some twenty were made in all, of which one or two cars shipped to America were powered by vee-eight Chevrolet units. The original engine in the Scott-Brown works car was tuned by Don Moore, and in its 3·8-litre form it gave around 300 b.h.p. on a 10:1 compression ratio. All other engines used in factory-sponsored cars were, however, prepared at Coventry by Jaguars.

Maurice Smith of *The Autocar*, who had a run in the original Lister-Jaguar in November 1957, compared its acceleration to that of the prototype Rover turbocar of 1950, and *Autosport* published some figures after a trial by John Bolster. A hundred and forty m.p.h. was obtainable with a 3·73:1 top gear, and with a higher-ratio back axle 200 m.p.h. was considered possible. As tested, the car would accelerate to 100 m.p.h. in 11·2 seconds, and to 120 m.p.h. in 15·2 seconds—by contrast, one of our modern 1-litre saloons takes over 15 seconds to reach 50 m.p.h. Bolster found the car quite docile, if a little too noisy for town work! During 1957, a few special Jaguar-powered cars were also built to the design of John Tojeiro, whose all-independently-sprung machines with M.G. engines had been raced successfully during the earlier 1950s. Tojeiro, of course, was responsible for the basic concept of the A.C. 'Ace' of 1954. The Lister-Jaguar sold at £2,750 complete—the Tojeiro car was £100 costlier.

Nineteen fifty-seven's Easter Goodwood Meeting saw the combination of Scott-Brown and Lister-Jaguar in splendid form, and he beat the new DBR.1 Aston Martins in the big sports car race. The *Autosport* race for series production sports cars was won by Sargent's XK120 from Maude's 300SL Mercedes-Benz—a creditable victory.

Ecurie Ecosse made their first big effort of the year in the Mille Miglia. This was to be the last real event to bear this name, for Portago's tragic accident at Mantua caused the Italian authorities to put an end to this, the last descendant of the 'town-to-town' races. Flockhart's D-type succumbed to fuel feed trouble after starting well up among the leaders, and the disc brakes of Richard Steed's Cooper-Jaguar became red-hot, forcing him to retire. At Spa, the Scottish cars met with no success either, though the D-types of Taylor and Rousselle finished third and fourth behind the works DBR.1 Aston Martins of Brooks and Salvadori. Aston Martin won at the Nurburgring again, beating the Ferraris, the Maserati vee-twelve, and the Jaguars of *Ecurie Ecosse*—these were never at their best on the curve-ridden German circuit, but Flockhart and Fairman finished seventh, the car 'running like clockwork'.

Le Mans reverted to its proper place in the calendar in 1957, being run again in June. The regulations specified the use of 92-octane fuel, and stipulated that 'a hood . . . shall effectively protect all the available seats', and that 'the windscreen shall have a minimum height of 15 cm. measured vertically', which engaging little rules produced some interesting and quite useless forms of weather protection and thus reduced maximum speeds, as was intended. Aston-Martin fielded two new 2·9-litre DBR1–300 models, and one example of the DBR2–370 3·7-litre type, the engine of which was later to be used in the DB.4 Grand Touring saloon. Maserati and Ferrari, however, had really gone to town. The former's cars, to be driven by Moss/Schell and Behra/Simon, were 4-litre vee-eights with four overhead camshafts, said to have 400 b.h.p. under the bonnet. The five-speed gearbox lived in the back axle, and, while Behra's car had a conventional open body, the Moss/Schell machine had bizarre aerodynamic coupé coachwork executed by Zagato to the ideas of Frank Costin. As if mistrustful of this monster, the Italian firm had also entered a 3-litre 'six' and a 2-litre 'four'. Ferrari's team-leader, Mike Hawthorn, had a scarcely less formidable machine in the shape of a 4-litre four o.h.c. vee-twelve, said to be good for 380 b.h.p. This was supported by a pair of 3·8-litre cars (Gendebien/Trintignant and Lewis-Evans/Severi).

Against this formidable array, five Jaguars were competing. Two of these were standard production cars, that driven by Lucas and 'Mary' wearing the blue of the French stable *Los Amigos*, and that of Frère and Rousselle the yellow of *Equipe Nationale Belge*. Of the remainder, two machines had 3·8-litre engines—Duncan Hamilton's own car, which he was sharing with Masten Gregory, and the *Ecurie Ecosse* entry assigned to Flockhart and Bueb. The second Scottish car was a 3·4-litre which Sanderson and Lawrence were to drive. All three British-entered Jaguars had the latest type of Dunlop disc brake with quickly replaceable pads, but fuel injection was used only on the two 3·8-litre machines. These bigger engines, incidentally, were not bored-out 3·4-litre units of the type used at Sebring earlier in the year, but were built up on new blocks evolved and supplied

by the factory. Full-width windscreens were, of course, worn and David Murray estimates that at least 10 m.p.h. was knocked off the maximum speed thereby. While Mike Hawthorn had been timed at 192 m.p.h. on the Mulsanne Straight in the 1956 race, the Scottish cars did not exceed 180 m.p.h. on the same stretch in 1957.

Five Jaguars started, and five Jaguars finished—*in first, second, third, fourth and sixth places*. Of the three Aston Martins, only Brooks made any impression, and he was unlucky enough to crash early on the morning of the second day, while still in second place. The Continental opposition disintegrated—almost literally. Within the first hour, the rear-axle gearbox of Moss's Maserati had given up the ghost, Simon crashed the open Maserati before Behra could even have a drive, and Hawthorn's Ferrari came to rest in a cloud of blue smoke. The Scarlatti/Bonnier 3-litre Maserati broke its transmission, eliminating the Orsi brothers' second line of defence, and by midnight the Gendebien/Trintignant 3·8-litre Ferrari had broken a piston. Flockhart and Bueb won for Coventry—and Scotland—at 113·85 m.p.h., Sanderson and Lawrence took second place at 111·16 m.p.h., and the French pair Lucas and 'Mary' were third at 110·17 m.p.h. Fourth place fell to Frère and Rousselle at 107·95 m.p.h., and Hamilton and Gregory were sixth. The Jaguar procession was broken only by the sole surviving Ferrari of Lewis-Evans and Severi, which averaged 104·38 m.p.h. to take fifth place,

Two generations from Browns Lane: a D-type with a 1966 4.2-litre E-type sports car.

The best of both worlds: an early E-type 3.8-litre sports car with the factory-built hardtop.

while Maranello also had the consolation of seeing one of their smaller cars—the 2-litre of Bianchi and Harris—come in seventh. As a British achievement, it was rivalled only by the 1-2-3-4 victory of the Bentleys in the 1929 race.

The late Ron Flockhart held that the D-type Jaguar had similar characteristics to the D-type E.R.A. on which he made his name. His recollections of the car in its 1957 form are most interesting:

'I found at Le Mans, particularly with the tail fin, that the faster it went the more stable the car became. It was my practice to relax completely down the Mulsanne Straight (race traffic permitting!), and flex my fingers and arms, the car steering itself at around 170 m.p.h. A good personal test of 'Chicken or Hero driver' was to take the slight right hand kink at the end of the Mulsanne Straight absolutely flat—no secret cheating by easing off a couple of hundred r.p.m., but an honest 5,800 r.p.m. on the 1957 3·8-litre. It could be done, but only just. If the track were damp, then this game was for Chicken drivers only. Both Ivor Bueb and I discovered this in our own fashion—something the spectators missed! However, in conditions of crosswind this was not possible, and I recall once at Goodwood one blustery day at practice where the Jaguar with tail fin was a handful through Fordwater and past the pits.'

Flockhart compared the 3·4-litre and 3·8-litre Jaguar engines to the 'Gipsy Major' and Rolls-Royce 'Merlin' aero-engines—it felt as if it would go on for ever. The 3-litre unit used later was, in his opinion, less reliable, especially above 6,000 r.p.m.

Anything would have been an anti-climax after this spectacular Jaguar success, but Archie Scott-Brown performed doughtily to win the sports-car race run in conjunction with the *Grand Prix de l'Europe* at Aintree on his Lister-Jaguar, and followed this up promptly with

two first places at Snetterton, and another at the August Bank Holiday meeting at Brands Hatch. At Aintree, Duncan Hamilton also finished third on his D-type. *Ecurie Ecosse*, however, were fully employed elsewhere.

Their alibi was not, as might have been expected, Rheims, for this Jaguar's paradise had succumbed to the prevailing trend, and the 12-Hour race was confined to Grand Touring Cars. In 1957, this type of machine as yet commanded relatively little interest, except from Enzo Ferrari, who had always built G.T. cars anyway. *The Motor* described Rheims as 'dull, processional, and poorly attended'. The only Jaguar entry was the XK140 coupé of Baillie and Jopp, and this was slower than the 1,300 cc Alfa-Romeo 'Giuliettas'. Scotland had, in fact, gone to Italy for that not-quite-credible event known to historians as 'Monzanapolis'.

The old-fashioned style of banked speedway had gone into a decline in the post-war years, in Europe, at any rate. Brooklands had been killed off, and Montlhéry, though very much alive, was regarded mainly as a testing-ground and as a venue for long-distance record attempts. Berlin's Avus track had never been popular with drivers, and anyway access to Berlin was difficult. Monza had fared perhaps better than its rivals, for it still saw the annual Motorcycle Grand Prix of the Nations. But where cars were concerned, it now catered, as did Montlhéry, for the smaller type of event and for records and tests of new machinery. A rebuilding programme had, however, been put in hand in 1955, and for 1957 the track's controller decided to organize a 500-mile 'Cup of Two Worlds' over the very fast, banked 'Speed Circuit'.

This idea had met with very little approval. The makers of

Formula I cars had elected not to support it. The professional drivers' union had not only declined support, but had ordered its members to boycott it. The entry was therefore made up of a collection of machinery from America, of the type run in the annual Indianapolis 500-Mile Race, which, be it said, was recognized as a World Championship event, though none of the cars which usually took part would have stood a hope of any normal Formula I event. The opposition was furnished by three *Ecurie Ecosse* Jaguars, a sporting gesture by David Murray.

The American cars, though they bore strange names such as 'John Zink Special' and 'Mirror Glaze Special', nearly all used the same engine, the 4·2-litre four-cylinder twin o.h.c. Meyer-Drake, the genesis of which went back to Harry Miller's late-Vintage Indianapolis power units. Two-speed gearboxes were universal, as was fuel-injection. The Jaguars came straight from Le Mans, and ran in standard trim, Fairman driving the 3·8-litre car, and Sanderson and Lawrence the two 3·4-litre machines. The only modification carried out concerned the air scoops, which were altered to cool the tyres instead of the brakes. They were, of course, outclassed, as naturally they would be. Murray sportingly ran them high on the

track, to prevent them obstructing the faster American cars. But they astonished the visitors from Indianapolis. Though Jimmy Bryan on the Dean Van Lines Special came home to win at 160·1 m.p.h., the Jaguars circulated quietly round to take fourth, fifth and sixth places, Fairman leading Lawrence and Sanderson. The former, on the Le Mans-winning car, put in a qualifying lap at 152 m.p.h., and a wealthy American sponsor was heard to mutter plaintively: 'Hell, my car cost $40,000; those things I can buy around $7,000, I guess, and they are darn nearly as fast as mine.'

The 3·8-litre car was stripped down on its return to Edinburgh, and no noticeable wear was found in the engine, despite the completion of 5,000 racing miles—the equivalent of 30,000 miles on the road; this in spite of the fact that maintenance between Le Mans and 'Monzanapolis' had been confined to a very hasty decoke.

Ecurie Ecosse achieved nothing in the Swedish Sports Car Race, and no better than eighth at Spa, though Naylor on another D-type took fifth place. In September, the indefatigable Mrs Anderson made the best performance by a British car in the Mobilgas Round Australia Rally, finishing seventh on a Mk. VIII saloon. The end of the season saw further Jaguar successes at Silverstone, Goodwood and Snetterton. At Silverstone, Hawthorn won the production touring-car race at an average speed of 82·19 m.p.h. with his 3·4-litre saloon. Salvadori won the big sports-car race for Aston Martin, but Scott-Brown's Lister-Jaguar was second, tying with Salvadori for fastest lap. This performance he promptly followed up by a victory in the Goodwood Trophy Race from the Tojeiro-Jaguars of Brabham and Taylor. Finally, at Snetterton, Bekaert's C-type was second in a three-hour night race, counting towards the *Autosport* championship, behind Rudd's A.C.-Bristol.

It had also been quite a good year for Norman Buckley, despite some trouble with 'Miss Windermere III' during the 'Championship of the World' races at Lugano. At home, however, in July 1957, he raised the World's Speed Record for 1,200-kg. boats over the straight kilometre to 113·57 m.p.h.

The main improvement in the 1958 Jaguar range was the introduction of disc brakes as an optional extra on the 2·4-litre and 3·4-litre saloons. These were of the Dunlop type as used on the XK150, and cost £36 15s. a set. Wire wheels added a further £52 10s. to the price. Mk. VIII was continued unchanged, and the 2·4-litre was now available with automatic transmission as well as with the standard manual and overdrive gearboxes. Allards introduced an attractive Jaguar-engined 'Gran Turismo' coupé to supplement their 'Palm Beach II'—it had a De Dion rear axle, in the manner of earlier sporting Allards, but at £2,551 it was a lot more expensive than the XK150 with full *de luxe* equipment, and 1957 was to be the last Earls Court Show at which the London firm showed cars.

In March 1958, Jaguars at last produced an open version of the XK150. This was initially 'for export only', and was made to three basic specifications; the 'standard' model with 190 b.h.p. engine, twin carburetters, and drum brakes; the 'special' model, with the 210 b.h.p. 'Blue Top' engine, twin carburetters, twin exhausts, and disc brakes; and the new XK150S, which had the 'Gold Top' engine, three S.U. HD.8 carburetters, twin exhausts, and disc brakes. This

last-mentioned unit incorporated a Weslake-designed and patented straight-port head, and developed 250 b.h.p. at 5,500 r.p.m. Disc wheels were still standard equipment on the cheapest model, but almost all customers specified the wire type, irrespective of other requirements. Buyers of 'standard' and 'special' models had the choice of the three standard transmissions, but the S-type came with a four-speed manual gearbox and overdrive only, ratios being 3·19, 4·09, 4·95, 7·16 and 12·2 to 1. Prices for the 'special' series started at $4,495, and the S-type roadster listed at $5,090. No sterling prices were quoted.

Nineteen fifty-eight racing regulations imposed a limit of 3-litres' capacity, and Jaguars fitted the *Ecurie Ecosse* cars with a new unit of 83 × 92 mm. (2,986 cc). The factory quoted an output of 254 b.h.p., and it would rev. up to 7,000 r.p.m. Brian Lister came out with a revised car with more aerodynamic bodywork and larger Girling disc brakes, two of these being ordered by Briggs Cunningham. Three-litre engines were of course used, and Halford and Bueb were retained to drive the works entries. Scott-Brown, who had gone to New Zealand for the Dominion's racing season, won the Lady Wigram Trophy at Christchurch—the first occasion on which that event had been won by a sports car.

Sir William Lyons was, as usual, cautious in his annual report for 1958, despite a record profit and record sales. He reminded the shareholders that there was always the danger of rising costs; on the credit side, however, sales to the U.S.A. had risen by 6%, and this was especially creditable, 'having regard to the fact that the models which sell more readily in that country suffered most in the fire'—by which, we may take it, he meant the 3·4-litre saloon, regarded by the American monthly *Sports Cars Illustrated* as an excellent compromise between the rather ponderous Mk. VIII and the 'underpowered' 2·4-litre. (By any other standards, of course, the smallest Jaguar had plenty of power, but 112 b.h.p. sounded pretty small beer to an American at a time when even the lowest-powered American cars such as six-cylinder Chevrolets advertised 140 b.h.p.) Nineteen fifty-eight also saw the opening of a new central Jaguar spares depot in the U.S.A., and most American Jaguar dealers now carried a stock of parts to the value of $60,000. The United States might be passing through one of its periodic trade recessions, but at the New York Importers' Show in April, Mk. VIII and the 3·4-litre had doubled their sales, and XK150 roadsters were selling at the rate of one an hour. It was noted with interest that only three out of six hundred recent customers had asked for 'time payments'.

Deliveries shot up from 12,952 in 1957 to 17,552 in 1958. Disc brakes were now specified on 95% of the 2·4-litre and 3·4-litre cars ordered, *The Autocar* commenting, when it tested the latter that June, that it would be 'a false economy to specify one without'. World exports were up 42% in the first eight months of the year, and American exports rose by 27%. In July, Reutter adjustable front seats became optional on the Mk. VIII at an additional cost of £42 10s., and Sir William Lyons presented a 2·4-litre saloon as a prize in a competition intended to raise £13,000 for the Motor Trades Benevolent Fund.

The Autocar tested an XK150 'special equipment' fixed-head

A masterpiece of stretching: the E-type 2 plus 2 as introduced at the 1966 Geneva Show had lost none of the elegance of its two-passenger forebear, and was the first of the series to be offered with the option of Borg-Warner automatic transmission.

coupé in February 1958. This had the 210 b.h.p. engine, wire wheels, disc brakes, and the optional overdrive, and cost £2,008 in this form. It recorded 123·7 m.p.h. in overdrive, 114 m.p.h. in direct top, and 91 m.p.h. on third gear. 0–30 m.p.h. acceleration was the best so far achieved by any Jaguar subjected to the weekly press' full test routine, the C-type included, at 2·8 seconds; and the car could reach 60 m.p.h. in 8·5 seconds and 100 m.p.h. in 25·1 seconds—rather slower than the C-type, and appreciably slower than the XK-SS. Fuel consumption was a moderate 20·5 m.p.g., and the testers considered it 'undeniably one of the world's fastest and safest cars', as well they might. The suspension was free from roll and pitch, and no fault could be found with the disc brakes, these being fade-free, light in normal operation, progressive in action, and capable of pulling the car up square from high speeds without judder or shake. The handbrake, now operated, as on all disc-braked-Jaguars ever made, *via* additional pads on the rear-wheel discs, was by no means as satisfactory, though, but speeds of 100 m.p.h. were possible at night with the aid of the long-range-beam headlamps. It is indicative of the changes which the XK series had wrought in the concept of the sports car that the quite generous luggage space was no longer considered adequate, while the gearbox rated only qualified approval. The ratios, apart from the wide gap between bottom and second, were admirable, and it was conceded that 'the movement between the ratios is sweet'; Jaguar's box, however, continued to please the customers if it sometimes worried the critics.

Nineteen fifty-eight was a mixed year for Jaguar in rallies. Thirty examples of the *marque* ran in the 'Monte', but none of them finished higher than twenty-fourth place. By contrast, they won the two biggest 'series production' classes in the R.A.C. event—gone were the days of the simple division between 'open' and 'closed' cars. Waddilove (2·4-litre) and Brinkman (3·4-litre) were the successful competitors. The Tulip Rally was a disappointment for the British contingent, but Morley's 2·4-litre was the best British car, taking eighth place and winning its class, while Jaguar were again successful in the big-car classes of the Scottish event. Sir Gawaine Baillie's 3·4-litre saloon finished third in the touring-car class of the *Tour de France*.

Saloon-car races became very popular in 1958, and with them came a further crop of Jaguar victories. The lighter 3·4-litre lent itself far better to this kind of sport than had the big Mk. VIIs, and the events were taken more seriously than hitherto, even acquiring their own annual championship which, be it said, was to be won in 1960 by Jack Sears on T. E. B. Sopwith's Jaguar. No longer did one encounter the motley assortment of vehicles that used to be seen at Goodwood a few years previously. The Lincoln-Zephyrs and similar machinery had been relegated to stock-car racing, and really heavy metal such as the vee-twelve Lagonda was now regarded as too rare and precious for mere 'circuit-bashing'.

At Aintree in April, Sir Gawaine Baillie and Ron Flockhart, both on 3·4-litres, headed the unlimited class, and Blond's 2·4-litre won the 2,600 cc class. Hawthorn was victorious at Silverstone's *Daily Express* meeting in May, averaging 84·22 m.p.h. with his 3·4-litre, and at Brands Hatch in June, T. E. B. Sopwith won his race. His average speed of 63·3 m.p.h. reflects the tortuous nature of the circuit in its original form, but compares quite favourably with the 74·93 m.p.h. lap of a Formula II Cooper at the same meeting. At Silverstone in July, another saloon race was staged on the same day as the British Grand Prix, and this time the laurels went to the American, Walter Hansgen, on a Jaguar, of course. This sport was popular in Australia, and the event staged at Melbourne's Albert Park meeting in November was won by David McKay on a 3·4-litre car, though the fastest practice lap was made by a Holden, presumably tuned. While some of their drivers ran in Production Touring Car events, *Ecurie Ecosse* as a team never supported them. It is of interest to note

An E-type in action at Spa.

that T. E. B. Sopwith, at any rate, favoured the standard manual gearbox, overdrive being used only at Snetterton.

The racing season was marred by the death of Archie Scott-Brown at Spa in May. In little more than twelve months, he had swept to fame with his Lister-Jaguar—in 1957 he had entered fourteen races, won eleven of them, and finished second in another, and in 1958 he won five races, three of them in New Zealand. He also fought a spirited duel with Stirling Moss's Aston Martin at the Goodwood Easter Meeting, before retiring, and finished third behind the works Aston Martins of Moss and Brooks in the British Empire Trophy Race, averaging 85·39 m.p.h. to the winner's 87·45 m.p.h. The whole racing world was shocked by Archie's death. He was a man who had succeeded against odds that would have deterred almost anyone else.

Ecurie Ecosse again fielded three D-types, driven by Gregory/Flockhart, Fairman/Lawrence and Bueb/Sanderson, at the Nurburgring that May, but they were no match for the 3-litre works Aston-Martins and the twelve-cylinder 'Testa Rossa' Ferraris, though only half a minute slower on their practice laps. The Fairman/Lawrence car, however, finished seventh.

At Le Mans in 1958, of course, both the Scottish *équipe* and Duncan Hamilton used the 3-litre engine, with normal Weber carburetters. A 10:1 compression ratio was made possible, as the organizers specified a fuel of 95–100 octane in place of the 92 octane used in 1957. With 50 b.h.p. less available from the engines, though, speed was down, and David Murray estimates the top speed of these cars to have been 160 m.p.h. The D-type's well-known reliability and controllability in the wet augured well for an *Ecurie Ecosse* hat-trick, but it was not to be, both the Sanderson/Lawrence and Fairman/Gregory cars going out early on with piston failure. This left Hamilton, who was in the lead at the eight-hour mark—regrettably, he inverted his car in a cloudburst at Arnage while trying to avoid a small Panhard. A Ferrari won.

The Jaguars were inevitably outclassed again at 'Monzanapolis', though this year David Murray and Brian Lister collaborated to evolve a 3·8-litre *monoposto* car for Jack Fairman to drive. The engine was offset to the left in the Lister-built frame, while *Ecurie Ecosse* was responsible for the body. Dunlop disc wheels and Dunlop outboard disc brakes were used at the front. Rear suspension was by De Dion axle, but the rear wheels were wire, and the rear disc brakes mounted inboard. Dunlops produced special racing tyres for this machine, and 200 m.p.h. was spoken of. Unfortunately, despite the lower frontal area, it turned out to be no faster than the standard D-types, as the size of front wheel fitted was out of proportion to the size of the car.

Despite rumours of possible Russian participation, the Americans again made the running at Monza, and Bueb had to be content with ninth place on the 3·4-litre D-type. Fairman, in spite of breaking a camshaft at the end of his heat, took eleventh place, and Masten Gregory's D-type with 3·8-litre engine was twelfth. The single-seater was later converted into a sports two-seater for Gregory, who subsequently crashed it.

Stirling Moss drove a Lister-Jaguar in the sports-car event that featured in the programme of the British Grand Prix meeting at Silverstone in July, and won, averaging 97·98 m.p.h. Bueb's Tojeiro-Jaguar was fourth, but the highest-placed D-type was only ninth, the driver being a comparatively unknown young man by the name of Innes Ireland. It is noticeable that nearly all the younger generation of British drivers have cut their teeth on Jaguars. *Ecurie Ecosse* used a Lister-Jaguar and a Tojeiro-Jaguar in the T.T., but neither distinguished itself. September, however, saw Ivor Bueb win the Scott-Brown Memorial Trophy at Brands Hatch, appositely enough on a Lister-Jaguar. At the Brighton Speed Trials too, G. Tyrer lowered the sports-car record to 25·11 seconds with his C-type,

Graham Hill on a lightweight competition E-type, winning his race at the International Trophy Meeting, Silverstone, May, 1963.

and in November the Australians held a race for big sports cars at Albert Park, Melbourne. As we have seen, the saloon-car event on the same day saw a Jaguar victory, and Pitt's D-type was third in the main race behind Whiteford's 300S Maserati and Phillips's Cooper-Jaguar. Walter Hansgen was acclaimed America's sports-car champion in his class for the second year in succession, but changing times were reflected by the fact that in 1958 he used a Lister-Jaguar, whereas his 1957 mount was a D-type. *Ecurie Ecosse* put their D-types up for sale, though one was retained, running at Le Mans in 1959 and again in 1960.

Norman Buckley took the one-hour World's Record for 800-kg. boats from Von Mayenburg, with a speed of 89·08 m.p.h. He was now using a D-type engine with 9·6:1 compression ratio.

Nineteen fifty-eight saw also two of the most welcome additions to my Museum at Beaulieu—one of the first D-types of 1954, and a 1931 Austin Seven Swallow saloon, both loaned by Jaguars. They were driven in under their own power, Bob Berry bringing the D-type. At last the D-type, though by no means a museum piece, was showing signs of age, after five years of racing, three wins at Le Mans, two second places and two thirds. The lessons learnt from this model were still, however, being put into practice. The 1958 Earls Court Show saw the arrival of Mk. IX, a development of Mk. VIII. Jaguars now offered a model in each group—sports car, fast touring saloon, and executive carriage, all with disc brakes on all four wheels.

The Cunningham/Salvadori E-type which finished fourth at Le Mans in 1962, at a speed that would have been more than sufficient for an outright win six years before.

CHAPTER 12

'A Special Kind of Motoring . . .'

1959–61

'*In the Mk. IX, the ticking of the clock made the interior seem all the more like a luxurious smoking room.*'

Ronald Barker, *The Autocar*, October 1958

'*Nimble as a kitten in town traffic, the highway is the true domain of the SP.250. To feel its eager response as it opens up is to know a new motoring adventure.*'

Daimler catalogue, 1959

THOSE who went to Earls Court in 1958 expecting to see a brand-new sports model on the Jaguar stand were doomed to disappointment. Aston Martin had their 3·7-litre DB.4 Gran Turismo saloon, but Jaguar's contribution was executive transport *par excellence*. It was, however, technically important, for this new Mk. IX was the first touring car from Browns Lane to offer disc braking as standard equipment. It also introduced power-assisted steering to the Jaguar range, while it was the first of their saloon models to use the 3·8-litre engine—a capacity used for racing in 1957 and 1958.

In the Mk. IX this power unit developed 220 b.h.p. at 5,500 r.p.m. on an 8:1 compression, though a 7:1 ratio was available for use in those countries where only low-octane fuels could be obtained. The braking system incorporated a vacuum reservoir as an insurance in the event of the engine's stalling, while power for the steering derived from a Hobourn-Eaton pump driven off the rear end of the generator. This extra assistance, incidentally, commended itself to the more sporting driver, for it enabled the steering to be geared up to a mere three-and-a-half turns from lock to lock, an appreciable improvement not only on Mk. VIII, but also on the original 3·4-litre, which demanded four-and-a-third turns, or rather more than is appreciated by the average rally competitor. Maintenance on Mk. IX was also simplified, the nineteen greasing points on the chassis requiring attention only at intervals of 2,500 miles. Transmission options were as usual, and the car sold at £1,995 with manual gearbox, £2,063 with overdrive, and at £2,163 if automatic transmission was specified.

The Motor tried one of the latter in September 1958. Surprisingly enough, it turned the scales at some 30 lbs. lighter than the 1957 model Mk. VIII, while the use of the bigger engine not only boosted maximum speed to 113·5 m.p.h. but also rendered cruising speeds of 100 m.p.h. well within the car's compass. Acceleration figures were likewise impressive, for the Mk. IX would attain 30 m.p.h. in four seconds, 60 m.p.h. in eleven seconds, and 100 m.p.h. in 32·5 seconds. Not so pleasing was an overall thirst of 13·5 m.p.g.—*The Autocar*, incidentally, tried the same example and recorded 1 m.p.g. more!—but the testers were prepared to forgive this, as they asked:

'What other model or make, of any nationality, or at any price, combines space for six passengers, a really large luggage locker, automatic transmission, power steering, disc brakes to all four wheels, the ability to reach 90 m.p.h. from rest in considerably less than half a minute, and the power to cover a mile in less than thirty-one seconds?'

No other 1959 model tested by *The Motor* was to incorporate all these features, and this reflects Lyons' skill as a compromiser. Jaguars had their failings. Time and time again, the Jaguar gearbox was slated as slow by the critics, but the vast majority of Jaguars were no longer sports cars, nor were their owners sports-car drivers—they used Jaguars because they were fast, smooth, durable, and superbly finished, not to mention the fact that they undersold all their competitors by a good 50%. Jaguar steering, especially on the saloons, inclined towards the low-geared, but this ensured that even the biggest Mk. VII and Mk. VIII models could be driven comfortably by a woman. A girl enthusiast of my acquaintance was lent a Continental Post-Vintage Thoroughbred with impeccable manners and an illustrious competition background. She described it as 'hard work in town', and was thankful to return to her everyday Mk. V! And Sir William had not forgotten that his very first cars—the Austin Seven Swallows of 1927—had appealed especially to the fair sex. However, the more critical customer can rest assured that his plaints are not taken lightly, for up to his retirement in 1972 he was apt to telephone down to the despatch bay with the instruction that: 'I want a 4.2 automatic XJ to take home tonight.' Thus did Sir William himself ensure that the finished product does not carry compromise beyond the limits of acceptability.

Late in 1958, I replaced my Mk. VIII with a 3·4-litre automatic saloon—needless to say, I specified disc brakes. I took this step partly because the Mk. VIII occupied more parking space than was generally available outside either my London office or my flat, and partly as a result of Mike Hawthorn's persuasions. During the 1958 season he had been running his own car, VDU 881, in saloon-car events, and this he had modified to give rather more brake horse-power—around 225. Pressure of work prevented me from returning my car to Mike to have it similarly tuned, but in the end we arranged that he was to have it early in January 1959—the work would be carried out while I was crewing for Robert Glenton in his Ford 'Zephyr' in the Monte Carlo Rally. When I arrived at Monte Carlo, I was appalled to hear of Mike's tragic death on the Guildford by-pass. The journey back to Farnham to collect the Jaguar was a poignant one—I felt, as I know everyone else did, that motoring would never be the same without him.

I ran my 3·4-litre some 20,000 miles in the next twenty months, including two continental trips. In deference to the ground clearance, I did not take it on my honeymoon to Greece, as I felt that this was an occasion on which I might be excused road-making! After the Mk. VIII, it felt a real sports car, and I agree with Mike Hawthorn and Duncan Hamilton that one 'could really throw it about'. The disc brakes never gave me a moment's trouble, and the 120 m.p.h. came up easily wherever road conditions permitted. When really pressed she was rather an oil-burner, but my only other criticism concerned a feeling of directional instability at high speeds. The car seldom did anything frightening, but I often had the feeling that it might, and certainly it was much stabler with a full complement of passengers. The fitting of Dunlop 'Durabands' in the spring of 1959 did a great deal to improve road adhesion. I never owned the manual gearbox version, though I drove one, and formed the impression that very little was lost by leaving the normal selection of ratios to the Borg-Warner device. The box on this overdrive car seemed very much slower than on other Jaguars I have driven, though this may well have been the fault of an individual machine. More probably it was only slow in relation to the car's fantastic acceleration. In spite of these minor failings, the 3·4-litre fully deserved its tremendous success, which is reflected in some statistics for 1958—17,552 cars delivered, and a profit of £1,487,981 on the financial year, or an increase of nearly £900,000 on 1957. This was, of course, the first year in which Jaguar profits soared over the million-pound mark. 17,335 of the original model 3·4-litre saloons were made between early 1957 and 1960, when production was tapered off in favour of the improved Mk. II type. In the circumstances, it is not surprising that Jaguar shares rose ten shillings to 55s. in twenty-four hours in February 1959, in anticipation of an increase in annual profit.

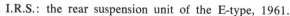

I.R.S.: the rear suspension unit of the E-type, 1961.

In March 1959, the Institution of Mechanical Engineers awarded its James Clayton Prize to W. M. Heynes, and during the next two seasons more and more eminent people bought Jaguars. When President de Gaulle of France paid a state visit to Canada in the spring of 1960, the official cars used in the 'motorcade' were not the usual Cadillacs or Lincolns, but Mk. IX Jaguars, and also during that year the Nigerian Government ordered forty cars of this type, cellulosed in the national colours of green and white, for official use. Not that the *marque* was unknown to West Africans—indeed it had all but succeeded the Cadillac as a success-symbol.

No fewer than thirty 2·4-litre saloons had been sold to private customers in Nigeria during 1957, and in modern pidgin the word 'Jagwah' denotes a smart man-about-town. A Swedish enthusiast carried this principle even further by entering in rallies under the *nom-de-guerre* of 'Jag', but honesty compels me to record that his usual mount was a Volvo. The Jaguar sign appeared on a public house in 1960, when the Jaguar dealers at Stourbridge, Worcestershire, took over a hostelry and renamed it 'The Jaguar Inn'.

Brian Lister produced a revised Lister-Jaguar for the 1959 season, retaining Bruce Halford and Ivor Bueb to drive for him. A new low-drag body was used, and the 3-litre engine was standardized to conform with the international regulations. Rumours even spoke of a works 'E-type' for the Sebring Twelve-Hour Race, but this did not materialize, and the Coventry *marque*'s representation in Florida was confined to a Cunningham-prepared 1959 Lister-Jaguar, entered by Listers themselves for Moss and Bueb to drive, and two 1958 cars (Thompson/Hansgen/Boss and Cunningham/Furno/Underwood). The former was tried in practice with Momo-Raybestos water-cooled brakes, but these gave trouble and were not used in the race. The engines used in these Cunningham entries were not the 3-litre type as raced in 1958, but a new 'bored and stroked' 2·4-litre evolved by Jaguars. None of the cars finished, the 1958 models retiring and Moss incurring disqualification for an alleged infringement of the refuelling rules. He ran out of petrol on the course and borrowed a motor-cycle to return to the pits. A capacity limit of 3 litres effectively eliminated Jaguars from the Gran Turismo class.

Bueb's Lister-Jaguar finished third in the race for big sports cars run in conjunction with the International Trophy at Silverstone in May, but 1959 was not a good year at Le Mans for Jaguar. Two Lister-Jaguars, a Tojeiro-Jaguar and a D-type started, but none of these finished. Broken connecting-rods accounted for Bueb and Halford's Lister-Jaguar, which went out while lying fourth, the Hansgen/Blond Lister-Jaguar succumbing to this failing also, as did Gregory and Ireland on the D-type, which was in second place at 10 p.m. The *Ecurie Ecosse* Tojeiro-Jaguar hung on till 3 a.m., when a warped cylinder head forced its withdrawal.

Saloon-car racing, however, proved more fruitful, and the 3·4-litre model proved almost unbeatable. At the Easter Goodwood meeting the victor was Ivor Bueb, who had a good day, winning the Sussex Trophy Race as well on a Lister-Jaguar from Blond on a

Big car with unitary construction: from the front Mk.X gives no evidence of a length of 202 inches or a weight of 3,930 pounds.

similar car. He followed this up by another saloon-car win at Aintree in April, and the event which featured in the programme of Silverstone's International Trophy meeting in May brought forth that overworked *cliché*, 'a Jaguar benefit', the 3·4-litre saloons of Bueb, Salvadori and Baillie finishing in that order. Bueb, as we have seen, was placed in a sports-car race that day as well, but his 3·4-litre had to give best in the Gran Turismo event to Stirling Moss's DB.4 Aston Martin, a car costing more than twice as much as the Jaguar.

Jaguars also made their mark on the rallies of 1959. Though they were unlucky in the 'Alpine', Parkes and Howarth finished eighth at Monte Carlo, while Morley spearheaded a British victory in the Tulip Rally, his 3·4-litre Jaguar taking first place in general classification in front of a Triumph and a Dagenham Ford.

In March 1959 the XK150S became available on the home market, though at first only the coupés were offered; prices were £2,187 for the fixed-head model and £2,217 for the drophead. *The Motor* tried an example of the former that August—it had, of course, the Weslake straight-port head, three S.U. HD.8 carburetters, and a new optional modification in the form of a Powr-Lok limited-slip differential. The testers found that it was the fastest closed car their journal had ever tested—at 132 m.p.h. it was only 12 m.p.h. slower than the overtly racing C-type tried in 1952, speeds on the other gears being 113 m.p.h. in direct top, 86 m.p.h. in third (or no faster than could be obtained by the intermediate 'hold' on an automatic box), and 59 m.p.h. in second. Speed, however, was not everything, and the XK150S matched it with remarkable acceleration, 30 m.p.h. being attainable in 2·9 seconds, 100 m.p.h. in 20·3 seconds and 120 m.p.h. in 36·2 seconds, while the time taken for the standing quarter-mile—16·2 seconds—actually equalled the figure obtained for the old C-type! Dunlop 'Roadspeed' R.S.4 tyres were fitted, and with them cornering was 'excellent, though not perhaps so tidy as one or two quite exceptional sports cars'.

No temperament was manifested by this Jaguar, but it did require 100-octane fuel, while starting from cold was rendered easy by the automatic choke, a legacy from the original pushrod 3½-litre of 1938. The gear-change, in *The Motor*'s opinion, afforded room for improvement. Overall fuel consumption was 18·5 m.p.g., but cruising at a sustained 70 m.p.h. would return a frugal 25·5 m.p.g. The new limited-slip differential eliminated wheelspin, though axle patter could still be induced if the car were cornered on the limit. This acclaim from the technical press was to be echoed nearly two years later by the old brigade, for, writing in *Motor Sport*, no less a personage than Cecil Clutton, former President of The Vintage Sports Car Club, described his standard XK150 as 'a really splendid car . . . and one which is giving me the utmost satisfaction and enjoyment', though he did confess to a dislike for Jaguar's standard shock-absorbers.

For 1960, Jaguar came out with the Mk. II saloon, a redesigned version of the unit-construction 2·4-litre and 3·4-litre cars. Many points that had come in for criticism on the earlier models were eliminated—the front suspension was modified to give a higher roll centre, and the track widened by 3¼in. at the rear. Disc brakes were also standardized. The original body structure had suffered from blind rear quarters, and rearward vision was vastly improved by the new wrap-around window at the back. The whole instrument panel was redesigned; the speedometer and rev. counter were positioned directly in front of the driver, the switches (now including a brake level fluid warning light) were transferred to a central panel, and the selector lever on automatic-transmission models returned to the steering-column. The odds and ends—radio and heater controls—were moved out of harm's way on to a console underneath the centre of the dash, and the ashtray, another irritating space-waster, was moved to the top of the transmission tunnel. Fog lamps were standard on cars for the home market, but wire wheels, radio and whitewall tyres remained optional extras. Ten exterior colours were standardized. Engines available were an improved 2·4-litre

Mk.X's successor, the 420G saloon of 1967. At a basic price of £2,238 on the home market, it is still highly competitive.

with B-type head giving 120 b.h.p. at 5,750 r.p.m., the 210 b.h.p. 3·4-litre as used in the previous model, and the 220 b.h.p. 3·8-litre unit already standardized for Mk. IX. Cars with the last-mentioned engine had a limited-slip differential as standard.

Though Mk. VIII was no longer offered, the Jaguar buyer could select his car from an impressive variety of models, which was reaching such complexity that the manufacturers put out a colour folder entitled *Choosing a Jaguar*. To begin with, there were the existing 2·4-litre and 3·4-litre saloons unchanged from 1959, with drum brakes as standard equipment, though disc brakes, wire wheels, overdrive and Borg-Warner automatic transmission were available as optional equipment. There was Mk. IX, with the choice of three transmissions. Then there was the XK150, available in standard and 'special equipment' forms with 3·4-litre engine and with special equipment and the 3·8-litre engine, and the XK150S, available with the overdrive transmission only, but with the choice of 3·4-litre or 3·8-litre engines. There were, of course, still the three standard body styles on this chassis—the roadster, the fixed-head coupé and the drophead coupé.

Nonetheless, some people felt that Jaguars had lost their way. They did not deny the truth of the Jaguar slogan, 'A Special Kind of Motoring, that no other car in the world can offer', but they felt that this 'special kind of motoring' was aimed at V.I.P.s, executives, and ordinary motorists of discrimination. Jaguars, they argued, were drifting away from their own public towards the Rover, Armstrong-Siddeley and Daimler *clientèle*. *The Veteran and Vintage Magazine* voiced their misgivings in its report upon the 1959 Show:

'Black marks to Jaguar—not for the cars they display, which, as ever, represent astonishing value and performance for money, but for the sports cars they didn't see fit to display. All the saloons were in dreadfully executive shades, too.'

It is unlikely that such people were much comforted by *The Autocar*'s eminently favourable report on a 3·8-litre Mk. II saloon tested in February 1960. The car's town-carriage manners and luxurious family appointments were mated to a Gran Turismo performance accentuated by the combination of a manual gearbox with overdrive. This dual personality was reflected in a willingness to run up to 6,000 r.p.m. in the indirect gears, and yet cruise happily and silently in overdrive top at 100 m.p.h. 125 m.p.h. was available if required, thanks to a ratio of 2·93:1. The 3·77:1 direct top gear gave 120 m.p.h., third was 4·84:1, giving 98 m.p.h., and 64 m.p.h.

Camouflaged prototype: careful 'uglification' cannot, however, really conceal the identity of this Mk.X on test in France. One wonders what the crew of the Berliet truck in the background thought.

could be attained on the 7·01:1 second. Bottom was, as usual, very low at 12·73:1, hence only 35 m.p.h. was possible in this ratio. Acceleration was well up to Jaguar standards, and the car reached 60 m.p.h. in only 8·5 seconds; it is a sobering thought to realize that this elegant carriage, weighing very nearly 33 cwt., was over 25 m.p.h. faster than the stark 3½-litre '100' of 1938, and took five seconds less to accelerate to 60 m.p.h., while 100 m.p.h., or fractionally more than the '100''s two-way maximum as tested, took only 25·1 seconds to attain. The power curve was remarkably even, and the 3·8-litre would accelerate in top gear from 60 m.p.h. to 80 m.p.h. in 6·3 seconds, while the real hustlers could lop a second off this by staying in third. Overall fuel consumption was slightly on the wrong side of 16 m.p.g., but there was a modest 25 m.p.g. available for those who were content to cruise steadily at 60 m.p.h., and even motorway users could return 15·5 m.p.g. at a sustained 100 m.p.h. I bought one of these cars with automatic transmission from John

Coombs in the autumn of 1960, and found it not only faster, but much stabler than my 1958 3·4-litre, all the worst faults having been ironed out. Incidentally, I seem to be in the minority over my preference for automatic, for Jaguars tell me that only 21–22% of orders on hand early in 1961 for 3·8-litre Mk. II cars specified automatic transmission. On the smaller models, the proportion is even lower—18–20% on the 3·4-litre, and a mere 10–12% for 2·4-litre cars. My car was to standard specification except for a special colour scheme—white, with black upholstery and chrome wire wheels. As delivered, it had a 8:1 compression ratio, later raised to 9:1 for 1961.

Norman Buckley also adopted a 3·8-litre engine in 1959, and with the 300 b.h.p. now available, 'Miss Windermere III' raised the straight kilometre record for 1,200-kg. boats to 120·63 m.p.h. In 1960, he installed a version of this unit with the D-type's dry-sump lubrication in a new hull ('Miss Windermere IV'), and took the one-hour record in the same class at 84·83 m.p.h. This record was still

Close relation of the Mk. II Jaguar was the 2½-litre Daimler introduced by this firm under Jaguar management. Power came from Daimler's own V-8 engine, and initially this version was available only with automatic transmission.

standing in April 1961, as were the one-hour and three-hour records taken by Buckley in the 800-kg. category, and the unlimited one-hour record which 'Miss Windermere III' had broken in 1956 with a speed of 79·66 m.p.h.

The 1960 rally season started badly for Britain, for the 'Monte' was almost as much of a benefit for Mercedes-Benz as Le Mans, 1957 had been for Jaguar, the cars from Stuttgart taking first, second, third and fifth places. The position improved thereafter, though. There were many more classes to win, as, in addition to divisions based on cubic capacity alone, there were also three separate categories for *types* of car—touring, improved touring, and *Gran Turismo*—which in fact helped Jaguars to bring home three class wins from the 1960 Tulip Rally, in which Haddon and Vivian took ninth place overall. The *marque* also returned to form in the 'Alpine', Behra (not the famous Jean, who was killed at Avus in 1959) winning the Touring Car class in his Mk. II 3·8-litre, with the Parkes/Howarth combination third. Not only did they vanquish the Mercedes-Benz opposition; they earned *Coupes* as well. 3·8-litre cars again swept the board in the *Tour de France*, winning the Touring Car category outright for the

second year in succession. Consten's victory was backed by a second place for the Jopp/Baillie car, and a fourth place for the Behra/Monneret combination. Jack Sears and William Cave took a 3·8-litre Mk. II saloon through the R.A.C. Rally in November, finishing fourth in general classification and heading their class. The soundtrack of their car in full cry was recorded in the Castrol film *Highland Fling*, and was music to those who alleged that Jaguars had gone 'all executive'.

The 3-litre limit had its effect on racing, and the small cars were coming to the fore in Gran Turismo and full sports-car events alike. In Australia, this was reflected by the victory of Jolly's Lotus XV in the Commonwealth's Tourist Trophy, Whiteford's Maserati beating Matich's D-type for second place. Sebring was even worse, for no Jaguars, or even Jaguar-engined cars, competed in 1960, while the Easter Goodwood meeting caused even Jaguar devotees to shake their heads—in the race for production touring cars, the DB.4 Aston Martins beat the 3·8-litre Jaguars, and in the Gran Turismo race one of Colin Chapman's 1,200 cc Lotus 'Elites' led an XK150S home. In June, however, the positions were reversed, for

The Daimler 'Sovereign' of 1967 is really only a Type 420 Jaguar with Daimler grille, even down to the famous twin o.h.c. six-cylinder engine.

at Oulton Park Don Parker's XK150S defeated Sir Gawaine Baillie who had forsaken his Jaguar for a Lotus, and Jaguars had an even sweeter revenge at Silverstone two months later. Here the production touring-car race was won by Mr Chapman in person, but his mount was a 3·8-litre Mk. II Jaguar saloon, and he subsequently bought one for his own use. I should add that I saw another sports-car manufacturer in attendance on his products at Goodwood's Guild of Motoring Writers' Test Day in 1960—he was driving a Jaguar.

At Silverstone in May, the Aston Martins did not turn out for the Production Touring car event, and Salvadori brought John Coombs's 3·8-litre Jaguar saloon into first place, not only averaging 87·55 m.p.h. but beating Stirling Moss into the bargain. John Coombs lent me his car for a weekend shortly afterwards, and I had an exhilarating time with it, the racing clutch making 'cog-swapping'

and spectacular starts a delight. I am afraid the inhabitants of Beaulieu found it a little too exciting—but amusingly enough, one of my tenant farmers approached me in the village a week later:

'Did you have the Salvadori car down here last weekend?' he asked.

I was puzzled at the question, and said so.

'Well, I recognized the exhaust note from the television,' was his reply.

Otherwise that Silverstone meeting was not very inspiring for Jaguar. The main sports-car event saw Coundley's Lister-Jaguar beat Flockhart on the *Ecurie Ecosse* D-type, now with a 'luggage boot' at the rear and a touring windscreen in deference to Appendix C in their class, but he could manage only fifth place overall behind the Coopers and Lotuses, and his average of 93·29 m.p.h. was appreciably lower than the 100·73 m.p.h. of Salvadori's winning

The S-type, in its turn, left another gap in the market, which was plugged
in 1966 by the introduction of the '420' with S-hull and rear suspension,
4.2 litre engine, and 420G frontal and interior treatment.

Cooper. Down among the back-markers, Jack Sears's DB.4GT Aston Martin coupé was faster than Sargent's three-litre D-type Jaguar!

The Jaguar Drivers' Club ran a joint meeting with the Aston Martin Owners' Club at Brands Hatch, also in May, on which occasion the dynamic Martini company sponsored a race between six Aston Martins and six Jaguars. There seems to have been some dispute over this, for victory was first awarded to the Aston Martins, but the decision was later reversed. The S.S. 100s, too, were beginning to figure in V.S.C.C. events, Michael Wilcock winning the Montagu Trophy at the Beaulieu Rally.

The big racing news of the year was, once again, Le Mans. After ill-luck in 1958, and a poor record in 1959, there seemed a hope that Jaguars might stage a comeback. Not that the outlook was very promising—Aston Martin, admittedly, had won the Constructors' Championship in 1959 and were no longer officially participating, but Brian Lister had also withdrawn both from racing and car manufacture in 1960, and *Ecurie Ecosse* were now down to one elderly D-type. Briggs Cunningham was running a Chevrolet 'Corvette', but those who studied the entry list also observed with interest that he had also entered a '3-litre Jaguar'. The press called this 'the new E-type', but it was in fact a development model which Cunningham had persuaded Sir William Lyons to release specially for Le Mans. Observant people read its registration number (VKV 752) and deduced that it had been on the road for some time.

In construction, this new car was very similar to the older D-type; the body and frame were integral from the scuttle rearwards, the nose-section being a tubular frame on which engine, suspension and steering-gear were mounted. The engine was an 85 × 88 mm. 3-litre, said to develop 295 b.h.p. on a 10:1 compression ratio, and the Lucas port-type fuel injection of the later works D-types was used. A four-speed all-synchromesh gearbox featured, the ratios being 3.31, 4.23, 5.44, and 7.1:1, while the Borg and Beck triple-plate clutch followed the accepted Jaguar racing practice. All four wheels were, however, independently sprung, with wish-bones and torsion bars at the front and a coil-and-wishbone arrangement at the rear. Disc brakes operated on all four wheels, and the Dunlop alloy wheels wore 6.50 × 16 tyres. The wheelbase was eight feet. A windscreen of the statutory 9.84-inch height ensured conformity with the prevailing sports-car regulations. Though the car appeared to be a closed coupé, it was not strictly anything of the sort. Jaguars had made the best of the rules by fitting a 'tonneau cover' extending from the top of the windscreen to behind the seats. This, coupled with perspex side-curtains, gave the 'saloon' effect. On trial over the Sarthe circuit it managed a lap of 121.37 m.p.h., comparative tests with a Ferrari and Cunningham's Chevrolet producing 125.37 and 112.18 m.p.h. respectively. The weight of 18.8 cwt. compared favourably with the Chevrolet's 26.7 cwt., but not so well with the Ferrari, which turned the scales at only 16.9 cwt.

By contrast, *Ecurie Ecosse*'s D-type was running in its fourth Le Mans—it had finished second in 1957, driven by Sanderson and Lawrence. For this occasion, however, Murray and Wilkinson had forsaken Jaguar's 'factory' 3-litre unit for one of their own devising, which, like the engines used in the Lister-Jaguars at Sebring in 1959, was a 'bored and stroked' 2.4-litre of 86 × 86 mm. Like Cunningham's experimental machine, it made use of an outsize 'tonneau cover' to reduce drag, while in deference to the regulations it still wore the farcical 'luggage boot' with which it had run at Silverstone in May. As ever, *Ecurie Ecosse* preferred normal carburation, and this car had the triple Weber set-up of the original D-types. It weighed half a hundredweight less than the new VKV 752, and was driven by Flockhart and Halford.

Neither car lasted the race. Walter Hansgen on the new machine made fastest practice lap at 124.11 m.p.h., but in the process it had a minor collision with a Ferrari, and in the race itself, a further 'shunt' damaged the fuel-injection pipes, forcing it to retire. The D-type proved faster while it was running, lying fourth after four hours, and fifth at eight hours—alas, the crankshaft broke after it had run more than half the race.

In August, however, Hansgen and the experimental car turned

Bridging the gap between Mk.II and Mk.X was the S-type introduced for the 1964 season, and here seen in 1968 form.

out again for the Road America race at Elkhart Lake, and this time it managed third place behind Causey and Stear's Maserati and the Pabst/Wuesthoff Ferrari. Briggs Cunningham supported the United States Grand Prix meeting later in the year, but this time he concentrated on the saloon-car race to good effect, the works-prepared 3·8-litre Mk. IIs of Hansgen and Pabst finishing first and second in front of another British car, Peter Harper's Sunbeam 'Rapier'. The seal was set on Jaguar's touring-car successes when the British Saloon-Car Championship was awarded to Jack Sears for his performances on T. E. B. Sopwith's 3·8-litre.

But 1960 had seen a far more important step. Sir William Lyons had never aspired to mass-production. While Jaguar had attained a position in the British motor industry only just below that of the 'Big Five'—B.M.C., Rootes, Ford, Vauxhall, and Standard-Triumph—

Low-priced item: the 1968 '240', a simplified 2.4-litre Mk.II saloon selling on the home market for £1,469. This 1960 redesign of a 1956 model was, however, still popular, and rightly so.

he was interested only in building quality cars at competitive prices. To achieve this end, he relied on more efficient production methods and longer runs, and not upon cheaper materials. Jaguars did not want to build 100,000 cars a year—what they did want was to be able to build a quarter of that number more economically, and in less cramped quarters, without skimping one iota of their basic standard of material and finish. Already, in 1959, they had bought the Browns Lane factory from the Ministry of Supply, while the enforced abandonment of their Mexican assembly plant had been offset by the establishment of another plant in South Africa, in addition to one in Ireland dating back to the days of Mk. V. The first Mk. II built up from 'completely knocked down' parts rolled off the South African assembly line in November 1960, and buyers who had hitherto been limited by import restrictions to either the cheapest 2·4-litre model or nothing could now have their choice of the complete Mk. II range.

But space was sorely needed. There was no room whatever for physical expansion at Browns Lane, where the factory was set in the middle of a housing estate, and Government policy laid stress on the diversion of any new industry to the distressed areas. Already Rootes were planning a new plant on Clydeside, and B.M.C. were also moving northwards in quest of expansion, despite hints of a recession on the horizon. Not that recession worried Jaguar, who had sat out several previous ones with unimpaired sales, but they did not want to manufacture their specialized product in an area divorced from the main motor industry. There was nothing to stop them buying an existing Midland company, and this is what they proceeded to do. In May 1960, negotiations were completed for the purchase of the Daimler Co. Ltd. from the B.S.A. Group for the sum of £3,400,000.

'The Daimler' was an institution in Coventry. It had been in existence there since 1896, and its roots went back to the very beginnings of Britain's motor industry, the original Daimler Motor Syndicate Ltd. having been established in 1893. Manufacture of complete cars had started in 1897, and by the time Jaguars took over, some families had served the company for three generations.

The name Daimler is associated in England with Royal patronage, and four Sovereigns—Edward VII, George V, Edward VIII, and

Power by Jaguar: the famous combination of the late Archie Scott-Brown and his Lister-Jaguar winning the 1957 British Empire Trophy Race at Oulton Park.

George VI—rode in Daimlers. But despite this, the firm took a keen interest in competitions in the early years of the century, and their big chain-driven cars were quite fast—fast enough, at any rate, for Daimler advertising to take the form of a 'Weekly Win' for some time. In 1908, however, they adopted Charles Yale Knight's double-sleeve valve engine, and this unit was to dominate their thinking until 1932.

The B.S.A. Co. Ltd. absorbed Daimlers in 1910, whereupon they scrapped their own car programme, and used the Knight engine instead. It is fashionable now to laugh at these vast, funereal carriages, trailing their smokescreen astern—one never decarbonized a Knight engine, for it 'improved with use'—but in their day they were a byword for smoothness, silence and flexibility. Daimlers might be conservative, but they pioneered the Vulcan-Sinclair Fluid Flywheel transmission, which was a much better system than some of the early American 'automatics' and did at least give the driver full control over the ratios at his disposal. They were also early in the field in Britain with independent front suspension, offering it in 1938 on both their own Fifteen and the 14 h.p. built by the old Lanchester Motor Co., which they had bought up in 1931. Their 1939 range was, in contrast to their Vintage productions, not devoid of performance, for they offered both a 90 m.p.h. 4-litre straight eight sports saloon and a fast tourer on the independently-sprung 2½-litre chassis that had replaced the Fifteen.

Despite serious damage in the Coventry 'Blitz', Daimlers were quick to resume production after the second World War, but thereafter a form of indecisiveness crept into their policy, and model followed model with disconcerting speed. They continued to cater for the carriage trade with a vast 5½-litre straight eight which weighed over two and a half tons, though handling beautifully—but at the same time they plunged into curious side-issues such as a 100 m.p.h. sports roadster on the 2½-litre 'Century' chassis, and an abortive attempt to build a medium-priced light car, the Lanchester 'Sprite'. In 1956, a change of management seemed to indicate some degree of stabilization, and for a while Daimler reverted to the manufacture of stately carriages with some performance, the 3·8-litre 'Majestic' of 1958 combining this with Dunlop disc brakes all round and automatic transmission. In the spring of 1959, it seemed that a new and progressive era for 'The Daimler' was being heralded with the introduction of the S.P.250 at the New York Importers' Show.

This was a sports two-seater with a short-stroke (76·2 × 69·85 mm.) 2½-litre vee-eight engine designed by Edward Turner and developing 140 b.h.p. at 5,800 r.p.m. Allied as it was to a close-ratio

Few people have made a custom-bodied Jaguar that can match the original article. Here is one of the best, Bertone's FT-type two-door saloon based on the 3.8-litre S-type, and shown at Geneva in 1966.

gearbox, it gave the new car an impressive top speed of 121 m.p.h., and *The Autocar* found that it would also accelerate from a standing start to 60 m.p.h. in 10·2 seconds, and to 100 m.p.h. in 26·3 seconds. The vee-eight unit gave the new Daimler a degree of top-gear flexibility worthy of any Jaguar, but the bodywork was not to everyone's liking, on grounds of styling and rigidity alike. At £1,395 complete, however, it was an inviting little car, and would have sold admirably from the start, had Daimlers been in a better position to manufacture and market it in quantities. The firm's other private-car offerings were the 3·8-litre 'Majestic' saloon and a stately 4·6-litre 'Majestic Major' vee-eight which had not attained production status when Jaguar took over.

The Daimler programme had possibilities. None of their products competed directly with the Jaguars, the S.P. 250 being a halfway house between such offerings as the Triumph and Austin-Healey and the XK150, while the big saloons catered for the market served by such machinery as the 3-litre Rover and the just-defunct Armstrong-Siddeley 'Sapphire'. Further, Daimlers had been doing a steady business for years with their diesel-powered omnibus chassis and armoured cars. Most important of all, 'The Daimler' was a large factory which was not being utilized to capacity. Jaguar, therefore, elected to carry on the Daimler tradition, retaining all the Daimler products, but aiming eventually to rationalize production by centering machining operations for the whole range at one plant and assembly at the other.

I was delighted to hear that Sir William Lyons had decided to lead Daimlers back to a place in the sun, instead of merely absorbing them, for the connection between my family and Daimlers goes back a very long way, almost to the beginning. My father had bought his first Daimler—a 6 h.p. twin-cylinder machine—in 1898, and a year later he became the first Englishman to drive a British car in a race on the Continent of Europe. It is apposite that the race was the Paris-Ostend event of 1899, and that therefore his 12 h.p. Daimler must have passed quite close to the site of that same Jabbeke-Aeltre Motorway on which the XK120 Jaguar was to have its baptism of fire nearly half a century later. In addition to this, he had also been largely responsible for introducing King Edward VII—then the Prince of Wales—to the delights of motoring, and in advising him as to the purchase of his first car—possibly that same Daimler now preserved in the Royal Collection at Sandringham. The Montagu association with Daimlers continued for some years—my father ran one up to 1907—and he can claim to have been the first person to drive a reigning monarch of England in a motor car: in April 1902, when King Edward VII landed at Bucklers' Hard, and was taken for a drive in the New Forest.

It was announced that no changes would be made in Daimler cars for 1961, apart from bodywork improvements on the S.P. 250, and very few on the Jaguars, though power-assisted steering was now to be an optional extra on the Mk. II saloons, and an additional selection of metallic colour schemes was to be available.

The Jaguar and Daimler apprenticeship organizations were merged, to mutual benefit. Daimler's Apprentice Association had for some time been devoting themselves to a labour of love—the restoration of the company's Veteran and Edwardian vehicles, including the King Edward VII's car, which now stands gleaming in the showroom at the Radford Works. They had also formed a Daimler Register with the aim of preserving as many Veteran, Vintage, and post-Vintage Daimlers as could be found—and none too soon, as the fabulous 'Double Six' of the later 1920s and early 1930s is all but extinct. Jaguar's apprentices went from strength to strength, causing *The Autocar* to remark, in August 1958:

'Parents seem to want to get their boys into one of four places these days—Winchester, Eton, Rolls-Royce or Jaguar.'

Jaguar showed no sports cars at Earls Court in 1960, though Daimlers compensated for this by making a good display with the S.P. 250. In the meantime, however, Colonel Rixon Bucknall, a loyal supporter of the company's products since he bought his first Swallow sidecar in 1922, had decided to make his ideal car. After approaching various manufacturers on the subject of such a 'bespoke' vehicle—most of them wanted him to buy *their* idea of one—he approached Jaguars, who agreed to supply him with a XK140 chassis, complete with C-type engine, close-ratio gearbox and competition-type drum brakes. A two-seater sporting body, modelled on the Colonel's 1930 '18/80' M.G., was built by the Hastings Motor Sheet Metal Works, considerable care being taken to ensure that all parts were accessible without removing the coachwork and that rattle-proof locker space was provided for everything, from tools to medical chest, umbrella and 'odds and ends'. Later modifications included disc brakes, a Powr-Lok limited-slip differential, and the tuning of an XK150S engine to far beyond the normal standard. Even more interesting, the owner and Bill Slack, that well-known Jaguar specialist, fitted a handbrake of undoubted efficacy. In place of the usual Jaguar system operating on the rear wheels, they installed a differential transmission brake (*not* the usual type operating on a drum behind the gearbox) from Jowett parts.

The Bucknall Jaguar Special aroused interest wherever it went, and with its S.S. 100-like radiator and 'pure 1930' lines it confused a lot of people, who imagined that they had unearthed a spotlessly preserved 1936 prototype! At a weight of under 24½ cwt., it was capable of close on 150 m.p.h., would accelerate from a standing start to 100 m.p.h. *and back again to a dead stop* in less than twenty-five seconds, and turned in 17½ m.p.g. in normal road use. As one man's idea of a really fast and manoeuvrable touring car, it forms an interesting contrast with both Jaguar's commercial productions and the Jaguar-based specials evolved simply for competition work. It is interesting to note that at least one American 'classic' enthusiast has attained his ideal car by fitting a twin-overhead-camshaft Jaguar engine in one of those legendary Lincoln 'Continentals' evolved by the late Edsel Ford and made in limited numbers between 1940 and 1948.

Late in 1960, the British motor industry suffered another recession. Workers went on short time and the fields surrounding the bigger

car factories began to fill up with unsold vehicles. The only plant unaffected was Jaguar, where work continued at the usual pitch, and notices were put up in the shops adjuring the staff not to be 'like the others'. Not that these were needed—Jaguars sailed through the dark winter of 1960-1 without a single day's short-time working.

The first splash of news from 1961 concerned the 3·8-litre; it was announced that a fleet of these cars, painted white, was to be issued to the police on M.1, Britain's first long-distance motorway, as replacements for the station wagons they had hitherto used. Evidently the malefactors' cars had proved too rapid for the guardians of the law! Rumours of a new Jaguar sports car were, however, in circulation again—this was to be much faster than even the XK150S. The company issued no denials; and certainly the rumours were

having an interesting effect on the Continent, where Enzo Ferrari was stepping up production of his 250GT model, and Mercedes-Benz were equipping their 300SL roadster with disc brakes. The entry lists for Le Mans closed, and enthusiasts read something that they had not seen since 1949—there was not a single Jaguar entered, nor any variation on a theme by Jaguar.

Editors of motoring papers began to sharpen their pencils. They had a feeling that Sir William Lyons was about to spring on them the kind of surprise that would rate not only a four-page illustrated description and a detailed road-test report, but an editorial as well.

They were right. On 16 March 1961, the new E-type was officially unveiled at the Geneva Show.

Jaguars at the shows. New York, 1950, featured a white and gold XK120. Paris, 1952, had as its centre of attraction the Montlhery record XK120 hardtop. Behind the Iron Curtain at Poznan in 1964 a representative range was exhibited.

CHAPTER 13

The E-Type and Beyond

1961

'A glittering new sports machine, of impeccable manners, that will go a long way towards repairing and restoring our slightly tarnished prestige throughout the world.'
Maxwell Boyd, *The Sunday Times*, March 1961

'It will be a winner everywhere, I am convinced. If ever there is a model which can persuade Jaguars back to racing, this is it.'
Denis Holmes, *The Daily Mail*, March 1961

It was 16 March 1961.

Film director Jacques Charrier, better known as the husband of the legendary Brigitte Bardot, flew in from Rome, where he was on location, to Geneva to ensure first place in the queue for the new Jaguar. In Jaguar's Piccadilly showrooms in London, a customer requested a demonstration run on the new car, only to be told that all the demonstrators were in Geneva.

'Put through a 'phone call, will you?' was his reply; 'If you'll reserve me a trial for tomorrow, I'll fly out.'

The motoring papers burst into editorials. *Autosport*, under the headline 'Jaguar Enterprise', hailed the new E-type as 'a true conception of the modern sports car displaying features which could only have resulted from intensive development work and a racing history'. The journal also issued a warning to Jaguar's competitors:

'The launching of the "E" will assuredly give the manufacturers of far more expensive G.T. cars something of a headache, and for prestige purposes it may be necessary for them to support certain international races and rallies in order to maintain their sales, both in their home markets and abroad.'

Note that the suggestion did not enjoin *Jaguar* to resume racing—this was hardly necessary.

The Motor's leader was succinctly entitled 'Half The Price', and pointed out that:

'More than ever will the Continental engineers shrug their shoulders and comment: "We cannot see how Lyons does it", with a mixture of admiration and envy.'

The old, old story going back to the Mk. VII, the XK120, and '100' models, and even to the S.S. I of 1932! At the same time *The Motor* reminded the public of the value of a 150 m.p.h. car as a means of imparting the principles of road safety to drivers.

'Congratulations, Jaguar!', proclaimed *Motor Sport*, which only a few months previously had upbraided Britain's motor industry for its backwardness in the face of fierce foreign competition and a recession. The E-type, it stated, was 'a stupendous achievement of British automobile engineering and craftsmanship', which worthily ushered in the Motorway Age.

Lyons' knowledge of what was required was, as ever, matched by that uncanny skill in choosing a time and a place for the unveiling of his new model. He selected Geneva rather than Brussels or London for two reasons—firstly, Switzerland was a true free market, with no native motor industry in need of State protection by tariff, and therefore within its boundaries the world's automobiles could compete on merit alone; and secondly, it was a market in which Britain's prestige had sunk to a painfully low ebb. During 1960, her share of the Swiss market was a mere 7,674 cars, or less than 10%, as against Germany's sales of 45,971 vehicles, France's 22,165, and Italy's 8,240. Further, the sales of Volkswagen alone amounted to more than double the number of British cars of all types imported in the course of 1960, while two other individual makes—Opel and Renault—also exceeded the British grand total. Jaguar, it is true, were making substantial headway—their 1960 sales were 476, or 180 more than in 1959—but this was a drop in the ocean beside the 2,479 cars sent to Switzerland in 1960 by Mercedes-Benz; though it must be conceded that the German firm's vast ascendancy probably stemmed from the sale of the smaller and cheaper '180' and '190' four-cylinder models, which were matched by no corresponding Jaguar variant.

What manner of car was it that evoked this flood of superlatives? Perhaps the car's outstanding feature was its independent rear suspension. Though Steyr and Austro-Daimler had been using this

Moulding the Swallow shape. Sidecar bodies under construction at Fole-shill in the late 1920's. The Zeppelin motif is still much in evidence, though by this time more conventional styles can be seen in the process of erection.

in the Vintage era, as had Alvis on their short-lived front-wheel-drive '12/75' of 1928, British manufacturers generally had left such advanced practices severely alone. It was universal on Mercedes-Benz models in 1955, but even by 1939 the sole British representative of this system had been the Atalanta—ancestor of the R.G.S.-Atalanta with Jaguar engine seen on the circuits in 1954. Production had, however, been on a very small scale, and even when Lagonda came out with independently-sprung rear wheels on their 1946 2½-litre the feature was not adopted on the parent company's Aston Martins. The Lagonda went out of production in 1958, and it was not until a year later that Standard–Triumph offered this feature to the general public on a mass-production car with their Triumph 'Herald'. Independent rear suspension was, in fact, quietly dismissed by the British motor industry as too expensive, and not conferring enough advantages to warrant its widespread adoption.

Among those who had outwardly ignored it were Jaguars. As a consequence, the C- and D-types had been at a serious disadvantage on such circuits as the Nurburgring, but then, as we have seen,

Lyons and Heynes had set their sights at Le Mans, where such luxuries were unnecessary. Not that they had been idle. Not only had an extensive development programme been carried out on Cunningham's Le Mans car, VKV 752, but in addition the new system had been tested on the road in a Mk. II saloon.

Structurally, the E-type showed close affinities not only with the Cunningham car, but with the D-type that had preceded it. The basic structure was a welded and stressed shell of 20-gauge steel sheet, bracing being furnished by box-section members comprising the door sills, scuttle assembly, the propeller-shaft tunnel and cross-members. As on the D-type, the engine, steering gear and front suspension units were carried on a detachable tubular front section. Front suspension likewise derived from the D-type, being by torsion bars and wishbones. The rear suspension was, as we have seen, entirely new.

It was not, however, quite the novelty it at first appeared, for way back in 1944 independent coil suspension at the rear had been tried on the 'VA' and 'VB' experimental light vehicles designed for the

War Office. The E-type, however, used twin-coil springs each side, incorporating Girling telescopic dampers, while the wheels were located by parallel transverse links of unequal length and longitudinal radius arms. The whole of this suspension system, together with the inboard disc brakes, was mounted for ease of assembly and servicing in a detachable bridge-piece. Steering was by rack-and-pinion, and retardation was, of course, taken care of by Dunlop disc brakes. Those at the rear were mounted inboard, and duplication of the master cylinders ensured that at least two wheels were still braked in the event of a failure, while the driver was advised of such a situation by the provision of a brake fluid warning light on the dashboard—a feature inherited from the Mk. II saloons. A separate handbrake operated on the rear wheels only.

The engine was basically the same 3·8-litre unit used in the XK150S, developing 265 b.h.p. at 5,500 r.p.m. in its latest form, with two interesting new design features. First, the three S.U. HD.8 carburetters were fed by a Lucas electric pump working in the tank immersed in the fuel; and second, a Lucas electrically-driven radiator fan was used—Jowetts had used such a device on their last 'Jupiter' model, the R.4 of 1954, but it had been intended as an auxiliary only. Only one transmission was offered, a four-speed gearbox which had synchromesh on the top three gears. Ratios were 3·31, 4·246, 6·156 and 11·177:1, but alternative axle ratios of 2·93, 3·07, and 3·54:1 were available if required. The clutch was of Borg and Beck single dry plate type, and the Salisbury hypoid final drive unit incorporated a Powr-Lok limited-slip differential as standard equipment.

Styling was fully aerodynamic, fixed-head coupé and open two-seater models being available, the latter with the option of a detachable hard-top—shades of the original Austin Seven Swallow of 1927. No attempt was made to carry more than two people, the large luggage shelf behind the seats was accessible on the closed car by swinging up the rear panel, and tools were housed in a special circular box mounted inside the spare wheel under the floor. The entire front section hinged up, in the fashion of the C- and D-types, to give access to the engine, and Jaguars solved the problem of keeping a curved windscreen clean by installing triple-blade wipers. The wire wheels wore 6·40 × 15 Dunlop R.S.5 types, R.5 racing

Sports racer transformed: a D-type creation by Michelotti (who styled the modern Triumph range) seen at the 1963 Geneva Show.

tyres being specified for maximum-speed work. On the E-type, the company had incorporated all the improvements learnt from racing and normal roadwork—all-round independent suspension, disc brakes, wire wheels, a limited-slip differential, and even a heater, though no starting handle was provided. The only officially-listed extras were radio, racing tyres, chromium-plated wire wheels, and a hardtop for the open model; and all this cost—£2,098 for the roadster, and £2,197 for the fixed-head coupé, inclusive of purchase tax!

No wonder five hundred were sold at the Geneva Show, and that the car's appearance at the New York Importers' Exhibition in April resulted in six being sold within half an hour of the doors opening. Subsequent orders at New York, incidentally, amounted to eleven million pounds' worth. Sir William Lyons announced further appointments at the factory, Arthur Whittaker being promoted to Deputy Chairman, W. M. Heynes to Vice-Chairman (Engineering), and three Executive Directors joining the Board. These were F. R. W. England, who also became Assistant Managing Director, R. W. Grice, the Works Director, and J. Silver, the Production Director. The competition world took a long look at the E-type, and made up its mind. T. E. B. Sopwith, after a successful season with his 3·8-litre Mk. II saloons, decided to add two E-types to his *Equipe Endeavour* (named after the famous yacht raced by his father T. O. M. Sopwith), and Peter Berry formed a racing team made up of two Mk. IIs and two E-types for Gran Turismo events. The John Coombs racing organization also added E-types to the Mk. II saloons already in use.

Sopwith was rewarded for his faith in the new model by a victory in the E-type's very first race—the twenty-five-lap Oulton Park Trophy Race for Grand Touring Cars in April 1961. Despite opposition from such formidable machinery as the 2·9-litre Ferraris of Graham Whitehead and Jack Sears, and Innes Ireland's DB.4 GT Aston Martin, the Jaguar emerged victorious, Graham Hill on the *Equipe Endeavour* car winning at 83·22 m.p.h. from the Aston Martin, and Salvadori on John Coombs' E-type which led at the start but fell back on the last lap. The *Equipe Endeavour* car achieved the almost unprecedented distinction of being collected from the factory on the Friday and winning its first race on the Saturday.

How did the car measure up on the road? Jaguars submitted their new car to the press in the weeks preceding the announcement, and while the first production batch was going through the works, the two finalized pre-production models—a roadster and a fixed-head coupé—were doing the rounds of the motoring journalists. The statistics were electrifying—there is no other word. In open form, as tried by *The Motor*, the car turned the scales at 24 cwt., *The Autocar*'s closed version being fractionally heavier. Maximum speeds were 149·1 m.p.h. for the roadster and 150·4 m.p.h. for the coupé, speeds on the indirects being 107 and 116 m.p.h. respectively on third, and 74 and 78 m.p.h. on second. The open car accelerated from a standing start to 30 m.p.h. in 2·6 seconds, to 60 m.p.h. in 7·1 seconds, and to 90 in 13·4 seconds. The 'ton' came up in 15·9

seconds, and 130 m.p.h. in a fraction over half a minute. A gradient of one-in-five could be surmounted at steady speed in top gear, and fuel consumption worked out at 19·7 m.p.g. It is interesting to compare these figures with two notable milestones from the past, the 3½-litre S.S. 100 of 1938, and the original 1949 model XK120 two-seater. The 1938 car was fractionally lighter than the E-type, at 23¾ cwt., but could attain no more than 98·1 m.p.h., 82 m.p.h. coming up in third gear. Acceleration through the gears to 30 m.p.h. occupied 3·8 seconds, or the time taken for the E-type to reach 40 m.p.h. 10·4 seconds from the start, the '100' was doing 60 m.p.h., and the E-type about 75 m.p.h. The superior aerodynamics of 1961, however, ensured a superior fuel consumption, as the '100' would not better 18 m.p.g. in normal tune, whereas even at a sustained 100 m.p.h. the E-type would return 21 m.p.g. Perhaps it would be fairer to compare the new model with the XK120; the 1949 type was nearly 25 m.p.h. slower at 124·5 m.p.h. on top gear, and 16 m.p.h. slower on third with a figure of 80 m.p.h. There was relatively little difference in acceleration at low speeds, but at 50 m.p.h. the E-type would already have gained an advantage of 1½ seconds, increased to three seconds by the time 60 m.p.h. was attained. In the 27·3 seconds required to push an XK120 up to 100 m.p.h. the E-type would have been doing well over 120 m.p.h., or close on the older car's absolute maximum in normal trim. Overall fuel consumption of the two cars was much the same.

True, the E-type came in for some criticisms from the testers. The gear-change was still on the slow side, and the seats were a little lacking in comfort for tall drivers. An amusing point concerned the fitting of number plates. Both the cars submitted for test had their registration numbers painted on the bodywork, a procedure which is legal in Great Britain provided that certain standards of legibility and size are met. It is not, however, legal in the U.S.A., and alterna-

A fastback created by Malcolm Sayer as an aerodynamic exercise, which was never followed up. Sold by the factory to Dick Protheroe, a Jaguar dealer, it was raced successfully by him. As of 1980, it was in private hands in Florida.

tive sites for number-plates are hard to find on the E-type, and in any case would be conducive to drag. *The Autocar* commented that the car's maximum speed of 150-odd m.p.h. proved elusive for some time, being suddenly attained without any apparent change of conditions. This was traced to the car's having shed its front trade-plate on the road—an explanation of why the limited trade regis-trations of the works C- and D-type Jaguars were always *painted* on!

But these criticisms apart, the car enjoyed a press which went beyond mere appreciation in its comments. Said *The Motor*:

'Admittedly it is quite easily the fastest car ever tested ... but the roadholding is entirely capable of handling the power, the springing is more comfortable than that of many sober touring cars, and the engine is extremely flexible and devoid of temperament.'

The Autocar expressed the view that:

'It offers what drivers have so long asked for, namely, sports-car performance and handling, combined with the docility, gentle suspension, and appointments of a town car.'

In *Autosport*, John Bolster showed his appreciation of the Jaguar's method of progression:

'Figures are all very well, but these almost incredible times are recorded in a silky silence that has hitherto been utterly foreign to the sports car ... The Jaguar's hypoid is totally inaudible, which can be said of hardly any orthodox back axle to-day.'

And William Boddy, after a short run in the fixed-head coupé, summarized his findings thus in *Motor Sport*, having staggered him-self and his readers by making the car accelerate from 10 m.p.h. to 100 m.p.h., *in top gear*, in twenty-five seconds:

'The E-type is a staggering motor car on all counts ... safety, acceler-ation, speed, equipment, appearance, all are there, for a basic price of only £1,480 ... I extend to Sir William Lyons, his design team, tech-nicians, and workers my humble congratulations.'

Once again, Jaguars were making their own bodies—or rather body-chassis units—on this model. Assembly, likewise, was con-ducted on a different plan from that used for the saloons and XK150

More like a standard E in appearance, this is the lightweight owned by Atkins and raced by Roy Salvadori. It subsequently passed into the private collection of Guy Griffiths in Chipping Campden, Glos.

types. With these, chassis (or mechanical components, in the case of the Mk. II) proceeded to a central point on the assembly line known as 'Clapham Junction', where the Mk. IXs and XK150 frames received their bodies. The Mk. II components were mounted on special spaced jigs on to which the painted, but only partially-trimmed hulls were lowered. The E-types, however, were assembled in three separate sections—the main hull, the front body section, and the front subframe—which were brought together at a point well up on the assembly line.

Jaguar had, in fact, re-attained that same position of pre-eminence which they had held in 1949. They had built a car which provided that same combination of super-sports performance and smoothness and docility that had singled out the original XK120 from its exciting and complex counterparts of pre-war days—the plug oilers, the rain-traps, and the gearboxes which demanded not only double-declutching but a skilful technique into the bargain.

Even by the autumn of 1961, the E-type was still a rarity on British roads, and it would have been pardonable for Sir William Lyons to make it the centre-piece of his display at Earls Court in October. Not that Jaguars had ceased to occupy the headlines, by any means, for early in October it was announced that they had purchased Guy Motors of Wolverhampton, a commercial vehicle firm with a long and illustrious record going back to 1914. Guys had been in financial difficulties for some time, and had lately gone into receivership. The acquisition of this company strengthened Jaguar's foothold in the heavy vehicle field, and *The Commercial Motor* reported in December 1961 that no fewer than 5,762 buses built by the Jaguar Group (Daimler and Guy) were being operated by British municipalities, this figure being fractionally under one-third of the total of 17,390 vehicles in service.

Further, it was known that a successor to Mk. IX was on the way. Already I had encountered a heavily disguised saloon in black primer circulating inside the factory grounds and had been careful not to ask too many questions on the subject of its identity. Nobody, however, pretended that it was anything but the new Mk. X.

With their new model, announced on the eve of the Earls Court Show, Jaguars had finally discarded the principle of a separate chassis, retained on the Mk. VII and its successors, Mks. VIII and IX, in favour of a true monocoque structure, of remarkable rigidity. This rigidity was ensured by the use of two large fabricated box sections running the length of the 'body', another large box-section cross-member forming the scuttle. The strength of this framework was such that it was found possible to use much thinner windscreen pillars and thus give the Mk. X better driving-seat visibility, and less bulky lines than its predecessors.

Even more important, the Jaguar design office had adapted the E-type's independent rear suspension by transverse links and coils to the new saloon, thus showing a healthy contempt for the long-held view that such systems were uneconomic. Gone also was the torsion-bar front suspension inherited from the Mk. VII, coil springs being used instead. As might have been expected, Dunlop disc brakes with quick-change pads were used on all four wheels, the rear brakes being mounted inboard. The self-adjusting handbrake still worked on the rear wheels only, and the Mk. X, like other disc-

The prototype S.S.90 sports car, 1935, showing the curved tail which contrasts with the classically British 'Le Mans slab tank' of production models. At the wheel is the Hon. Brian Lewis (later Lord Essendon).

braked Jaguars, had a fluid warning light on the dashboard.

Despite the usual crop of rumours to the contrary, Jaguars retained the XK-type unit in the new car, but a really brisk performance was ensured by using the 3·8-litre version as fitted in the E-type. This developed 265 b.h.p. at 5,500 r.p.m., and was fed with three S.U. HD.8 carburetters. Even more important, automatic transmission was not compulsory, the engineers at Browns Lane recognizing that even in the luxury class there are still owners who prefer to *drive* their cars. The principal change was the provision of a Powr-Lok limited-slip differential as standard, a feature also found in the 3·8-litre Mk. II and XK150S models: but buyers still had the choice of a four-speed manual gearbox, with or without overdrive, and Borg-Warner automatic transmission with the driver-controlled 'intermediate hold'. Top-gear ratio with the manual box was 3·54 : 1.

Equipment was, as ever, lavish. The instrumentation followed the layout adopted for the Mk. II saloons in 1960, and the interior offered reclining seats, a comprehensive fresh-air heating and demisting system, and folding tables. Despite the provision of twin headlights, the exterior styling remained unadorned, and proved a refreshing contrast to the 'sculpturing' affected by some of the Jaguar's competitors in the executive class.

The critics, as usual, began to wonder how it was all done, but were astounded to find that the Mk. X's weight of 35 cwt. was only half a hundredweight more than that of the original Mk. VII, and that this combination of luxury and performance could be bought for £2,392 in England (£1,640 basic). The makers' performance figures were an interesting contrast with Mk. VII in 1952 form: Mk. X was 19 m.p.h. faster with a top speed of 120 m.p.h., it could attain 60 m.p.h. in 10·2 seconds whereas the original big saloon had taken 13·7 seconds, and the no-longer-magic 'ton' could be reached in less than half a minute, which compared favourably with the 32 seconds taken by Mk. VII to work up to 90 m.p.h. Fuel consumption was estimated at 16–18 m.p.g., which was an improvement on the figures recorded by its immediate predecessor, the Mk. IX.

The usual 'rave' notices appeared. *The Autocar* stressed the importance of the application of independent rear suspension to a sports saloon, while *The Motor* struck an apposite note by observing that 'the toughest rival for any coachbuilder is ... Sir William Lyons, whose ability to produce the right line at the right price is quite remarkable'. Even the diehard *Veteran and Vintage Magazine* admired the new Jaguar's unadorned lines and described the car as 'our idea of a collector's piece in 1992'. At a rather gloomy Motor Show, overshadowed by doubts about Britain's proposed entry into the European Common Market, and a paralysing strike at one of the Rootes Group factories, Jaguars were cheerfully promising their employees full-time working through the winter. The company's robust health was evidenced by the admission that tooling costs for Mk. X ran to a cool £4 million, whereas the 2·4-litre, their original essay into unitary construction touring-cars, had required an investment of a mere million pounds. There were no major changes in the Daimler programme, though the long-wheel-base limousine version of the 4½-litre Vee-Eight 'Majestic Major', originally shown in 1959, before the Jaguar take-over, was put into production, thus restoring the old-established Coventry firm to its former prominent position in the field of chauffeur-driven carriages.

With a brace of winners in the stable—the E-type and the new Mk. X—it was hardly surprising that profits for the 1961/2 financial year soared by over £216,000 to well above the two million-pound mark. Changing times were, however, reflected in the appearance of a handful of the big new saloons on the home market as early as February, 1962—contrast this with the eighteen months' wait to which the first British buyers of the XK 120 had been condemned. Manual-transmission versions of Mk. X were slower in coming through, owing to the small demand for this type of gearbox.

The Big Cat's influence in racing was on the wane. Nineteen sixty-two was a patchy year, and 1963 no better. Ferrari dominated the G.T. class which had superseded the out-and-out sports-racers of an earlier era. Not that the E-type was incapable of giving a good account of itself, as witness the fifth place achieved by Cunningham and Salvadori at Le Mans in 1962. Their average speed of 108·87 m.p.h. would have been more than sufficient for an outright victory in 1956, and it was not lost on observers that the Jaguar was a road-

Stirling Moss with the C-type in which he won the 1951 T.T. at Dundrod.

going machine selling for one-third of the list price of a *touring* Ferrari. None the less, Maranello's win that year gave them the best aggregate at Le Mans, with six victories to the five of Jaguar and Bentley. As might have been expected, the T.T. was also a Ferrari benefit, the Lightweight G.T.O.s having 310 b.h.p. to the E-type's 265. Salvadori on the fastest Jaguar had to be content with fourth place.

Nineteen sixty-three followed the same trend. True, John Coombs's lightened E-type coupé, in the hands of Graham Hill, achieved a brief ascendancy over the Ferraris in national events, a victory at the Goodwood Easter Monday Meeting being capped at Mallory Park in July. But Briggs Cunningham's entry of three cars at Le Mans was destined to be his swan-song, and ninth place was scant reward for a doughty challenger who had come a long way since his début with a brace of Cadillacs in 1950. The T.T. at Goodwood saw Salvadori and Sears trailing behind the Ferraris of Hill and Parkes.

More significant still was the change in saloon-car racing. Nineteen sixty-two remained a Jaguar year, with the 3·8-litre Mk. IIs dominant, but the writing was already on the wall. At the Crystal Palace Whit Monday Meeting, Kelsey's Chevrolet gave Salvadori a run for his money, while at Snetterton's Archie Scott-Brown Memorial Meeting second place fell to Sachs's 'Chevy II', even if Graham Hill won for Jaguar. By September, a Chevrolet actually won a race over the tortuous London circuit, albeit in the absence of the cars from Coventry. Already the big American sedans were moving in for the kill, and the inevitable happened the following year at Silverstone's International Trophy Meeting—only it was Ford, and not General Motors, who were responsible for bringing an end to the hegemony that dated back to the days of Mk. VII. Goliath, in the shape of Jack Sears at the wheel of 6·9-litres of Dearborn-made 'Galaxie', defeated David, and followed up this advantage with other wins at Aintree in May, and at the Crystal Palace in June. Not that the Americans were as yet infallible; *The Motor's* Six-Hour Saloon Car Race at Brands Hatch, a truly international affair which attracted Lancias and Alfa-Romeos from Italy, German-entered B.M.W.s and Jaguars, and Volvos and 'Minis' from Belgium, saw Sir Gawaine Baillie's very fast Ford trounced in appalling weather by the 3·8-litre of Salmon and Sutcliffe, appropriately registered BUY 12. Though this car was disqualified, the first two places were awarded to Jaguars—Roy Salvadori being followed home by the German partnership, Lindner and Nocker.

This was, however, destined to be the 3·8's last major win in

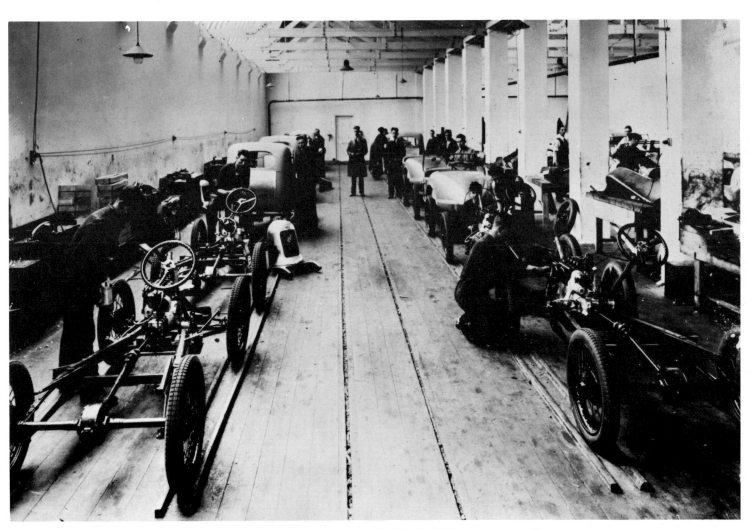

The Austin Seven assembly line at Foleshill, 1929. The chassis are radiatorless, the rounded-nose type being peculiar to William Lyons's custom version of the breed.

England: they could still score up class victories after the 'Galaxies' had been upgraded into a larger-capacity group, but generally saloon-car racing was becoming the preserve of smaller machinery, such as the twin o.h.c. Ford 'Lotus-Cortinas' and the ubiquitous 'Mini-Cooper', a development of Alec Issigonis's brilliant design for B.M.C. which had first appeared at the 1959 London Show. In Germany the name of Jaguar was still feared, thanks to the endeavours of Peter Lindner. Though his good fight in the 1963 1,000-Kilometre Race at the Nurburgring on an E-type ended in retirement, he and his co-driver Nocker defeated five works-entered Mercedes-Benz to win the Six-Hour Touring Car event on the same circuit. That year's Monte Carlo Rally saw only three Jaguars entered, as against sixteen Mercedes-Benz, fifteen Alfa-Romeos, and no fewer than twenty-two Citroens—and these made no impression, the big-car class being annexed by the American Fords. But while Ferrari might mop up the G.T. category of the *Tour de France*, the 3·8s were still unbeatable in the touring class, despite the presence of three 'Galaxies'. Consten's win was backed by the second place awarded to Mlles. Soisbault and Texier, who also annexed the *Coupe des Dames*. At Prescott, Scragg's E-type was a regular winner

of the G.T. class, and at Brighton the old familiar 'Jaguette' was joined by an unusual Jaguar-powered 'special', S.H. Richardson's A.C. 'Ace' with 3·8-litre engine.

But if the giants had edged the compacts out of the money in racing, Jaguar were able, in March, 1963, to put on a demonstration of the same sort of scheduled, high-speed service that had won them so many laurels at Le Mans. Five drivers, led by Geoff Duke, ran a 3·8-litre Mk. II saloon at Monza for four days and four nights, averaging 106·62 m.p.h. Four International Class 'C' records were annexed, including 10,000 miles at 106·58 m.p.h.—an interesting contrast with the performance of the late Leslie Johnson and his team with the XK 120 coupé LWK 707, which had averaged only 100·68 m.p.h. over this distance in 1952. The 3·8 used a 2·93:1 axle ratio with the overdrive locked out of action, and overall fuel consumption was 14·9 m.p.g. *The Autocar* tried the car afterwards, and found it 'a very fine special car for grand touring', but Jaguar did not rise to the bait. Another 1963 success was victory in the European Touring Car Challenge, which fell to the German Peter Nocker driving a 3·8 Mk. II entered by Peter Lindner; this was the first of a series that has gained increasingly in importance in subsequent years.

Devotees of the *marque* might complain that its image was fading into 'just another expensive car', but export figures gave the lie to

Export by air: an E-type goes abroad.

this. Jaguars were not only selling well—they were competitive. In 1962 a 3·4-litre saloon could be bought in Italy for the equivalent of £2,114, or £69 less than the cost of a 220SE Mercedes-Benz. The price also compared quite favourably with the more expensive products of the home industry—the Alfa-Romeo '2600 Sprint' at £1,857, the Lancia 'Flaminia' at £1,778, and the Fiat 2300S coupé at £1,552. Of these three, only the Lancia offered anything like the Jaguar's accommodation. The Mk. X retailed for £2,988, and had no competitors—as yet Maserati's eight-cylinder *quattroporte* was a thing of the future. No wonder Italian sales rose by 30 per cent in 1962, and by a staggering 114 per cent the following year—this in the face of a trade recession, though no doubt the great Dr. Giuseppe Farina's business connections with the Italian distributors helped.

In Germany, where sales rose by 50 per cent in 1963, Jaguar also emerged with credit. Obviously neither the Mk. II (£1,940) nor the Mk. X (£2,640) could compete against Daimler-Benz on their native heath, where a 220 could be bought for just over £1,000, and a 300SE for £2,210, but the energetic competition programme pursued by the company's distributor, Peter Lindner, had its effect.

France was a rather easier market, if only because that country no longer offered anything remotely competitive with either Coventry or Stuttgart. Even the Chrysler-powered Facel Vega, last survivor of the race of Gallic *grand'routiers*, was moribund. Thanks to the Common Market, a '2·4' cost £350 more than a 220S, but in the G.T. Category positions were reversed, and the E-type at £2,739 was a more attractive proposition than Mercedes-Benz's new 230SL at £2,760. Mk. X at £2,883 was a real bargain as against the £4,300 asked for a Cadillac. No wonder 53 per cent more Jaguars were sold in France in 1963, a better-than-average figure when compared with the overall European increase of 40 per cent. Even in Switzerland, traditionally the toughest nut to crack, the 2·4-litre was only £50 more expensive than the rival Mercedes-Benz model in March 1964. In the sporting category, the E-type at £2,175 furnished fierce and effective competition for Chevrolet's

'Corvette Stingray' (£2,546), while Aston Martin (£4,383) and Ferrari (£3,988) were in a different price-bracket altogether. Jaguar's Swiss sales in 1964 were 465, ahead of Porsche with 410 cars, but understandable enough well behind the firmly-established Mercedes-Benz, which sold 3,050 units—the majority of these, however, were the ubiquitous 190 and 190D models used as taxis. Rover sold 1,160 vehicles, which suggests an alarming challenge from Solihull's new and exciting o.h.c. four-cylinder '2000' until one realizes that the figure includes the evergreen and popular Land-Rover.

As for the United States, Sir William Lyons was able to tell his shareholders in April 1963 that this market was taking one-third of all the company's private-car production, and a national poll taken by the magazine *Car and Driver* voted the E-type the best all-rounder, while the 3·8-litre Mk. II (a 1960 design of a model laid down in 1957!) was considered to be the best 'luxury compact'. What is more, Americans not only talked Jaguar, they bought Jaguar as well, and sales were up by 44·5 per cent on the previous year. When nuclear-powered freighter *Savannah* made her maiden voyage across the Atlantic in June 1964, part of her cargo consisted of Jaguars and Daimlers.

There were no changes in the Jaguar range for 1963, though seat belt anchorages had become standard equipment during the past season. To compensate for this *status quo*, however, there was an interesting addition to the Daimler programme in the shape of a 2½-litre saloon listing at £1,786, or £108 more than the corresponding Jaguar model. It combined the Mk. II hull with Daimler's effective 140 b.h.p. Vee-8 engine as used in the SP.250 sports car since 1959. The diehard *Veteran and Vintage Magazine* could not resist a crack about 'slamming a Daimler grille on the nose of a Mk. II Jaguar', but this model, which was supplied only with split-bench seats and a Type 35 Borg-Warner automatic gearbox, soon carved a niche for itself in the market. On test it proved capable of 110 m.p.h., and could turn in 20 m.p.g. on a long run.

Nineteen sixty-two/three was a record season for Jaguar production, and again it was found necessary to expand the company's

The C-type marches on: Gordon Mackenzie of New York owned this car in 1968, its roll-bar hidden behind a headrest in the D-type manner.

scope. In March 1963, the old-established firm of Coventry-Climax Engines Ltd. was acquired. This concern had undergone an astonishing *volte face* in the 1950s. In the inter-War years its reputation had been based on a long line of stolid, reliable power units, found under the bonnets of such uninspired cars as Clyno, Swift, and the earlier Triumphs. True, the i.o.e. engines built for Triumph and the Morgan 4/4 in the 1930s were rather more potent, but the War years had involved Coventry-Climax in the production of trailer pumps for the National Fire Service, initially a convenient means of using up stocks of 8 h.p. side-valve units left over from Swift's bankruptcy in 1931!

But from the workhorses of Civil Defence had stemmed an exciting generation of single and twin o.h.c. engines which had spearheaded Britain's domination of Formula I, as well as consolidating the impact of Colin Chapman's road-going Lotuses. The firm also had a major hand in the development of the 875 cc o.h.c. engine of Rootes's endearing little Hillman 'Imp', launched a month after the Jaguar take-over. The presence of a new régime at the Widdrington Road Works aroused hopes of a return to serious competition work, but though Coventry-Climax produced an ingenious flat-sixteen engine during the last year of the 1½-litre Grand Prix Formula, the new owners made it clear that they did not propose to pursue this line of development. The purchase of Coventry-Climax was followed two years later by the acquisition of that factory's former rivals in the proprietary-engine field, Henry Meadows of Wolverhampton. Meadows, however, had long been involved with commercial vehicles—their last effort to see service in a private car had been a 3-litre twin o.h.c. 'six' made in very small numbers for Invicta in 1946—and Jaguar were merely taking advantage of Meadows's proximity to the Guy works at Fallings Park. In 1966, they were building American Cummins diesels for installation into Daimler buses and Guy lorries, the ultimate goal being the manufacture in Britain of both Vee-6 and Vee-8 versions.

All the existing models—three variations on the Mk. II theme, the Mk. X, the E-type, and the 2½-litre and 4·6-litre Daimlers—were continued for 1964, but there was also a new Jaguar, the S-type saloon. This was somewhat of an intermediate type, based on the Mk. II but with the Mk. X's design of independent rear suspension. Other changes included a restyled front end, larger side lamps, wrap-around direction indicators, twin rear tanks with a total capacity of fourteen gallons, and a much bigger boot holding nineteen cubic feet as against the Mk. II's twelve. It could be had in the accustomed three forms—manual, manual with overdrive, and automatic—but only with the two bigger sizes of engine (3·4-litre and 3·8-litre). List prices were £1,669 and £1,758 respectively, and Edward Eves, writing in *The Autocar*, expressed the view that it would be 'impossible to find as sound a high-speed touring saloon . . . offering such a degree of development and reliability'. Unfortunately it took a long time to reach large-scale production, a fact admitted in the Annual Report issued by the company in March, 1965, in which Sir William Lyons also commented: 'Obviously all cost increases have to be absorbed by the company, and can only be offset by the extent to which we can still further improve our manufacturing efficiency'. Would that other captains of industry adopted the same far-sighted attitude! Sir William proceeded to implement this policy further by building a new body-painting plant at a cost of £350,000, and this came into operation that August. Henceforward bodies were no longer fully sprayed before being offered up to their mechanical components, but given a first colour coat and road-tested, the finishing process following once they had been passed out by the engineering side. Thus the rectification bay hitherto required for touching-in operations became redundant.

Nineteen sixty-four saw a strong challenge from America. While to the trans-Atlantic enthusiast the sports car remained, as always, the imported car, Chevrolet's 'Stingray' version of the long-established 'Corvette' was quite an impressive piece of machinery, capable of 146 m.p.h.—it could also out-accelerate the E-type fractionally. The fact that it required 5·3 litres and eight cylinders to do it was offset by its lower price on the home market; the brakes, however, were not up to the performance, an inevitable consequence of many years of 'blanket' speed limits in the U.S.A. There was also Ford's new 'Mustang'. At home, this was certainly not aimed at the *connoisseur*, but rather at the up-and-coming young executive with a taste for something different. Even with the optional 4·7-litre Vee-8 engine (a modest and not over-urgeful 'six' was standard equipment) it could only attain 116 m.p.h., thanks to low overall gearing; it was heavy, at 31 cwt., and proved thirsty, at 12·8 m.p.g., when tested by the British motoring press. Handling in the wet was likewise tricky, but it was a full four-seater, and unlike some other American 'personal cars', it was a genuine compact, measuring only 15 ft. 2 ins. from stem to stern—six-and-a-half inches longer

Formal Jaguar: the executive edition of Mk. X with division introduced for 1966.

than the E-type. Further, though the 'Mustang' sold to the kind of American who might never have heard of the Jaguar, its position in export markets was rather different. The ever-present dollar shortage gave it scarcity value, while its unusual appearance appealed to the less sporting fringe of specialist buyers. It was backed by world-wide Ford service, and even in England it could be sold, fully-equipped, for £1,925 in October, 1964. What is more, it caught on at home in an unprecedented manner, half a million being produced in less than eighteen months. A monthly output of 40,000 makes an interesting contrast with the 250,000 twin o.h.c. Jaguar engines of all types turned out between 1949 and the early part of 1966. The 'Mustang' was also making itself felt in European competition. In the 1964 Tour de France one of the newcomers from Dearborn, albeit in highly modified guise, ousted Consten from his accustomed first place in the touring category, and 1965 saw the breed's first saloon-car win in Britain, at Brands Hatch. Such a contender would surely provoke an answer from Jaguar.

Mk. X, too, stood in need of some advancement. For the first time in many years, a Jaguar had received less than 'rave' notices in the British press. *The Motor* said of the overdrive version tested in 1963 that 'in many ways it looks better than it is'. Most of the plaints were levelled at the gearbox, which was considered 'elderly in design, and, to most drivers, out of place in such plush surroundings'. Also singled out for criticism were the slippery front seats with their lack of lateral support, and the handbrake mounted under the dash, a feature which I must confess I disliked, too. The car was also rated as expensive to run, but the overall fuel consumption of 13.6 m.p.g. remains, to my mind, creditable for a six-seater saloon turning

the scales at nearly 36 cwt., and capable of taking three-figure cruising speeds in its stride. My automatic version was quite appreciably thirstier. *The Autocar* also took issue over the front seats, and felt that the power-assisted steering was undergeared, though its testers compared the interior trim to 'the cosily affluent air of an Edwardian library'. About the brakes, 'there were no reservations—they were 'superb''. Personally, I liked my Mk. X, which was uncannily quiet without losing any of the urge that had characterized the 3.8-litre Mk. II that had preceded it. The handling, likewise, was incredibly sure-footed for a very big machine, and it could be thrown about on winding roads with an exuberance that I would never have dared unleash on a Mk. VII or Mk. VIII.

The answer was not long in coming, and when it came it surprised a lot of the wiseacres who had dreamed of Vee-12 engines and five-speed gearboxes. Jaguar wisely adhered to the well-tried and indestructible twin-cam 'six', now available in 4.2-litre (92.07 × 106 mm) form. This engine, available in both Mk. X and E-type for the 1965 season, was not just a bored-out '3.8', but had a completely redesigned block with re-spaced bore centres; the two end cylinders were further apart, and the middle four were closer together. Other improvements included the provision of an alternator, a new one-piece cast aluminium manifold, and revised ancillary drives. On the Mk. X installation a triangular belt drive took care of water pump, fan, and a separate pump for the hydraulic power-assisted steering. A Lucas pre-engaged starter motor also featured in the specification. On a 9:1 compression ratio output was unchanged at 265 b.h.p., but the new engine gave better bottom-end torque, and consequently superior acceleration in the middle-speed ranges. The

Victor at Le Mans, 1951: Whitehead takes the checkered flag.

Jaguar from the Air: Browns Lane is the former Daimler Shadow Factory to which Jaguar moved in 1952.

main chassis improvement on Mk. X was the adoption of the advanced Marles-Varamatic variable-rate power-assisted steering, which effectively overcame earlier criticisms in this department.

Even more important were those changes which concerned the transmission. Options on Mk. X were unchanged, and the E-type was still listed only with a four-speed manual box, but both manual and automatic versions were entirely new. The former now had synchromesh on all four forward ratios, and a Laycock-Hausserman diaphragm-spring clutch replaced the Borg and Beck type hitherto used. This box was also standardized on manual-transmission models of the S-type. The new automatic was the Borg-Warner Model-8 with a choice of two drive ranges, 'D1' and 'D2'. 'D1' made used of all forward gears, but if 'D2' were selected, bottom gear was eliminated, making for a smoother if more leisurely take-off. Prices were only slightly increased, the increment ranging from £98 in the case of the E-type up to £132 for the automatic Mk. X. For

Radford, known to generations of Coventry's car workers as 'The Daimler', now houses machine shops, tool rooms, press shops, and engine assembly and testing departments, as well as the Daimler 'bus plant.'

the time being the 3·8-litre variants were continued.

Road test reports confirmed the all-round improvement. Maximum speed was scarcely affected—the 4·2-litre with automatic gearbox as tested by *The Motor* recorded 118·2 m.p.h. as against the 120 m.p.h. of the 3·8-litre overdrive version as tried in 1963. But the magazine made ample amends for its earlier strictures, admitting that 'after several years of production . . . it has developed into an extremely good car'. The new Borg-Warner box gave very smooth changes, both upward and downward. *The Autocar* was delighted by the car's performance in the middle ranges—the 4·2-litre would accelerate from 60 to 100 m.p.h. in the same time as the 3·8-litre had needed to go from 30 to 70 m.p.h. The top gear

ratio, at 3·54:1, was perhaps a little on the low side, but the testers admitted that a higher ratio would have had an adverse effect on the car's overall performance in direct drive. 'There is no lumpiness', they observed, 'to make the driver feel that it should have changed down'. With the latest steering gear only three turns were needed from lock to lock. As for the brakes, these 'have been developed relentlessly to keep abreast of rising performance, and good though they were on the 3·8 Mk. X, these are even better'. A new type of oil-control ring had reduced the oil consumption, once an Achilles' heel of twin-cam Jaguars, and no fault could be found with the heater, either.

The E-type, as ever, taxed the journalists' stock of superlatives,

A '420' on its way by air to the U.S.A. Note the chromed wire wheels and whitewalls.

especially now that they could no longer poke fun at the gearbox. If the overall performance figures showed no noticeable change, it was found possible even on a 3·07:1 axle ratio to start in top gear! Commented *The Motor*: 'Handling, steering, and brakes are of such a high order that sensible drivers will never find the power/weight ratio of 220 b.h.p. per ton an embarrassment; indeed this is one of the rare high-performance cars in which every ounce of power can be used on the road.' The gear lever could 'now be whisked into any gear as fast as the hand can move'. There was little change in fuel consumption, which went up from 19·7 to 18·5 m.p g. with the introduction of the bigger engine; while at a steady 100 m.p.h., the E-type would turn in 20 m.p.g., giving the car a range of close on 300 miles under motorway conditions—before, that is, the 70 m.p.h. speed limit inflicted on the unhappy British motorist at the close of 1965. *The Autocar*, while sharing its sister journal's general approval of the 4·2-litre car, considered the fourteen-gallon fuel tank 'a little mean'.

Otherwise the Jaguar and Daimler ranges continued as before, the only casualty being the latter concern's SP.250 sports two-seater, which despite its adoption by a number of Police forces had never made any appreciable inroads into Triumph or Austin-Healey sales.

Jaguars made no impression in racing during the 1965 season. Two E-types, a 3·8-litre and a 4·2-litre, ran at Sebring without success, there were no Jaguar entries at all at Le Mans, and the best the E-type could do in the T.T. was eighth place in the G.T. category, behind an A.C. 'Cobra', two Ferraris, and four more 'Cobras'. For all the switch of emphasis to *gran turismi*, road-going machinery was well and truly squeezed out, leaving the field to Ferrari, and to specialized vehicles with American Vee-8 power units. Though cars of this type could be used for shopping, such usage was more often the basis for some off-beat publicity, whereas the E-type was first and foremost a fast tourer.

A series of strikes at Coventry prevented the appearance of Jaguar's expected show-stopper at Earls Court in October, 1965. The principal changes for 1966 were found in the Mk. II range, which was given a new lease of life with an all-synchromesh gearbox for the manual versions. Mk. X was made available in an executive model with electrically-operated division, a tacit admission by the factory that their chauffeur-driven carriages were not all Daimlers. Also available was a highly-effective air-conditioning installation

'We run them in'. A familiar sight in Britain is the Mk.II saloon as used by the police.

by Delaney Gallay Ltd., which added £275 10s. to the list price.

But if the G.T. version of the 4·2-litre E-type could not be ready in time for the London Show, it made its *début* at Geneva the following Spring, and the end-product was a genuine '2 plus 2', unlike some of its rivals. The wheelbase was lengthened from 8 ft to 8 ft 9 ins, the car was given two inches of extra height, and the doors were widened to give easier access to the back. A divided rear-seat squab could be folded down, in which case a really useful luggage platform was available when only two people were being carried. Structural strength was assured by utilizing the transverse tunnel carrying the rear suspension units both as main rear cross-member for the lower part of the body, and as support for the back seat. There were no major mechanical changes, but G.T. buyers had a choice of two transmissions—four-speed all-synchromesh, or the D1-D2 Borg-Warner automatic.

The new model as tested by *The Motor* proved to be 14 m.p.h. slower than the two-seater, but its maximum speed of 136·2 m.p.h. was more than adequate, while twenty stops undertaken at one-minute intervals from 85 m.p.h. failed to induce any noticeable brake fade. The automatic box was a trifle jerky by Borg-Warner standards, especially when changes were made at above 3,000 r.p.m. This criticism was echoed by Denis Jenkinson in *Motor Sport*. 'If you are going to drive the car properly', he observed, 'it is anything but automatic, relying on a lot of stirring about by the driver'—which is really an admission that he considered manual more suitable for such a machine. In his view the E-type, even with

Jaguar on the water: Norman Buckley with Miss Windermere III'.

four seats, was not really a G.T. either—he preferred to call it 'a refined touring car for Touring in the grand manner'—the sort of thing people used to say about Hispano-Suizas in the 1920s. But the report ended with an accolade: 'Unless you have just parted from a two-seater E-type coupé you would not know the difference when driving it, and I feel that Sir William Lyon's engineers have once again done a splendid job.'

Also at Geneva was Frua's version of the E-type, with five inches clipped off the nose, a not-altogether-happy radiator grille, some extra brake horses, modified suspension, and stronger bumpers, which Coombs of Guildford were considering putting on the British market. But more important was Bertone's two-door sports saloon, using the basic platform and mechanical components of the 3·8-litre S-type. The radiator grille had a hint of Mk. X about it, but though *The Autocar* rated this model as 'perhaps the best-looking Jaguar saloon ever', many of the magazine's readers disagreed strongly. As import duty was chargeable only on the body and trim, it was listed in England at £3,673 inclusive of tax. My own opinion is that factory styling is still preferable to the efforts of Italian *haute couture*, even if the end-product is an individualistic four-seater, and not merely a '2 plus 2'.

The march of events would, however, soon lead Jaguar-fans to wonder how long this individuality would remain.

E-type from the front: few ordinary motorists see this in their mirrors for any length of time.

CHAPTER 14

Joining the Big Battalions

One of the strengths of the specialist car manufacturer used to lie in his ability to provide exactly what the customer required. The large volume producer completely lacked this flexibility. To-day, everything has changed. The immense resources of the largest manufacturers and the use of computers for stock control, enable the giants to offer a staggering variety of options at extremely competitive prices and to sell them in very large volume.

Sir William Lyons, Lord Wakefield Gold Medal Paper, 1969.

In the mid 60s there was talk about the leading British motor manufacturers getting together so that as an industry we would be better able to face world competition. I was an enthusiastic protagonist as I believed that this was both necessary and desirable.

ibid.

On 12 July 1966, the British public was surprised to find headlines in their daily papers that had nothing to do with the war in Vietnam, the economic crisis, or even the World Football Cup—all burning questions of the hour. The *Daily Telegraph*'s announcement 'Jaguars Merge With B.M.C.' was typical.

The news was received with surprise, to put it mildly. For thirty years the Big Cat had stood for an individuality that was typically British, and from the fulfilment of this had come a recognition that was understood in any language. Even the joint statement by Sir William Lyons and Sir George Harriman of the British Motor Corporation that this was a merger rather than a take-over failed to reassure the more enthusiastic motorist, who had not forgotten the fate of the Riley.

Operation of the new group would be administered by a company to be known as British Motor (Holdings) Ltd. Its eight makes of private car and four makes of commercial vehicle would command 44 per cent of the home market where the basic B.M.C. combine had enjoyed 42 per cent, while the addition of Jaguar to the family would carry B.M.C.'s penetration into two new categories—the luxury-sporting saloon and the heavy truck. The only real overlap between the two ranges concerned the Vanden Plas 'Princess', never a very significant model, and by no means competitive with Daimler, let alone Jaguar. The Jaguar group would continue under the chairmanship of Sir William Lyons, and would retain 'the greatest possible degree of autonomy'.

That B.M.C. would benefit by the prestige value of Jaguar was unquestionable. Britain's biggest car manufacturer had long been strongest in the small-car class, where Alec Issigonis's brilliant Morris 'Minor' of 1948 had been worthily followed up eleven years later by the 'Mini'. Though the similar '1100' of 1963 had also turned out to be a best-seller, Ford's 'Cortina' derivatives had steadily been edging B.M.C.'s bigger saloons out of the 1½–2-litre category, traditionally a stronghold of the Corporation's two principal partners from the days of the Austin Twelve and Morris-Cowley in the 1920s. Further, while Jaguar had enjoyed a goodly share of dollar exports since the days of the push-rod cars, B.M.C. had never been able to sell their 'bread-and-butter' models on the same relative scale as their sporting machinery. M.G's 'TC', 'A', and 'B', and the Austin-Healey family might have become part of the American motoring scene but there had been no consolidation of the original Austin A.40's almost meteoric impact in 1948: not even the 'Mini' could captivate the heart of the trans-Atlantic motorist. Jaguar, with a weekly output of 500–600 cars, were earning £7,000,000 a year in the United States, whereas B.M.C., turning out nearly 20,000 a week, had to be content with a mere £21,000,000.

The step was, moreover, a logical one. The countries of the Old World, faced with the necessity of importing more and more raw materials, were becoming increasingly dependent on exports to maintain their balance of payments, while Japan was bulking steadily larger in the export field. Model changes cost more as tooling costs rose, and though a specialist manufacturer could rely on longer runs in terms of actual time—the Mk. VII Jaguar lasted from 1951 until early 1957, and the basic design survived for another four seasons—the situation would eventually arise in which he would have to retool, possibly with funds insufficient to enable him to keep abreast of the opposition. This had already happened in America, and not to specialist makers, either: the independents—Hudson, Studebaker, Packard, and Willys—had been relentlessly squeezed out despite their endeavours to remain competitive with the Big Three. The advent of the Common Market had accelerated the pace in Europe, as witness the combined operation by Daimler-Benz and Volkswagen to salvage Auto-Union, the Chrysler-Simca and Citroën-Panhard amalgamations, and the close liaison between Peugeot and Renault. Even in Japan, still regarded as a rising industrial nation, Nissan and Prince first joined forces and ultimately amalgamated in 1966. An obstinate independence might earn the accolade of the fanatic, but it could also mean either an unromantic decadence as a mere assembler of other people's parts, or a succession of half-hearted model changes which would eventually disillusion even the loyalists. The last years of Sunbeam in Wolverhampton

S.S.100 against a wintry background.

and Stutz in Indianapolis illustrate this point: neither had anything new to offer after 1930, and both died in the same year, 1935, making to the last admirable but outmoded motor cars.

Nor was the assembled vehicle still viable, since in these days most 'manufactured' cars are in fact assembled from major components bought out. The difference is that these are now made to the so-called manufacturer's design and thus are not proprietary parts in the old sense. And those component-suppliers not directly con-

trolled by the Big Battalions are invariably geared to their custom. In Jaguar's case B.M.C. owned the Pressed Steel Company, who have for many years been responsible for the production of all Jaguar saloon hulls. Thus a sudden slump in B.M.C's own press-work orders could adversely affect the price that Jaguar would have to pay. Further, Jaguar has always been a family concern, and thus the question can well be asked: 'After Sir William Lyons, who?'.

As if to emphasize their continuing independence, Jaguar had two

E-type sports car with 4.2-litre background.

A batch of E-types, awaiting delivery to clients, outside the administrative block at Browns Lane.

new models on show at Earls Court in October, 1966. One of these, the 420G, was merely the old Mk.X renamed and improved in detail, mainly in respect of additional crash padding on the dashboard, and the replacement of the traditional spotlamps by a brace of neat, matching grilles. The companion 420, however, was designed to bridge the gap between the 'S' range and the big cars, and could best be described as an S-type with the 4·2-litre engine and the appointments and frontal treatment of the 420G. Twin S.U. HD.8s replaced the triple-carburetter installation of the larger version, while on both the latest Jaguar variants customers had the choice of three transmission options—four-speed all-synchromesh with or without overdrive, and the Borg-Warner Type-8 automatic imported from

Jaguar without a name. The 3-litre car (VKV 752) built for Briggs
Cunningham to drive at Le Mans, 1960. It was a halfway house between
the D- and E-types.

America. Marles Varamatic power-assisted steering was standard on the 420G and optional on the 420, and prices were competitive as ever, prices in basic form being £2,238 and £1,930 respectively. At the same time a new big Daimler was unveiled: this car, the 'Sovereign', was in all essentials a Type-420 Jaguar, though it was listed only with overdrive and automatic.

Essentially the same range was continued into 1968, though the 3.8 Mk. II disappeared, and the two smaller variants were redesignated 240 and 340, respectively. Much was made of the 240's greater power—133 b.h.p. as against 112—in relation to its 1956 prototype: it was also pointed out that it retailed for only £133 more. The two oldest members of the family had, however, been stripped of some of their luxury. Trim was now Ambla rather than leather, and chromium-plated ancillary grilles replaced the foglamps of more

affluent days. The 340 lasted only one season, but the little Jaguar saw the decade out.

Also downgraded, though for a different reason, was the E-type. True, American sales had been holding up well, a rise in California balancing a mean 20 percent drop in other states, but the Nader-inspired safety-consciousness was now overlaid by tougher emission standards and California, with its built-in smogs, led the way. Within a few years, native makers would be offering 'Californian specials' on virtually every chassis, so much so that 'stick shift' addicts would be virtually confined to the smaller foreign imports.

Jaguar was not to be left behind. Some £250,000 were expended on making the E-type not only safe, but 'clean', with the mandatory air pump. First came the 4.2-litre 'emission' engine, featuring two dual-choke Zenith carburetters in place of the regular triple S.U.s,

Last of the compacts: 1968's 240 saloon. Upholstery is now Ambla instead of leather and foglamps are extra, but in twelve years the base price has risen barely £200.

The wider line: a 1957 XK150 coupé, last of the basic XK family, though the name was carried on in America, where the E-type was known as the 'XK-E'.

plus an extra small-diameter choke tube effective at low revs: this reduced output to 245 b.h.p. gross, or 171 net. At the same time, key-starting and hazard warning flashers were incorporated.

Inevitably, performance suffered. The car was three seconds slower to 100 m.p.h. and 125 m.p.h. now represented the maximum. By the time the 1968 London Show came round, the true Series II had arrived, also with detoxed power unit, but with crossflow radiator and twin fans as well. The brakes were now of Girling make, and power-assisted steering joined the list of options.

Worse, safety was now incompatible with the unadorned Lyons elegance. Gone were the slim sidelamps and bumpers, replaced by heavier metalware. Large rectangular tail-lights lived beneath the raised rear bumper and American-style number plate. The steering column now incorporated a collapsible section, and perhaps the sole aesthetic improvement was the more deeply-raked screen. By mid-1970, the roadster had vanished from catalogues, though these 'prostitutions' kept exports flowing. By the time the E family finally disappeared at the beginning of 1975, 49,032 out of a total of 72,584 cars had found customers in the U.S.A. The home market took 12,320, or well under 20 percent, a figure which compares interestingly with perhaps 4,000 assorted XKs delivered to British clients between 1950 and 1961. It is also fair to say that 'federalisation'

helped the E-type to survive and write yet another distinguished chapter into the Jaguar saga.

Overall, the export picture remained happy. Early in 1968, the press office reported sales worth £56 million in the previous four years, a creditable showing in those halcyon days when the most expensive Jaguar still *retailed* for less than £2,500. 52 per cent of all production went abroad, thanks to careful tailoring and 'horses for courses'. In Germany, the late Peter Lindner's agency was doing brisk business with the 420, local customers getting, of course, the specification ordained by their government—laminated screens and dual wing mirrors. Also indulged were their personal preferences— automatic, high-ratio back axles for *autobahn* work, heated rear windows, and wire wheels, though on these last, the locally-illegal eared hub caps had to be sacrificed.

If racing were apparently a thing of the past, the twin-cam. engine now scaled new heights of versatility. If Dennis's ingenious front-wheel drive ambulance with Jaguar power came to nothing, the unit had performed successfully in their fire engines and in Daimler's Ferret and Fox armoured cars. Now, from the summer of 1968, there was a new seven-seater Daimler in the classical idiom, built by B.M.H's Vanden Plas subsidiary on a lengthened 420G floor pan, and purest Jaguar beneath the skin: it was a Lyons creation,

The price of safety. On the Series II E-type, the Lyons line is still unmistakable, and those much-criticized bumpers look sylph-like in the safety-conscious 'eighties. But something has been lost . . .

too. The vehicle measured 226 inches from stem to stern and weighed over two tons dry. Further, it could be had for £3,824 at a time when a Phantom V Rolls-Royce already cost more than ten thousand pounds, and Marles Varamatic power steering and automatic transmission were part of the package. The modest sales potential (around 300 a year) and a conservative clientele have assured the model's survival into the 1980s. Since the first stage of Vanden Plas's work transformed the car into a driveable 'chassis', it was easily modified to the needs of the funeral trade.

A major cloud had, however, appeared on the horizon. May 1968 saw the consummation of the merger to end all mergers, between British Motor Holdings and the Leyland Group, now embracing Rover and Triumph cars (Alvis's private-car production had ceased during 1967), as well as vast commercial-vehicle interests. Sir William Lyons's dream of 'getting together to face world competition' had come true.

Seen from hindsight, British Leyland must rate as a catastrophe. In 1968, however, it looked good, even from the Jaguar standpoint. The new consortium could claim 40 per cent (roughly double 1979 levels!) of all home-market car sales, and on paper its winners outnumbered its losers. Lord Stokes, the Leyland chief of the period, would soon axe such needless duplications as the aged 4-litre Vanden Plas limousine (*née* Austin Princess) and the wholly meaningless Riley line, but this still left the Mini, the 1100/1300 family, the sporting TRs and Spitfires from Triumph, the M.G-B, the Rover 2000 and its four-wheel drive stablemates, and of course the Jaguar Daimler family. That it also landed the group with three separate Vee-eight programmes—Triumph had one in the pipeline to join the Rover-Buick and the Daimler—was still overlooked, by the laity at any rate.

Jaguar was promised 'the greatest possible degree of autonomy'. Sir Williams Lyons remained at the helm, and would control the

Ultimate versatility. Vanden Plas's 1968 Daimler limousine, here seen in an appropriate setting. It featured Jaguar's twin-cam six in place of a Daimler-built vee-eight.

firm's destiny until his retirement in 1972. All they apparently lost was their recently acquired empire—Daimler's buses and Guy passed to Leyland's Truck and Bus Division, and Coventry-Climax to Special Products. But the new structure had its effect in other ways. The giant would soon prove unmanageable; the Jaguar had to suffer for the sins of other departments. As late as 1970, the management, while admitting the loss of 5,000 cars by strike action, could also claim a new record of 29,507 units delivered. Further, only a tiny minority of the stoppages were attributable to 'industrial action within our organisation'.

This was not, however, the whole story. Leyland might leave the factory alone, but they had their own ideas of foreign distribution, and these were not Jaguar's. By the early 1970s such former stalwarts as Mme. Bourgeois in Belgium and Emil Frey in Switzerland had switched their allegiance to Japanese Toyotas, though the latter had continued for a while in charge of Leyland's new Swiss subsidiary. Ironically, this was happening at a time when Leyland management was flirting with Toyota and seeking (vainly, as it transpired) to market Jaguars through a section of Toyota's domestic dealer-network.

The painful saga of British Leyland has been amply dealt with in Graham Turner's *The Leyland Papers* and elsewhere. Worse was to follow: soon Jaguar would cease to have a corporate existence, while Lord Ryder's famed report on the ailing giant would advocate more and more rationalisation. Production figures, however, show that Jaguar came through the worst phase of Leylandism relatively unscathed. Annual deliveries stayed at or above the 25,000 level, rising to 1974's peak of 35,826 units. Five years after the XJ6's introduction at the 1968 London Show, a two-year wait was the norm, and when Jaguar suffered its first big lay-off in the winter of 1974–75, it was no fault of Leyland policy. The energy crisis had coincided infelicitously with the work-up of the magnificent V12. At long last Americans were turning towards frugal compacts, a change from the on-off love affair that had punctuated the Detroit scene since 1960.

But in 1968 the problem seemed to be too many models rather than Trades Unions or Leyland meddling. At that time the press office reckoned that 189,024 Jaguar/Daimler permutations—or roughly seventeen years' production—existed within the catalogue. Thus, some tidying was indicated, and the groundwork for this was laid at Earls Court with the introduction of the XJ6 (not, of course, to be confused with the earlier four-cylinder prototype of that name).

Basically the new car was an update of the compact unitary saloon theme launched in 1955, with the E-type rear springing dating back

When is an XJ not an XJ? When it is a closely guarded pre-production prototype being tested over the rough stuff. But even the plastic patches can't quite conceal the shape, and those Coventry trade plates give the game away.

to 1964's S-family. For all the cross-hatch grille and the Big Cat's final banishment from the bows, it was unmistakably William Lyons, and unmistakably Jaguar. In fact, the new style gave a 'crouching beast' look, brilliantly exploited on the cover of the 1973 Show catalogue. The car was also a twin-cam. six, though shrewd observers measured the bonnet width and noted how well a vee-engine would fit.

The revolution came beneath the surface. Coils and wishbones with anti-dive characteristics replaced torsion bars at the front, while the hull itself was conceived on three-box principles. Torsional strength was concentrated below the waistline, which reconciled a rigid centre-section with narrow screen pillars and plenty of glass.

Sills and propeller-shaft tunnel were main structural members, reinforced by a double-skinned bulkhead and extra cross-members, under the front seats and just ahead of the rear seat pan. Separate rubber mounts were used for each front suspension unit, and there were further box sections built into the bonnet sides, into the frontal radiator support, and as rear suspension supports. The traditional, wing-mounted fuel tanks were now fully sealed compartments.

From the mechanical standpoint, the rack and pinion steering of bigger-engined cars was power assisted, brakes were the servo-assisted Girling discs from the Series II E-type, and buyers had the usual choice of transmissions—manual, manual with overdrive, and Borg-Warner three-speed automatic. (In fact, though 'straight' manual

An increasingly executive image spelt fewer wire-wheel options and
a higher percentage of automatics, but the XJ6 still wears the former
happily. However, a casualty is the traditional Big Cat mascot.

In the early XJ days, Jaguars were still within reach of constabulary budgets, and the Ayrshire Force received this car at a time when there were still formidable home-market queues.

was nominally listed as late as 1974, it hardly ever happened.) Wood-and-leather trim survived, but switches were now of rocker type and hazard warning flashers were standard equipment. Also provided were a heated rear window, two-speed wipers, electric screen-washers, seat belt anchorages (belts themselves were still extra), and an air-blending heater which, it was hoped, would still the time-honoured grouses over Jaguar ventilation. It did not: when air conditioning joined the extras list in 1972, it was welcomed with open arms by the press.

Standard engine was the faithful 4.2-litre, credited with 245 b.h.p. at 5,500 r.p.m., but for those in quest of economy there was a new, smaller unit, in effect an 'opened-up' 2.4, with dimensions of 83 x 86 mm. (2,792 c.c.), rated at 180 b.h.p. Prices were still astoundingly low, from £1,797 for a basic 2.8-litre up to £2,254 for a 4.2 with full de luxe equipment.

Predictably, it was the old familiar story we have heard since the first Jaguar's début in 1935: rave notices and the Car of the Year awards which latter did not, of course, happen in the 1930s. An automatic 4.2 tested by Autocar in June 1969, attained 120 m.p.h. and 17 m.p.g., while acceleration times were close to those of the original XK120 two-seater: less than a second slower (3.9 as against 3.2) to 30 m.p.h., a quarter-second slower to 50, and a 0–100 m.p.h. figure of 30.4 seconds. The 'ton' in half-a-minute on a luxury, automatic-equipped saloon would have been unthinkable a few years back. Since by this time the old 120 was becoming an object of reverence, nobody drew unkind parallels in the braking department! A superb ride was allied to an absence of those thumps characteristic of too many expensive unitary offerings, handling was considered better than the E-type's, and there was no kick-back from the steering, even on pavé. Only the hydraulic steering pump intruded into the general silence. No wonder Roger Bell, in those days a member of Motor's test staff, would later sum the XJ up as the outstanding car of the 1970s, in spite of the fact that it was fifteen months old when the decade opened.

The 2.8, by contrast, proved somewhat of a lemon. Piston failures were not unknown, and the car was quietly played down by Jaguar themselves. A Daimler edition (from the end of 1969 the Sovereign label would be attached to more luxurious XJs with fluted grilles) was tested by Autocar as a used model, and returned only 18–21 m.p.g. Admittedly, this one was an automatic, but since the main object of the smaller power unit was fuel economy, there seemed to be little advantage in the loss of performance (around 105 m.p.h. maximum) and acceleration. After 1972, sales were restricted to a few export markets with capacity taxes and other small-car biasses, and a year later the 2.8 was quietly dropped.

In the meantime the problem was to lay hands on any XJ6. Someone had to be getting them, and though American shipments

hit a new overall high of 3,536 units in the first half of 1970, Jaguar was reduced to running 'Don't blame your Dealer' advertisements. They also comforted Britons with reminders that production was running at 400 cars a week when, in fact, it was nearer 150, as was later admitted! The factory was, however, up to the 650 level by the autumn of 1971, at which time 50,000 cars had been made, and 28,000 of them exported.

The demise of the 420G at the end of the 1970 season (the S-types and the 420 had faded out two years before) suggested that something new might be brewing. 1971 saw the season's no. 1 sensation, a 5.3-litre V12. The press sharpened its pens once more.

The genesis of this one went back a long way—to 1956—when Jaguar retired from racing. They had intended to return in 1958, but the fire at the factory scotched these plans, and since then they had been too busy with touring models. In the early 1960s, however, Walter Hassan and W. M. Heynes, assisted by Derrick White on the chassis side and by Malcolm Sayer as aerodynamicist, went to work on a mid-engined monocoque racer, the XJ13. The engine (its code-name, with deliberate confusion, was XJ6!) first ran in August 1964, though the car itself was not ready until 1966.

Its integral structure had D and E affiliations: front suspension was by double wishbones, with twin parallel trailing arms and coils

Daimlers were no longer 'Distinctively Different'. This 1970 4.2-litre Sovereign was excellent value at £2,714, and it wore the right grille, though everything further aft was unadulterated Jaguar.

Forgotten dreams . . . or would it have upset the Ford-Ferrari applecart at Le Mans? Mid-engined XJ13 racer with the original four-cam V12 unit, 1966.

at the rear. Girling ventilated disc brakes were to be expected, while the new engine location dictated a transaxle, in which the gearbox was the same ZF five-speeder used in Ford's GT40 racing coupés: a twin-plate clutch was utilized to transmit the extra power of the V12 engine. This last was a new departure, and indeed the first Jaguar engine totally uninfluenced by the old R.A.C. horsepower formula jettisoned at the end of 1946. Cylinder dimensions were 87 × 71 mm for a capacity of 4,994 cc, and the blocks were angled at sixty degrees. The four overhead camshafts (two per block) had chain primary drive, with secondary drive by gears. Cooling was assisted by an electric fan, and the Lucas mechanical fuel injection fed by twin Lucas electric pumps. The car weighed 2,478 lbs. dry, and was designed for 170 m.p.h., with 143 m.p.h. coming up in fourth and 116 in third. Tests at the M.I.R.A. track produced a new 161 m.p.h. lap record, and the car was timed at 175 m.p.h. down the straight. Alas, a crash put paid to further development, though the XJ13 has since been rebuilt and survives in the factory's own collection. Inevitably its existence remained a distant rumour: any press release would have set off an impossible demand for road-going Twelves.

Now a modified edition of this engine went into the E-type. Dimensions of the production model were 90 × 70 mm (5,343 cc) and in the interests of simplicity one chain-driven camshaft per block sufficed, with bowl-in pistons. Making the integral block and crankcase of alloy saved 116 lbs. over the old cast-iron six, and in fact

The last sports car, here seen with factory hardtop option. There is a hint of XJ about the twelve-cylinder E-type's radiator grille.

the complete engine came out only 80 lbs. heavier. Cooling was assisted by twin electric fans, the unit conformed with American emission standards, and though fuel injection was tried, the designers settled for four dual-choke downdraught Zenith carburetters. Output in standard form was 272 b.h.p. as against the 502 b.h.p. of the XJ13, and new ground was broken by the use of Lucas-Opus transistorised ignition, the first time such a system had been applied to a volume-production engine.

Jaguar were clearly taking the V12 seriously, and the £3 million expended on a new engine plant at the Radford works went a long way to explaining why William Lyons had chosen to abdicate his independence. This plant was currently turning out 170 engines a week, but had a 'stretch' potential of four figures. This suggested, indeed, that Jaguar might be after the world's record for volume-production, twelve-cylinder cars: 179,041 Lincolns of the Zephyr family turned out between 1936 and 1948.

First recipient of the new masterpiece was, of course, the E-type. The longer, 2 + 2 wheelbase was standardised, and the roadster reinstated in the range, with an automatic option now available on this as well as on the coupé. At the same time, the cockpit was updated for greater safety, and wings were wider. Otherwise the changes were undramatic: a stiffened structure, the latest split-circuit disc braking ventilated at the front, and energy-absorbing steering column of collapsible type, and Adwest power steering as standard. Wheels were pressed-steel disc or wire to order, while on roadsters, at any rate, the longer 'chassis' made for more *lebensraum*. Early publicity referred to an alternative Series III model using the well-tried 4.2-litre six, but this existed only in prototype form. One such car survived to win Peter Taylor the *Autosport* Production-Car Championship in 1974.

The latest cross-hatch grille was hardly attractive, and purists lamented the demise of the old, wood-rim steering wheel. But the latest E-type made up for all the power losses caused by the last, detoxed sixes. One reporter summarised the car as 'new wine in an old bottle', and the result was vintage, if not in a strictly motoring sense. Handling was almost unimpaired, flexibility was incredible (a 10–30 m.p.h. *top-gear* acceleration time of 7.3 seconds was recorded), and over 140 m.p.h. came up in top. The car would hurtle up to 120 in 26.5 seconds, while a long-term fuel consumption of 14.3 m.p.g. was, in *Autocar*'s view, 'entirely acceptable in relation to the colossal performance available'. The only let-down was the ventilation—the through-flow system provided on coupés seemed to make precious little difference. As for price, Sir William Lyons was still in command, and at the £3,857 quoted in 1972 it undercut such opposition as Aston Martin, B.M.W., Jensen and Porsche. Only the Aston could beat it in terms of sheer speed, though up to 60 m.p.h. Porsche's latest 911S was slightly ahead. Price comparisons of the period are interesting, although slightly unrealistic if British import duty is taken into consideration. B.M.W.'s 3.0CS coupé cost £5,118, the Mercedes-Benz 350SL £5,379, and the cheapest Aston Martin (the six, by now on its way out) £6,447. Yet in a free market such as Switzerland, the Jaguar roadster at 33,500 francs could

Safety cockpit: this shot of the twelve-cylinder E-type shows the
rocker-type switches on the dash. For the USA, air-conditioning was
added; the outlets can be seen under the facia.

hold its own against even the B.M.W. at 37,600, or a few hundred francs more than the British car in coupé form. Jaguar was back on the map.

History was soon to repeat itself. Though the twelve-cylinder E-type was always regarded as more than a roadgoing test-bed (it would account for 15,292 units in four seasons), the engine had been designed around the XJ saloon, and in June 1972, it duly took its place under that conveniently wide bonnet. Its flat torque curve was tailor-made for automatic and, in fact, there would be no manual alternative to Borg-Warner's Type-12 box.

Otherwise changes were minimal: an engine-driven fan in place of the E-type's twin electric installation, and stainless steel guards under the bonnet to cope with high temperatures. The XJ front suspension was reinforced to cope with the extra weight—some 300 lbs. installed—of the new model. Pricewise, the car was a real bargain, at £3,725. This time a Daimler version appeared immediately: it carried the Double Six label, in commemoration of Europe's first series-production V12, released from Radford back in the autumn of 1926.

There was, however, no comparing two generations of Daimler, except in terms of flexibility and maybe fuel consumption. The old Double-Six-50 had a 155-inch wheelbase, weighed two-and-a-half tons even in owner-driven form, and was flat out at 80 m.p.h. It was also aimed at paid chauffeurs, while its price (1970's inflation

Built to travel fast and far. A V12 E-type coupé hastens north at dusk.

notwithstanding) was barely £1,000 lower than the new model. This latter proved as fast as the latest E-type (the road-test figure of 146 m.p.h. was actually higher), and not much less accelerative, needing only nineteen seconds to reach 100 m.p.h. Silence attracted comparisons with the Rolls-Royce, the car cruised at way over a Silver Shadow's maximum of 112–115 m.p.h. (not that many countries still permitted such indulgence!), and one critic commented that 'the only sensation of having a propulsive unit under the bonnet is that of speed and acceleration'. Unlike its Daimler ancestor, the new V12 was not an oil-burner—some 700 miles per pint was the norm as against the 300 ascribed (somewhat less than justly) by the press to twin-cam. Jaguar sixes. In any case, in 1972 the world could still take an 11 m.p.g. thirst for petrol in its stride: a factor which may well win Jaguar the sad honour of launching the last of the series-production Twelves.

By the autumn, an extra four inches of wheelbase were available on the XJ12L, this one offering rear-seat legroom worthy of so splendid a carriage. Long-wheelbase Double Sixes could be had in Vanden Plas form with vinyl roofs and built-in air conditioning for £5,439. A year later came the Series II XJ family, with reinforced bulkheads and doors, raised bumpers conforming to the latest American rules, and improved heaters. Instruments were now grouped in front of the driver, a centralised door locking system was fitted, and the twelve's cooling system was now applied to the six, as were

Soon after the marriage of the V12 engine and XJ hull came some extra length and rear seat leg-room. Jaguar's XJ12L (above) had a running-mate in the Daimler Double Six (below), here seen in luxury Vanden Plas guise with vinyl top.

ventilated front disc brakes. Power-Lok differentials, standard on V12s, became optional in the six-cylinder range, all now with 4.2-litre engines.

Most important of all, the Lyons touch would be seen in all its glory for the last time on a new body style: a two-door, five-seater coupé using the original short 'chassis'. To many people, it was the most beautiful car to come out of Browns Lane since the first XK120 coupé in 1951. There was only one fly in the ointment: you couldn't buy one. Deliveries would not begin until February 1975.

What with 1972's summer strike, which had delayed deliveries of the first XJ12s, people were beginning to wonder what was happening at The Jaguar. A new £15,000 landaulette on the big Vanden Plas Daimler chassis was scant consolation: only two were made.

Grace and pace . . . though there's not a lot of space in the back of the Series III E-type 2+2 coupé. Even the Moscow militiaman is not immune to its beauty, though.

CHAPTER 15

Jaguar Without Lyons

How many people who can afford to spend over £12,000 on a car are prepared to put up with manual transmissions?

XJ-S Road Test, *Autocar,* May 1977

This question has been posed with increasing vehemence by the press since automatics first gained the upper hand in the early 1960s. The Jaguar answer ran to 15–20 per cent out of a clientele of perhaps 30,000 a year. More frightening, however, was the thought of a £12,000 Jaguar—and one which would cost close on £20,000 by the beginning of 1980!

The early days of the Leyland regime had little outward effect on Browns Lane. The old pattern continued—a show-stopper followed by a year or two of steady consolidation. There had been the XJ6 in 1968, the twelve-cylinder E-type in 1971, the XJ12 in 1972, and the coupé in 1973. Boss might succeed boss at Leyland, but the world still wanted Jaguars and still had to put up with the waiting list.

But change was in the air. The old ream was breaking up. Heynes had already retired, Malcolm Sayer's untimely death in 1971 had deprived Jaguar of an inspired aerodynamicist, and in 1972 not only Walter Hassan, but William Lyons himself would step down, the latter after fifty distinguished years in the motor industry. That he continued as President of Jaguar Cars was merely a courtesy gesture to a great figure. The circle was completed in January 1974, when F.R.W. (Lofty) England, Lyon's successor as Chairman, also departed. Geoffrey Robinson, the next in line, had a short reign, since he found himself violently out of sympathy with Leyland's increasing policy of rationalisation.

On the car side, a notable casualty was the E-type: the last of over 72,000 was laid down late in 1974, the final batch of fifty carrying commemorative plaques. No. 1 of this series would fetch £15,000 at auction in December 1979: the last of them all, appropriately painted black, made but one short journey, from the end of the assembly line to the factory's showroom. Open Jaguars had been relegated to the past.

This did not deter specialist industry. Best-known of all the Jaguar-based specialty items was the J72 introduced in 1972 by Robert Jankel's Panther West Winds Ltd. of Weybridge. The wide-rim wheels apart, it could easily have been taken for an SS100, and all the essential mechanics were Jaguar—a 3.8-litre or 4.2-litre engine, a four-speed overdrive gearbox of XJ6 type, and all-disc brakes. The tubular chassis was to Panther's own design, with coil-spring i.f.s, a live axle and coils at the rear, and recirculating-ball steering gear. Speeds of 115–120 m.p.h. were possible, and subsequent V12 editions were quite a lot faster, though not very manageable. Panther sold some 380 of these cars in the first four seasons, though later efforts were perhaps less felicitous. Of these, the Lazer—a bizarre, Jaguar-engined beach buggy—never got beyond a Motor Show appearance, but the fantastic De Ville of 1974 was actually made in fair numbers.

This mid-1930s style four-door sports saloon with its horseshoe radiator attracted comparisons with the Bugatti Royale, and a typical show time comment in those auction-oriented years was: 'What's the reserve?' Construction was traditional: a Panther-built chassis frame and body panels in hand-beaten aluminium. It was trimmed in Connolly leather with carpeting by Wilton, and equipment included air conditioning, electric windows and sun roof, radio-stereo, a radio-telephone, and a television set in the rear compartment. Initial price was £17,650, but the 1976 drophead coupé edition would be the season's most expensive British car at £31,941.

Mechanics were Jaguar XJ12, down to brakes, steering, suspension and final drive unit. The car had a certain appeal to pop stars and the like, but nostalgia has always been a sticky wicket, and Panther were in receivership by the end of 1979.

Others were sportier. Bryan Wingfield's Deetype and Guy Black's Lynx were convincing replicas of the original D-type using similar monocoque hulls allied to E-type mechanical elements. Customers willing to pay £15,000–20,000 for such vehicles could also choose which D-type shape they wanted, and in 1978 Wingfield was talking in terms of an XJ13 replica, though presumably without the

On its way out – the open Jaguar. No sports cars would be made after
1974, though the V12 E-type coupé still had some months to run.

From the side the shape has suffered little, even in the 1970s. V12
E-type with automatic transmission.

four-cam engine. The Guyson was an individualistic wedge shape built up around an E-type centre-section, its six-cylinder engine giving 330 b.h.p. with the aid of six-dual-choke Weber carburetters. Dick Crosthwaite and John Gardiner called *their* Big Cat a Kougar: this one was a marriage of S-type mechanics (cheap and plentiful) to their own multi-tubular frame and glassfibre bodywork. The general effect was Le Mans Replica Frazer Nash rather than any named variety of Jaguar.

Alas, the *pur sang* was now seen only in Club events. There was, however, one brief renaissance—predictably in America, where six-cylinder E-types continued to give a good account of themselves in amateur hands. Not that there was anything amateur about Bob Tullius's approach.

Tullius had made his name with a long string of victories at the wheel of TR Triumphs, and later with Dodges in Trans Am events. In 1974, he teamed up with Leyland-America to run V12 E-types under SCCA rules. The complications of coast-to-coast coverage were circumvented by mounting two *équipes*—his own Group 44 in the East, and Huffaker Engineering's, with Lee Mueller as driver, in California. Results were generally good, despite a defeat at the hands of the Chevrolet Corvettes in the finals at Atlanta. In 1975, however, Tullius personally won the SCCA Championship. What a pity that there were no longer any E-types to sell, especially as the energy crisis was biting, and the XJ12 was suffering a recession!

Nostalgia-machine. Panther West Winds always denied that their J72 was a replicar but, its wide-rim wheels apart, it was very like the old SS100 of pre-war days. Bonnet bulges indicate a V12 engine within.

The pinnacle of beauty. What a pity the XJ coupé took so long to
reach the public. Here is a Series II V12 with raised bumpers.

With the new coupés still unavailable, the nostalgia brigade made most of 1974's headlines, but in 1975 there were some further improvements to the XJ range. These included an important 'first' for Jaguar: factory-fitted stainless steel exhausts. Axle ratios were raised in the interests of economy (the XJ12's went up from 3.31 to 3.07), power steering was officially standardised throughout the range, and all XJ12s now featured vinyl roofs. These latter were also to be fitted with Lucas electronic fuel injection, though short-chassis cars continued to be delivered in carburetter form until later in the year. With the formal demise of the 2.8-litre, a new 'economy' XJ appeared, powered by an old friend, the 3.4-litre unit as used from 1949 to the end of the sixties. In its latest guise with twin S.U. HS.6 carburetters, it gave 161 b.h.p., and was the first Jaguar Six of the modern generation on which 'straight' manual was no longer even quoted. This 3.4-litre came only as a short-chassis saloon: its list price of £4,795 was more than double 1968's form. Capacity, rather than

'cylinder' designations, took over from July, when the cars became the XJ 3.4, 4.2 and 5.3, respectively.

Though the fuel-injected V12 is considered by many to be the best Jaguar engine so far, these novelties were but Kings and Queens in the pack: Jaguar was saving their Ace for Earls Court. September 19, 1975, was summarised by the factory as 'A Black Day for Modena, Stuttgart and Turin'. Bob Knight and Harry Mundy, now in charge of engineering at Browns Lane, had come up with the XJ-S.

To most of us, the shape was a horrid disappointment. The Lyons touch had, it seemed, been lost from a bulky coupé resembling an overblown and less-than-sporting Ferrari, though some people saw traces of Bertone's one-off 1968 show car, the Piranha, on an E-type floor plan. (They were wrong: the Piranha was irrelevant to Jaguar thinking.) At £8,900, too, it did not seem exactly cheap: gone were the days when one inspected the latest model and asked how in heaven's name Bill Lyons did it. One of Leyland's platforms, however, was that Jaguars were unrealistically priced. In their view, an inexpensive prestige car must wear the Rover badge, and that division's vee-eights consistently undercut the XJ family. Still, the cheapest Ferrari cost £10,520, their V12s ran at around the £16,000 mark in Britain, and even Lamborghini's relatively modest P250 came out at £9,434. And if you wanted your Italian masterpiece serviced, it was wise to make tracks for London.

Problems of built-in safety, of course, ruled out any updating of the old E-type: that car's boot-mounted fuel tank would have been illegal anyway. Thus from the sills downward the XJ-S was a short-chassis XJ, its wheelbase further abbreviated to 8 ft. 6 in. The bulkhead and engine compartment sides formed a triangulated structure, while the doors (as on Series II saloons) were reinforced against lateral impact. Plastic bumpers of 5 m.p.h. type were fitted, the fuel tank spanned the rear suspension arch forward of the luggage locker, and the Adwest power steering was an E-type legacy, though higher gearing had been adopted in the interests of more 'feel'. Reflective aluminium panels were used under the bonnet, brakes were split-circuit Girling discs, and the 154-inch wheels were of die-cast alloy.

The power train was little changed, though by this time electronic fuel injection was used on all twelve-cylinder engines. Quoted output was a respectable 285 b.h.p., and buyers had a choice of four-speed synchromesh or a Borg-Warner 12 automatic box. Air conditioning, centralised door locks, inertia reel seat belts, and a laminated glass windscreen were inclusive, though only seat facings were now of leather: p.v.c. sufficed for the rest of the trim. A sign of the times was a galaxy of eighteen warning lamps on the facia—shades of Duesenberg's legendary 'box of tricks' or those 2300S Fiat coupés which so infuriated testers in the early 1960s. Matters were, however, simplified by two 'overall' lights, one in red which called for an immediate stop, and the second in amber, which spelt 'investigate when convenient'.

The XJ-S's looks might not appeal, but the car certainly went, attaining 153 m.p.h. in complete safety and uncanny silence. Wind noise supervened at 80 m.p.h., but acceleration set new standards once more for touring Jaguars: 0–50 in 5.2 seconds, 0–100 in 16.9 seconds, and 0–140 m.p.h. in 45 seconds. Further, a manual car could be driven off in top gear and reach this same velocity in 70 seconds, though one hopes that drivers with such habits would have specified automatic! Not that self-shifting was an appreciable penalty: the difference to 100 m.p.h. was a mere $1\frac{1}{2}$ seconds in the manual car's favour, or no more than could be accounted for by weather conditions and variations between individual vehicles.

The XJ-S was not raced in Europe, though across the Atlantic Bob Tullius had his own modifications ready in time for the 1977

Executive express. The XJ-S coupé.

season. These consisted in the main of scrapping fuel injection in favour of six carburetters and converting the power unit to dry-sump lubrication, thus eliminating problems of oil surge. That this cost some £6,000 to do was offset by a top speed of 180 m.p.h. and ten seconds lopped off the 0–120 m.p.h. acceleration time. Tullius was well rewarded with the Trans Am drivers' championship, though in the constructors' section Jaguar lost out fractionally to Porsche. Less publicised, for obvious reasons, was another XJ-S victory, that of Dave Heinz and Dave Yarborough in the 1979 Cannonball Race.

This event commemorated the great American marathon driver, E. G. ('Cannonball') Baker, whose last transcontinental record was taken in 1933, when he averaged nearly 60 m.p.h. at the wheel of a Graham Eight. Such dashes were almost certainly illegal then, but in the age of safety and emission laws they were positively criminal. This did not prevent 46 starters from leaving New York, or 42 of them from making it to Los Angeles. The winning Jaguar was lucky enough to dodge police traps, and did the run in 32 hours 51 minutes, an average of 87.25 m.p.h. The second-place 6.9-litre Mercedes-Benz was only eight minutes slower.

The irony of Tullius's triumphs was not lost on the home front, where Jaguar's racing renaissance was having a rough passage. On paper, prospects looked excellent when the Broadspeed 5.3 coupé took its bow in February 1976. Ralph Broad (to whom the work was entrusted by Leyland) had modified the suspension and fitted a full anti-roll cage, though much of the wood-and-leather trim was retained. Wheels were of wide-rim, magnesium-alloy type, thirteen-inch diameter at the front, and $13\frac{1}{2}$ in. at the rear, while in the best Edwardian manner the brakes were to be water-cooled. In practice they were not: Group 2 regulations forbade this.

The engine, overbored to a little over 5.4 litres, ran on an 11.51:1 compression, used racing-type fuel injection, and was said to give at least 480 b.h.p. Unlike Tullius, Broad could not use dry-sump lubrication; once again regulations would defeat him until it was too late. Curiously, though, the four-speed close-ratio manual box (unobtainable on the stock article) was successfully homologated. Drivers were to be Derek Bell, David Hobbs, Steven Thompson, and British touring-car champion Andy Rouse. A full season's sport was promised.

But race after race came—with no Jaguars. The cars ran precisely once in 1976, in the T.T., and even then only one car (Bell/Rouse) came under starter's orders. It won pole position and led from the start, coming out on top in an early tussle with Nilsson's B.M.W. It was then delayed by a flat tire on the circuit, and though Rouse resumed the race, he would later shed a wheel. *Motor Sport* called it 'a promising debut'.

At least a full programme was attempted in 1977. The use of nineteen-inch wheels should have solved the tire problems, while the cars now acquired a spoiler for their boot lids. This had to become a factory extra, though few stock coupés were seen with it. Some useful publicity was gained when a replica (with standard engine) was featured in television's *Avengers* series, but reliable lubrication and drive-shafts would have been more of an asset, and

the Jaguars never won through. The latter ailment eliminated Bell and Rouse at the Salzburgring, and the cars were scratched from Mugello and Enna while a remedy was sought. Things looked better at Brno, where Schenken and Fitzpatrick were timed at over 170 m.p.h. on the straights. When the former blew a tyre at full speed, the car was at least able to continue, finishing well down the list in sixteenth place. Bell and Rouse retired after assorted top-end and transmission troubles.

At least a Jaguar had finished, and at the Nürbúrgring there was actually a second place for Bell and Rouse behind the Alpino-B.M.W. of Nilsson/Quester, even if *Autocar* hinted at 'five engine changes and oil surge galore'. The other car had a short life and a merry one: a lap record straight off followed by the almost immediate departure of oil pressure.

By the time Zandvoort came round, Broad had secured homologation for the dry-sump engine, but only one car went to Holland in this form, and ironically it was the old-type 5.3 (Bell/Rouse) which worked its way into second place before retiring once more. The T.T. looked more hopeful, though it took Schenken only an hour to shed the now-mandatory wheel, leaving Rouse to tackle the B.M.W. opposition. This he did in fine style, though veteran racegoers could not help noting sadly that these days it was the German cars that had the brakes, while the British Jaguars relied on speed. Was this the true heir of the old C- and D-types?

It was not. Eight laps from the end, the Jaguar gave up the ghost, and Leyland called it quits. The renaissance had gone out with a T. S. Eliot whimper and a sizable bill to the taxpayer now that Leyland was state owned. *Autocar* suggested 'well over £100,000': *Motor Sport* hinted at more than twice this sum. The Leyland albatross had struck again.

Jaguar-fans, however, took heart when a further upheaval at Leyland put Michael Edwardes into power. With a truly Hanoverian regularity, the new broom promptly reversed all the old policies. The car division was reshuffled into three groups—Austin-Morris, the specialised Jaguar-Rover-Triumph range, and Land Rover Ltd., henceforward to guide the destinies of Rover's all-wheel drive range. The new J.R.T. set up had an impressive array of plants: in Coventry it controlled Browns Lane (Jaguar), Radford (Daimler), and Canley (Triumph), to which could be added the Rover complex at Solihull, Triumph's two Merseyside factories at Speke, and the small, London-based Vanden Plas operation with only 290 employees. One of the Speke factories and Vanden Plas were, however, shortly destined for the axe.

Jaguar got the best of the deal. Rover lost those profitable cross-country vehicles which had kept them out of the merger game for so long in the 1950s and 1960s, and the unhappy M.G., irrevocably wedded to Cowley and Longbridge, embarked upon a one-way trip to the condemned cell. But the Edwardes regime believed firmly in *marque* identity, so J.R.T. was once again a corporate undertaking and not just a faceless division. If E. P. Thompson, the American-born overall head of the new group, had relatively little automobile experience, Jaguar itself was in the hands of Bob Knight, with over

1976's tragedy, the Broadspeed XJ12 racing coupé, sole XJ model to
match the big engine with a manual gearbox.

thirty years at the factory behind him, most of these in responsible
situations. A J.R.T. handout released for the 1978 Motor Show was
explicit. 'Because', it said, 'of the traditions and history of the *marques* and because of their unique and enduring individualities, the
new company does not seek to impose a uniform identity across the
whole organisation'. Nonetheless, the formidable impact of Rover's
new 3½-litre SP saloon made it clear that Jaguar had gone up-
market for good.

In the midst of all these alarums and excursions, a 1977 success
passed almost unnoticed. Tony Fahey's hydroplane with XJ12 engine
set a new international 5-to-7-litre class inboard record at 128.375
m.p.h. His *Vladivar I* was none other than a rebuild of the late
Norman Buckley's *Miss Windermere V,* with the Jaguar in place of a
6½-litre Maserati. (Buckley had been unable to extract a Twelve
from the works.) There were other links with the past; preparation
of Fahey's engine was by Ron Beaty's Forward Engineering under

the supervision of retired Jaguar experimental-shop foreman Phil
Weaver. Weaver had been closely associated with Buckley's engines
in six-cylinder days.

Exports still bulked large. Despite the changing economic climate, Americans were now taking 6,000 XJ saloons a year, while
yet another onslaught was made on the Japanese market. This time
there was a new importer, Mitsui, with ten distributors and one
hundred ancillary outlets. Jaguars had always been the mainstay of
Leyland's limited Japanese sales—about 1,600 a year—and now
local customers were apparently willing not only to pay £24,000 for
a 5.3 saloon, but also to put up with left-hand drive, necessary
since Japan's emission rules closely paralleled America's. The cars
were still competitive in Switzerland, where the 39,000 francs asked
in 1979 for a 4.2 ran close to such offerings as B.M.W.'s most
expensive saloon (38,200) and the Cadillac Seville, now economically viable at 39,200 fr. (thanks to the fall of the dollar). True,

Mercedes-Benz could market their 280 for less than 30,000 francs, but this was hardly a prestige car. The 350, more valid competition, slotted halfway between the 4.2 and 5.3 at 44,800 fr. At nearly 60,000 fr, the XJ-S sounded very expensive, but one had to remember that full-size Maseratis worked out at 68,800, and the 400 Ferrari at 83,200.

On the production side, little of moment was happening. A casualty of the first months of 1978 was the delightful coupé, which had never made up the leeway lost by early window-sealing problems. As by this time the short-chassis saloons had been dropped, the car was out on a limb. (Leyland's excuse for scrapping the design was that it would have been uneconomic to tool for a restyled Series III version.) Happily it would have a descendant in the form of a drophead conversion by SS's old rivals, Avon. This company, after many vicissitudes and a spell of hearse-making, had come under the control of Graham Hudson. Their Jaguar ragtop, created by Anthony Stevens, became available during 1979. The pity was that it had not happened during the coupé's lifetime.

Also during 1979 the Borg-Warner 12 transmission was supplanted on 5.3s and XJ-Ss by the General Motors 400. There had been too many complaints of jerky shifts, something that Turbohydramatic, with nearly forty years of continuous development behind it, had finally eliminated. In other respects, however, the XJ family still rated *The Motor*'s past label of 'British and Best'. *Autocar*'s team, trying the latest 4.2 that October, noted with 'astonishment' that 'so old a design should remain not merely competitive, but should still set the highest of standards in the toughest of classes'.

The following March, at Geneva, Jaguar took a step that many people had been requesting for years: they offered the 4.2 with Rover's five-speed gearbox incorporating an overdrive top, an arrangement preferable to a separately-controlled overdrive. Italian makers, notably Alfa Romeo and Fiat, had long adopted such a method. Initially five-speeders were reserved for the Swiss market, and they were to be confined to six-cylinder models. Harry Mundy, who would retire in 1980, had devised an admirable five-speed transmission for the twelves, but money was short, and demand limited: a cool 85 per

Open Jaguars today: Pininfarina's XJ-S Spyder was strictly for the 1978 Birmingham Motor Show, with little or no hope of replicas. By contrast Ladbroke Avon, Graham Hudson's revival of SS's one-time rivals, was prepared to sell you this XJ drophead (opposite), converted from an existing coupé. The stylist is Anthony Stevens.

cent of Jaguar's clientele now specified automatic. By the end of 1978 it had become apparent with the advent of the Rover box, that 'stick-shift' XJ-Ss would continue only as long as supplies of the old-type transmissions lasted.

There was even less hope of production for Pininfarina's lovely XJ-S Spyder, the star of that year's Motor Show. Mechanically it was stock, but it was as close to a true roadster as was now viable, with its unobtrusive anti-roll hoop trimmed to match the two-piece hood, and doubling as seat-belt anchorage. The facia was an electronic masterpiece with rows of warning lights, horizontal speedometer, and rev-counter. On later cars (should they happen), deformable plastic nose and tail pieces were promised. Show visitors drew favourable comparisons with the maestro's last one off Jaguar, an overblown XJ saloon somewhat resembling an overblown N.S.U. R080.

Customers would, however, profit from Italian influence, though the subject never made the headlines. Hitherto, others had followed Jaguar, sometimes almost slavishly, as in the case of De Tomaso's Ford-engined Deauville sports saloon. Now, in the post-Lyons era, Jaguar would invoke the aid of Pininfarina for the XJ's latest facelift, announced in the spring of 1979.

All these Series III cars were four-door saloons on a common 9 ft. 4¾ in. wheelbase, and the three engines were continued, though the 4.2 received Lucas-Bosch L-Jetronic fuel injection, carburetters being retained on the 3.4. The Rover five-speeder was the staple manual option, and cruise control was available on 5.3s and automatic 4.2s. Another timely option was a headlamp wash-wipe.

Styling was subtly updated, with a higher roofline, but no increase in actual body height, flush-fitting door handles, and redesigned bumpers. The old cross-hatch grille gave way to a more attractive design with central vertical bar—as on the first S.S. I of 1932! But for all the Italianisation, cars were still unmistakably Jaguars or Daimlers. The latter breed was continued, albeit only with the two larger engines, while customers who wanted something 'distinctively different', in pursuit of the old Daimler company's slogan, could have their saloons with Vanden Plas trim. For state occasions there was still £22,213 worth of 4.2-litre limousine, now put together at Browns Lane since the closure of the Kingsbury coachworks. In Britain, alas, nothing, be it Jaguar or Daimler, now cost less than £13,000, in spite of which annual sales still topped the 25,000 mark. Whatever lay in the future, it would not be another obituary.

Jaguar has held its head above water through the turmoil of the 1970's. Some of the Lyons imprint remains, even if detailed execution is no longer his.

On the 1st April 1980, Jaguar's first full-time Chairman for five years was appointed. That was John Eagan. After making his name as the force behind British Leyland's 'Unipart' he went to Massey Ferguson in 1976 before returning to British Leyland. Also in 1980, after nearly 8 years, the company was granted its former title of Jaguar Cars Ltd. again.

Anything to do with British Leyland carries an outsize question mark if only because a state owned undertaking is swayed by the views of the party in power – and in any case the energy crisis means that the automobile's future hangs in the balance.

No sector of the car market is exempt from the necessity to conserve energy and to provide economy conscious motoring. In 1981, after five years' development, a unique HE cylinder-head design was introduced. Jaguar was the first manufacturer to use this so-called 'fireball' combustion chamber in volume production. Along with a substantial increase in power on V12 models, fuel economy improvements of 20 per cent or more were obtained. This coupled with a new pricing policy has led in the second half of 1981 to increased sales in the USA and UK – which in turn have led to the company returning to the black.

In March 1961, my son and heir, Ralph Douglas-Scott-Montagu, made his first road journey at the age of five days in the Mk.II saloon I was then driving. I see no reason why I should not live to see a grandchild of mine begin his motoring career in a Jaguar – even if it be a battery-electric governed to 50 m.p.h.

Shape for the 1980s: the Series III XJ saloon shows off its new divided grille.

What most people see of the Series III XJ saloon — where the law
permits! The higher roof line and flush-fitting door handles are
clearly in evidence on this 4.2-litre example.

APPENDIX I

S.S. AND JAGUAR MODELS 1932-81

Model	Years Current	Model	Years Current
S.S. I (including S.S. 90)	1932–36	E-type 3.8-litre	1961–65
S.S. II	1932–36	Mk. X 3.8-litre	1962–65
S.S. Jaguar 1½-litre (side valve)	1936–37	S-type 3.4-litre	1964–68
S.S. Jaguar and Jaguar 2½-litre (including '100' models)	1936–48	S-type 3.8-litre	1964–68
S.S. Jaguar and Jaguar 1½-litre (o.h.v.)	1938–48	Mk. X 4.2-litre	1965–67
S.S. Jaguar and Jaguar 3½-litre (including '100' models)	1938–48	E-type 4.2-litre	1965–68
2½-litre Mk. V	1949–51	E-type 4.2-litre 2 + 2	1966–68
3½-litre Mk. V	1949–51	420	1967–68
XK120	1949–54	420G	1967–70
Mk. VII (all types)	1951–57	240	1968–69
C-type	1951–54	340	1968
D-type	1955–57	E-type 4.2-litre Series II	1968–71
XK140	1955–57	XJ6 2.8-litre	1969–73
2·4-litre (excluding Mk. II models)	1956–60	XJ6 4.2-litre	1969–73
Mk. VIII	1957–59	E-type Series III	1971–74
XK-SS	1957	XJ12	1972–73
3·4-litre (excluding Mk. II models)	1957–60	XJ6 and 12 Series II	1974–79
XK150	1957–61	XJ 3.4, 4.2 and 5.3	1975–79
Mk. IX	1959–61	XJ-S	1976
Mk. II 2.4-litre	1960–67	XJ Series III, 3.4, 4.2 and 5.3	1979
Mk. II 3.4-Litre	1960–67	XJS Series III, 5.3 HE	1981
Mk. II 3.8-litre	1960–67	XJS HE	1981

APPENDIX II

SWALLOW SPECIAL COACHWORK ON
PROPRIETARY CHASSIS 1927-1933

Date	Make	Model	No. of Cyls.	C.C.	Styles Listed and Prices	Remarks
1927	Austin	Seven	4	747·5	2-seater, £175 Hardtop coupé, £185	
	Morris	Cowley	4	1,550	2-seater, £210	
1928	Austin	Seven	4	747·5	2-seater, £175 Hardtop coupé, £185	With hard and soft tops, £190
1929	Austin	Seven	4	747·5	2-seater, £170 10s. Hardtop coupé, £180 10s. Saloon, £187 10s.	With hard and soft tops, £185 10s.
	FIAT	509A	4	990	Saloon, £250	
1930	Austin	Seven	4	747·5	2-seater, £170 10s. Hardtop coupé, £180 10s. Saloon, £187 10s.	With hard and soft tops, £185 10s.
	FIAT	509A	4	990	Saloon, £250	Discontinued March 1930
	Standard	Nine	4	1,287	Saloon, £245	
	Swift	Ten	4	1,190	Saloon, £275	
1931	Austin	Seven	4	747·5	2-seater, £165 Hardtop coupé, £175 Saloon, £187 10s.	With hard and soft tops, £185 De luxe models £5 extra
	Standard	Big Nine	4	1,287	Saloon, £250	
	Standard	Ensign	6	2,054	Saloon, £275	Introduced May 1931
	Swift	Ten	4	1,190	Saloon, £278	Discontinued May 1931
1931	Wolseley	Hornet	6	1,271	2-seater, £220	Introduced Jan. 1931
1932	Austin	Seven	4	747·5	2-seater, £150 Hardtop coupé, £160 Saloon, £165	With hard and soft tops, £165
	Standard	Big Nine	4	1,287	Saloon, £250	
	Standard	Sixteen	6	2,054	Saloon, £275	
	Wolseley	Hornet	6	1,271	2-seater, £225 4-seater, £225	
	Wolseley	Hornet Special	6	1,271	2-seater, £255 4-seater, £255	Introduced May 1932
1933	Wolseley	Hornet Special	6	1,271	2-seater, £255 4-seater, £260	

APPENDIX III

STANDARD SERIES PRODUCTION S.S. AND JAGUAR MODELS 1932-1981

Prices quoted for post-war models include Purchase Tax unless otherwise stated, and are those ruling on the earliest date in the given year on which the model was available.

Data given relate to the basic model of each standard type. Engine and transmission options are quoted in the 'Remarks' column where applicable.

S.D.P.—Single dry plate (clutch).
S/E—Special Equipment (model).

Date and Model	Price	No. of Cylinders and Engine Dimensions	Output (B.H.P. at R.P.M.)	Carburetter	Valves	Ignition	Cooling	Lubrication
1932 S.S.I	£310	6 65·5 × 101·6 mm. 2,054 c.c.	48 at 3,600	Solex	Side	Coil	Thermo-syphon and fan	Force feed
S.S.II	£210	4 60·25 × 88 mm. 1,006 c.c.	28 at 4,000	Solex	Side	Coil	Thermo-syphon and fan	Force feed
1933 S.S.I 16 h.p.	£325	6 65·5 × 101·6 mm. 2,054 c.c.	48 at 3,600	S.U. or R.A.G.	Side	Coil	Thermo-syphon and fan	Force feed
S.S.I 20 h.p.	£335	6 73 × 101·6 mm. 2,552 c.c.	62 at 3,600	S.U. or R.A.G.	Side	Coil	Thermo-syphon and fan	Force free
S.S.II	£210	4 60·25 × 88 mm. 1,052 c.c.	28 at 4,000	Solex	Side	Coil	Thermo-syphon and fan	Force feed
1934 S.S.I 16 h.p.	Coupé, £335 Saloon, £340 Tourer, £335	6 65·5 × 106 mm. 2,143 c.c.	53	R.A.G.	Side	Coil	Pump and fan	Force feed
S.S.I 20 h.p.	Coupé, £340 Saloon, £345 Tourer, £340	6 73 × 106 mm. 2,663·7 c.c.	68	R.A.G.	Side	Coil	Pump and fan	Force feed

S.S.II 10 h.p.	Coupé, £260 Saloon, £265	4 63·5 × 106 mm. 1,343 c.c.	32 at 4,000	R.A.G.	Side	Coil	Pump and fan	Force feed
S.S.II 12 h.p.	Coupé, £265 Saloon, £270	4 69·5 × 106 mm. 1,608 c.c.	38 at 4,000	R.A.G.	Side	Coil	Pump and fan	Force feed
1935 S.S.I 16 h.p.	Saloon, £340 Tourer, £335 Airline saloon, £360 Drophead coupé, £380	6 65·5 × 106 mm. 2,143 c.c.	53	2 R.A.G.	Side	Coil	Pump and fan	Force feed
S.S.I 20 h.p.	Saloon, £345 Tourer, £340 Airline saloon, £365 Drophead coupé, £385	6 73 × 106 mm. 2,663·7 c.c.	68	2 R.A.G.	Side	Coil	Pump and fan	Force feed
S.S.90	£395	6 73 × 106 mm. 2,663·7 c.c.	90	2 R.A.G.	Side	Coil	Pump and fan	Force feed
S.S.II 10 h.p.	Saloon, £265 Tourer, £260	4 63·5 × 106 mm. 1,343 c.c.	32 at 4,000	2 R.A.G.	Side	Coil	Pump and fan	Force feed

Date and Model	Gearbox and Ratios	Clutch and Final Drive	Brakes	Suspension	Wheels and Tyres	Wheelbase and Track	Remarks
1932 S.S.I	4-speed 4·66, 6·15, 9·75, 16·08:1	S.D.P. Spiral bevel	Bendix cable-operated	½–E : ½–E	R.W. wire 28 × 5·50	9ft. 4ins. 4ft. 1in.	Standard engine. 20 h.p. unit £10 extra
S.S.II	3-speed	S.D.P. Spiral bevel	Bendix cable-operated	½–E : ½–E	R.W. wire 27 × 4·75	7ft. 5½ins. 3ft. 9ins.	Standard engine
1933 S.S.I 16 h.p.	4-speed 4·66, 6·15, 9·75, 16·1:1	S.D.P. Spiral bevel	Bendix cable-operated	½–E : ½–E	R.W. wire 5·50 × 18	9ft. 11ins. 4ft. 3ins.	Standard engine
S.S.I 20 h.p.	4-speed 4·66, 6·15, 9·75, 16·1:1	S.D.P. Sprial bevel	Bendix cable-operated	½–E : ½–E	R.W. wire 5·50 × 18	9ft. 11ins. 4ft. 3ins.	Standard engine
S.S.II	4-speed 5·43, 7·5, 13·3, 20·68:1	S.D.P. Spiral bevel	Bendix cable-operated	½–E : ½–E	R.W. wire 27 × 4·75	7ft. 5½ins. 3ft. 9ins.	Standard engine
1934 S.S.I 16 h.p.	4-speed, synchro. 4·75, 6·52, 10·04, 17·1:1	S.D.P. Spiral bevel	Bendix cable-operated	½–E : ½–E	R.W. wire 5·50 × 18	9ft. 11ins. 4ft. 5½ins.	Standard engine
S.S.I 20 h.p.	4-speed, synchro. 4·75, 6·52, 10·04, 17·1:1	S.D.P. Spiral bevel	Bendix cable-operated	½–E : ½–E	R.W. wire 5·50 × 18	9ft. 11ins. 4ft. 5½ins.	Standard engine
S.S.II 10 h.p.	4-speed, synchro. 5·29, 7·68, 12·84, 20·85:1	S.D.P. Spiral bevel	Bendix cable-operated	½–E : ½–E	R.W. wire 4·75 × 18	8ft. 8ins. 3ft. 10½ins.	Standard engine
S.S.II 12 h.p.	4-speed, synchro. 5·29, 7·68, 12·84, 20·85:1	S.D.P. Spiral bevel	Bendix cable-operated	½–E : ½–E	R.W. wire 4·75 × 18	8ft. 8ins. 3ft. 10½ins.	Standard engine

1935							
S.S.I 16 h.p.	4-speed, synchro. 4·5, 6·18, 9·51, 16·2:1	S.D.P. Spiral bevel	Bendix cable-operated	½-E: ½-E	R.W. wire 5·50 × 16	9ft. 11ins. 4ft. 5⅜ins.	Standard engine. Drophead coupé introduced March 1935
S.S.I 20 h.p.	4-speed, synchro. 4·25, 5·83, 8·98, 15·3:1	S.D.P. Spiral bevel	Bendix cable-operated	½-E: ½-E	R.W. wire 5·50 × 18	9ft. 11ins. 4ft. 5⅜ins.	Standard engine. Drophead coupé introduced March 1935
S.S.90	4-speed, synchro. 4·5, 5·83, 8·98, 15·3:1	S.D.P. Spiral bevel	Bendix cable-operated	½-E: ½-E	R.W. wire 5·50 × 18	8ft. 8ins. 4ft. 6ins.	Standard engine. Introduced March 1935. Available with 4·25 and 3·75 rear axles
S.S.II 10 h.p.	4-speed, synchro. 5·29, 7·68, 12·84, 20·85:1	S.D.P. Spiral bevel	Bendix cable-operated	½-E: ½-E	R.W. wire 4·75 × 18	8ft. 8ins. 3ft. 10½ins.	Standard engine

Date and Model	Price	No. of Cylinders and Engine Dimensions	Output (B.H.P. at R.P.M.)	Carburetter	Valves	Ignition	Cooling	Lubrication
1935								
S.S.II 12 h.p.	Saloon, £270 Tourer, £265	4 69·5 × 106 mm. 1,608 c.c.	38 at 4,000	2 R.A.G.	Side	Coil	Pump and fan	Force feed
1936								
S.S.I 20 h.p.	Saloon, £325 Airline saloon, £350	6 73 × 106 mm. 2,663·7 c.c.	68	2 R.A.G.	Side	Coil	Pump and fan	Force feed
S.S.II 12 h.p.	£240	4 69·5 × 106 mm. 1,608 c.c.	38 at 4,000	2 R.A.G.	Side	Coil	Pump and fan	Force feed
S.S. Jaguar 1½-litre	£285	4 69·5 × 106 mm. 1,608 c.c.	65 at 4,500	S.U.	Side	Coil	Pump and fan	Force feed
S.S. Jaguar 2½-litre	Saloon, £385 Tourer, £375	6 73 × 106 mm. 2,663·7 c.c.	104 at 4,500	2 S.U.	Overhead pushrod	Coil	Pump and fan	Force feed
S.S.100	£395	6 73 × 106 mm. 2,663·7 c.c.		2 S.U.	Overhead pushrod	Coil	Pump and fan	Force feed
1938–40								
S.S. Jaguar 1½-litre	Saloon, £298 Drophead coupé, £318	4 73 × 106 mm. 1,776 c.c.	65 at 4,500	S.U.	Overhead pushrod	Coil	Pump and fan	Force feed
S.S. Jaguar 2½-litre	Saloon, £395 Drophead coupé, £415	6 73 × 106 mm. 2,663·7 c.c.	102 at 4,600	2 S.U.	Overhead pushrod	Coil	Pump and fan	Force feed
S.S.100 2½-litre	£395	6 73 × 106 mm. 2,663·7 c.c.		2 S.U.	Overhead pushrod	Coil	Pump and fan	Force feed
S.S. Jaguar 3½-litre	Saloon, £445 Drophead coupé, £465	6 82 × 110 mm. 3,485 c.c.	125 at 4,250	2 S.U.	Overhead pushrod	Coil	Pump and fan	Force feed
S.S.100 3½-litre	£445	6 82 × 110 mm. 3,485 c.c.		2 S.U.	Overhead pushrod	Coil	Pump and fan	Force feed

1946–8 Jaguar 1½-litre	1946: Saloon, £684 S/E saloon, £729 1947: Saloon, £787 S/E saloon, £838 1948: Saloon, £865 S/E saloon, £921	73 × 106 mm. 1,776 c.c.	4	65 at 4,500	S.U.	Overhead pushrod	Coil	Pump and fan	Force feed

Date and Model	Gearbox and Ratios	Clutch and Final Drive	Brakes	Suspension	Wheels and Tyres	Wheelbase and Track	Remarks
1935 S.S.II 12 h.p.	4-speed, synchro. 4·86, 7·06, 11·8, 19·18:1	S.D.P. Spiral bevel	Bendix cable-operated	½–E: ½–E	R.W. wire 4·75 × 18	8ft. 8ins. 3ft. 10½ins.	Standard engine
1936 S.S.I 20 h.p.	4-speed, synchro. 4·25, 5·83, 8·98, 15·3:1	S.D.P. Spiral bevel	Bendix cable-operated	½–E: ½–E	R.W. wire 5·50 × 18	9ft. 11ins. 4ft. 5⅜ins.	Standard engine. 16 h.p. engine available for £5 less
S.S.II 12 h.p.	4-speed, synchro. 4·86, 7·06, 11·8, 19·18:1	S.D.P. Spiral bevel	Bendix cable-operated	½–E: ½–E	R.W. wire 4·75 × 18	8ft. 8ins. 3ft. 10½ins.	Standard engine. 10 h.p. engine available for £5 less
S.S. Jaguar 1½-litre	4-speed, synchro. 4·86, 7·06, 11·8, 19·18:1	S.D.P. Spiral bevel	Girling rod-operated	½–E: ½–E	R.W. wire 4·75 × 18	9ft. 0ins. 4ft. 0ins.	Standard engine. Continued for 1937, price £295
S.S. Jaguar 2½-litre	4-speed, synchro, 4·25, 5·83, 8·98, 15·3:1	S.D.P. Spiral bevel	Girling rod-operated	½–E: ½–E	R.W. wire 5·50 × 18	9ft. 11ins. 4ft. 6ins.	Standard-built engine. Listed also with 2-litre engine, 1936, but none made. Continued for 1937 with gear ratios 4·5, 6·18, 9·51 and 16·2 to 1
S.S.100	4-speed, synchro. 4, 5·48, 8·45, 14·4:1	S.D.P. Spiral bevel	Girling rod-operated	½–E: ½–E	R.W. wire 5·25 × 18	8ft. 8ins. 4ft. 6ins.	Standard-built engine. Continued for 1937
1938–40 S.S. Jaguar 1½-litre	4-speed, synchro. 4·86, 7·06, 11·8, 19·1:1	S.D.P. Spiral bevel	Girling rod-operated	½–E: ½–E	R.W. wire 5·25 × 18	9ft. 4½ins. 4ft. 6ins.	Standard-built engine. 1940 saloon price, £325
S.S. Jaguar 2½-litre	4-speed, synchro, 4·5, 6·16, 9·5, 16·2:1	S.D.P. Spiral beve	Girling rod-operated	½–E: ½–E	R.W. wire 5·50 × 18	10ft. 0ins. 4ft. 8ins.	Standard-built engine
S.S.100 2½-litre	4-speed, synchro. 4·5, 5·48, 8·45, 14·4:1	S.D.P. Spiral beve	Girling rod-operated	½–E: ½–E	R.W. wire 5·50 × 18	8ft. 8ins. 4ft. 6ins.	Standard-built engine. Fixed-head coupé listed 1939 at £545, but none made. 1940 price £435
S.S. Jaguar 3½-litre	4-speed, synchro. 4·25 5·12, 7·9, 13·45:1	S.D.P. Spiral bevel	Girling rod-operated	½–E: ½–E	R.W. wire 5·50 × 18	10ft. 0ins. 4ft. 8ins.	Standard-built engine. 1940 saloon price, £490
S.S.100 3½-litre	4-speed, synchro. 3·8, 4·58, 7·06, 12·04:1	S.D.P. Spiral bevel	Girling rod-operated	½–E: ½–E	R.W. wire 5·50 × 18	8ft. 8ins. 4ft. 6ins.	Standard-built engine. Fixed-head coupé listed 1939 at £595, but only one made. 1940 price £490
1946–8 Jaguar 1½-litre	4-speed, synchro. 4·875, 7·08, 11·84, 19·21:1	S.D.P. Hypoid bevel	Girling rod-operated	½–E: ½–E	wire 5·25 × 18	9ft. 4½ins. 4ft. 4ins.	Last Jaguar model with Standard-built engine

Date and Model	Price	No. of Cylinders and Engine Dimensions	Output (B.H.P. at R.P.M.)	Carburetter	Valves	Ignition	Cooling	Lubrication
1946-8 Jaguar 2½-litre	1946: £889 1947: £991 1948: £1,089	6 73 × 106 mm. 2,663·7 c.c.	102 at 4,600	2 S.U.	Overhead pushrod	Coil	Pump and fan	Force feed
Jaguar 3½-litre	1946: £991 1947: £1,099 1948: £1,199	6 82 × 110 mm. 3,485 c.c.	125 at 4,250	2 S.U.	Overhead pushrod	Coil	Pump and fan	Force feed
1949 Jaguar 2½-litre Mk.V	1949: £1,189 1950: £1,247	6 73 × 106 mm. 2,663·7 c.c.	102 at 4,600	2 S.U.	Overhead pushrod	Coil	Pump and fan	Force feed
3½-litre Mk.V	£1,263	6 82 × 110 mm. 3,485 c.c.	125 at 4,250	2 S.U.	Overhead pushrod	Coil	Pump and fan	Force feed
XK120	1950-1: 2-seater, £1,263 1952: 2-seater, £1,678 F.h. coupé, £1,694 1953: 2-seater, £1,759 F.h. coupé, £1,775 1954: 2-seater, £1,601 F.h. coupé, £1,644 D.h. coupé, £1,660	6 83 × 106 mm. 3,442 c.c.	160 at 5,000	2 S.U. horizontal	Twin overhead camshafts	Coil	Pump	Force feed
1951 Mk.VII	1951: £1,276 1952: £1,694 1953: £1,775 1954: £1,616	6 83 × 106 mm. 3,442 c.c.	160 at 5,000	2 S.U. horizontal	Twin overhead camshafts	Coil	Pump	Force feed
C-type	£2,327	6 83 × 106 mm. 3,442 c.c.	200 at 5,800	2 S.U. horizontal	Twin overhead camshafts	Coil	Pump	Force feed
1952 XK120 Special Equipment	£1,255 (not incl. P.T.)	6 83 × 106 mm. 3,442 c.c.	180 at 5,750	2 S.U. horizontal	Twin overhead camshafts	Coil	Pump	Force feed
1955 Mk.VIIM	1955: £1,616 1956: £1,711	6 83 × 106 mm. 3,442 c.c.	190 at 5,600	2 S.U. horizontal	Twin overhead camshafts	Coil	Pump	Force feed

Date and Model	Gearbox and Ratios	Clutch and Final Drive	Brakes	Suspension	Wheels and Tyres	Wheelbase and Track	Remarks
1946-8 Jaguar 2½-litre	4-speed, synchro. 4·55, 6·12, 8·82, 15·36:1	S.D.P. Hypoid bevel	Girling rod-operated	½–E: ½–E	wire 5·50 × 18	10ft. 0ins. 4ft. 6ins.	Jaguar-built engine. Drophead coupé for export only from Dec. 1947
Jaguar 3½-litre	4-speed, synchro. 4·27, 5·74, 8·28 14·41:1	S.D.P. Hypoid bevel	Girling rod-operated	½–E ½–E	wire 5·50 × 18	10ft. 0ins. 4ft. 6ins.	Jaguar-built engine. Drophead coupé for export only from Dec. 1947
1949 Jaguar 2½-litre Mk.V	4-speed, synchro. 4·55, 6·21, 9·01, 15·35:1	S.D.P. Hypoid bevel	Girling 2LS hydraulic	Independent wishbone and torsion bar: ½–E	disc 6·70 × 16	10ft. 0ins. 4ft. 9½ins.	Saloon and drophead coupé. In production till 1951. This and subsequent models have Jaguar-built engines
3½-litre Mk.V	4-speed, synchro. 4·3, 5·87, 8·52, 14·5:1	S.D.P. Hypoid bevel	Girling 2LS hydraulic	Wishbones and torsion bars: ½–E	disc 6·70 × 16	10ft. 0ins. 4ft. 9½ins.	Saloon and drophead coupé. Production till 1951
XK120	4-speed, synchro. 3·64, 4·98, 7·22, 12·29:1	S.D.P. Hypoid bevel	Lockheed 2LS hydraulic	Wishbones and torsion bars: ½–E	disc 6·00 × 16	8ft. 6ins. 4ft. 3ins.	Fixed-head coupé, March 1951. Drophead coupé, April 1953
1951 Mk.VII	4-speed, synchro. 4·27, 5·84, 8·56, 14·4:1	S.D.P. Hypoid bevel	Girling 2LS hydraulic with servo assistance	Wishbones and torsion bars: ½–E	disc 6·70 × 16	10ft. 0ins. 4ft. 9½ins.	Borg-Warner 2-speed automatic transmission optional on export models from Jan. 1953: Laycock de Normanville overdrive from Jan. 1954 on home and export models
C-type	4-speed, synchro. 3·31, 3·99, 5·78, 9·86:1	S.D.P. Hypoid bevel	Lockheed 2LS hydraulic	Wishbones and torsion bars: torsion bars	wire 6·00 × 16 front 6·50 × 16 rear	8ft. 0ins. 4ft. 3ins.	Drum brakes on production models
1952 XK120 Special Equipment	4-speed, synchro. 3·54, 4·84, 7·01, 11·93:1	S.D.P. Hypoid bevel	Lockheed 2LS hydraulic	Wishbones and torsion bars: ½–E	wire 6·00 × 16	8ft. 6ins. 4ft. 3ins.	Drophead coupé from April 1953. Known in U.S.A. as XK 120 M.C.
1955 Mk.VIIM	4-speed, synchro. 4·27, 5·17, 7·44, 12·73:1	S.D.P. Hypoid bevel	Girling 2LS hydraulic with servo assistance	Wishbones and torsion bars: ½–E	disc 6·70 × 16	10ft. 0ins. 4ft. 10ins.	Available with overdrive; ratios 3·53, 4·55, 5·5, 7·82, 13·56:1 and with Borg-Warner 3-speed automatic transmission

Date and Model	Price	No. of Cylinders and Engine Dimensions	Output (B.H.P. at R.P.M.)	Carburetters	Valves	Ignition	Cooling	Lubrication
1955–7 XK140	1955: 2-seater, £1,598 F.h. coupé, £1,616 D.h. coupé, £1,644 1956–7: 2-seater, £1,692 F.h. coupé, £1,711 D.h. coupé, £1,741	6 83 × 106 mm. 3,442 c.c.	190 at 5,600	2 S.U. horizontal	Twin overhead camshafts	Coil	Pump	Force feed
D-type	£3,878	6 83 × 106 mm 3,442 c.c.	250 at 6,000	3 twin-choke Weber	Twin overhead camshafts	Coil	Pump	Force feed: dry sump
1956 2·4-litre	1956: £1,344 (S/E, £1,375) 1957: £1,430 1958–9: £1,495 1960: £1,445	6 83 × 76·5 mm. 2,483 c.c.	112 at 5,750	2 d/d Solex	Twin overhead camshafts	Coil	Pump	Force feed
1957 Mk.VIII	£1,830	6 83 × 106 mm. 3,442 c.c.	210 at 5,500	2 S.U. HD.6	Twin overhead camshafts	Coil	Pump	Force feed
XK-SS	£1,570 (in U.S.A.)	6 83 × 106 mm. 3,442 c.c.	250 at 6,000	3 twin-choke Weber	Twin overhead camshafts	Coil	Pump	Force feed: dry sump
3·4-litre	1957–9: £1,672 1960: £1,579	6 83 × 106 mm. 3,442 c.c.	210 at 5,500	2 S.U. HD.6	Twin overhead camshafts	Coil	Pump	Force feed
XK150	1958–9: £1,763 1960: £1,666	6 83 × 106 mm. 3,442 c.c.	190 at 5,500	2 S.U. HD.6	Twin overhead camshafts	Coil	Pump	Force feed
1958 XK150S	£2,065	6 83 × 106 mm. 3,442 c.c.	250 at 5,500	3 S.U. HD.8	Twin overhead camshafts	Coil	Pump	Force feed
1959 Mk.IX	1959: £1,994 1960: £1,884	6 87 × 106 mm. 3,781 c.c.	220 at 5,500	2 S.U. HD.6	Twin overhead camshafts	Coil	Pump	Force feed
1960 2·4-litre Mk.II	£1,534	6 83 × 76·5 mm. 2,483 c.c.	120 at 5,750	2 d/d Solex	Twin overhead camshafts	Coil	Pump	Force feed

Date and Model	*Gearbox and Ratios*	*Clutch and Final Drive*	*Brakes*	*Suspension*	*Wheels and Tyres*	*Wheelbase and Track*	*Remarks*
1955–7 XK140	4-speed, synchro. 3·54, 4·28, 6·2, 10·55:1	S.D.P. Hypoid bevel	Lockheed 2LS hydraulic	Wishbones and torsion bars: ½-E	disc 6·00 × 16	8ft. 6ins. 4ft. 3½ins.	Available with overdrive, and with automatic in 1956–7. Special Equipment version has 210 b.h.p. engine and wire wheels
D-type	4-speed, synchro. 3·54, 4·52, 5·82, 7·61:1	Triple dry plate Hypoid bevel	Dunlop disc	Wishbones and torsion bars: torsion bars	alloy 6·50 × 16	7ft. 6ins. 4ft. 2ins.	
1956 2·4-litre	4-speed, synchro. 4·55, 6·21, 9·01, 15·35:1	S.D.P. Hypoid bevel	Lockheed Brakemaster 2LS servo-assisted hydraulic	Independent coil and wishbone: cantilever ½-E	disc 6·40 × 15	8ft. 11½ins. 4ft. 6⅝ins.	Unitary construction Standard model listed only in 1956. Overdrive optional; automatic, disc brakes and wire wheels optional from 1958
1957 Mk.VIII	4-speed, synchro. 4·27, 5·16, 7·47, 12·73:1	S.D.P. Hypoid bevel	Girling 2LS hydraulic, servo-assisted	Independent wishbones and torsion bars: ½-E	disc 6·70 × 16	10ft. 0ins. 4ft. 10ins.	Overdrive or 3-speed automatic optional
XK-SS	4-speed, synchro. 3·5, 4·5, 5·8, 7·6:1	Triple dry plate Hypoid bevel	Dunlop disc	Wishbones and torsion bars: torsion bars	alloy 6·50 × 16	7ft. 6⅝ins. 4ft. 3½ins.	
3·4-litre	4-speed, synchro. 3·54, 4·54, 6·58, 11·95:1	S.D.P. Hypoid bevel	Lockheed Brakemaster 2LS servo-assisted hydraulic	Coil and wishbones: cantilever ½-E	disc 6·40 × 15	8ft. 11⅜ins. 4ft. 6⅝ins.	Unitary construction. Overdrive or automatic optional. Disc brakes, and wire wheels available as optional equipment from 1958. Introduced February 1957
XK150	4-speed, synchro. 3·54, 4·54, 6·58, 11·95:1	S.D.P. Hypoid bevel	Lockheed 2LS hydraulic	Wishbones and torsion bars: ½-E	disc 6·00 × 16	8ft. 6ins. 4ft. 3⅜ins.	Introduced May 1957, in fixed-head and drophead coupé forms: special equipment models have 210 b.h.p. engine, wire wheels, Dunlop disc brakes. Overdrive and automatic available in standard and special equipment ranges. Roadster introduced March 1958
1958 XK150S	4-speed, synchro. with overdrive 3·18, 4·09, 5·247, 7·60, 13·81:1	S.D.P. Hypoid bevel	Dunlop servo-assisted disc	Wishbones and torsion bars: ½-E	wire 6·00 × 16	8ft. 6ins. 4ft. 3⅜ins.	Disc brakes standard. Overdrive transmission only. 'Gold Top' engine with straight-port head. 3·8-litre engine optional, 1959
1959 Mk.IX	4-speed, synchro. 4·27, 5·48, 7·94, 14·42:1	S.D.P. Hypoid bevel	Dunlop servo-assisted disc	Wishbones and torsion bars: ½-E	disc 6·70 × 16	10ft. 0ins. 4ft. 10ins.	Power steering. Overdrive or automatic optional
1960 2·4-litre Mk.II	4-speed, synchro. 4·27, 5·48, 7·94, 14·42:1	S.D.P. Hypoid beve	Dunlop servo-assisted disc	Coil and wishbones: cantilever ½-E	disc 6·40 × 15	8ft. 11⅜ins. 4ft. 7ins.	Unitary construction. Overdrive or automatic optional. Power steering available as optional extra, 1961. All synchromesh gearbox, 1966.

Date and Model	Price	No. of Cyls. and Engine Dimensions	Output (B.H.P. at R.P.M.)	Carburetter	Valves	Ignition	Cooling	Lubrication
1960 3·4-litre Mk.II	£1,669	6 83 × 106 mm. 3,442 c.c.	210 at 5,500	2 S.U. HD.6	Twin overhead camshafts	Coil	Pump	Force feed
3·8-litre Mk.II	£1,779	6 87 × 106 mm. 3,781 c.c.	220 at 5,500	2 S.U. HD.6	Twin overhead camshafts	Coil	Pump	Force feed
1961 E-type	Roadster, £2,098 Coupé, £2,197	6 87 × 106 mm. 3,781 c.c.	265 at 5,500	3 S.U. HD.8	Twin overhead camshafts	Coil	Pump	Force feed
1962 Mk. X	£2,392	6 87 × 106 mm. 3,781 c.c.	265 at 5,500	3 S.U. HD.8	Twin overhead camshafts	Coil	Pump and fan	Force feed
1964 3·4-litre S-type	£1,669	6 83 × 106 mm. 3,442 c.c.	210 at 5,500	2 S.U. HD.6	Twin overhead camshafts	Coil	Pump	Force feed
3·8-litre S-type	£1,758	87 × 106 mm. 3,781 c.c.	220 at 5,500	2 S.U. HD.6	Twin overhead camshafts	Coil	Pump	Force feed
1965 4·2-litre Mk. X	£2,156	92·07 × 106 mm. 4,235 c.c.	265 at 5,400	3 S.U. HD.8	Twin overhead camshafts	Alternator	Pump	Force feed
4·2-litre E-type	£2,033	92·07 × 106 mm. 4,235 c.c.	265 at 5,400	3 S.U. HD.8	Twin overhead camshafts	Alternator	Pump	Force feed
1966 4·2-litre E-type '2+2'	£2,245	92·07 × 106 mm. 4,235 c.c.	265 at 5,400	3 S.U. HD.8	Twin overhead camshafts	Alternator	Pump	Force feed
1967 420	£1,930	6 92·07 × 106 mm. 4,235 c.c.	245 at 5,500	2 S.U. HD.8	Twin overhead camshafts	Alternator	Pump, fan and thermostat	Force feed
420G	£2,238	6 92·07 × 106 mm. 4,235 c.c.		3 S.U. HD.8	Twin overhead camshafts	Alternator	Pump, fan and thermostat	Force feed

Date and Model	Price	No. of Cycles and Engine Dimensions	Output (B.H. at R.P.M.)	Carburation	Valves	Ignition	Cooling	Lubrication
1968 240	£1,365	6 83 × 76.5 mm 2,483 c.c.	133 at 5,500	2 S.U. HS.6	Twin overhead camshafts	Coil	Pump	Force feed
340	£1,442	6 83 × 106 mm 3,442 c.c.	213 at 5,500	2 S.U. HD.6	Twin overhead camshafts	Coil	Pump	Force feed
1969 XJ6 2.8	£1,797*	6 83 × 86 mm 2,792 c.c.	180 at 6,000	2 S.U. HD.8	Twin overhead camshafts	Alternator	Pump, fan, thermostat	Force feed
XJ6 4.2	£2,253*	6 92.07 × 106 mm 4,235 c.c.	245 at 5,500	2 S.U. HD.8	Twin overhead camshafts	Alternator	Pump, fan, thermostat	Force feed
1971 E Series III	Roadster, £3,123* Coupé, £3,369*	12 90 × 70 mm 5,343 c.c.	272 at 5,850	4 Zenith 175 CDSE	One overhead camshaft per block	Tran- sistorised	Pump and 2 fans	Force feed
1972 XJ12	£3,726*	12 90 × 70 mm 5,343 c.c.	265 at 6,000	4 Zenith 175 CDSE	One overhead camshaft per block	Tran- sistorised	Pump and 2 fans	Force feed
1975 XJ 3.4	£4,795*	6 83 × 106 mm 3,442 c.c.	161 at 5,000	2 S.U. HS.8	Twin overhead camshafts	Alternator	Pump, fan, thermostat	Force feed
1976 XJ-S	£8,900*	12 90 × 70 mm 5,343 c.c.	285 at 5,500	Electronic fuel injection	One overhead camshaft per block	Tran- sistorised	Pump and 2 fans	Force feed
1979 XJ 3.4 Series III	£11,189*	6 83 × 106 mm 3,442 c.c.	161 at 5,000	2 S.U. HS.8	Twin overhead camshafts	Alter- nator	Pump, fan, thermostat	Force feed
XJ 4.2 Series III	£12,326*	6 92.07 × 106 mm 4,235 c.c.	205 at 5,500	Electronic fuel injection	Twin overhead camshafts	Alter- nator	Pump, fan, thermostat	Force feed
XJ 5.3 Series III	£15,015*	12 90 × 70 mm 5,343 c.c.	285 at 5,750	Electronic fuel injection	One overhead camshaft per block	Tran- sistorised	Pump and 2 fans	Force feed

*at introduction

Date and Model	Gearbox and Ratios	Clutch and Final Drive	Brakes	Suspension	Wheels and Tyres	Wheelbase and Track	Remarks
1960 3·4-litre Mk.II	4-speed, synchro. 3·45, 4·54, 6·58, 11·95:1	S.D.P. Hypoid bevel	Dunlop servo-assisted disc	Coil and wishbones: cantilever ½–E	disc 6·40 × 15	8ft. 11⅜ins. 4ft. 7ins.	As above. All synchromesh gearbox, 1966.
3·8-litre Mk.II	4-speed, synchro. 3·54, 4·54, 6·58, 11·95:1	S.D.P. Hypoid bevel	Dunlop servo-assisted disc	Coil and wishbones: cantilever ½–E	disc 6·40 × 15	8ft. 11⅜ins. 4ft. 7ins.	As above. Wire wheels available as optional equipment on Mk. II models. All synchromesh gearbox, 1966.
1961 E-type	4-speed, synchro. 3·31, 4·246, 6·156, 11·177:1	S.D.P. Hypoid bevel	Dunlop servo-assisted disc	Coil independent: independent lower wishbones and coils	wire 6·40 × 15	8ft. 0ins. 4ft. 2ins.	Racing tyres optional, front 6·00 × 15, rear 6·50 × 15
1962 Mk. X	4-speed, synchro. 3·54, 4·54, 6·58, 11·95:1	S.D.P. Hypoid bevel	Dunlop servo-assisted disc	Coil independent: independent lower wishbones and coils	disc 7·50 × 14	10ft. 0ins. 4ft. 10ins.	Unitary construction. Overdrive or automatic available
1964 3·4S	4-speed, synchro. 3·54, 4·54, 6·58, 11·95	S.D.P. Hypoid bevel	Dunlop servo-assisted disc	Coil and wishbones: independent lower wishbones and coils	disc 185 × 15	8ft. 11½ins. 4ft. 8¼ins.	Overdrive, automatic, power assisted steering, wire wheels optional: all synchromesh gearbox from 1965.
3·8S	4-speed, synchro. 3·54, 4·54, 6·58, 11·95	S.D.P. Hypoid bevel	Dunlop servo-assisted disc	Coil and wishbones: independent lower wishbones and coils	disc 185 × 15	8ft. 11½ins. 4ft. 8¼ins.	As above.
1965 4·2	4-speed, all-synchro. 3·54, 4·7, 6·98, 10·76	Laycock-Hausserman diaphragm	Dunlop servo-assisted disc	Coil and wishbones: independent lower wishbones and coils	disc 6·40 × 15	10ft. 0ins. 4ft. 10½ins.	Overdrive, automatic optional. Power assisted steering standard.
4·2E	4-speed, all-synchro. 3·07, 3·9, 5·34, 8·23	Laycock-Hausserman diaphragm	Dunlop servo-assisted disc	Torsion bars and wishbones: independent lower wishbones and coils	wire 6·40 × 15	8ft. 0ins. 4ft. 2ins.	From late 1968, revised Series II, 'emission' engine 245 b.h.p. gross, 171 b.h.p. net. 2 Stromberg dual-choke carburetters for U.S. market cars. Girling disc brakes.
4·2E '2 + 2'	4-speed, all-synchro. 3·07, 4·07, 6·06, 9·33	Laycock-Hausserman diaphragm	Dunlop servo-assisted disc	Torsion bars and wishbones: independent lower wishbones and coils	wire 185 × 15	8ft. 9ins. 4ft. 2ins.	Automatic optional. From late 1968, revised Series II, 'emission' engine 245 b.h.p. gross, 171 b.h.p. net. 2 Stromberg dual-choke carburetters for U.S. market cars. Girling disc brakes.
1967 420	4-speed, all-synchro. 3·54, 4·7, 7·44, 10·76:1	Laycock diaphragm type Hypoid bevel	Dunlop servo-assisted disc	Coil and wishbones: lower tubular links and coils	disc 185–15	8ft. 11½ins. 4ft. 7½ins.	Unitary construction; overdrive or automatic optional
420G	4-speed, all-synchro. 3·54, 4·7, 6·98, 10·76:1	Laycock diaphragm type Hypoid bevel	Dunlop servo-assisted disc	Coil and wishbones: lower tubular links and coils	disc 205–14	10ft. 4ft. 10ins.	Unitary construction; overdrive or automatic optional

Date and Model	Gearbox and Ratios	Clutch and Final Drive	Brakes	Suspension	Wheels and Tyres	Wheelbase and Track	Remarks
1968 240	4-speed, all-synchro. 4.27, 5.66, 8.42, 13:1	S.D.P. Hypoid bevel	Dunlop servo-assisted disc	Coil and wishbones: cantilever ½-ell.	disc 6.40 × 15	8ft. 11¾ ins. 4ft. 7ins.	Overdrive and automatic options
340	4-speed, all-synchro. 3.45, 4.54, 6.58, 11.95:1	S.D.P. Hypoid bevel	Dunlop servo-assisted disc	Coil and wishbones: cantilever ½-ell.	disc 6.40 × 15	8ft. 11¾ ins. 4ft. 7ins.	As above.
1969 XJ6 2.8	4-speed, all-synchro. 4.27, 5.93, 8.14, 12.5:1	S.D.P. Hypoid bevel	Girling servo-assisted disc	Coil and wishbones: independent lower tubular links and coils	disc 7.50 × 15	9ft. 1in. 4ft. 11ins.	As above.
XJ6 4.2	4-speed, all-synchro. 3.54, 4.92, 6.74, 10.38:1	S.D.P. Hypoid bevel	Girling servo-assisted disc	Coil and wishbones: independent lower tubular links and coils	disc 7.50 × 15	9ft. 1in. 4ft. 11ins.	Overdrive and automatic options, but overdrive virtually standard on manuals. Coupé from 1970, when S.II saloons given longer, 9 ft. 4¾ ins. wheelbase.
1971 E.III	4-speed, all-synchro. 3.31, 4.54, 6.3, 9.69:1	S.D.P. Hypoid bevel	Girling servo-assisted disc	Torsion bars and wishbones: independent lower tubular links and coils	pressed steel E70-VR15	8ft. 11ins. 4ft. 6¼ ins.	Automatic and wire wheel options.
1972 XJ12	3-speed, automatic. 3.31, 4.8, 7.94:1	— Hypoid bevel	Girling servo-assisted disc	Coil and wishbones: independent lower tubular links and coils	disc E70-VR15	9ft. 1in. 4ft. 11ins.	Coupé from 1974, when S.II saloons given longer, 9ft. 4¾ ins. wheelbase.
1975 XJ 3.4	4-speed, all-synchro. With overdrive, 2.76, 3.54, 4.32, 6.74, 11.46:1	S.D.P. Hypoid bevel	Girling servo-assisted disc	Coil and wishbones: independent lower tubular links and coils	disc E70-VR15	9ft. 4¾ ins. 4ft. 10½ ins.	Series II specification: automatic option.
1976 XJ-S	4-speed, all-synchro. 3.07, 4.26, 5.85, 9.94:1	S.D.P. Hypoid bevel	Girling servo-assisted disc	Coil and wishbones: independent lower tubular links and coils	alloy 205-70-VR15	8ft. 6ins. 4ft. 10½ ins.	Automatic option, compulsory from mid-1979
XJ 3.4 Ser. III	5-speed, all-synchro. 2.94, 3.54, 4.98, 7.4, 11.75:1	S.D.P. Hypoid bevel	Girling servo-assisted disc	Coil and wishbones: independent lower tubular links and coils	disc E70-VR15	9ft. 4¾ ins. 4ft. 11ins.	Automatic option.
SJ 4.2 Ser. III	5-speed, all-synchro. 2.74, 3.31, 4.63, 6.92, 11:1	S.D.P. Hypoid bevel	Girling servo-assisted disc	Coil and wishbones: independent lower tubular links and coils	disc E70-VR15	9ft 4¾ ins. 4ft. 11ins.	Automatic option.
XJ 5.3 Ser. III	3-speed, automatic. 3.07, 4.63, 7.7:1	— Hypoid bevel	Girling servo-assisted disc	Coil and wishbones: independent lower tubular links and coils	disc 205-70-VR15	9 ft. 4¾ ins. 4 ft. 11ins.	HE cylinder head introduced 1981

APPENDIX IV

S.S. AND JAGUAR COMPETITION SUCCESSES
1934-65

A list of the major successes won by S.S. and Jaguar cars up to 31 December 1965.

Only first, second, and third places, and winner's average speeds and times are given.

Date	Event	Model	Drivers	Placing	Av. Speed or Time	Date	Event	Model	Drivers	Placing	Av. Speed or Time
1934 Jan.	Monte Carlo Rally	S.S.I	S. H. Light	1st Unlimited Open Cars, *Concours de Confort*		**1936** July	Marne Sports Car G.P.	S.S. Jaguar 2½-litre	F. J. McEvoy	1st 2,000–3,000 c.c. class	69·98 m.p.h.
							Welsh Rally	S.S. Jaguar 2½-litre	D. S. Hand E. H. Jacob 2nd	1st Class 1 (Large Closed Cars)	
Aug.	Internationa Alpine Trial	S.S.I	Works team: C. M. Needham S. H. Light A. G. Douglas Clease	3rd Group 2 (teams) Silver-Gilt Plaque				S.S. Jaguar 1½-litre	R. E. Sandford	1st Class 2 (Small Closed Cars)	
		S.S.I	F. W. Morgan	Silver Gilt Plaque Awarded in individual competition		Aug.	International Alpine Trial	S.S.100 2½-litre	T. H. Wisdom Mrs E. M. Wisdom	Best individual performance irrespective of class Best performance in 2,000–3,000 c.c. class Glacier Cup	
1935 Jan.	Monte Carlo Rally	S.S.I	Hon. B. E. Lewis	1st Unlimited Open Cars, *Concours de Confort*		Sept.	Shelsley Walsh Hill-Climb	S.S.100 2½-litre	S. H. Newsome	1st 3,000 c.c. Unsupercharged	51·62 sec.
March	R.A.C. Eastbourne Rally	S.S.I	W. G. V. Vaughan	1st Class Award	Class awards only this year	**1937** March	R.A.C. Rally	S.S.100 2½-litre	J. Harrop	1st General Classification 1st Open Cars over 15 h.p. Buxton Starting Control Prize	
		S.S.I	A. H. G. Hooper	1st Class Award							
		S.S.I	V. L. Parry	1st Class Award							
		S.S.I	G. W. Olive	1st Class Award				S.S.100 2½-litre	T. H. Wisdom	2nd General Classification 2nd Open Cars over 15h.p. Leamington Starting Control Prize	
		S.S.I	S. H. Newsome	1st Class Award							
		S.S.I	A. G. Douglas Clease	1st Class Award							
		S.S.I	R. D. Hunnam	1st Class Award							
		S.S.II	Mrs E. M. Wisdom	1st Class Award							
May	Shelsley Walsh Hill-Climb	S.S.90	Hon. B. E. Lewis	3rd Sports Cars up to 3,000 c.c.	54 sec.						

Date	Event	Model	Drivers	Placing	Av. Speed or Time
		S.S.100 2½-litre	T. H. Wisdom E. W. Rankin E. H. Jacob Hon. B. E. Lewis	Manufacturers' Team Prize	
July	Welsh Rally	S.S.100 2½-litre	E. H. Jacob	Best overall performance 1st in class for Open Cars over 15 h.p.	
		S.S.100 2½-litre	E. H. Jacob E. W. Rankin G. E. Matthews	Manufacturers' Team Prize Club Team Prize (S.S. Car Club)	
Sept.	Shelsley Walsh Hill-Climb	S.S.100 3½-litre	S. H. Newsome	2nd 5-litre Class fastest unsupercharged car	45·94 sec.
Oct.	B.A.R.C. Meeting, Brooklands: First October Long Handicap	S.S.100 3½-litre	T. H. Wisdom	1st	111·85 m.p.h
1938 Jan.	Monte Carlo Rally	S.S. Jaguar 3½-litre	J. O. H. Willing	*Concours de Confort Grand Prix d'Honneur* 1st Closed Cars over 1,500 c.c.	
May	R.A.C. Rally	S.S.100 3½-litre	J. Harrop	1st Open Cars over 15 h.p.	
July	Welsh Rally	S.S.100 3½-litre	Mrs V. E. M. Hetherington	1st Open Cars over 15 h.p.	
Sept.	Paris–Nice Trial	S.S.100 2½-litre	T. H. Wisdom	1st 3-litre class	
1939 Jan.	Monte Carlo Rally	S.S. Jaguar 3½-litre	J. Harrop	10th equal	
May	R.A.C. Rally	S.S.100 3½-litre S.S.100 2½-litre S.S.100 3½-litre	S. H. Newsome A. D. C. Gordon C. J. Gibson C. Mann	2nd Open Cars over 15 h.p. 2nd Club Team Prize	
June	Shelsley Walsh Hill-Climb	S.S.100 3½-litre	S. H. Newsome	1st 3,001–5,000 c.c. Unsupercharged Cars	42·95 sec.
July	Welsh Rally	S.S.100 3½-litre S.S.100 3½-litre	W. C. N. Norton Miss V. Watson	1st Open Cars over 15 h.p. Ladies' Prize (Open Cars)	
1946 May	Bo'ness Speed Trials	S.S.100 3½-litre	N. A. Bean	F.t.d.	40 sec.
June	Shelsley Walsh Hill-Climb	S.S.100 3½-litre	S. H. Newsome	2nd 5,000 c.c. class	46·95 sec.

Date	Event	Model	Drivers	Placing	Av. Speed or Time
Aug.	Prescott Hill-Climb	S.S.100 3½-litre	R. M. Dryden	1st 3,001–5,000 c.c. Sports Car class	59·7 sec.
	Craigantlet Hill-Climb	S.S.100 3½-litre	J. W. Patterson	1st Unlimited Unsupercharged Cars	99 sec.
1947 May	Bo'ness Hill-Climb	S.S.100 3½-litre	N. A. Bean	1st Unlimited Sports Car class	43·4 sec.
June	Prescott Hill-Climb	S.S.100 3½-litre	R. M. Dryden	1st Unsupercharged Sports Cars over 3,000 c.c.	
July	Bouley Bay Hill-Climb, Jersey	S.S.100 3½-litre	Mrs E. M. Wisdom	Best Performance by a Lady	72 sec.
	J.C.C. Eastbourne Rally	S.S.100 3½-litre S.S.100 3½-litre S.S.100 3½-litre	H. E. Matthews E. I. Appleyard L. Parker	1st Class Award 1st Class Award 1st Class Award	
1948 July	International Alpine Rally	S.S.100 3½-litre	E. I. Appleyard	1st over 3,000 c.c. class *Coupe des Alpes*	
Sept.	Jabbeke–Aeltre Motorway, Belgium	M.G. Special (Jaguar XJ 2-litre engine)	Major A. T. G. Gardner	International Class E (2-litre records) 1 km. f.s. 1 m. f.s. 5 km. f.s.	176·72 m.p.h. 173·66 m.p.h. 170·52 m.p.h.
1949 April	Tulip Rally, Holland	S.S.100 3½-litre	E. I. Appleyard	2nd General Classification 1st Over 1,500 c.c. class	
Aug.	One-Hour Production Car Race, Silverstone	XK120	L. G. Johnson P. D. C. Walker	1st 2nd	82·80 m.p.h.
1950 Jan.	Palm Beach Production Car Race, U.S.A.	XK120	L. G. Johnson	4th	
April	Mille Miglia, Italy	XK120	L. G. Johnson	5th	
June	Santa Ana Races, California	XK120 XK120	P. Hill J. McAfee	2nd 3rd	
July	International Alpine Rally	XK120	E. I. Appleyard	1st Over 3,000 c.c. Best individual performance *Coupe des Alpes*	

Date	Event	Model	Drivers	Placing	Av. Speed or Time
Aug.	Bouley Bay Hill-Climb, Jersey	L.G.S. (3½-litre Jaguar engine)	F. Le Gallais	3rd Over 2,000 c.c. class	
	One-Hour Production Car Race, Silverstone	XK120	P. D. C. Walker	1st Over 2,000 c.c. and Over 3,000 c.c. classes	881·8 m.p.h.
			A. P. R. Rolt	2nd Over 2,000 c.c. and Over 3,000 c.c. classes	
Sept.	Shelsley Walsh Hill-Climb	XK120	P. D. C. Walker	1st Production Cars over 3,000 c.c.	44·61 sec.
	Tourist Trophy, Dundrod	XK120	S. Moss	1st 1st Unlimited class	75·15 m.p.h.
		XK120	P. N. Whitehead	2nd	
		XK120	S. Moss P. N. Whitehead L. G. Johnson	Team Prize	
Nov.	Pebble Beach Cup Race, California	XK120	P. Hill	1st	
		XK120	Parkinson	2nd	
	M.C.C. 1,000-Mile Rally	XK120	E. I. Appleyard	2nd General Classification 1st Over 3,000 c.c. class	
1951 Jan.	Monte Carlo Rally	3½-litre Mk.V	C. Vard	3rd	
		3½-litre Mk.V	W. H. Waring	9th	
April	Rallye Soleil, France	XK120	Peignaux	1st	
		XK120	Taylor	2nd	
		XK120	Bray	3rd	
	Tulip Rally, Holland	XK120	E. I. Appleyard	1st General Classification 1st Over 1,500 c.c. class	
May	Morecambe Rally	XK120	E. I. Appleyard	1st	
	Silverstone International Trophy Meeting: Production Car Race	XK120	S. Moss	1st	84·5 m.p.h.
		XK120	C. J. P. Dodson	2nd	
		XK120	J. Duncan Hamilton	3rd	
	R.S.A.C. Scottish Rally	XK120	L. Wood	1st General Classification 1st in class	
	Bremgarten Preis, Berne	XK120	Scherrer	1st Production Sports Cars over 1,500 c.c.	78·12 m.p.h.
	M.C.C. Edinburgh Rally	XK120	W. F. Mead	1st Large Sports Cars	
June	Production Car Race, Spa	XK120	J. Claes	1st	81·22 m.p.h.

Date	Event	Model	Drivers	Placing	Av. Speed or Time
	R.A.C. Rally	XK120	E. I. Appleyard	1st Open Cars over 3,000 c.c.	
		XK120	Miss M. Newton	Best Open-car Performance by a Lady	
	Le Mans 24-Hour Race	C-type	P. N. Whitehead P. D. C. Walker	3rd on Index of Performance	93·49 m.p.h.
July	International Alpine Rally	XK120	E. I. Appleyard	1st Over 3,000 c.c. class Best individual performance *Coupe des Alpes*	
		XK120	Habisreutinger	2nd Over 3,000 c.c. class *Coupe des Alpes*	
		XK120	Appleyard Habisreutinger Soler	Team Prize	
	Bouley Bay Hill-Climb, Jersey	XK120	R. L. Sangan	1st Sports Cars over 3,000 c.c.	
		XK120	A. Owen	2nd Sports Cars over 3,000 c.c.	
Aug.	Liège–Rome–Liège Rally	XK120	J. Claes/J. Ickx	1st General Classification 1st Over 3,000 c.c. class	
		XK120	Herzet/Baudvin	2nd General Classification 2nd Over 3,000 c.c. class	
	Johore Grand Prix, Malaya	XK120	B. R. Hawes	2nd	
		XK120	F. M. Ferguson	3rd	
Sept.	Tourist Trophy, Dunrod	C-type	S. Moss	1st	82·55 m.p.h
		C-type	P. D. C. Walker	2nd	
		C-type	L. G. Johnson/ A. P. R. Rolt	3rd	
		C-type	S. Moss/ P. D. C. Walker	Team Prize	
		C-type	L. G. Johnson/ A. P. R. Rolt		
	Tour de France	XK120	Hache/Crespin	1st Over 3,000 c.c. class	
		XK120	Simone/Schlee	2nd Over 3,000 c.c. class	
		XK120	Descollas/Gignoux	3rd Over 3,000 c.c. class	
	N.W. London M.C. London Rally	XK120	E. I. Appleyard/ G. Wilkins	1st	
	Watkins Glen G.P., U.S.A.	XK120	S. Johnston	1st 3,001–4,000 c.c. class	
Oct.	Reno Road Race, U.S.A.	XK120	D. Parkinson	1st	
	Palm Springs Road Race, U.S.A.	XK120	D Parkinson	2nd	

Date	Event	Model	Drivers	Placing	Av. Speed or Time
1951 Nov.	M.C.C. National Rally	XK120	F. P. Grounds/ J. B. Hay	1st Open Cars over 3,000 c.c.	
1952 Jan.	Monte Carlo Rally	Mk.VII Mk.VII	R. Cotton J. Herteaux	4th 6th	
March	Sebring 12-Hour Race	XK120	C. Schott/ M. Carroll	2nd on distance	
April	R.A.C. International Rally	XK120	J. C. Broadhead	2nd Open Car class	
		XK120	Miss M. Newton	Best Performance by a Lady	
	Jersey Speed Trials	XK120	Lord Louth	Fastest Production Car over 1,800 c.c.	8.4 sec.
	Goodwood Easter Monday Meeting: 1st Sports Car Handicap	XK120	E. W. Holt	1st	70.24 m.p.h.
			J. B. Swift	2nd	
	S.S.C.C. Highland Three Days Rally	XK120	G. P. Denham-Cooke	1st General Classification 1st Open Cars over 1,800 c.c.	
	Rallye Soleil, France	XK120	D. O'M. Taylor/ Mrs Taylor	1st Sports Cars over 2,500 c.c.	
		XK120	R. Habisreutinger/ W. Horning	2nd Sports Cars over 2,500 c.c.	
	Tulip Rally, Holland	Mk.VII	E. I. Appleyard/ Mrs Appleyard	2nd General Classification 1st Touring Cars over 3,000 c.c.	
		XK120	R. Habisreutinger/ W. Horning	1st Sports Cars over 3,000 c.c.	
		XK120	F. P. Grounds/ Mrs Grounds	2nd Sports Cars over 3,000 c.c.	
	S.S.C.C. Turnberry Meeting Sports Car Race, over 2,500 c.c.	XK120	I. Stewart	1st	62 m.p.h.
		XK120	P. J. Kenneth	2nd	
	Formule Libre Race	XK120	I. Stewart Sir J. Scott-Douglas	2nd 3rd	
May	Silverstone International Trophy Meeting Production Touring Car race	Mk.VII	S. Moss	1st Production Touring Cars over 3,000 c.c.	75.22 m.p.h.
	Production Sports Car race	C-type	S. Moss	1st Production Sports Cars over 3,000 c.c.	84.02 m.p.h.
	Morecambe Rally	XK120	Mrs E. I. Appleyard	Ladies' Prize	

Date	Event	Model	Drivers	Placing	Av. Speed or Time
	Prescott Hill-Climb	H.W.M.-Jaguar	O. Moore	1st Unsupercharged Sports Cars over 3,000 c.c.	49.11 sec.
	Lisbon Rally	Mk.VII	Sosa	2nd Unlimited class	
	British Empire Trophy Race, Isle of Man	XK120	Sir J. Scott-Douglas	1st Over 3,000 c.c. class	65.22 m.p.h.
	Bridgehampton Races, U.S.A. Hayground Cup (Unlimited Cars)	XK120	W. Hansgen	2nd	
		XK120	P. Timmins	3rd	
	Bridgehampton Cup (Modified Sports Cars)	XK120	J. Fitch	3rd	
	Hampton Cup (Production Cars)	XK120	M. B. Carroll	1st	
		XK120	J. Koster	2nd	
		XK120	W. H. Saunders	3rd	
June	R.S.A.C. Scottish Rally	XK120	G. P. Denham-Cooke	1st Open Cars over 2,200 c.c.	
	Bo'ness Speed Trials	XK120	F. S. Mort	1st Sports Cars over 3,000 c.c.	41.27 sec.
		XK120	Mrs S. Black	Fastest Time by a Lady	43.31 sec.
	Grand Prix de France, Rheims: Sports Car Race	C-type	S. Moss	1st Over 2,000 c.c. class	98.2 m.p.h.
July	R.S.A.C. Hill-Climb, Rest-and-be-Thankful	XK120	J. Neilson	1st Sports Cars over 3,000 c.c.	63.89 sec.
	Jersey International Sports Car Race	C-type	I. Stewart	1st	87.82 m.p.h.
	International Alpine Rally	XK120	M. Gatsonides	2nd General Classification 1st Over 3,000 c.c. class Coupe des Alpes	
		XK120	E. I. Appleyard	Coupe des Alpes Alpine Gold Cup	
	Bouley Bay Hill-Climb	XK120	Lord Louth	1st Sports Cars over 2,000 c.c.	64.4 sec.
		L.G.S. (XK engine)	F. Le Gallais	2nd f.t.d. 1st Racing Cars over 2,000 c.c.	56.2 sec.
Aug.	West Essex C.C. Daily Mail Meeting, Boreham: 34-lap Sports Car Race	C-type	S. Moss	1st Over 3,000 c.c.	88.09 m.p.h.

Date	Event	Model	Drivers	Placing	Av. Speed or Time
	Montlhéry	XK120	L. G. Johnson, H. L. Hadley, S. Moss, J. E. G. Fairman	World's and Class C International Records 72 hours	105·55 m.p.h.
				4 days	101·17 m.p.h.
				15,000 km.	101·94 m.p.h.
				10,000 miles	100·65
				10,000 km.	107·31 m.p.h.
	Goodwood Nine Hours' Race Liège–Rome–Liège Rally	C-type XK120	S. Moss/ P. D. C. W lker Laroche/Radix	1st Over 3,000 c.c. class 2nd General Classification 1st Over 3,000 c.c. class	
	S.S.C.C. Meeting, Turnberry: Sports Cars over 1,500 c.c.	C-type C-type C-type	S. Moss J. Duncan Hamilton I. Stewart	1st 2nd 3rd	75·56 m.p.h.
	Shelsley Walsh Hill-Climb	C-type	P. D. C. Walker	1st Sports Cars over 3,000 c.c. Best Performance by a Production Sports Car	41·14 sec.
Sept.	Brighton Speed Trials	Alta-Jaguar	E. P. Scragg	1st Sports Cars over 2,500 c.c.	29·13 sec.
		Jaguette 2,663 c.c. (s/c)	W. Coleman	1st Unlimited Sports Cars F.t.d. by a Sports Car	28·45 sec.
		L.G.S. (XK engine)	F. Le Gallais	1st Formula I category Racing Cars	27·31 sec.
		XK120	Mrs R. Sarginson	F.t.d. by a Lady	30·76 sec.
	I.M.R.C. Wakefield Trophy Race, The Curragh	C-type XK120	I. Stewart Sir J. Scott-Douglas	1st (1st in handicap race for O'Boyle Trophy) 3rd (2nd in O'Boyle Trophy)	80·39 m.p.h.
	Prescott Hill-Climb	C-type	P. D. C. Walker	1st Sports Cars over 3,000 cc Fastest sports car	47·53 sec.
	Elkhart Lake Race, U.S.A.	C-type	P. Hill	1st 3,001–4,000 c.c. class	
	Goodwood September B.A.R.C. Meeting 5-lap Sports Car race	C-type C-type	A. P. R. Rolt S. Moss	1st 2nd	83·62 m.p.h.
	2nd September Handicap for sports cars	XK120 XK120	W. A. Dobson M. W. Head	1st 2nd	77·76 m.p.h.

Date	Event	Model	Drivers	Placing	Av. Speed or Time
	Seneca Cup Race, Watkins Glen, U.S.A.	C-type	J. Fitch	1st Unlimited class	76·5 m.p.h.
Oct.	Bristol M.C. and L.C.C., Castle Combe	C-type H.W.M.-Jaguar	I. Stewart O. Moore	1st Sports Cars over 1,500 c.c. 2nd	78·66 m.p.h.
	International Charterhall Meeting	C-type C-type	I. Stewart S. Moss	1st Unlimited Sports Cars 2nd	77·5 m.p.h.
	Coupe du Salon, Montlhéry	XK120	Simone	1st Touring Cars over 3,000 c.c.	81·85 m.p.h.
	M.C.C. Rally	XK120 XK120	D. O'M. Taylor/ Mrs Taylor S. Moss/ J. A. Cooper	1st Open Cars over 3,000 c.c. 1st Closed Cars over 3,000 c.c.	
1953 Jan.	Monte Carlo Rally	Mk.VII Mk.V 3½-litre Mk.VII	E. I. Appleyard C. Vard Air Vice-Marshal D. C. T. Bennett	2nd 5th 9th	
March	Sebring 12-Hour Race	C-type	S. Johnston/ R. Wilder	3rd	
	R.A.C. Rally	XK120 Mk.VII	E. I. Appleyard/ Mrs Appleyard D. G. Scott	1st General Classification 1st Sports Cars over 1,500 c.c. 1st Touring Cars over 2,600 c.c.	
April	Bristol M.C. and L.C.C., Castle Combe	H.W.M.-Jaguar	O. Moore	1st Unlimited Sports Cars	78·26 m.p.h.
	Goodwood Easter Meeting 1st Sports Car Handicap	XK120	E. Protheroe	2nd	
	2nd Sports Car Handicap	XK120	M. W. Head	2nd	
	S.S.C.C. Highland Three Days Rally	XK120	J. M. Cringean	1st Open Cars over 1,500 c.c.	
	West Hants and Dorset C.C., Ibsley 7-lap Sports Car Scratch Race	C-type C-type	I. Stewart J. Stewart	1st 3rd	73·86 m.p.h.
	Tulip Rally, Holland	Mk.VII	E. I. Appleyard	1st Touring Cars, 2,400–3,500 c.c.	

Date	Event	Model	Drivers	Placing	Av. Speed or Time
May	Silverstone International Trophy Meeting	Mk.VII	S. Moss	1st Production Touring Cars 1st Production Touring Cars over 3,000 cc	74·12 m.p.h.
	Morecambe Rally	XK120	E. I. Appleyard	1st	
	Charterhall National Meeting	C-type	N. Sanderson	2nd Unlimited Sports Cars	
		C-type	J. Stewart	3rd	
	R.S.A.C. Coronation Scottish Rally	XK120	J. H. Cunningham	1st Open Cars over 2,500 c.c.	
	West Essex C.C., Snetterton: Unlimited Sports Car Race	C-type	I. Stewart	1st	81·45 m.p.h
		C-type	J. Stewart	3rd	
June	Le Mans 24-Hour Race	C-type	A. P. R. Rolt/ J. Duncan Hamilton	1st	105 85 m.p.h.
		C-type	S. Moss/ P. D. C. Walker	2nd	
	West Essex C.C., Snetterton: Unlimited Sports Car Race	C-type C-type H.W.M.-Jaguar	I. Stewart J. Lawrence O. Moore	1st 2nd 3rd	74·58 m.p.h.
July	Rheims 12-Hour Race	C-type	S. Moss/ P. N. Whitehead	1st	105·45 m.p.h.
	Leinster Trophy Race, Wicklow	C-type C-type C-type	I. Stewart J. Lawrence Sir J. Scott-Douglas	Club Team Prize	
	International Alpine Rally	XK120	E. I. Appleyard/ Mrs Appleyard	1st Over 2,600 c.c. Coupe des Alpes	
		XK120	Fraikin/Gendebien	2nd Over 2,600 c.c. Coupe des Alpes	
		XK120	J. Mansbridge/ Mrs Mansbridge	3rd Over 2,600 c.c. Coupe des Alpes	
	Belgian 24-Hour Race, Spa	C-type	Sir J. Scott-Douglas/ G. Gale	2nd	
		C-type	H. Roosdorp/ T. Ulmen	3rd	
	Bouley Bay Hill-Climb, Jersey	XK120	Lord Louth	1st Sports Cars over 2,500 c.c.	61·8 sec.
		L.G.S. (XK engine)	F. Le Gallais	1st Racing Cars over 2,500 c.c. 3rd f.t.d.	55·2 sec.
	U.S.A.F. Trophy Meeting, Snetterton: Sports Car Race	XK120	J. Farrow	2nd	
Aug.	Evian–Mont Blanc Rally	XK120	Air Vice-Marshal D. C. T. Bennett/ Mrs Bennett	1st Over 3,000 c.c. class	
	International Charterhall Meeting: Sports Car Race	C-type C-type	I. Stewart J. Stewart	2nd 3rd	
	Swiss Grand Prix, Berne: Sports Car Race	XK120	I. Balaracco	1st Production Sports Cars over 1,500 c.c.	75·50 m.p.h.
	Goodwood Nine Hours' Race	C-type	J. Stewart/ B. Dickson	3rd	
	Shelsley Walsh Hill-Climb	H.W.M.-Jaguar	G. E. Abecassis	1st Sports Cars over 3,000 c.c.	45·01 sec.
	Liège–Rome–Liège Rally	XK120	Fraikin/Gendebien	2nd General Classification	
Sept.	Tourist Trophy, Dundrod	C-type	S. Moss/ P. D. C. Walker	1st 3,001–5,000 c.c. class	
	Brighton Speed Trials	Jaguar 3,442 c.c. (s/c)	G. D. Parker	1st Unlimited Supercharged Sports Cars Fastest sports car	26·88 sec.
	Wakefield Trophy, The Curragh	C-type	J. Kelly	2nd	
	Prescott Hill-Climb	C-type	P. D. C. Walker	1st Sports Cars over 3,000 c.c.	49·69 sec.
		L.G.S. (XK engine)	F. Le Gallais	1st Racing Cars up to 4,500 c.c. (not s/c)	46·44 sec.
	Goodwood Meeting: Sports Car Race (over 1,500 c.c.)	H.W.M.-Jaguar	G. E. Abecassis	1st	83·00 m.p.h.
Oct.	Coupe du Salon, Montlhéry	C-type XK120	Simone A. Hug	2nd 1st Production Cars over 1,300 c.c.	
	Lisbon Rally	XK120	E. I. Appleyard	2nd General Classification	
	M.C.C. Rally	Mk.VII	Maj. J. E. Osborne/ F./Lt. D. Brown	1st Production Closed Cars over 2,600 c.c.	
		XK120	J. Hally/Mrs Hally	1st Modified Production Closed Cars over 2,600 c.c.	
	Great American Mountain Rally	XK120	W. Dewess	2nd	
1954 Jan.	Monte Carlo Rally	Mk.VII Mk.VII	R. Adams C. Vard	6th 8th	
April	Castle Combe: Unlimited Sports Cars	C-type H.W.M.-Jaguar	J. Stewart G. E. Abecassis	2nd 3rd	
	Goodwood Easter Monday Meeting: Sports Car Handicap	C-type	J. Stewart	1st	82·11 m.p.h.
		C-type	A. P. R. Rolt	2nd	

Date	Event	Model	Drivers	Placing	Av. Speed or Time
	Tulip Rally, Holland	Mk.VII	J. P. Boardman/ J. A. Duckworth	4th General Classification / 1st Touring Cars over 2,600 c.c.	
May	W.H.D C.C. Ibsley	XK120	G. Tyrer	2nd Closed Car Race (over 1,500 c.c.)	
		C-type	J. Stewart	1st Sports Car Race (over 2,500 c.c.)	80·91 m.p.h.
		C-type	N. Sanderson	2nd	
		C-type	H. Davids	3rd	
		C-type	J. Stewart	2nd	
		C-type	N. Sanderson	Formule Libre Race 3rd	
	Prescott Hill-Climb	Alta-Jaguar Jaguar	E. P. Scragg	1st Unsupercharged Sports Cars over 3,000 c.c.	47·63 sec.
	National Capitol Races, Washington D.C.: Abraham Lincoln Trophy Race	C-type	E. Erickson	2nd	
	Silverstone International Trophy Meeting Sports Car Race	H.W.M.-Jaguar	G. E. Abecassis	2nd	
		C-type	P. D. C. Walker	3rd	
	Production Touring Car Race	Mk.VII	E. I. Appleyard	1st	75·55 m.p.h.
		Mk.VII	A. P. R. Rolt	2nd	
		Mk.VII	S. Moss	3rd	
	Daily Telegraph Aintree Meeting: Sports Car Race	C-type	J. Duncan Hamilton	1st	73·97 m.p.h.
		C-type	J. Stewart	3rd	
June	Goodwood Meeting: Johnson Challenge Trophy	C-type	J. Stewart	1st	82·52 m.p.h.
		C-type	N. Sanderson	2nd	
		C-type	G. Dunham	3rd	
	Sports Car Handicap Race 'A'	XK120	E. Protheroe	2nd	
		C-type	M. W. Head	3rd	
	West Essex C.C. Meeting, Snetterton: Unlimited Sports Car Race	C-type	R. F. Salvadori	1st	84·26 m.p.h.
		C-type	J. D. Titterington	3rd	
	Sports Car Handicap Race, 5 laps, over 1,500 c.c.	C-type	R. F. Salvadori	1st	85·29 m.p.h.
	Le Mans 24-Hour Race	D-type	A. P. R. Rolt/ J. Duncan Hamilton	2nd	

Date	Event	Model	Drivers	Placing	Av. Speed or Time
	Oulton Park National Meeting: Unlimited Sports Cars	C-type	J. D. Titterington	1st	71·65 m.p.h.
	Formule Libre Race	C-type	N. Sanderson	2nd	
		C-type	N. Sanderson	3rd	
	R.S.A.C. Scottish Rally	XK120	J. Hally	1st Sports Cars over 2,600 c.c.	
		Mk.VII	J. M. C. Shand	1st Touring Cars over 2,600 c.c.	
	Shelsley Walsh Hill-Climb	Alta-Jaguar	E. P. Scragg	1st Sports Cars over 2,500 c.c.	40·98 sec.
	Bo'ness Speed Trials	XK120	M. Salmon	1st Sports Cars over 3,000 c.c.	41·03 sec.
July	Rheims 12-Hour Race	D-type	P. N. Whitehead/ K. Wharton	1st	104·55 m.p.h.
		D-type	A. P. R. Rolt/ J. Duncan Hamilton	2nd	
		C-type	Laurent/Swaters	3rd	
	Leinster Trophy Race, Wicklow	C-type	J. Kelly	2nd	
	International Alpine Rally	XK120	E. Haddon/ C. Vivian	1st Over 2,600 cc class	
	Bouley Bay Hill-Climb	XK120	Lord Louth	1st Sports Cars over 2,500 c.c.	63·4 sec.
		L.G.S. (XK engine)	F. Le Gallais	1st Racing Cars over 2,500 c.c.	55·2 sec.
Aug.	Crystal Palace: Unlimited Sports Car Race	H.W.M.-Jaguar	F. A. O. Gaze	1st	69·69 m.p.h.
	International Meeting, Snetterton: Sports Car Race, (over 3,000 c.c.)	Cooper-Jaguar	P. N. Whitehead	1st	83·44 m.p.h.
		C-type	M. W. Head	2nd	
		XK120	R. E. Berry	3rd	
	Dutch Sports Car Race, Zandvoort	C-type	N. Sanderson	2nd / 1st Over 3,000 c.c. class	79·19 m.p.h.
		C-type	R. Laurent	3rd	
	Wakefield Trophy, The Curragh	Cooper-Jaguar	P. N. Whitehead	1st	82·87 m.p.h.
		C-type	J. Kelly	Equal 2nd	
		C-type	J. Duncan Hamilton	Equal 2nd	
	O'Boyle Trophy Handicap Race, The Curragh	XK120	R. E. Berry	2nd	
		C-type	J. Kelly	3rd	
	Ohio Valley Cup Production Car Race, Lockbourne, Ohio	XK120	C. Wallace	1st	86 m.p.h.
		XK120	J. Manning	2nd	
		XK120	L. Katskee	3rd	

Date	Event	Model	Drivers	Placing	Av. Speed or Time
Sept.	Brighton Speed Trials	Jaguara 3,442 c.c. (s/c)	G. D. Parker	1st Unlimited s/c Sports Cars	30·06 sec.
	International Charterhall Meeting: Unlimited Sports Car Race	C-type	R. F. Salvadori	1st	78·94 m.p.h.
		C-type	N. Sanderson	2nd	
	Bo'ness Speed Trials	XK120	M. Salmon	1st Sports Cars over 3,000 c.c.	42·29 sec.
		XK120	R. L. Fraser	1st Production Cars over 3,000 c.c.	44·69 sec.
	Goodwood Trophy Meeting: Unlimited Sports Car Race	C-type	R. F. Salvadori	1st	83·88 m.p.h.
		H.W.M.-Jaguar	G. E. Abecassis	3rd	
	WATKINS GLEN RACES, U.S.A. Glen Trophy (Production Cars over 1,250 c.c.)	XK120	R. Perrin	1st	73·6 m.p.h.
		XK120	G. Constantine	2nd	
		XK120	W. Smith	3rd	
	Seneca Cup	C-type	M. R. J. Wyllie	1st	73·6 m.p.h.
		Hansgen-Jaguar	W. Hansgen	2nd	
	Buenos Aires Sports Car Race	XK120	F. C. Cranwell	3rd	
Oct.	Aintree International Meeting: 5-lap Sports Car Race	R.G.S.-Atalanta	R. G. Shattock	1st	72·14 m.p.h.
	SNETTERTON MEETING: 5-lap Sports Car Handicap	XK120	J. Sears	3rd	
	5-lap Scratch Sports Car Race	XK120	D. Kasterine	1st Over 3,000 c.c. class	76·97 m.p.h.
Nov.	M.C.C. Round Britain Rally	Mk.VII	E. R. Parsons/ Mrs J. G. M. Vann	1st General Classification	
		XK120	E. Haddon/ C. Vivian	1st Open Sports Cars over 2,600 c.c.	
		XK120	L. S. Stross/ Mrs Stross	1st Closed Sports Cars over 2,600 c.c.	
Dec.	Brands Hatch Boxing Day Meeting: Albatross Trophy, Unlimited Sports Cars	C-type	D. Margulies	3rd	
1955 Jan.	Monte Carlo Rally	Mk.VII	R. J. Adams/ E. McMillen	8th	
		Mk.VII	R. J. Adams C. Vard E. I. Appleyard	Charles Faroux Team Trophy	
Mar.	Dakar G.P.	D-type	J. Duncan Hamilton	3rd	
	R.A.C. Rally	Mk.VII	L. S. Stross/ K. F. Pointing	1st Production Touring Cars over 2,600 c.c.	

Date	Event	Model	Drivers	Placing	Av. Speed or Time
	Sebring 12-Hour Race	D-type	J. M. Hawthorn/ P. Walters	1st	79·3 m.p.h.
	Snetterton Spring Meeting: Sports Car Race, over 2,700 c.c.	XK120	E. Haddon	1st	72·81 m.p.h.
		XK120	D. Hewitt	2nd	
April	Coupe de Paris, Montlhéry	D-type	J. Duncan Hamilton	1st Sports Car class	
	Goodwood Easter Meeting: Sports Car Race, over 2,000 c.c.	D-type	J. Duncan Hamilton	3rd	
May	SILVERSTONE INTERNATIONAL TROPHY MEETING: Sports Car Race	D-type	A. P. R. Rolt	3rd	
	Production Touring Car Race	Mk.VII	J. M. Hawthorn	1st	78·92 m.p.h.
		Mk.VII	J. Stewart	2nd	
		Mk.VII	J. D. Titterington	3rd	
	Helsinki Sports Car Race	D-type	M. W. Head	1st	
		C-type	Lincoln	2nd	
	G.P. des Frontières, Chimay	XK120	Meunier	3rd	
	Sardinia Trophy Race	C-type	D. Margulies	3rd	
	Tulip Rally, Holland	Mk.VII	J. P. Boardman/ J. W. Whitworth	1st Touring Cars, 2,600–3,500 c.c.	
	Ulster Trophy Race, Dundrod	D-type	J. D. Titterington	1st	89·86 m.p.h.
		C-type	W. T. Smith	2nd	
	GOODWOOD WHITSUN MEETING: 10-lap Race, Sports Cars over 2,000 c.c.	D-type	J. Duncan Hamilton	1st	83·72 m.p.h.
		D-type	R. E. Berry	2nd	
		C-type	E. Protheroe	3rd	
	Johnson Challenge Trophy Race	D-type	J. Duncan Hamilton	1st	84·41 m.p.h.
		D-type	R. E. Berry	3rd	
June	G.P. of Portugal Oporto	D-type	J. Duncan Hamilton	3rd	
	Le Mans 24-Hour Race	D-type	J. M. Hawthorn/ I. L. Bueb	1st	107 m.p.h.
		D-type	J. Claes/ J. Swaters	3rd	
July	Bouley Bay Hill-Climb, Jersey	XK120	Lord Louth	1st Sports Cars over 3,000 c.c.	61 sec.
		L.G.S. (XK engine)	F. Le Gallais	1st Racing Cars over 2,000 c.c.	54·4 sec.
	Munster '100' Handicap Race, Cork	XK120	M. D. Heather	1st	79·69 m.p.h.

Date	Event	Model	Drivers	Placing	Av. Speed or Time
Aug.	Charterhall International Meeting: Unlimited Sports Car Race	D-type	J. D. Titterington	1st	81·52 m.p.h.
	SNETTERTON INTERNATIONAL MEETING: 25-lap *Formule Libre*	D-type	J. D. Titterington	3rd	
	Scratch Race for Sports Cars over 2,750 c.c.	D-type / D-type / C-type	J. D. Titterington / N. Sanderson / W. T. Smith	1st / 2nd / 3rd	84·14 m.p.h.
	Goodwood Nine Hours' Race	D-type	J. D. Titterington / N. Sanderson	2nd	
Sept.	Brighton Speed Trials	Cooper-Jaguar	C. Wick	1st Sports Cars over 2,500 c.c.	25·30 sec.
		Jaguar a 3,442 c.c. (s/c)	G. D. Parker	1st Supercharged Sports Cars, unlimited	28·2 sec.
	Autumn International Meeting, Aintree: Unlimited Sports Car Race	D-type / D-type	N. Sanderson / J. D. Titterington	1st / 2nd	80·97 m.p.h.
	Prescott Hill-Climb	H. W. M.-Jaguar	E. P. Scragg	1st Sports Cars over 3,000 c.c.	47·4 sec.
	Silverstone B.R.D.C. and B.R.S.C.C. Meeting: Unlimited Sports Cars	D-type / D-type / C-type	J. Duncan Hamilton / M. W. Head / J. Barber	1st / 2nd / 3rd	74·97 m.p.h.
	Watkins Glen G.P., U.S.A.: Seneca Cup	D-type / C-type	S. Johnston / M. R. J. Wyllie	1st / 1st	81·92 m.p.h. 69·6 m.p.h.
Oct.	Castle Combe Meeting: Unlimited Sports Car Race	H.W.M.-Jaguar	G. E. Abecassis	1st	82·10 m.p.h.
Dec.	Governor's Trophy, Nassau, Bahamas	D-type	S. Johnston	3rd	
	Brands Hatch Boxing Day Meeting: Martini Trophy Race	C-type	W. A. Scott-Brown	3rd	
1956 Jan.	Ardmore Sports Car Race, N.Z.	Cooper-Jaguar / H.W.M.-Jaguar	P. N. Whitehead / F. A. O. Gaze	2nd / 3rd	
	Christchurch Sports Car Race, N.Z.	H.W.M.-Jaguar / XK140	F. A. O. Gaze / Archibald	1st / 2nd	
	Lady Wigram Trophy Race, N.Z.	Connaught-Jaguar	L. Marr	3rd	
	Monte Carlo Rally	Mk.VII	R. Adams / F. Biggar	1st	

Date	Event	Model	Drivers	Placing	Av. Speed or Time
March	R.A.C. Rally	XK140	E. I. Appleyard	2nd General Classification	
	Sebring 12-Hour Race	D-type	R. Sweikert / Ensley	3rd	
	Snetterton: 15-lap race for Unlimited Sports-Racing Cars	D-type / H.W.M.-Jaguar / D-type	R. Flockhart / G. E. Abecassis / A. Brown	1st / 2nd / 3rd	88·36 m.p.h
	Goodwood Easter Meeting: Sports-Car Handicap Race	D-type	R. Flockhart	1st	86·77 m.p.h.
April	Aintree International Meeting: Unlimited Sports Car Race	D-type / D-type	J. D. Titterington / N. Sanderson	2nd / 3rd	
	Coupe de Paris, Montlhéry	D-type	J. Duncan Hamilton	1st	
May	Prescott Hill-Climb	Jaguar a 3,442 c.c. (s/c)	G. D. Parker	1st Sports Cars over 3,000 c.c.	47·16 sec.
	SILVERSTONE *Daily Express* MEETING: Sports Car Race Production Touring Race	D-type / Mk.VII / 2·4-litre	R. E. Berry / I. L. Bueb / J. Duncan Hamilton	3rd / 1st / 2nd	80·01 m.p.h.
	Belgian Production Car Races, Spa	D-type / 2·4-litre	N. Sanderson / P. Frère	1st Sports Car class / 1st Touring Car class	110·35 m.p.h. 96·64 m.p.h.
	G.P. des Frontières, Chimay	D-type	J. Duncan Hamilton	2nd	
	Whitsun Trophy Race, Goodwood	D-type / D-type	J. D. Titterington / R. Flockhart	1st / 3rd	87·65 m.p.h.
	Cumberland One-Hour Race, Maryland, U.S.A.	D-type	W. Hansgen	1st	
June	Shelsley Walsh Hill-Climb	H.W.M.-Jaguar	G. E. Abecassis	1st Sports Cars over 2,500 c.c.	46·48 sec.
	Aintree National Meeting: Unlimited Sports-Car Race	D-type / D-type	J. D. Titterington / I. L. Bueb	2nd / 3rd	
July	Rheims 12-Hour Race	D-type / D-type / D-type	J. Duncan Hamilton/I. L. Bueb / J. M. Hawthorn/P. Frère / J. D. Titterington/J. E. G. Fairman	1st / 2nd / 3rd	110·94 m.p.h.
	R.S.A.C. Rest-and-be-Thankful Hill-Climb	H.W.M.-Jaguar / H.W.M.-Jaguar	R. Fielding / Mrs R. Fielding	1st Sports Cars over 2,000 c.c. / Best Performance by a Lady	62·24 sec. / 68·92 sec.

Date	Event	Model	Drivers	Placing	Av. Speed or Time
	Silverstone British Grand Prix Meeting: 25-lap Sports Car Race	D-type	J. D. Titterington	3rd	
	Leinster Trophy Race, Wicklow	C-type	A. C. O'Hara	3rd	
	Le Mans 24-Hour Race	D-type	R. Flockhart/ N. Sanderson	1st	104·46 m.p.h.
Aug.	B.A.R.C. Crystal Palace Meeting: 7-lap Sports Car Race	Tojeiro-Jaguar	E. Protheroe	1st	68·68 m.p.h.
		C-type	J. M. Trimble	2nd	
	5-lap Invitation Handicap Race	C-type	J. M. Trimble	2nd	
		Tojeiro-Jaguar	E. Protheroe	3rd	
	Shelsley Walsh Hill-Climb	H.W.M.-Jaguar	R. Fielding	1st Sports Cars over 2,500 c.c.	47·05 sec.
Sept.	Brighton Speed Trials	Tojeiro-Jaguar	J. L. E. Ogier	1st Sports Cars over 2,500 c.c.	25·36 sec.
	Goodwood Meeting: Goodwood Trophy	D-type	R. Flockhart	3rd	
	5-lap Sports Car Handicap	D-type	J. Lawrence	1st	84·44 m.p.h.
		H.W.M.-Jaguar	E. Protheroe	2nd	
	Prescott Hill-Climb	H.W.M.-Jaguar	R. Fielding	1st Sports Cars over 2,500 c.c.	49·4 sec.
Nov.	M.C.C. National Rally	Mk.VII	R. W. Russell	1st Production Touring Cars over 2,600 c.c.	
1957 March	Sebring 12-Hour Race	D-type 3·8-litre	J. M. Hawthorn/ I. L. Bueb	3rd	
	Snetterton Sports Car Race (over 2,700 c.c.)	Tojeiro-Jaguar	E. Protheroe	1st	85·11 m.p.h.
		D-type	P. Blond	2nd	
		D-type	J. M. Trimble	3rd	
April	British Empire Trophy Race, Oulton Park	Lister-Jaguar	W. A. Scott-Brown	1st	84·21 m.p.h.
	Easter Monday International Meeting, Goodwood: *Autosport* Series Production Sports Car Race	XK120	P. J. Sargent	1st Over 2,700 c.c. class	74·80 m.p.h.
	Sussex Trophy Race	Lister-Jaguar	W. A. Scott-Brown	1st	89·42 m.p.h.
	Nottingham S.C.C. Mallory Park Easter Monday Races	Cooper-Jaguar	C. Murray	1st Sports Cars over 2,000 c.c.	74·27 m.p.h.
	W.E.C.C. National Sprint	Lister-Jaguar	W. A. Scott-Brown	F.t.d.	19·64 sec.

Date	Event	Model	Drivers	Placing	Av. Speed or Time
	Meeting, Snetterton	Tojeiro-Jaguar	J. L. E. Ogier	2nd F.t.d.	20·05 sec.
		Tojeiro-Jaguar	Miss P. Burt	F.t.d. by a Lady	23·38 sec.
		C-type	J. Bekaert	1st Sports Cars over 2,700 c.c.	23·26 sec.
		C-type	P. M. Salmon	1st Sports Cars (any trim) over 3,000 c.c.	22·42 sec.
May	Prescott Hill-Climb	H.W.M.-Jaguar	E. P. Scragg	1st Sports Cars over 3,000 c.c.	46·7 sec.
	Spa Sports Car Race	D-type	H. Taylor	3rd	
	Forez Sports Car Races, Ste. Etienne	D-type	R. Flockhart	1st	91·16 m.p.h.
		D-type	N. Sanderson	2nd	
		D-type	J. Duncan Hamilton	3rd	
	Snetterton Meeting: 5-lap Production Car Scratch Race	XK140	E. Pantlin	1st Class E	
	15-lap Unlimited Sports Car Race	Lister-Jaguar	W. A. Scott-Brown	1st	88·09 m.p.h.
		Tojeiro-Jaguar	E. Protheroe	2nd	
	10-lap Invitation Race	Lister-Jaguar	W. A. Scott-Brown	1st	89·67 m.p.h.
June	Crystal Palace: Unlimited Sports Car Race	Lister-Jaguar	W. A. Scott-Brown	1st	73·50 m.p.h.
		H.W.M.-Jaguar	L. Leston	2nd	
	Goodwood Whit-Monday Meeting: Unlimited Sports Car Race, 26 laps	Cooper-Jaguar	M. W. Head	1st	85·58 m.p.h.
		D-type	M. Charles	3rd	
	Le Mans 24-Hour Race	D-type 3·8-litre	R. Flockhart/ I. L. Bueb	1st	113·85 m.p.h.
		D-type 3·8-litre	N. Sanderson/ J. Lawrence	2nd	
		D-type	J. Lucas/'Mary'	3rd	
		D-type	P. Frère/ J. Rousselle	4th	
		D-type 3·8-litre	J. M. Hawthorn/ M. Gregory	6th	
	R.S.A.C. Rest-and-be-Thankful Hill-Climb	H.W.M.-Jaguar	R. Fielding	1st Sports Cars over 2,000 c.c.	60·96 sec.
		XK140	Miss E. Griffin	Best Performance by a Lady	75 sec.
July	Aintree Sports Car Race	Lister-Jaguar 3·8-litre	W. A. Scott-Brown	1st	78·81 m.p.h.
		D-type 3·8-litre	J. Duncan Hamilton	3rd	
	Snetterton Meeting: Vanwall Trophy Race	Lister-Jaguar 3·8-litre	W. A. Scott-Brown	1st	89·39 m.p.h.

Date	Event	Model	Drivers	Placing	Av. Speed or Time
	15-lap Race for Series Production Sports Cars over 2,700 c.c.	D-type	H. Taylor	1st	80·01 m.p.h.
		C-type	J. Bekaert	2nd	
		C-type	P. Mould	3rd	
	10-lap Race for Unlimited Sports Cars	Lister-Jaguar 3·8-litre	W. A. Scott-Brown	1st	90·72 m.p.h.
		Tojeiro-Jaguar	P. Gammon	2nd	
		H.W.M.-Jaguar	P. Blond	3rd	
Aug.	B.R.S.C.C. Brands Hatch Meeting: Series Production Sports Car Race	XK140	J. Bekaert	3rd	
	Kingsdown Trophy Race	Lister-Jaguar 3·8-litre	W. A. Scott-Brown	1st	71·79 m.p.h.
		Tojeiro-Jaguar	G. Hill	2nd	
	Shelsley Walsh Hill-Climb	L.G.S. (XK engine)	F. Le Gallais	1st Racing Cars over 2,500 c.c.	38·2 sec.
		H.W.M.-Jaguar	E. P. Scragg	1st Sports Cars over 2,500 c.c.	39·29 sec.
Sept.	Snetterton Autumn Meeting: Sports Car Race (over 2,700 c.c.)	Lister-Jaguar	W. A. Scott-Brown	1st	
		Lister-Jaguar	T. Kyffin	3rd	
	Bouley Bay Hill-Climb, Jersey	L.G.S. (XK engine)	F. Le Gallais	F.t.d.	53 sec.
	Brighton Speed Trials	XK-SS	J. Coombs	1st Production Sports Cars over 1,500 c.c. Fastest Production Sports Car	26·63 sec.
	Prescott Hill-Climb	Jaguara 3,442 c.c. (s/c)	G. D. Parker	1st Sports Cars over 3,000 c.c.	47·02 sec.
		L.G.S. (XK engine)	F. Le Gallais	1st Formule Libre Racing Cars	45·63 sec.
	Daily Express Meeting, Silverstone: Sports Car Race	Lister-Jaguar 3·8-litre	W. A. Scott-Brown	2nd	
	Production Touring Car Race	3·4-litre	J. M. Hawthorn	1st	82·19 m.p.h.
		3·4-litre	J. Duncan Hamilton	2nd	
	Mobilgas Round Australia Rally	Mk.VIII	Mrs Anderson	1st Over 2,500 c.c. class	
	B.A.R.C. Goodwood National Meeting: Goodwood Trophy Race	Lister-Jaguar	W. A. Scott-Brown	1st	88·84 m.p.h.
		Tojeiro-Jaguar	J. Brabham	2nd	
		D-type	H. Taylor	3rd	
Oct.	Snetterton 3-Hour Night Race	C-type	J. Bekaert	2nd	

Date	Event	Model	Drivers	Placing	Av. Speed or Time
Dec.	Brands Hatch Boxing Day Meeting: John Davy Trophy	3·4-litre	T. E. B. Sopwith	1st	61·61 m.p.h.
		3·4-litre	Sir G. Baillie	2nd	
1958 Jan.	Australian Mobilgas Economy Run	Mk.VIII	M. Dunning/ J. M. Cash	1st Automatic Transmission class	
	Lady Wigram Trophy Race, New Zealand	Lister-Jaguar 3·8-litre	W. A. Scott-Brown	1st	83·93 m.p.h.
March	R.A.C. Rally	2·4-litre	B. R. Waddilove/ G. Wood	1st Series Production Cars, 2,001–2,600 c.c.	
		3·4-litre	E. N. Brinkman	1st Series Production Cars, 2,601 c.c. and over	
	Snetterton March Meeting: 8-lap Sports Car Race	Lister-Jaguar	W. A. Scott-Brown	1st Over 2,700 c.c.	87·35 m.p.h.
	Formule Libre Race	Lister-Jaguar	W. A. Scott-Brown	1st	88·83 m.p.h.
	Saloon Car Race	3·4-litre	T. E. B. Sopwith	1st Over 2,700 c.c.	75·32 m.p.h.
April	Goodwood Easter Monday Meeting: Sussex Trophy	D-type	J. Duncan Hamilton	3rd	
	B.R.D.C. Empire Trophy Race, Oulton Park	Lister-Jaguar	W. A. Scott-Brown	3rd	
	Aintree '200' Meeting: Production Saloon-Car Race	3·4-litre	R. Flockhart	2nd	
		2·4-litre	P. Blond	1st 1,600–2,600 c.c. class	66·28 m.p.h.
	Sports Car Race, over 1,100 c.c.	Lister-Jaguar 3·8-litre	W. A. Scott-Brown	1st	86·1 m.p.h.
		Lister-Jaguar 3·8-litre	M. Gregory	3rd	
	Tulip Rally, Holland	2·4-litre	D. J. Morley/ G. E. Morley	1st Series Production Cars, 2,000–2,600 c.c.	
May	Silverstone Daily Express Meeting: Sports Car Race	Lister-Jaguar 3·8-litre	M. Gregory	1st	99·54 m.p.h.
		Lister-Jaguar 3·8-litre	W. A. Scott-Brown	2nd	
	Production Touring Car Race	3·4-litre	J. M. Hawthorn	1st	84·22 m.p.h.

Date	Event	Model	Drivers	Placing	Av. Speed or Time
June	Prescott Hill-Climb	H.W.M.-Jaguar	E. P. Scragg	1st Sports Cars over 3,000 c.c.	46·82 sec.
	Spa Sports Car G.P.	Lister-Jaguar 3·8-litre	M. Gregory	1st	121·24 m.p.h.
	Goodwood Whit-Monday Meeting: Whitsun Trophy	Lister-Jaguar D-type	A. G. Whitehead	1st	84·41 m.p.h.
			J. Duncan Hamilton	2nd	
	Production Saloon Car Race	3·4-litre	J. Duncan Hamilton	1st	78·95 m.p.h.
		3·4-litre	T. E. B. Sopwith	2nd	
		3·4-litre	Sir G. Baillie	3rd	
	Whitsun 10-lap Handicap Race	Lister-Jaguar D-type	B. Halford	1st	87·3 m.p.h.
			J. Duncan Hamilton	3rd	
	Shelsley Walsh Hill-Climb	Emeryson-Jaguar (2·4-litre special)	P. Emery	1st Racing Cars, 1,501–2,500 c.c.	45·97 sec.
		H.W.M.-Jaguar	E. P. Scragg	1st Sports Cars over 2,500 c.c. Fastest sports car	43·09 sec.
	Brands Hatch: Production Saloon Car Race	3·4-litre	T. E. B. Sopwith	1st Over 2,700 c.c.	63·3 m.p.h.
	Bridgehampton Sports Car Race, U.S.A.	Lister-Jaguar	W. Hansgen	1st	79·5 m.p.h.
July	B.R.C.S.C. Crystal Palace Meeting: London Trophy	Lister-Jaguar 3·8-litre	I. L. Bueb	1st	76·96 m.p.h.
		Lister-Jaguar 3·8-litre	B. Halford	2nd	
	Saloon Car Race	3·4-litre	T. E. B. Sopwith	1st	66·88 m.p.h.
		3·4-litre	Sir G. Baillie	2nd	
		3·4-litre	D. J. Uren	3rd	
	Leinster Trophy Race, Wicklow	Lister-Jaguar	P. N. Whitehead	1st Over 2,000 c.c.	74·67 m.p.h.
	British Grand Prix Meeting, Silverstone: Sports Car Race	Lister-Jaguar 3·8-litre	S. Moss	1st	97·92 m.p.h.
	Saloon Car Race	3·4-litre	W. Hansgen	1st Over 3,000 c.c.	83·92 m.p.h.
	Snetterton Meeting: Sports Car Race	Lister-Jaguar	W. Hansgen	1st Over 2,700 c.c.	92·37 m.p.h.
	Saloon Car Race	3·4-litre	T. E. B. Sopwith	1st Over 3,000 c.c.	69·05 m.p.h.
Aug.	Brands Hatch August Bank Holiday Meeting: Kingsdown Trophy	Lister-Jaguar 3·8-litre	I. L. Bueb	1st	72·59 m.p.h.
		Lister-Jaguar 3·8-litre	R. Jensen	2nd	
		Lister-Jaguar 3·8-litre	B. Halford	3rd	
	Saloon Car Race	3·4-litre	T. E. B. Sopwith	1st Over 2,700 c.c.	62·5 m.p.h.
	Snetterton National Benzole Meeting: Sports Car Race	XK120	R. A. Gibson	1st Over 3,000 c.c.	75·78 m.p.h.
	National Benzole Trophy, Appendix C Sports Cars	H.W.M.-Jaguar	J. Bekaert	1st Over 1,500 c.c.	88·41 m.p.h.
	International Brands Hatch Meeting: Saloon Cars	3·4-litre	T. E. B. Sopwith	1st Over 2,700 c.c.	63·84 m.p.h.
Sept.	Brighton Speed Trials	C-type	G. Tyrer	1st Sports Cars over 2,500 c.c.	25·11 sec.
	Snetterton September Meeting: Scott-Brown Memorial Trophy 10-lap Sports Car Race	Lister-Jaguar	I. L. Bueb	1st	93·92 m.p.h.
		Lister-Jaguar	R. Jensen	1st Over 2,700 c.c.	89·09 m.p.h.
	Oulton Park: Sports Cars over 1,100 c.c.	Lister-Jaguar 3·8-litre	I. Bueb	2nd	
		Lister-Jaguar	B. Halford	3rd	
	Tour de France	3·4-litre	Sir G. Baillie/ P. Jopp	3rd Touring Category	
Oct.	Snetterton: One-Hour Saloon Car Race	3·4-litre	T. E. B. Sopwith	1st	78·85 m.p.h.
	Riverside G.P., U.S.A.	D-type 3·8-litre	B. Krause	3rd	
Nov.	Victorian T.T., Melbourne	Cooper-Jaguar	D. Whiteford	2nd	
		D-type	W. Pitt	3rd	
1959 Jan.	Monte Carlo Rally	3·4-litre 3·4-litre 3·4-litre	Parkes Brinkman Walton	Charles Faroux Team Trophy	

Date	Event	Model	Drivers	Placing	Av. Speed or Time
March	Snetterton Spring Meeting: *Formule Libre* Scratch Race	Lister-Jaguar 3·8-litre	R. Flockhart	2nd	
		Lister-Jaguar 3·8-litre	J. Bekaert	3rd	
	Goodwood Easter Meeting: Sports Car Race (over 1,100 c.c.)	Lister-Jaguar 3·8-litre	I. L. Bueb	1st	78·64 m.p.h.
		Lister-Jaguar 3·8-litre	P. Blond	2nd	
	Saloon Car Scratch Race	3·4-litre	I. L. Bueb	1st	78·40 m.p.h.
		3·4-litre	R. F. Salvadori	2nd	
		3·4-litre	Sir G. Baillie	3rd	
	Mallory Park Easter Meeting: Unlimited Sports Car Race	Lister-Jaguar	J. Clark	1st	81·18 m.p.h.
April	Daytona Beach Sports Car Race, U.S.A.	D-type	A. Pabst	3rd	
	Aintree International Meeting: Sports Car Race (over 1,100 c.c.)	Lister-Jaguar 3·8-litre	M. Gregory	3rd	
	Saloon Car Race	3·4-litre	I. L. Bueb	1st	74·99 m.p.h.
		3·4-litre	R. F. Salvadori	2nd	
		3·4-litre	Sir G. Baillie	3rd	
	Silverstone International Trophy Meeting: Sports Car Race	Lister-Jaguar 3·8-litre	M. Gregory	3rd	
	Production Touring Car Race	3·4-litre	I. L. Bueb	1st	86·57 m.p.h
		3·4-litre	R. F. Salvadori	2nd	
		3·4-litre	Sir G. Baillie	3rd	
	Tulip Rally, Holland	3·4-litre	D. J. Morley/ W. Hercock	1st General Classification 1st Production Touring Cars over 2,600 c.c.	
May	Goodwood Whitsun Meeting: Touring Car Race	3·4-litre	Sir G. Baillie	2nd	
	Whitsun Trophy Race	Tojeiro-Jaguar	R. Flockhart	1st	88·51 m.p.h.
		Lister-Jaguar	J. Bekaert	2nd	
		Lister-Jaguar	P. Blond	3rd	
June	Shelsley Walsh Hill-Climb	H.W.M.-Jaguar	E. P. Scragg	1st Sports Cars over 2,500 c.c.	42·38 sec.

Date	Event	Model	Drivers	Placing	Av. Speed or Time
July	Vanwall Trophy Meeting, Snetterton: *Autosport* Championship Race Sports Car Race	XK120	R. Protheroe	1st Over 2,000 c.c.	81·14 m.p.h.
		Lister-Jaguar 3·8-litre	P. Mould	1st 1,101–3,000 c.c.	86·77 m.p.h.
	Saloon and G.T. Race	3·4-litre	Sir G. Baillie	1st equal	80·88 m.p.h.
		XK120	R. Protheroe	1st equal	
Aug.	B.R.S.C.C. Brands Hatch August Bank Holiday Meeting: Touring Cars over 1,300 c.c.	3·4-litre	Sir G. Baillie	1st	63·41 m.p.h.
	Series Production Sports Cars over 1,600 c.c.	XK120	E. Protheroe	1st	65·36 m.p.h.
	Snetterton August Bank Holiday Meeting: Production Sports Car Race	XK120	R. Protheroe	1st Over 2,000 c.c.	80·34 m.p.h
	Formule Libre Race	Lister-Jaguar 3·8-litre	W. F. Moss	2nd	
	Brands Hatch International Meeting: Race for Special Touring Cars	3·4-litre	J. Sears	1st Over 2,600 c.c.	64·86 m.p.h.
Sept.	Scott-Brown Memorial Trophy Meeting, Snetterton: 8-lap Scratch Race for Sports Cars over 1,100 c.c.	Lister-Jaguar 3·8-litre	W. F. Moss	1st	89·30 m.p.h.
	Saloon and G.T. Race	XK120	R. Taylor	1st Over 2,000 c.c.	77·53 m.p.h.
	Prescott Hill-Climb	H.W.M.-Jaguar	E. P. Scragg	1st Sports Cars over 3,000 c.c.	46·58 sec.
	Oulton Park International Gold Cup Meeting: Closed Car Race	3·4-litre	R. F. Salvadori	1st	75·80 m.p.b
		XK140	R. Protheroe	2nd	
	Tour de France	3·4-litre	Da Silva Ramos/ Estager	1st Touring category 3rd on Index	
Oct.	Snetterton: 3-Hour Night Race	XK120	R. Protheroe	1st Over 2,000 c.c.	75·47 m.p.h.
Dec.	Brands Hatch Boxing Day Meeting: Silver City Trophy for Sports and Racing Cars over 1,200 c.c.	Lister-Jaguar	G. Lee	1st Sports Car class	62·22 m.p.h.

Date	Event	Model	Drivers	Placing	Av. Speed or Time
1960 March	Australian T.T., Tasmania	D-type	K. Matich	3rd	
	SNETTERTON SPRING MEETING: Sports Car Scratch Race	Lister-Jaguar 3·8-litre	D. Wilkinson	1st Over 3,000 c.c.	89·63 m.p.h.
	G.T. Race	XK150S	D. Parker	1st Over 2,000 c.c.	78·24 m.p.h.
April	Goodwood Easter Meeting: Fordwater Trophy for Closed Cars	3·8-litre Mk.II	R. F. Salvadori	2nd	
		3·8-litre Mk.II	J. Sears	3rd	
	B.R.S.C.C. Brands Hatch Meeting: G.T. Race	XK120	R. Gibson	1st Over 1,600 c.c. class	66·06 m.p.h.
	B.R.S.C.C. Norfolk Trophy Meeting, Snetterton: Touring Car Race	3·8-litre Mk.II	Sir G. Baillie	1st	81·96 m.p.h.
	Tulip Rally, Holland	XK150S	E. Haddon/ G. Vivian	1st G.T. Cars, 3,000–4,000 c.c.	
		3·8-litre Mk.II	J. P. Boardman/ J. W. Whitworth	1st Improved Production Touring Cars, 1,600–4,000 c.c.	
		3·8-litre Mk.II	Parkes/Howarth	1st Normal Series Production Touring Cars, 2,501–4,000 c.c.	
	Prescott Hill-Climb	Lister-Jaguar 3·8-litre	E. P. Scragg	F.t.d. by a sports car	45·19 sec.
May	SILVERSTONE *Daily Express* TROPHY MEETING: Unlimited Sports Car Race	Lister-Jaguar 3·8-litre	J. Coundley	1st Over 3,000 c.c.	93·29 m.p.h.
	Production Touring Car Race	3·8-litre Mk.II	R. F. Salvadori	1st	87·55 m.p.h.
		3·8-litre Mk.II	S. Moss	2nd	
		3·8-litre Mk.II	G. Hill	3rd	
	Shelsley Walsh Hill-Climb	Lister-Jaguar 3·8-litre	E. P. Scragg	1st Sports Cars over 2,500 c.c.	38·43 sec.
July	R.S.A.C. Rest-and-be-Thankful Hill-Climb	XK150S	A. McCracken	1st Sports Cars over 2,000 c.c.	65·47 sec.

Date	Event	Model	Drivers	Placing	Av. Speed or Time
	International Alpine Rally	3·8-litre Mk.II	Behra/Richard	1st Touring Car category 1st Over 2,000 c.c. Coupe des Alpes	
		3·8-litre Mk.II	Parkes/Howarth	3rd Touring Car category Coupe des Alpes	
	SCOTT-BROWN MEMORIAL TROPHY MEETING, SNETTERTON: 10-lap Scratch Race, Sports Cars	Lister-Jaguar 3·8-litre	J. Bekaert	1st	
	Touring and G.T. Race	XK140	D. Hobbs	1st Unlimited class	
	Silverstone British Grand Prix Meeting: Production Touring Car Race	3·8-litre Mk.II	A. C. B. Chapman	1st	86·50 m.p.h.
		3·8-litre Mk.II	J. Sears	2nd	
		3·8-litre Mk.II	Sir G. Baillie	3rd	
Aug.	Aintree August Bank Holiday Meeting: Sports Car Race	Lister-Jaguar 3·8-litre	G. Ashmore	2nd	
		D-type	M. Salmon	3rd	
	B.R.S.C.C. SILVERSTONE MEETING: Unlimited Sports Car Race	Lister-Jaguar	G. Lee	1st	83·12 m.p.h.
	Touring Car Race	3·4-litre	W. A. Powell	1st	72·34 m.p.h.
	W.E.C.C. NATIONAL BENZOLE MEETING, SNETTERTON: G.T. Race	XK140	D. Hobbs	1st	80·16 m.p.h.
	Sports Cars over 1,100 c.c.	Lister-Jaguar 3·8-litre	J. Bekaert	2nd	
	Saloon Cars	3·4-litre	W. Aston	1st	79·98 m.p.h.
		3·4-litre	P. Sargent	2nd	
		3·4-litre	W. A. Powell	3rd	
	International Brands Hatch Meeting: Farningham Trophy Race (Touring Cars)	3·8-litre Mk.II	J. Sears	1st	74·05 m.p.h.
		3·4-litre	W. A. Powell	2nd	
		3·4-litre	W. Aston	3rd	
Sept.	Angola G.P., West Africa	D-type	Love	1st	
	Brighton Speed Trials	Lister-Jaguar	M. Anthony	1st Sports Cars over 2,500 c.c.	26·15 sec.
		Jaguette 2,663 c.c. (s/c)	W. Coleman	1st Unlimited Supercharged Sports Cars	30·25 sec.

Date	Event	Model	Drivers	Placing	Av. Speed or Time
Sept.	Prescott Hill-Climb	Lister-Jaguar	E. P. Scragg	1st Sports Cars over 3,000 c.c.	55·19 sec.
	Tour de France	3·8-litre Mk.II	Consten/Renel	1st Touring category	
		3·8-litre Mk.II	Jopp/Baillie	2nd Touring category	
Oct.	British Empire Trophy Meeting, Silverstone: Saloon Car Race	3·8-litre Mk.II	Sir G. Baillie	1st	84·20 m.p.h.
		3·8-litre Mk.II	D. Taylor	2nd	
	G.T. Race	XK120 (3·8-litre engine)	R. Gibson	1st	79·76 m.p.h.
	B.R.S.C.C. Snetterton Meeting: Sports-Racing Cars	Lister-Jaguar 3·8-litre	J. Bekaert	1st	91·65 m.p.h.
	Saloon Cars	3·4-litre	W. Aston	1st Over 2,600 c.c.	78·83 m.p.h.
	Lewis-Evans Trophy Meeting, Brands Hatch: Sports Car Race, over 1,500 c.c.	Lister-Jaguar	B. Halford	1st	76·25 m.p.h.
		Lister-Jaguar	J. Bekaert	2nd	
	Touring Car Race	3·4-litre	W. A. Powell	1st	66·95 m.p.h.
Nov.	U.S. Grand Prix Meeting, Riverside: Compact Car Race	3·8-litre Mk.II	W. Hansgen	1st	
		3·8-litre Mk.II	A. Pabst	2nd	
	R.A.C. Rally	3·8-litre Mk.II	J. Sears/W. Cave	1st Touring Cars over 2,500 c.c.	
Dec.	Brands Hatch Boxing Day Meeting: Touring Car Race	3·8-litre Mk.II	Sir G. Baillie	1st	64·21 m.p.h.
1961 March	B.R.S.C.C. Spring Meeting, Snetterton: Unlimited Sports Car Race	Lister-Jaguar	G. Lee	1st	87·93 m.p.h.
	Saloon Car Race	3·4-litre	P. Sargent	1st	80·93 m.p.h.
April	Oulton Park: G.T. Trophy Race	E-type	G. Hill	1st	83·22 m.p.h.
		E-type	R. F. Salvadori	3rd	
	Goodwood Easter Meeting: St. Mary's Trophy Saloon Car Race	3·8-litre	M. Parkes	1st	76·3 m.p.h.

Date	Event	Model	Drivers	Placing	Av. Speed or Time
May	Spa: G.T. Race, cars over 2,000 c.c.	E-type	M. Parkes	2nd	
June	Goodwood Whitsun Meeting: Sports Car Race	Lister-Jaguar	de Selincourt	2nd	
		D-type	M. Salmon	3rd	
July	B.A.R.C. British Grand Prix Meeting, Aintree: G.T. Race	E-type	J. Sears	2nd	
	B.R.D.C. British Empire Trophy Race Meeting, Silverstone: Production Touring Car Race	3·8-litre	M. Parkes	1st	73·14 m.p.h.
		3·8-litre	G. Hill	2nd	
Aug.	August Bank Holiday International Meeting, Brands Hatch: G.T. Race	E-type	B. McLaren	2nd	
		E-type	R. F. Salvadori	3rd	
	Touring Car Race	3·8-litre	M. Parkes	1st	77·73 m.p.h.
		3·8-litre	R. F. Salvadori	2nd	
		3·8-litre	J. Sears	3rd	
Sept.	Brighton Speed Trials	H.K.-Jaguar Special	G. Parker	f.t.d. (cars)	24·63 secs.
		Tojeiro-Jaguar	Mrs. V. Lewis	1st Ladies' class	
		Jaguette	W. Coleman	1st Supercharged sports cars	
	Snetterton M.R.C.: Three Hours' Sports Car Race	D-type	M. Salmon	1st	81·53 m.p.h.
		E-type	P. Sargent	3rd	
Oct.	Coupe du Salon Meeting, Montlhéry: Touring Car Race, cars over 2,000 c.c.	3·8-litre	B. Consten	1st	
		3·8-litre	C. de Guezac	2nd	
1962 March	B.R.S.C.C. Spring Meeting, Snetterton: G.T. Cars over 2,000 c.c.	E-type	R. P. G. Sturgess	1st	85·45 m.p.h.
	Saloon Cars over 3,000 c.c.	3·8 litre	P. J. Sargent	1st	80·35 m.p.h.
April	B.A.R.C., Oulton Park: G.T. Race	E-type	G. Hill	2nd	
	Snetterton: Saloon Car Race over 2,000 c.c.	3·8-litre	M. Parkes	1st	87·34 m.p.h.

Date	Event	Model	Drivers	Placing	Av. Speed or Time
May	Goodwood, Sussex Trophy Race	Lister-Jaguar	G. de Selincourt	2nd	
		Lister-Jaguar	J. Coundley	3rd	
	Saloon Car Race, over 3,000 c.c.	3·8-litre	G. Hill	1st	86·59 m.p.h.
	Aintree '200' Meeting: Saloon Car Race, over 3,000 c.c.	3·8-litre	G. Hill	1st	78·05 m.p.h.
	SILVERSTONE INTERNATIONAL TROPHY MEETING: Production Car Race, over 3,000 c.c.	3·8-litre	G. Hill	1st	85·87 m.p.h.
	Sports Car Race	D-type	P. Sutcliffe	3rd	
	Hockenheim Races: 56-Km Race	E-type	Neerpasch	2nd	
		E-type	Ruthardt	3rd	
	Saloon Cars	3·8-litre	P. Nocker	1st	
June	Crystal Palace Whit Monday Meeting: Saloon Cars over 3,000 c.c.	3·8-litre	R. Salvadori	1st	74·51 m.p.h.
	Mallory Park Whitsun Meeting: G.T. Race	E-type	G. Hill	2nd	
	Goodwood Whitsun Meeting: 10 lap Saloon Car Race	3·8-litre	P. Woodroffe	1st	81·85 m.p.h.
	Le Mans 24-hour Race	E-type	B. S. Cunningham / R. Salvadori	4th	107·87 m.p.h.
	Nurburgring 6-Hour Touring Car Race	3·8-litre	P. Lindner	1st	
		3·8-litre	Schadrack	2nd	
		3·8-litre	Kreft	3rd	
July	Nurburgring 12-Hour Touring Car Race	3·8-litre	P. Lindner / H. J. Walter	1st	72.25 m.p.h.
	Kirkiston Hawthorn Memorial Meeting: Sports Car Race	E-type	M. Smirfit	2nd	
	A.M.O.C. Silverstone Meeting: Saloons over 3,000 c.c.	3·8-litre	W. Powell	1st	76·75 m.p.h.
	U.S.A.F. Trophy Race	E-type	E. Protheroe	1st	91·76 m.p.h.
	Martini 100-Mile Race	Lister-Jaguar	J. Coundley	1st	91·97 m.p.h.
	SNETTERTON SCOTT-BROWN MEMORIAL MEETING: 14-lap Scratch Saloon Car Race	3·8-litre	G. Hill	1st	86·87 m.p.h.
August	British Grand Prix meeting, Aintree: Saloon Car Race	3·8-litre	J. Sears	1st	77·81 m.p.h.
	Brands Hatch, Molyslip Trophy Race (saloon cars)	3·8-litre	M. Parkes	1st	74·12 m.p.h.
		3·8-litre	J. Sears	2nd	
		3·8-litre	R. Salvadori	3rd	
	Shelsley Walsh Hill-Climb: Production Touring, Sports and G.T. Cars over 2,601 c.c.	E-type	E. P. Scragg	1st	39·02 sec.
Sept.	Nurburgring, Rheinland-Pfalz G.T. Race	E-type	Sir J. Whitmore	3rd	
	Crystal Palace, B.R.S.C.C. Meeting, 15-lap G.T. Race, over 2,600 c.c.	E-type	E. Protheroe	1st	77·02 m.p.h.
	Brighton Speed Trials: Sports Cars over 2,500 c.c.	E-type	J. A. Playford	1st	26·03 sec.
	Supercharged Sports Cars	Jaguette	W. Coleman	1st	26·58 sec.
	Circuit of Albi, G.T. Race	E-type	Garaud	3rd	
	Tour de France Touring Car Class	3·8-litre	B. Consten /Renel	1st	
		3·8-litre	Rosinski /Charon	2nd	
		3·8-litre	Richard /de Montaigu	3rd	
Oct.	Silverstone, Clubman's Championship Meeting: 10-lap G.T. and Production Sports Car Race	E-type	R. P. G. Sturgess	1st	
	10-lap Saloon Car Race, over 3,000 c.c.	3·8-litre	P. Woodroffe	1st	
	Brands Hatch, Motor International 6-Hour Saloon Car Race	3·8-litre	M. Parkes / J. Blumer	1st	75·37 m.p.h.
		3·8-litre	P. Lindner / P. Nocker	2nd	
	Geneva Rally, Touring Cars over 2,001 c.c.	3·8-litre	Kraft	1st	
Dec.	Brands Hatch, Boxing Day Meeting: Peco Trophy 10-lap Race	E-type	K. Baker	1st	71·77 m.p.h.
1963 March	Snetterton Meeting: 10-lap Touring-car Race	3·8-litre	C. McLaren	1st	84·54 m.p.h.

Date	Event	Model	Drivers	Placing	Av. Speed or Time
April	10-lap Sports-Racing Car Race Monza	Lister-Jaguar 3·8-litre	A. Dean	3rd	
			G. Duke, J. Bekaert and others	International Class C Records: 3 days: 107·023 m.p.h. 4 days: 106·662 m.p.h. 15,000 km: 106·615 m.p.h. 10,000 miles: 106·58 m.p.h.	
	Snetterton, International Trophy Meeting: Sports Cars over 2 litres	E-type	G. Hill	1st	79·37 m.p.h.
	Cars over 2 litres 2,000 c.c.	3·8-litre	R. Salvadori	1st	83·41 m.p.h.
	B.A.R.C. National Meeting, Oulton Park: Touring Car Race, over 2,000 c.c.	3·8-litre	G. Hill	1st	82·75 m.p.h.
	Goodwood, Easter Monday Meeting: 10-lap Touring Car Race	3·8-litre	G. Hill	1st	85·02 m.p.h.
		3·8-litre	R. Salvadori	2nd	
		3·8-litre	M. Salmon	3rd	
	Sussex Trophy Race for G.T. Cars	E-type	G. Hill	1st	97·18 m.p.h.
		E-type	R. Salvadori	3rd	
	Brands Hatch, John Day Trophy for G.T. Cars	XK 120	Falce	1st	65·32 m.p.h.
	Mallory Park, Easter Meeting: G.T. Cars over 2,500 c.c.	E-type	K. Baker	1st	
	Aintree '200' Meeting: Saloon Cars over 2,000 c.c.	3·8-litre	G. Hill	1st	78·86 m.p.h.
May	B.O.C. National Prescott Hill-Climb: Touring, Sports and G.T. Cars over 2,501 c.c.	E-type	E. P. Scragg	1st	56·43 sec.
	Silverstone, International Trophy Meeting: G.T. Cars	E-type	G. Hill	1st	101·02 m.p.h.
		E-type	R. Salvadori	2nd	
		E-type	E. Protheroe	2nd	
	Saloon Cars	3·8-litre	R. Salvadori	2nd	
		3·8-litre	P. Dodd	3rd	
	Japanese International Meeting, Suzuka: G.T. Race	E-type	T. Yokoyama	1st	
June	Crystal Palace, Whit Monday Meeting: Touring Car Race	3·8-litre	R. Salvadori	2nd	
		3·8-litre	G. Hill	3rd	
	Goodwood Whitsun Meeting, 10-lap Spring Grove Trophy Saloon Car Race	3·8-litre	M. Salmon	1st	85·77 m.p.h
	Shelsley Walsh National Hill-Climb: Production, Touring, Sports and G.T. Cars over 2,600 c.c.	E-type	E. P. Scragg	1st	39·93 sec.
	Nurburgring, 6-Hour Touring Car Race	3·8-litre	P. Lindner	1st	
July	Motor 6-Hour Production Car Race, Brands Hatch	3·8-litre	R. Salvadori	1st	
		3·8-litre	P. Lindner / P. Nocker	2nd	
	Silverstone, A.M.O.C. Martini Trophy Meeting: Saloon Cars over 3,000 c.c.	3·8-litre	W. Aston	1st	88·16 m.p.h.
	Mallory Park, Grovewood Trophy G.T. Race	E-type	G. Hill	1st	87·11 m.p.h.
		E-type	R. Salvadori	3rd	
	Snetterton National Meeting: 10-lap Saloon Car Race	3·8-litre	M. Salmon	2nd	
		3·8-litre	W. Aston	3rd	
	10-lap Touring Car Race	3·8-litre	J. Adams	2nd	
		3·8-litre	M. Pendleton	3rd	
	G.T. Race	E-type	P. H. Sutcliffe	1st	91·02 m.p.h.
		E-type	K. Baker	2nd	
	British G.P. Meeting Silverstone: Touring Car Race	3·8-litre	G. McDowell	3rd	
	118-Km G.T. Race	E-type	E. Protheroe	3rd	
August	B.R.S.C.C., Mallory Park Meeting: G.T. Cars over 2,500 c.c.	E-type	H. Walkup	1st	80·19 m.p.h.
	B.R.S.C.C., Aintree Meeting: G.T. Race	E-type	R. Mac	1st	83·6 m.p.h.
		E-type	J. Dean	2nd	
		XK.120	R. Beck	3rd	
	S.M.R.C., Snetterton Meeting: Sports Racing Cars	Lister-Jaguar	D. Beckett	2nd	
	G.T. Cars	E-type	M. Fruitnight	1st	
	Brands Hatch, Molyslip Trophy Meeting Race 'A', Saloon Cars	3·8-litre	A. Powell	2nd	
	Race 'B', Saloon Cars	3·8-litre	G. Hill	2nd	
		3·8-litre	R. Salvadori	3rd	

Date	Event	Model	Drivers	Placing	Av. Speed or Time
	Tourist Trophy Race, Goodwood	E-type	R. Salvadori	3rd	
Sept.	Brighton Speed Trials: Saloon Cars over 1,600 c.c.	3.8-litre	M. A. Runham	1st	29.21 sec.
	Sports-racing Cars over 1,600 c.c.	D-type	Mrs. P. Coundley	1st	24.90 sec.
	B.O.C. Prescott Hill Climb, Sports-racing Cars over 1,600 c.c.	Lister-Jaguar	D. Beckett	1st	53.86 sec.
	Sports, Saloon, and G.T. Cars over 1,601 c.c.	E-type	E. P. Scragg	1st	55.86 sec.
	Tour de France, Touring Car Class	3.8-litre	B. Consten/Renel	1st	(and 2nd in touring category)
	Coupe des Dames	3.8-litre	Mlle. A. Soisbault /Mlle. L. Texier	1st	
	Bridgehampton 500-km Race	E-type	W. Hansgen	3rd	
Nov.	Wills 60-Hour Touring Car Race, Pukehohe	3.8-litre	A. Shelly /R. Archibald	1st	
Dec.	Brands Hatch Boxing Day Meeting: John Davy Trophy, G.T. Cars over 2,500 c.c.	E-type	J. W. Dean	1st	66.27 m.p.h.
1964 May	Prescott Hill-Climb, Sports, GT, Saloon Cars over 1,600 c.c.	E-type	E. P. Scragg	1st	55 sec.
	Nottingham S.C.C. Meeting, Silverstone: 8-lap G.T. Race	E-type	A. J. Lambert	1st	82.73 m.p.h.
	8-lap Sports Car Race	E-type	A. J. Lambert	1st	82.87 m.p.h.
	8-lap Sports-racing Cars	XK120	R. Beck	1st	83.5 m.p.h.
	Coupe de Paris GT Race, Montlhéry	E-type	P. Sutcliffe	1st	82.63 m.p.h.
July	European G.P. Meeting, Brands Hatch: Ilford Trophy G.T. Race	E-type	J. Stewart	2nd	
	Limburg Grand Prix, G.T. Cars 2-5 litres	E-type	P. Sutcliffe	3rd	

Date	Event	Model	Drivers	Placing	Av. Speed or Time
Aug.	Shelsley Walsh National Hill-Climb: Production, Touring, Sports, and G.T. Cars over 2,600 c.c.	E-type	E. P. Scragg	1st	37.35 sec.
Sept.	Prescott Hill-Climb: Sports, Saloon, and G.T. Cars over 1,600 c.c.	E-type	E. P. Scragg	1st	52.96 sec.
	Brighton Speed Trials: Saloons, over 2,000 c.c.	3.8-litre	R. D. Jennings	2nd	
	Sports and G.T., over 2,500 c.c.	E-type	J. A. Playford	3rd	
	Sports-racing, over 2,500 c.c.	Lister-Jaguar	K. Wilson	2nd	
		Lister-Jaguar	D. A. Beckett	3rd	
	Ladies' Class	D-type	Mrs. P. Coundley	1st	24.47 sec.
	Snetterton, September Meeting: 3-Hour G.T. Race	E-type	R. Mac	2nd	
1965 Jan.	B.R.S.C.C., Brands Hatch Meeting: Redex Trophy 10-lap G.T. Race	E-type	W. R. Pearce	1st	62.61 m.p.h.
May	Prescott, R.A.C. Hill-Climb Championship Meeting: Sports, Saloon and G.T. Cars over 1,600 c.c.	E-type	E. P. Scragg	1st	53.74 sec.
	B.R.S.C.C., 1000-Mile Production Sports Car Race, Brands Hatch	E-type	J. Oliver /C. Craft	3rd	
June	Goodwood Whitsun Meeting: Sports Car Race	XK120	R. M. H. Bailey	2nd	
	Shelsley Walsh, Diamond Jubilee Hill-Climb: Production Touring, Sports, and G.T. Cars over 2,600 c.c.	E-type	E. P. Scragg	1st	37.6 sec.
July	Spa Cup, Touring Car Race	3.8-litre	J. Sparrowe	2nd	
August	Snetterton G.T. Race, over 2,500 c.c.	E-type	R. Ward	1st	79.45 m.p.h.

INDEX

For ease of reference this Index is, in some instances, sectionalized under classified main headings. Hence the various models of car will be found tabulated below *S.S. cars, S.S. Jaguar cars, Jaguar cars,* etc.; races and competitions are treated similarly; and most of the references to other countries, apart from competitive events, occur under *Export.*